PANIC

PANIC

Origins, Insight, *and* Treatment

EDITED BY
LEONARD J. SCHMIDT, M.D.
AND BROOKE WARNER

North Atlantic Books
Berkeley, California

Published by
North Atlantic Books
P.O. Box 12327
Berkeley, California 94712

Cover painting by Katie Meier
Book design by Jennifer Dunn
Cover design by Paula Morrison
Printed in the United States of America

This is issue #63 in the *Io* series.

Panic: Origins, Insight, and Treatment is sponsored by the Society for the Study of Native Arts and Sciences, a nonprofit educational corporation whose goals are to develop an educational and crosscultural perspective linking various scientific, social, and artistic fields; to nurture a holistic view of arts, sciences, humanities, and healing; and to publish and distribute literature on the relationship of mind, body, and nature.

North Atlantic Books are available through most bookstores. To contact North Atlantic directly, call 800-337-2665 or visit our website at www.northatlanticbooks.com.

Substantial discounts on bulk quantities of North Atlantic books are available to corporations, professional associations, and other organizations. For details and discount information, contact the special sales department at North Atlantic Books.

LIBRARY OF CONGRESS CATALOGING-IN-PUBLICATION DATA
Panic : origins, insight, and treatment / edited by Leonard J. Schmidt and Brooke Warner ; foreword by Peter A. Levine.
    p. cm. — (Io series ; no. 63)
Includes bibliographical references.
    ISBN 1-55643-396-4 (pbk.)
    1. Panic. 2. Hysteria. 3. Hysteria (Social psychology) 4. Social psychology. I. Schmidt, Leonard J. II. Warner, Brooke, 1976- III. Io ; no. 63.
    RC532 .P36 2002
    616.85'223—dc21
                                                                    2002006336

1 2 3 4 5 6 7 / 06 05 04 03 02

A panic attack is a discrete period in which there is
the sudden onset of intense apprehension, fearfulness,
or terror, often associated with feelings of impending doom.
During these attacks, symptoms such as shortness of
breath, palpitations, chest pain or discomfort, choking or
smothering sensations, and fear of "going crazy" or losing
control are present.

Panic Disorder without Agoraphobia
is characteristic by recurrent unexpected Panic Attacks about
which there is persistent concern. Panic Disorder with
Agoraphobia is characterized by both recurrent unexpected
panic attacks and agoraphobia.

"The Scream," 1895. **Edvard Munch**

DSM-IV CRITERIA FOR PANIC ATTACK

A discrete period of intense fear or discomfort, in which four (or more) of the following symptoms developed abruptly and reached a peak within 10 minutes:

1) palpitations, pounding heart, or accelerated heart rate
2) sweating
3) trembling or shaking
4) sensations of shortness of breath or smothering
5) feeling of choking
6) chest pain or discomfort
7) nausea or abdominal distress
8) feeling dizzy, unsteady, lightheaded, or faint
9) derealization(feelings of unreality) or depersonalization (being detached from oneself)
10) fear of losing control or going crazy
11) fear of dying
12) paresthesias (numbness or tingling sensations)
13) chills or hot flushes

DSM-IV CRITERIA FOR PANIC DISORDER

A) Both (1) and (2)

   (1) recurrent unexpected Panic Attacks

   (2) at least one of the attacks has been followed by 1 month (or more) of one (or more) of the following:
   • persistent concern about having additional attacks
   • worry about the implications of the attack or its consequences (e.g., losing control, having a heart attack, "going crazy")
   • a significant change in behavior related to the attacks

B) The Panic Attacks are not due to the direct physiological effects of a substance (e.g., a drug of abuse, a medication) or a general condition (e.g., hyperthyroidism).

C) The Panic Attacks are not better accounted for by another mental disorder, such as Social Phobia (e.g., occurring on exposure to feared social situations), Specific Phobia (e.g., on exposure to a specific phobic situation), Obsessive-Compulsive Disorder (e.g., on exposure to dirt in someone with an obsession about contamination), Posttraumatic Stress Disorder (e.g., in response to stimuli associated with a severe stressor), or Separation Anxiety Disorder (e.g., in response to being away from home or close relatives).

Contents

Foreword

W HILE THERE HAVE BEEN many volumes written on panic and anxiety, it is unusual to see one with such interdisciplinary breadth: Contributions range from the arts and literature, history, mythology, dreams, sleep, pharmacology, psychoanalysis, cognitive-behavioral therapies, and non-traditional approaches, including those that stake out the role of the "living experiential body" as healer. It is an anthology that speaks to the curious mind and to readers seeking practical guidance in dealing with anxiety states personally or as health professionals dealing with this common "malady."

In this age of more than "ordinary anxiety," clinicians, counselors, researchers, social thinkers, and the lay public can find much to contribute to their knowledge and practical resources in this volume. Through the historical and mythological treatments the reader may find a broader context with which to grasp the concept of panic and anxiety; and in addressing such questions as: When is anxiety a normal part of life and when does it become pathological?

An original and engaging essay on the phenomenology of panic (Grossinger) takes the reader on a broad experiential, existential, and philosophical voyage. There are several therapeutic chapters that address questions of treatment where anxiety has become a "disorder." They may serve as a guide for individuals and clinicians in addressing the problems associated with panic and in finding appropriate solutions. It is here that this book offers a range of conventional and alternative therapeutic avenues, including thoughtful pharmacological suggestions (Pande), as well as other complementary medications in the form of herbal and homeopathic remedies (Gaeddert, Lang). Recent, experiential therapies that focus upon the "felt body" in resolving anxiety states (i.e., Somatic Experiencing/Levine and Bioenergetics/Robins) are covered with generous case material. In addition, there is an excellent chapter that bridges these newer body-oriented approaches with the more established mental, cognitive-behavioral therapies (Resnick). In this way the article puts the head back on the body where it belongs, bringing together mind and body as a welded unity in effective, coherent, therapeutic action.

It should be noted that this is an anthology and contains a wide variety of approaches without a cohesive weaving of these disparate aspects. But whether a problem or not will depend largely on the readers curiosity and perseverance in bringing important parts together for themselves. There is not yet a unified theory of anxiety. And while this book can hardly make such a comprehensive claim, as a work in progress, it scopes out broad and seldom-explored realms. It may be a beginning in mapping out that vital territory, a critical need in these uncertain and turbulent times.

Peter A. Levine, Ph.D.
—Author of *Waking the Tiger, Healing Trauma.*

Editors' Introduction

T HIS IS A BOOK ABOUT PANIC—that terrible, profound emotion
that stretches us beyond our ability to imagine any experience more horrible. Physicians like to compare painful clinical conditions on some imagined "Richter scale" of vicious, mean hurt,
and usually the pain from a passing kidney stone wins that distinction. To the psychiatrist, there is no more vicious, mean hurt
than an exploding and personally disin-
tegrating panic attack. Panic commands
the attention of the sufferer in a way no
other emotion quite mimics. It devastates;
no wonder so much attention becomes
focused on avoidance.

pan·ic
Pronunciation: pa-nik
Function: adjective
Etymology: French panique, from Greek panikos,
literally, of Pan, from Pan
Date: 1603
1 : of, relating to, or resembling the mental or emotional
state believed induced by the god Pan <panic fear> 2 :
of, relating to, or arising from a panic <a wave of panic
buying> 3 : of or relating to the god Pan

—Merriam-Webster Dictionary

Throughout this book, our authors
describe states of anxiety, conditions of
panic, and panic disorder as they explore
its character from a startling array of perspectives. How frequently do these experiences occur—particularly if they endure
beyond a moment drawn from some murky epoch in our lives?

Epidemiologists want to know the *prevalence* of these anxious
states. Clinicians know (or should remember) that they are likely
to be deceived by their observations of the human parade of distress they encounter in their work. Sampling from clinic populations
is likely to yield a distorted view of the full dimensions of a phenomenon; Karno and colleagues discovered that obsessive-compulsive disorder was between 25–60 times more common than had
previously been estimated from clinical samples.

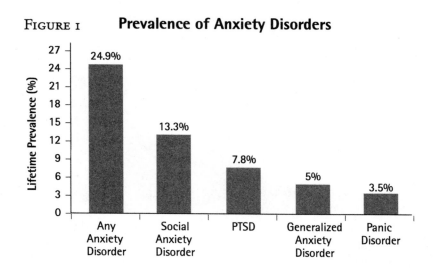

FIGURE I   **Prevalence of Anxiety Disorders**

The National Comorbidity Survey, modeled on the 1990 U.S. census, was the first canvas to administer a validated structured psychiatric interview to a representative sample (8,098 respondents between the ages of fifteen and fifty-four) to represent the population of the entire continental United States. The group of anxiety disorders accounted for 24.9 percent of all disorders over a lifetime. FIGURE 1 shows the relative distribution of the anxiety disorders studied. Obsessive-compulsive disorder was not evaluated in this survey but has reliably been estimated to have a 2.5 percent prevalence in both U.S. and world population studies. From this sample, panic disorder is shown to be the least frequent anxiety disorder (3.5 percent lifetime). FIGURE 2 provides us with a more detailed view of panic phenomenology.

More than 15 percent of persons surveyed reported they had a sudden experience of unexplained fear, i.e., a *fearful spell*, over their lifetimes. When these respondents were then asked if they had four or more symptoms characterizing a *panic attack* more than 11 percent responded affirmatively. *Panic attacks* are characterized by intense fearful spells with accompanying psycho physiological symptoms, reaching full intensity within ten minutes. *Recurrent panic attacks* occurred with a lifetime prevalence of 4.2 percent. When at least one of the recurrent attacks has occurred spontaneously (i.e., with no observable fearful stimulus) and has been followed by persistent worry about another attack, worry about the consequences of further attacks, or there is a significant behavioral change related to the attacks, the person meets the criteria for *panic disorder.* It is recurrence, actual or anticipated, that brings the phenomenon to a level that is considered clinically significant. Subtraction of persons with recurrent panic attacks without a spontaneous or unexpected attack reduced the lifetime rate for panic disorder to 3.5 percent. Of the remaining subjects, 2 percent did not have *agoraphobia.* This left a 1.5 percent lifetime occurrence of the most disabling form of the disorder—*panic disorder with agoraphobia.* Agoraphobia leads to fear or avoidance of places or situations from which escape may be impossible or help may not be available if one had a panic attack.

FIGURE 2
Prevalence of Panic Phenomenology

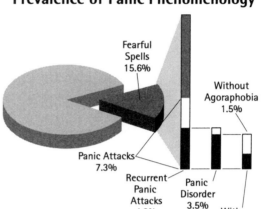

Fearful
Spells
15.6%

Without
Agoraphobia
1.5%

Panic Attacks
7.3%

Recurrent
Panic
Attacks
4.2%

Panic
Disorder
3.5%

With
Agoraphobia
1.5%

Two other characteristics of the National Comorbidity Survey are worth noting. Women are 2.89 times more likely to have a *panic attack* and 2.48 times more likely to have *panic disorder* than men. Those persons with fewer than twelve years of education were 4 times more likely to have a *panic attack* and 10 times more likely to have *panic disorder* than a comparison group with a college education.

As Joan Didion notes, "We tell ourselves stories in order to live." The root of these stories is a complex interaction of brain physiology, the work of the mind, and the coping strategies one uses to deal with our environment. With this work, our authors provide us with a rich and varied view of how this happens.

—Leonard J. Schmidt, M.D.

THIS ANTHOLOGY IS WIDE SWEEPING in its discourse on panic, not just as a disorder but as a cultural phenomenon and multi-faceted emotion. Panic exists on the most instinctual and primitive level as an alert, flooding the body with a rush of adrenaline that overwhelms the system and confronts us with what we know as the fight-or-flight reaction. Miraculous feats and tragic choices have occurred in moments of panic—the mother who lifted the tail end of her car to save her trapped child; the man who chose to jump to his death from the World Trade Center when faced with his option. Though we cringe to imagine ourselves in such situations, these reactions are still fear based and rational because they represent impulsive, survival-oriented thinking patterns. The more debilitating side of panic is the isolating, irrational, and distressing effects of panic disorder, whose victims exhibit avoidance behavior and develop life strategies to avert the onset of the volatile panic attack. The National Institutes of Health released their most recent numbers for panic disorder reporting that "three million adults—at least one in sixty-three—have or will have panic disorder in their lifetimes."

This book is meant to present the many layers of the panic experience rather than to suggest what to do about it, though various treatment options are outlined. The contributing authors, poets, and artists of this book come from various fields of interest, from literary and humanities backgrounds to psychological and medical. Divided into three main sections—origins, insight, and treatment—the texts function like spokes on a wheel whose central point is panic. They are disparate in their approach, but unified in focus.

Concepts represented in *Origins* include historical instances of panic, dating from the etymology of the word *panic* from the Greek god Pan, who struck panic into the hearts of travelers with his echoing screams, to modern psychoanalysis and Freudian concepts of panic-anxiety; the biology of panic is explained in an illustration of what we know of its physiological responses and bodily

Pan, god of fertility, fields, and lustful satyr, was notorious for striking sudden, unreasoning fear into the hearts of travelers camped in remote and desolate places. The Greeks blamed Pan for the inexplicable scary sounds that echoed across lonely valleys in the darkness and spooked people setting up camp for the night.

The Greeks called this fright *panikon deima*—literally, "panic fear." This later found its way into the French word *panique*, and on into English from there. It was first used as an adjective with varied spelling: *panique affrights, pannick fear,* and *panic dread.*

reactions; the co-existence of panic with other serious ailments and the ramifications of dismissive doctors and misdiagnoses; also, the personal struggles of contributors who have themselves suffered from panic disorder and their invaluable wisdom from years of coping and learning how to live with their demons.

Insight branches into literary, musical, cinematic, and artistic themes. The short story as a medium to express panic and instill panic reactions into the hearts of readers is considered—citing examples ranging from Edgar Allan Poe to Flannery O'Connor—as is the power of music to raise the hairs on the heads of its listeners as its resonating sounds send vibrations into the very core of the soul. The cinema with its visual effects and realism has a unique advantage when it comes to planting the seeds of panic, though these panic reactions are meant to thrill and delight, far from the devastating and life-altering suffering that accompanies true panic reactions based on real psychological fears or traumas.

Lastly, *Treatment* imparts the most straight-forward section of the anthology. The expertise of practitioners, doctors, and therapists—from pharmaceutical drug therapy options to Bioenergetic body therapy to an explanation of sleep-panic and on into homeopathic and herbal treatment remedies—is laid out to inform the reader and provide options.

panic (pan´ik) n.
A sudden overpowering terror, often affecting many people at once.

—American Heritage College Dictionary

Added to the mix are poems from sufferers of panic, from seventeen-year-old Amber Taylor, an aspiring poet, to Sylvia Plath and Anne Sexton, accomplished poets who were so haunted during their lives that they opted through suicide to cut them short. And finally there is art that portrays the experience of panic visually, including the claustrophobic feeling of isolation and entrapment (pp. 292, 385), the pensive expression on the face of a sufferer (p. 375), and the ultimate unleashing of emotional build-up in from Steve Markwell's mirroring demons (p. 342) to Edvard Munch's *The Scream* (p. vi).

The intent of this anthology is to convey how panic exists in the world. In an attempt to explore its pervasiveness and universal experience we take an interdisciplinary approach to the subject, emotion, experience, and existence of panic. The breadth of this anthology sheds light on the way panic manifests in the lives of the people it affects. The chapters have been written to capture the spectrum of emotion that panic embraces. From the thrill-seekers who want the "safe" panic reaction of a scary movie or an intense piece of music to the sufferers of panic disorder who endure the repetitive discomforts that accompany panic attacks, panic is an emotion that is impossible to define in one chapter, one anthology, or one personal experience. Most people relate to panic as a fleeting moment of spiked fear and subsequent release in the form of panic and anxiety attacks that affect us in relatively benign circumstances—speaking in front of a group of people, sleeping in on the morning of an important meeting, the moment right after flying past a concealed police car as we wait for the siren and consequent ticket. This thought-provoking subject will undoubtedly conjure emotions that will fascinate, haunt, and allure the reader as they sympathize, empathize, and likely relate to some or many of the observations of panic herewithin.

"Instead of being at the mercy of wild beasts, earthquakes, landslides, and inundations, modern man is battered by the elemental forces of his own psyche. This is the World Power that vastly exceeds all other powers on earth. The Age of Enlightenment, which stripped nature and human institutions of gods, overlooked the God of Terror who dwells in the human soul."

—Carl Jung

—Brooke Warner

ORIGINS

Culture-Bound Panic-Like Syndromes

Malaysia, Laos, Polynesia	**Amok** dissociative episode; period of brooding followed by outbursts of violent, aggressive behavior; often followed by a claim of amnesia
Latin Cultures	**Ataque de Nervios** uncontrollable shouting, attacks of crying, trembling, heat in the chest rising to the head, and verbal or physical aggression
West Africa, Haiti	**Boufée Delirante** outburst of agitated and aggressive behavior, marked cofusion, and psychomotor excitement
India, China, Sri Lanka	**Dhat** severe anxiety and hypochondriacal concerns associated with discharge of semen; feelings of sickness or exhaustion
Native American	**Ghost Sickness** preoccupation with death; bad dreams, feelings of danger, loss of appetite, confusion, suffocations, and feelings of futility
Malaysia, China, Thailand	**Koro** sudden and intense anxiety that the penis (or female vulva and nipples) will recede into the body and cause death

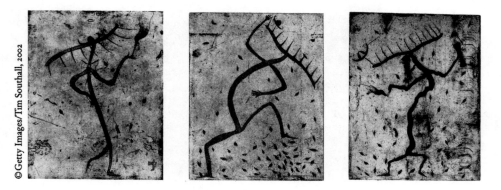

Arctic and Subarctic Eskimos	**Pibloktoq** dissociative episode; extreme excitement, seizures that lead to coma; during the attack victims have been known to have violent outbursts and perform dangerous and irrational acts
African-American, European-American, Caribbean	**Rootwork** cultural interpretations that ascribe illness to hexing, witchcraft, sorcery, or the evil influence of another person; anxiety-causing
China, Taiwan	**Shenkui** panic symptoms that accompany somatic complaints for which no physical cause can be demonstrated; includes fear of semen loss, feared because of its representation of vital life force
Ethiopia, Somalia, Egypt, Sudan, Iran and other North African and Middle Eastern countries.	**Zar** spirit-possessing of an individual; dissociative episodes include laughing, shouting, hitting the head against a wall, singing, or weeping; also apathy and withdrawal; not considered pathological locally

"The age-old method of curing the possessed and getting rid of undesirable entities which have invaded them follows the same sort of pattern as our drug abreaction treatments of battle neuroses. The 'possessed' patient is worked up into a condition of frenzied emotional excitement, in which he expresses intense anger and fear, and this leads very often to a collapse, which may be followed by a feeling of calm and release from the 'demon' which has been tormenting him, just as our patients felt released from traumatic memories."

—William Sargant, *The Mind Possessed: A Physiology of Possession, Mysticism and Faith Healing*

Historical Instances of Panic

P AN, A GREEK GOD, half-man and half-goat, was said to have appeared on the side of the Athenians in the Battle of Marathon and to have put the Persians to flight. Thereafter the adjective *panikos* (noun *panikon*) was to describe an extreme sense of irrational fear in an individual or a collective. In 1534, Rabelais had coined the term *peur panique,* and from there it spread to other modern European languages. As a technical medical term, its history is much shorter.

For the historian, an attempt to write an historical survey of panic is bound to cause anxiety, not an unrelated phenomenon.[1] This is partially due to the difficulties presented by the etymology of the word itself. The word *panic* differs from *fear* or *terror* because of the active sense it connotes. As a medical term, describing a pathological state of an individual, it is relatively new and not synonymous to its wider usage. Moreover, tracing the history of the medical concept of panic, we are led to many related phenomena: hysteria and neurasthenia, phobias (especially agoraphobia), soldier's heart and shell shock, melancholia and depression—and we have not yet exhausted the list. The historical relation between panic and anxiety is yet another, if not the chief, source of confusion.

Not unrelated is the problem of methodology, as it is hard to define precisely what the history of panic would look like, even if only the history of the medical concept. We could, for instance, search in the writings of past physicians for something that resembles panic as we know it *today,* the outcome of which would be a story of medicine's gradual understanding of panic as a separate

TO PAN

Muse, tell me about Pan, the dear son of Hermes, with his goat's feet and two horns—a lover of merry noise. Through wooded glades he wanders with dancing nymphs who foot it on some sheer cliff's edge, calling upon Pan, the shepherd-god, long-haired, unkempt. He has every snowy crest and the mountain peaks and rocky crests for his domain; hither and thither he goes through the close thickets, now lured by soft streams, and now he presses on amongst towering crags and climbs up to the highest peak that overlooks the flocks. Often he courses through the glistening high mountains, and often on the shouldered hills he speeds along slaying wild beasts, this keen-eyed god. Only at evening, as he returns from the chase, he sounds his note, playing sweet and low on his pipes of reed: not even she could excel him in melody—that bird who in flower-laden spring pouring forth her lament utters honey-voiced song amid the leaves. At that hour the clear-voiced nymphs are with him and move with nimble feet, singing by some spring of dark water, while Echo wails about the mountain-top, and the god on this side or on that of the choirs, or at times sidling into the midst, plies it nimbly with his feet. On his back he wears a spotted lynx-pelt, and he delights in high-pitched songs in a soft meadow where crocuses and sweet-smelling hyacinths bloom at random in the grass.

They sing of the blessed gods and high Olympus and choose to tell of such an one as luck-bringing Hermes above the rest, how he is the swift messenger of all the gods, and how he came to Arcadia, the land of many springs and mother of flocks, there where his sacred place is as god of Cyllene. For there, though a god, he used to tend curly-fleeced sheep in the service of a mortal man, because there fell on him and waxed strong melting desire to wed the rich-tressed daughter of Dryops, and there he brought about the merry marriage. And in the house she bare Hermes a dear son who from his birth was marvelous to look upon, with goat's feet and two horns—a noisy, merry-laughing child. But when the nurse saw his uncouth face and full beard, she was afraid and sprang up and fled and left the child. Then luck-bringing Hermes received him and took him in his arms: very glad in his heart was the god. And he went quickly to the abodes of the deathless gods, carrying his son wrapped in warm skins of mountain hares, and set him down beside Zeus and showed him to the rest of the gods. Then all the immortals were glad in heart, and Bacchic Dionysus in especial; and they called the boy Pan because he delighted all their hearts.

And so hail to you, lord! I seek your favour with a song. And now I will remember you and another song also.

—From Hesiod, *The Homeric Hymns and Homerica*, translated by H.G. Evelyn-White

The name Pan is here derived from *Pávr∑s* "all." Cp. Hesiod, *Works and Days* 80-82, *Hymn to Aphrodite* (v) 198.

phenomenon. However, from an epistemological point of view, it would not serve to consider panic outside of its historical context. We should not treat the medical concept of panic apart from the society and culture in which it was constructed as a distinct behavior. For this reason a separate cultural analysis of panic is really the reverse of the same error. Those two are inseparable, as what we usually refer to as *culture* is not merely the context in which the phenomenon of panic was medicalized but is rather intrinsic to this very process.

The present-day association of panic and anxiety, as defined by the DSM-IV (p. vii), may be in itself problematic for the historian: "Their association," writes Michael J. Clark, "has been variable and contingent from both a clinical and historical standpoint … anxiety and panic represent two very different kinds of experience." This contemporary classification is in itself an outcome of the history of panic. As we shall see, the history of panic is the history of the attempt to mark a distinction from anxiety, an attempt that was not always entirely successful. Schematically put, the history of the modern phenomenon of panic should begin, I think, with the nineteenth-century interest in anxiety, *in tandem* with the emergence of hysteria and neurasthenia as the *prima loci* of psychiatric interest in the second half of that century. We will then enter the twentieth century with the gradual dissolution of nineteenth-century psychiatric paradigms of the neuroses on the one hand and the experiences of psychiatry at war on the other, until the late 1900s when panic is finally defined as we know it today.

Although the Latin term *anxietas* was found in the medical literature in the early eighteenth century, it only after the 1850s that doctors began to discuss anxiety as a separate phenomenon, usually as symptoms of other nervous diseases or forms of insanity. Whereas in English and in German only one word existed, anxiety and angst respectively, in French there existed a subtle difference between *anxiété* and *angoisse,* which was not always clear.[2] Littré and Robin defined three intensities of anxiety in their *Dictionnaire de Médecine* (1858): *inquiètude, anxiété,* and *angoisse.* As German E. Berrios and Christopher Link rightly mention, the term *angst* acquired new significance after the publication of Kierkegaard's work in 1844, which differentiated between object-related fear and fear that has no object. But as Aubrey Lewis reminds us, the German *angst* implies a much stronger sense of fear than the English *anxiety,* and to translate one into another is wrong.

The second half of the nineteenth century, of course, was the golden age of hysteria. Although considered a disease since ancient times, the work of historians such as Jan Ellen Goldstein and Roy Porter has shown that nineteenth-century hysteria was a new phenomenon, constructed both by nineteenth-century bourgeois culture as well as by the rising profession of psychiatry. As Porter puts it, "the nineteenth century was hysteria's golden age precisely because it was then that the moral presence of the doctor became normative as never before in regulating intimate lives." Here the problems of the relation between body and mind manifested in such force that hysteria was not only one of the pillars upon which psychiatry constituted itself as a discipline but also a major source of embarrassment. Nineteenth-century physicians and psychiatrists deployed conflicting strategies in order to understand this phenomenon. Somatic models, which predominated medical thought during the nineteenth century, viewed hysteria as caused by some anatomical lesion, rendering hysteria a universal disease and therefore a legitimate matter of interest to the medical establishment. Psychological models emerged out of the politics of the clinical setting and as a result of problems in the somatic models. And finally, as Foucault and others have noted, hysteria was one of the focal points of nineteenth-century discourse on sexuality.

Although usually associated with femininity, hysteria in the male was already known even before its great theorizer, Jean Martin Charcot, came on the scene. Hysteria's twin, neurasthenia, is even more problematic. Coined by American Charles Beard to describe nervous fatigue among men and then picked up by Weir Mitchel to describe nervous diseases among middle-class women, the term enjoyed much success in Europe where it was used to designate different nervous diseases. Charcot, for instance, used to ascribe hysteria to working-class males and neurasthenia to his middle-class patients.

It was is in this medical world that the idea of anxiety as a separate phenomenon (not a separate condition!) started to gain merit. It was usually described as a symptom accompanying various disorders but especially neurasthenia, which was still conceptualized in physiogenetic terms toward the end of the century—far more than hysteria. Gradually, anxiety-related neuroses were seen as separated from the *grandes névroses,* hysteria and neurasthenia. For instance, in 1866, Morel identified a new set of neuroses, which he called *délire emotif* (emotional delirium), the etiology of which he thought to be pathological changes in the ganglionic nervous system.

This process reached its climax with the French publication of Freud's *The Justification for Detaching from Neurasthenia a Particular Syndrome: The Anxiety Neurosis* (1895). Here Freud suggested that what was known as neurasthenia should be broken into neurasthenia "proper" and anxiety-neuroses (*névrose d'angoisse*), which is defined by a state of anxiousness and anxiety attacks.[3] Freud's suggestion met hardly any resistance, and Berrios and Link might be right to suggest that this is because similar suggestions were already made, if only less overtly. Few have expressed opposing ideas: Pitres and Règis, for instance, suggested that what Freud was describing is really neurasthenia and melancholia. But not unexpectedly, Freud's sexual etiology of anxiety-neuroses, which he thought was only partially a hereditary predisposition, received a considerable amount of criticism, much less than the idea of anxiety-neuroses itself.

Jules Henry famously asserted that psychopathology is the outcome of all that is wrong with a culture. It is now well known that the fears of modernity and the uncertainty of changing times became an obsession among the nineteenth-century bourgeois culture, often manifesting itself in outbursts of hysteria and neurasthenia. Living in an era of accelerated changes, such as shifting of gender roles, the emergence of capitalist industrial society, the development of the railway train and speed travel, and the growing demands of modern society in general, have resulted in increased nervousness, and nervousness about nervousness, to use the words of one important analyst of nineteenth-century bourgeois culture, Peter Gay.

World War I posed new challenges to the medical establishments with the experience of what was eventually termed *shell shock*. To view these symptoms of war as the first epidemic of male hysteria would be to lose sight of some of the other dimensions of this phenomenon, especially in terms of medical practices of managing lives. Male hysteria on the battlefield was not entirely new to the medical authorities. Already in the American Civil War soldiers were diagnosed as suffering from soldier's heart and nostalgia. During the Russo-Japanese War in 1905, the Russians established the principles of military psychiatric treatment of nervous breakdown during war. Many of those original principles are still intact: Proximity, Immediacy, and Expectancy. The Russians were also the first to notice evacuation syndrome, the increase in cases of nervous breakdown once a legitimate cause for evacuation was established. It was, however, the experience of the First World War that brought significant changes in the military medical practices in the West.

During World War II numerous soldiers developed battle neuroses, including "shell shock." Shell shock is a predecessor of modern panic disorder that was caused by severe trauma and overload to the emotional system during and after the experience and witnessing of modern warfare. Symptoms included withdrawal, reexperiencing the terror locked in memories, and an inability to function in the real world. Ether and methedrine were prescribed to initiate intense emotional excitement which would then result in the desired emotional catharsis. The intent was to encourage an intense emotional release that would thereby "get it out of the system," so to speak.

To map out a few points of importance to our discussion on panic on the subject of shell shock, historians such as Eric Leed and Elaine Showalter have identified the new kind of warfare, with its impersonality and the soldier's sense of futility. Additionally, parallels between female and male hysteria have been drawn, establishing both as non-verbal expressions against war, as well as against the concept of manliness itself. Leed further suggests that shell shock was a compromise between the reluctant soldier and the authorities, who preferred to confront the soldier on medical rather than moral grounds. During the war, psychological models proved more favorable. This mentality allowed ideas about the characters of the British or French soldiers to remain intact, since heavier weight (often negative) was given to the physical medical conditions. The "pathological" conditions were often dismissed as less significant and easier to overcome. Shell shock would become combat stress in the Second World War and Posttraumatic Stress Disorder after the Vietnam War. In the First World War, however, shell shock was still discussed in terms of hysteria, and as much as the medical authorities were attempting to find a cure (which was aimed only at getting the soldier back to the battlefield), they were also occupied with the question of fear and anxiety in the context of the realities of war and the problem of anxiety and fear as, after all, normal conditions. Moreover, most historians agree that the experience of shell shock in World War I was one of the causes for the rise of psychiatry as a widespread civilian practice and for the growing reception of Freud's theories of the psyche.

Freud's separation of anxiety-neuroses recounted above is perhaps the most important event in the history of the formation of anxiety as a clinical entity. It could be seen, of course, as the outcome of a very anxious society. Peter Gay identifies anxiety and guilt as major psychic forces in this culture. What he sees as nervousness about nervousness, that is, endless discussions on the increasing cases of nervous disorders in times of significant change, is a symptom of an undercurrent of anxiety (and guilt) that lies beneath the notorious nineteenth-century bourgeois confidence. Auden's assertion that his century (the twentieth) was the Age of Anxiety is universally recognized. The nineteenth century, with its world wars, its accelerated progress in medicalization, and its gradual replacement of the accepted old-world psychiatric paradigms with new ones, began to increasingly pay more attention to anxiety as pathology. As Clark mentions, although Freud eventually gave up his sexual etiology to anxiety-neurosis, he did not alter his concept of anxiety-neuroses significantly, and he continued to view anxiety as the key to understanding the human psyche. And yet, although most of his successors have attempted to secure the distinctiveness of anxiety-neuroses from other pathological states, few of them have succeeded. As Lewis suggests, anxiety-related research became popular more as a result of the growing awareness of the role of anxiety in other clinical syndromes (such as depression) and less due to the growing success of anxiety-neuroses as a distinct clinical category. The history of anxiety, claims Clark, is for the most part the history of *normality*, a non-pathological response to living in world of escalating changes. The history of panic, on the other hand, would be less of panic itself but of measurements and practices to avoid it.4 But anxiety as *pathology* has a history too, not entirely distinct, I think, from that of anxiety as *normality*.

Consider, for instance, *agoraphobia,* defined by Westphal in his influential publication *Die Agoraphobie* (1871). Reviewing the case histories of three male patients, Westpahl defined a specific phobia from open spaces or from crowds. Although his etiology of the pathology was widely contested, his views became widely accepted among the psychiatric establishment. In the following decades, sociologists such as Simmel and urbanists such as Sitte were identifying the modern city as the cause of such pathological states. The spatial organization of the modern city was now in itself pathologized. Agoraphobia and its pair claustrophobia describe less of a pathological state than the normal existence of the modern urban dweller.

Is it time we move on—to the age of panic? In 1890, Brissaud, a neurologist, made another major step in the history of panic. He tried to differentiate between *anxiété,* which he thought to be of a psychological origin, and *angoisse,* which he described in terms of somatic lesions. In 1895, Freud separated the anxiety-neuroses from neurasthenia. And yet the term *panic,* as related to the individual, was only being used by one physician. In 1875, Maudsley proposed the term *melancholic panic* to describe something similar to Morel's *delirious emotions.* Later, in 1920, Kempf coined the term *homosexual panic* to describe a fragile schizophrenic personality marked by latent homosexuality. The wide acceptance of this category might have helped the term *panic* itself to rise in prominence as a commonly used technical term, particularly during World War II, and especially in the English-speaking world.

In 1962, American psychiatrist Donald Klein noticed that after administering Impramine[5] to patients who suffered from anxiety-neurosis complicated with agoraphobia, the drug suppressed acute anxiety attacks but not the long-lasting state of anxiety. He therefore concluded that they must be different phenomena, and ascribed to the first one what Freud himself termed in French *attaque d'angoisse*—the term *panic attack.* This differentiation, made on the basis of different reactions to a therapeutic action, was the basis for the definitions given in the DSM-III and the DSM-IV for panic attack, panic disorder, and anxiety disorders in general.[6]

Freud, we must remember, used the word panic only once—in his *Group Psychology and the Analysis of the Ego* (1921). Freud was not the only one who referred to panic when analyzing the behavior of the masses; in fact, it was used mainly in researches conducted by military psychiatry, but not only by them. In sociology, the term *moral panic* is now a common classification of certain epidemics that could be termed hysterical, or could be termed as panic reactions. Does the history of panic defy, too, any attempt to separate pathology and normalcy? Consider for instance the use of homosexual panic defense in the American legal system. As Eve Kosofsky Sedgwick puts it,

> [T]he homosexual panic defense rests on the falsely individualizing and pathologizing assumption that hatred of homosexuals is so private and so atypical a phenomenon in this culture as to be classifiable as an accountability-reducing illness.... [On] the contrary ... hatred of homosexuals is even more public, more typical, hence harder to find a leverage against than hatred of other disadvantaged groups.

Is panic disorder one of the characteristics of our culture? It may well be so. But the fact that panic (as anxiety) is related to so many other phenomena might suggest that there is a lesson to be learned from the widespread use of *panic* as an explanatory term for human behavior. I am not suggesting a nihilistic approach to medical knowledge, nor a criticism that is aimed at the individual. But I do think that we should ask critical questions when observing the recurrence of panic attacks, for indeed they can teach us a great deal about "all that is wrong with our culture." Our inquiry should not stop short of going a few steps ahead of the medical diagnostics. Put in a different way, we can do better than (just) panic about panic.

Endnotes

1. Unfortunately, there are only a few historical surveys on the history of panic and panic disorder. For the development of the medical category of panic I have found the article by Berrios and Link and the survey by Pichot very useful and my analysis is indebted to their excellent studies.

2. The Latin word *angustia* is the source of the English, French, and German words anguish, angoisse, and angst. However, only in French were both words used as technical terms. There is no German equivalent to the Latin *anxietas*.

3. Unlike German or English, no equivalent to anxiousness and ängstlichkeit exist. Freud has decided to term it *attente anxieuse*, which can be best translated as a tendency toward anxiety.

4. In this respect Clark's opinion gains weight from the fact that panic disorders, when treated psychologically, are generally treated with cognitive behavioral therapies.

5. See Drug-Specific Information for Panic Disorder Diagnois, pp. 284–288.

6. As Zal mentions, from the DSM-III onward, the psychiatric definitions are based on empirical somatic observation rather than psychological analysis. It is also important to mention that the concept of panic as a psychiatric disorder has caught on considerably in North America, whereas in other cultures certain forms of panic are not considered pathological locally.

FRANZ RENGGLI

Tracing the Roots of Panic to Prenatal Trauma

F OR THE PAST FIVE YEARS I have worked with a patient in my practice who suffers from panic attacks. I will call her Miriam. Her panic attacks usually begin with a feeling of tightness in her chest, as if "an elephant were sitting on it." Connected with this sensation of suffocation are heart palpitations so strong she believes she's suffering a heart attack, dying, or losing her mind. Miriam has always been a person who never let herself lose control in her life; otherwise she risked having a panic attack. Due to her overwhelmingly powerful anxieties our therapy sessions took place over the telephone.

The crisis that brought Miriam to therapy were panic attacks that were triggered by two car accidents, one shortly after the other. She suffered whiplash injury, which resulted in headaches and severe back and neck pain (sometimes so agonizing she thought of killing herself). The car accidents followed the end of a traumatic divorce that had gone on for two years and had threatened her with losing custody of her son.

Though the car accidents were stressful enough in and of themselves, it seemed there must have been an earlier cause for Miriam's distress. Miriam's traumatic family history holds the key: Prior to Miriam's birth, her mother had aborted a baby girl in the seventh month of pregnancy. The baby was aborted at home, survived for several hours without care or nourishment, and finally died. Miriam's mother's problems continued with Miriam; she was vomiting constantly, losing weight, and was ultimately thinner when she gave birth than she was when Miriam was conceived. Another crisis presented itself as the day of Miriam's birth approached. It was a Saturday night when her mother's labor started and she went to the hospital. Although her cervix had already dilated, because the hospital staff was tired they gave Miriam's mother morphine to stop labor. Ironically, the next day labor had to be induced to force the birth. During the birth her cervix ruptured and Miriam's mother nearly bled to death. Because of her mother's medical crisis and because Miriam appeared to be dead, the newly born baby was laid aside. Only later did someone notice that the baby girl was still alive, and only then was Miriam cared for. Because of her mother's critical condition, Miriam was separated from her for a week after birth. Another factor was that Miriam's mother suffered her whole life under a psychotic mother (Miriam's grandmother).

Were the whiplash injuries or the divorce and custody battle or Miriam's birth history the root of her panic attacks? It was the recapitulated physical and emotional pain of the fearfully traumatic divorce trial and the whiplash injuries that catapulted Miriam to reconnect with her mother's physical and emotional pain from the trauma before and during her pregnancy, and both their birth experiences which made it possible for Miriam to seek help in resolving her pain. An important question is whether Miriam's mother ever completely mourned for her aborted baby before Miriam was conceived? Because her mother probably had not been able connect with and resolve her feelings of grief, sadness, and probable guilt at the death of her first baby, Miriam was born with her mother's same unresolved feelings.

The History of Prenatal and Perinatal Psychology

Here I introduce the present knowledge of prenatal and perinatal psychology and psychotherapy. It began with the 1924 book by Otto Rank, *The Trauma of Birth*. Rank, together with his patients, recognized that the roots of neurotic development can always be traced back to the birth experience and that the neurotic pains of his clients could not be completely understood outside of this context. In the 1950s, Hungarian psychoanalyst Nandor Fodor, who was living in the United States, detected that every strong anxiety

"In his book on the trauma of birth, [Otto] Rank (1924) has made a determined attempt to establish a relationship between the earliest phobias of children and the impressions made on them by the event of birth. But I do not think he has been successful. His theory is open to two objections. In the first place, he assumes that the infant has received certain sensory impressions, in particular of a visual kind, at the time of birth, the renewal of which can recall to its memory the trauma of birth and thus evoke a reaction of anxiety. This assumption is quite unfounded and extremely improbable. It is not credible that a child should retain any but tactile and general sensations relating to the process of birth. If, later on, children show fear of small animals that disappear into holes or emerge from them, this reaction, according to Rank, is due to their perceiving an analogy. But it is an analogy of which they cannot be aware. In the second place, in considering these later anxiety-situations Rank dwells now on the child's recollection of its happy intra-uterine existence, now on its recollection of the traumatic disturbance which interrupted that existence—which leaves the door wide open for arbitrary interpretation. There are, moreover, certain examples of childhood anxiety which directly traverse his theory. When, for instance, a child is left alone in the dark one would expect it, according to his view, to welcome the re-establishment of the intra-uterine situation; yet it is precisely on such occasions that the child reacts with anxiety. And if this is explained by saying that the child is reminded of the interruption which the event of birth made in its intra-uterine happiness, it becomes impossible to shut one's eyes any longer to the far-fetched character of such explanations."

—Sigmund Freud, *Inhibitions,
Symptoms and Anxiety*

dream was ultimately a dream about one's own birth. Who isn't familiar with dreams of a terrifying flight without having the control to move or prevent the imminent danger? Or the dream of being swallowed by a huge swirling vortex and then falling to its furthest depths?

English psychoanalyst Francis Mott, a student of Fodor's, developed a psychology of the fetal self in the womb through analysis of his patients' dreams. Mott detected that the baby senses the negative feelings of the mother coming into its body through the blood of the umbilical cord. In response, the fetus returns these bad feelings to the mother through the same blood, running it back through the placenta. Thus a fight, or even war, can start early in life between a mother and her baby. Mott also worked on mythology

Walk Warily
D.H. Lawrence

Walk warily, walk warily, be careful what you say:
because now the Sunderers are hovering round,
the Dividers are close upon us, dogging our every breath
and watching our every step,
and beating their great wings in our panting faces.

The angels are standing back, the angles of the Kiss.
They wait, they give way now
to the Sunderers, to the swift ones
the ones with the sharp black wings
and the shudder of electric anger
and the drumming of pinions of thunder
and hands like salt
and the sudden dripping down of the knife-edge cleavage of the lightning
cleaving, cleaving.

Lo, we are in the midst of the Sunderers
the Cleavers, that cleave us forever apart from one another
and separate heart from heart, and cut away all caresses
with the white triumphance of lightning and electric delight,
the Dividers, the Thunderers, the Swift Ones, blind with speed
who put salt in our mouths
and currents of excitement in our limbs
and hotness, and then more crusted brine in our hearts.

It is the day of the Sunderers
and the angels are standing back.

*   *   *

to show that every god or godly figure in the world has something
to do with a baby in the womb—every god has a connection with
light, brightness, or fire—a symbol of the primary feeling of the
fetal self in the womb.

The field of prenatal and perinatal psychology continued with
the advancements of Czech psychiatrist Stanislav Grof, who
worked with LSD. This psychedelic drug often regresses people to

their birth and all the horrors and panics they experienced. Never is so much adrenaline secreted in a human being as when a woman goes into labor. This is the same hormone that is secreted in the fight-or-flight response. That means that the birth process is the utmost experience of anxiety in most people's lives. Grof also showed that the different traumata of life all center on the same feelings. Like the skin of an onion, one layer can be peeled away, but the essence and roots of the anxiety remain locked in the center with the trauma of birth. Grof called this phenomenon the COEX-system.

English psychiatrist and theologian Frank Lake also used LSD for his research and discovered that the origin of every trauma does not lie in birth, but rather in the experiences of a fetus during its first three months, beginning with conception. How parents react when they find out they are expecting a child is the first impacting experience. This means that early trauma of the first days and weeks repeats itself during the rest of pregnancy, becomes a pattern in the birth, and continues into infancy and childhood.

Ultrasound examinations provide firm evidence regarding the progression of the fetal psyche in the womb. Italian psychoanalyst Alessandra Piontelli witnessed a physician showing a mother her baby during her ultrasound and how she reacted to her baby and visa versa. In Piontelli's case histories we learn that a baby reflects the behavior of the mother like a mirror. The deepest imprinting for the personality of a human being develops during the time in the mother's womb.

American David Chamberlain was the next to make advances by putting children and their mothers under hypnosis and regressing them to their in utero and birth experiences. Chamberlain showed that the birth stories of the child and mother were identical. Children can vividly remember their birth and what they lived through before birth—marking a milestone in the development of prenatal and perinatal psychology and psychotherapy. With all of this knowledge to work from, therapist William Emerson began to work with babies and small children in the mid-1970s to help them to resolve their pregnancy and birth traumata.

To review, here's a summary of the main results of prenatal and perinatal psychology and psychotherapy:

- Birth represents the most intense experience of anxiety in most human lives. The body's inclination to stress originates from birth. Stress is *the* illness of our time.

- The most important imprinting of a human being happens in utero during the first nine months of existence, at birth, and during infancy and babyhood. Although we cannot consciously remember this as adults, our bodies store these memories.

- Because we don't consciously recall our prenatal and perinatal experiences, we are inclined to repeat them continuously throughout our lives, to stage them again and again in our professions, partnerships, and with our children and friends. Emerson calls this tendency recapitulation. The more traumatic the beginning of our lives, the more we tend so recapitulate our vulnerability. Peter Nathanielsz showed that the conditions in which we develop in the womb profoundly influence our susceptibility to coronary artery disease, stroke, diabetes, and obesity in later life, reiterating the notion that people seek out therapy to resolve issues that originate with prenatal and perinatal traumata.

- Most people live through a lot of traumata in their lives. While stories vary from case to case, the emotional charge is usually very similar (the COEX-system). Whiplash injuries, for instance, or other trauma connected with strong emotional and/or physical pain, should heal spontaneously or with professional help after a certain time. If not there is probably a hidden birth or pregnancy trauma beneath the present trauma. In my own practice working with babies, I see tendencies in both parents to suppress old hurt feelings, anxieties, and traumatic experiences. As adults we have the ability to repress these feelings, whereas babies do not yet have this capacity. They absorb all the unresolved feelings and problems of their parents—past family problems, unfinished business, unresolved conflicts between father and mother. I have found that parents are usually very willing to confront these traumatic experiences in their own lives as new parents. This is a good time to initiate the healing process for both parents and baby.

Panic in Relation to the Prenatal and Perinatal Eexperience

Before I begin my case studies, I would like to direct the reader's attention to the symptoms of the panic attack itself. All these symptoms can be compared to what a baby experiences at birth.

Panic is the outbreak of catastrophic anxieties. Difficulty in breathing is the center of this syndrome, as the body tells itself, "I want to get out of here, I cannot bear it any longer." The feeling of suffocating is one of the strongest symptoms of a panic attack. Connected with it are sensations of feeling restricted and tightness in the chest. Heart palpitation is generally perceived with same intensity and often causes people to think they are about to have a heart attack. Feelings of suffocating combined with heart palpitations can give the panic attack the added dimension of acute fear of death or of losing one's mind. The feeling of loss of control causes an intense sense of fear. This is experienced by the body as dizziness, fainting, or numbness. Can the feelings and experiences of birth be described more accurately and clearly?

In panic sweating can alternate with chills: It has been proposed that an infant experiences burning sensations on the skin when they leave the womb. Also, the feeling of losing the mother during or after birth is, according David Chamberlain, one of coldness or shivering, the physical symbol of separation and loneliness. The terrifying feeling of losing control can be explained by the influence of the medication administered to the mother in labor. The work of Emerson and Ray Castellino, a Craniosacral therapist based in Santa Barbara, has shown that the baby is often overwhelmed by pain and that the contact to the mother during labor is drastically weakened or completely interrupted, causing the baby to lose control of the movements and the force of its own body, which is extremely frightening.

Panic attacks are frequently accompanied by irritable bowel syndrome (i.e., digestive troubles, flatulence, diarrhea, or constipation). Let us be reminded that during and immediately after birth the intestines begin to function whereas during pregnancy the baby was fed directly through the blood of the mother. Migraines are one of the most common comorbidities of panic attacks, which

brings up the question as to whether an unresolved birth trauma is hidden behind migraines.

If we consider claustrophobia, the fear of narrow and crowded spaces, the symbolic meaning of childbirth is clear and evident. Agoraphobia can be understood as avoiding the anxiety-releasing mechanisms. Depersonalization and the loss of reality can be another symptom of panic attacks; through these symptoms the person speaks directly of the anxieties experienced at birth.

The main thesis of cognitive therapy is that body sensations are catastrophically misinterpreted. This assertion supports my argument that panic attacks are often the result of unresolved pregnancy or birth trauma. An apparently harmless situation has the capacity to trigger body sensations that originate within old traumas.

Case Studies

I would like to share several case studies that impressed me; but first I would like to share a personal experience. I was married and my wife and I had two children. During my long career as patient, mostly after my divorce, I recognized how much panic I felt about being close to and having a relationship with a woman, which at the same time was my deepest wish. These fears lay dormant in me as long as I was married, under a thick layer of symptoms. They gradually came to the surface the more I learned about myself. Being a therapist myself, I was desperate; I was close to giving up my practice. After all, how could I help other people if I couldn't help myself? My history: About six years ago, through a special regression therapy, I recognized that my mother, who had had two girls, did not want a third child. She thought of abortion but her religious beliefs did not allow her do it. About halfway through her pregnancy with me she suffered from such intense anxiety and terror that she tried to kill herself. When I was born we both nearly died. I then realized my inner formula was—when I open my heart to a woman that I love, I risk dying. This knowledge helped me to calm down and to come out of my depression and panic.

In the practice of two colleagues and friends I recently met a patient, I will call him James, who had three severe accidents in as many years. First he was caught in an avalanche, then he got stuck in his kayak after having suffered a prolapsed disk, and finally he was caught in a car between a truck and a wall on the highway and nearly died. Since then he's been suffering from a whiplash injury. James is in constant therapeutic treatment and takes strong medication against the pain, which is sometimes so strong he considers killing himself.

One of my friends worked with Craniosacral Therapy*, the other with Peter Levine's Somatic Experiencing**. Through them I had the opportunity to meet James. He shared his story, to which I replied that I could see that he could not free himself three times from a situation in which he was trapped. He shared that his mother

---

* Craniosacral Therapy is a treatment process that uses gentle touch to stop or manipulate skullbone sutures, with the goal of activating the self-healing process and reducing dependence on healthcare providers.

** Somatic Experiencing is a naturalistic approach to trauma healing through the observation that prey animals, though routinely threatened, are rarely traumatized.

had lost three children during pregnancy before she conceived him. From my experience I know that a mother losing a baby mostly lives through her own unresolved trauma and because of that she is unable to mourn. Often times her next baby has to mourn for her during the pregnancy and their own infancy and babyhood. I believe that James went through considerable mourning for his three siblings. He wanted to come out of the womb but was stuck. The strong painkillers prevented James from crying in the present time, but in the following session he could feel his tears again for the first time. He felt hope to free himself one day from the pains he had been suffering in the last years. James is an example of how a person restages the trauma of pregnancy and birth in their life.

A close friend of mine lives with the panic of having suicidal feelings if he does not take his antidepressants. His history: He is the youngest child of an East-European Jewish family that owned important weapon factories in their country. When Hitler occupied the country they negotiated the safety of the entire family by turning over their factories to the Third Reich. My friend was conceived during this time of utmost terror and the beginning of his life in the womb coincided with the family's escape to Switzerland.

Another case study involves a friend and colleague of mine who developed such intense pain—a panic equivalent—that she had to stop working. Her history: When her mother was near the end of her pregnancy, she fell down the stairs. This fall initiated my colleague's birth.

Another friend developed chronic fatigue syndrome three years ago. He just lies in bed and can't do any work—another panic equivalent. His history: His mother became so depressed during her pregnancy with him that she had to take antidepressants. Her depression had its origin in having been regularly beat up by her father. My friend had to be delivered by caesarian section and was immediately put in an incubator and completely separated from his mother for two weeks.

For several years one of my patients had such severe sweat attacks during the night that he had to change his pajamas and bed linens every night. His "conscious" panic was concentrated on birds, mostly on dead birds—creatures he managed to avoid. His history: He also came from an East-European country from which his parents had fled during an uprising against the Russian occupation. His mother wanted to go back but his father wanted to go as far away as he could. As a compromise they settled in Switzerland. My patient was conceived in the refugee camp where his mother was forced to do hard work. She fell in a pit, which was the event that initiated his birth.

Another patient experiences panic as a feeling of tightness in his chest and chronic pains in his neck. His first child memory: He was playing peacefully in his parent's garden. He turned back and saw a huge black dog behind him. He panicked and screamed as loud as he could, and was finally calmed down by his father who played the accordion for him. He experienced similar panic attacks throughout his life and at a certain period the awareness of his own being would cause a panic attack. Additionally, his mother suffered from a weak heart during his delivery and she nearly died.

Lastly, I would like to report about two young girls I saw as patients. The first, only two-and-a-half years old, had been suffering panic attacks during the night. The girl's mother and father had such a vehement quarrel in the middle of the mother's pregnancy that the father ended up smashing a glass onto a hard floor in an outbreak of rage. The splinters from the glass injured the mother's foot. She could not receive any treatment during her pregnancy, and after the birth it was too late to operate the tendons. The pains continued and resonated as resentment in the mother. After the husband's outbreak of rage the mother felt very lonely and abandoned. Once the parents were able to acknowledge their rage and speak about it, they were able to reconnect through their love. This resulted in their little girl being able to sleep without panic attacks.

The second girl was the adopted baby of some friends of mine. She was labeled a "heroin baby," as both of her real parents were shooting up heroin during the mother's entire pregnancy. After birth, the baby had to undergo heroin withdrawal. As a baby she had five to six panic attacks with wild screaming every night. By her sixth birthday they had decreased to about three per night. As a six-year-old, she was finally able to articulate the nightmares she was experiencing during these panic attacks: in the dream she lived through the experience of an older sister who died at the hands of her abusive, violent, heroin-addicted father. She was unconsciously aware of these memories, having been five months along in her own in utero development. In her dream she lived through her biological father's cruelty again and again—feeling as if she herself had been maltreated and killed.

With these stories I have attempted to show that our behavior and emotions are influenced and shaped to a major extent by circumstances and events of which we cannot be conscious. However, the memory of that early time is stored in our body, in our unconscious. Therefore, the "stories" our patients tell us may not always be the cause of panic. But connected to them is always the hidden trauma, the birth and pregnancy pattern in their body. For the healing process it is necessary to see, to feel, to be in contact with this body pattern. It is the via regia, the best way to the unconscious, to the old traumata, to the catastrophic anxieties and fantasies. Changing this old body pattern means healing. Therefore healing occurs through the changing of the body pattern.

Conclusion

Our perceptions, feelings, anxieties, and conflicts are deeply imprinted in our prenatal and perinatal experiences. This means changing the paradigm compared to the position of the sciences in the first five to eight decades of the last century, when scientists believed that a neonate baby was just a reflex bundle that did not perceive nor experience anything. Being able to see a baby as a fully conscious human being from conception on, we will better understand the basis of our feelings of tenderness and love and of warmth and security. For the basis of the human relationships and of our self-esteem on the one hand, to the sadness, desperation, anger, rage, violence, and terror on the other hand, lies in the vulnerability of these early days and months of each human being, which continues into babyhood and adult life.

PETER A. LEVINE

Panic, Biology, and Reason: Giving the Body Its Due

The Substitute Tiger

MY INTEREST in the essential role played by bodily responses in the genesis and treatment of panic-anxiety began quite accidentally in 1969.[1] A psychiatrist, knowing of my interest in "mind/body healing"—a fledgling arena at the time, had referred a young woman to see me. Nancy had been suffering from panic attacks for about two years. She had not responded to psychotherapy, while tranquilizers and antidepressant drugs gave her only minimal relief. The referring psychiatrist asked me to do some "relaxation training" with her. My attempts were equally unsuccessful. She resisted; I tried harder. We got nowhere. Since I knew almost nothing about panic attacks at the time, I asked her for more detailed information about the how and when of her attacks. Nancy revealed that the onset of her first attack occurred while she, along with a group of other students, was taking the Graduate Record Examination. She remembers breaking out in a cold sweat and beginning to shake. Forcing herself to complete the test, Nancy then ran out, frantically pacing the streets for hours, afraid to enter a bus or taxi. Fortunately, she met a friend who took her home. During the following two years her symptoms worsened and became more frequent. Eventually she was unable to leave her house alone and could not follow through with graduate school even though she had passed the exam and was accepted by a major university.

In our conversation, Nancy recollected the following sequence of events: Arriving early, she went to the café to have a coffee and smoke a cigarette. A group of students were already there, talking about how difficult the test was. Nancy, overhearing this, became agitated, lit another cigarette, and gulped a second coffee. She remembered feeling quite jittery upon entering the room. She recalled that the exams and marking pencils were passed out and that she wrote vigorously. She became almost breathless at this point and quite agitated—I noticed that her carotid (neck) pulse was increasing rapidly.

I asked Nancy to lie down and I tried to get her to relax. Relaxation was not the answer. As I naively, and with the best of intentions, attempted to help her relax, she went into a full-blown anxiety attack. Her heartbeat accelerated further to about 150 beats per minute. Her breathing and pulse rate then started to decrease. I was relieved, but only momentarily. Her pulse continued to drop, precipitously to around 50 beats per minute; she became still. Her face paled and her hands begin to tremble: "I'm real scared … stiff all over … I'm dying … I can't move … I don't want to die … help me … don't let my die." She continued to stiffen, her throat becoming so tight that she could barely speak. Nancy forced the words, "Why can't I understand this … I feel so inferior, like I'm being punished … there's something wrong with me … I feel like I'm going to be killed … there's nothing … it's just blank." (We had rather unfortunately co-discovered, some years before it was reported in the literature, "relaxation-induced panic syndrome.")

The session continued as follows:

"Feel the pencil," I requested without really knowing why.

"I remember now. I remember what I thought," she replied. *"My life depends on this exam."* Her heart rate increased now, moving back up into the eighties.

At this point, a dream image of a crouching tiger jumping through the bush flashed before me. Quite startled, a fleeting thought about a zoological article I had recently read on "tonic immobility" or "death feigning" prompted me to announce loudly: "You are being attacked by a large tiger. See the tiger as it comes at you. Run toward those rocks, climb them, and escape!"

Nancy let out a blood-curdling yell—a shout that brought in

a passing policeman (fortunately my office partner took care of the situation—perhaps explaining that I was doing "relaxation training"). She began to tremble, shake, and sob in waves of full body convulsions. I sat with her for almost an hour while she continued to shake. She recalled terrifying images and feelings from age four. She had been held down by doctors and nurses and struggled in vain during a tonsillectomy with ether anesthesia. She left the session feeling "like she had herself again." We continued relaxation, including assertion training, for a couple more sessions. She was taken off medication, entered graduate school, and completed her doctorate in physiology without relapse.

The Body Has Its Reasons

Aaron Beck and Gary Emery, in their seminal book, *Anxiety Disorders and Phobias,*[2] make the point that to understand fear, anxiety, and panic the person's *appraisal* of a situation is most important. In the chapter, "Turning Anxiety on Its Head," the authors consider cognitive appraisal to be a critical fulcrum in anxiety reactions. They argue that because anxiety has a strong somatic-emotional component, the subtler cognitive processing which occurs may be neglected both in theory and in clinical practice. Clearly Nancy's belief of the difficulty of the exam—based in part on the overheard conversation in the café—led to her thought: *my life depends on this,* an unconscious threat appraisal. By focusing narrowly on the cognitive aspects of anxiety, however, Beck and Emery overlook the fundamental role played by bodily responses and sensations in the experience of anxiety. When Nancy drank the coffee and smoked the cigarette (caffeine and nicotine, together, can be a robust stimulant), the physiological arousal of increased heart rate both fed into and was fed by her cognitive assessment of the "threat" from the exam driving her heart rate sharply up. Together, both assessment and physiological activation resonated with the *imprinted* bodily reaction of being terrorized and overwhelmed twenty years before during the tonsillectomy. The panic attack was triggered from that synergy.

In addition to recognizing the importance of cognitive factors, systematic study of bodily reactions and sensate experience is not only important, it is *essential.* This study needs to occur conjointly with the recognition and exploration of cognitive and perceptual factors. Appreciating the role of bodily experience illuminates the complex web called "anxiety" and connects many threads in understanding and modifying its physiological and experiential basis. In addition to turning anxiety on its head, we need also to *connect* the body with the head—recognizing the intrinsic psychophysiological unity that welds body and mind.

Cognitive theorists believe that anxiety serves primarily to signal the brain to activate a physical response that will dispel the source of anxiety. The role of anxiety is likened in this way to that of pain. The experience of pain impels us to do something to stop it. The pain is not the disease. It is merely a symptom of fracture, appendicitis, and so forth. Similarly, according to Beck, anxiety is not the disease but only a signal: "Humans are constructed in such a way as to ascribe great significance to the experience of anxiety so that we will be impelled to take measures to reduce it." He notes: "The most primal response depends on the generation of unpleasant subjective sensations that prompt a *volitional* intentional action designed to reduce danger. Only one experience of 'anxiety' is necessary to do this."[3] As examples Beck mentions the arousal of anxiety when a driver feels that he is not in complete control of the car and which prompts him to reduce his speed until he again feels in control. Similarly, a person approaching a high cliff retreats because of the anxiety.

What is the wisdom of an *involuntary,* primitive, global, somatic, and often immobilizing brainstem response?[4] Is it exclusively for calling the individual's attention to making varied and specific *voluntary* responses? Such an inefficient arrangement is highly doubtful. A lack of refinement in appreciating the essential nuances played by bodily responses and sensations in the structures and experience of anxiety is typical of cognitive approaches. Beck, for example, flatly states that "a specific combination of autonomic and motor patterns will be used for escape, a different combination for freezing, and a still different pattern for fainting. However, the subjective sensation—anxiety—will be approximately the same for each strategy." In the following paragraph of this same article he adds, "An active coping set is generally associated with sympathetic nervous system dominance, whereas a passive set, triggered by what is perceived as an overwhelming threat, is often associated with parasympathetic dominance. . . as in a blood phobic. In either case the subjective experience of anxiety is similar."[5]

Beck's statements reveal a significant glitch in the cognitive phenomenology of anxiety highlighting its paradoxical nature. According to his reasoning, the same body signal is relayed to the brain's cognitive structures for all forms of threat. The "head" (cognitive) structures are then somehow expected to decide on an appropriate course of action. This top-heavy, Cartesian holdover goes against the basic biological requirements for an immediate, precise, and unequivocal response to threat. It is a view that is quite confusing because it requires that distinctly different kinesthetic, proprioceptive, and autonomic feedback be experienced as the same signal. We have tended, in the post-Cartesian view of the world, to identify so much with the rational mind that the wider role of instinctive, bodily responses in orchestrating and propelling behavior and consciousness has been all but ignored.

Beck's statements that "a specific combination of autonomic and motor patterns will be used for escape, a different combination for freezing, and a still different pattern for fainting" and that "the subjective sensation—anxiety—will be approximately the same for each strategy" contradict both evolutionary imperative and subjective experience. In my thirty-five years of experience in what is now called somatic psychology, these statements simply do not fit the *subjective facts* and would have had William James turning over in his grave. If you ask several anxious people at random what they are feeling, they may all *say* that they are feeling "anxiety." However, if they are then queried with the epistemological question: "How do you *know* that you are feeling anxiety," you will get several different responses. One, for example, could be, "because something bad will happen to me." Another may be that they are feeling strangled in their throat; still another that their heart is leaping out of their chest; another that they have a knot in their gut. Other people might report that their neck, shoulders, arms, and legs are tight; others might feel ready for action; and still others that their legs feel weak or their chest collapsed. All but the first answer are specific and varied *physical* sensations. And if the person who said what he thought ("… like something bad will happen to me") was directed to a scan of her body, she would have discovered some *somatic/physical* sensation driving and directing the thought.

If we feel threatened and assess that we can escape or fight back, we will feel one set of physical sensations. If, on the other hand, we feel threatened and perceive that we cannot escape or fight back then we feel something quite different. Now here is the key factor: both the assessment of danger and the perception of our capacity to respond are not primarily conscious. Let's look to our distant ancestors to illuminate these questions.

Instinct in the Age of Reason

Animals possess a variety of orientation and defensive responses that allows them to respond automatically to different, potentially dangerous situations rapidly and fluidly. The sensations involving escape are profoundly different from those of freezing or collapse. I am in agreement with Beck in describing panic and posttraumatic anxiety states as having in common "the experience of dread with the perception of inescapability." What I first gleaned from Nancy thirty-five years ago, and later confirmed by the ethological analysis of predator/prey behaviors, was that the singular experience of *traumatic panic-anxiety* that Beck talks about occurs only where the normally varied and active defensive responses have been unsuccessful, that is, when a situation is both dangerous and inescapable.[6] Anxiety, in its pathological panic form (as distinguished from so-called signal anxiety), represents a profound failure of the organism's innate defensive structures to mobilize and thus allow the individual to escape threatening situations actively and successfully. Where escape is possible, the organism responds with an active pattern of coping. There is the continuous experience of danger, running, and escape. When, in an activated state, escape is successfully completed, anxiety does not occur. Rather a fluid (felt) sense of "biological competency" is experienced. Where defensive behaviors are unsuccessful in actively resolving severe threat, anxiety is generated. It is where active forms of defensive response are aborted and incomplete that anxiety states ensue. Beneath the monolithic lable of anxiety are camouflaged a wealth of incomplete and identifiable somatic responses, sensations, and bodily feelings. These body experiences represent the individual's response to past experience, but also to their "genetic potential" in the form of unrealized defensive responses. The recognition that these instinctive orientation and defensive behaviors are organized motor patterns, that is, prepared motor acts, helps to return the body to the head. Anxiety derives ultimately from a failure to complete motor acts.

Jean Genet, in his autobiographical novel, *Thief's Journal*, states this premise in bold prose: "Acts must be carried through to their completion. Whatever their point of departure, the end will be beautiful. It is (only) because an action has not been completed that it is vile." When orienting and defensive behaviors are carried out smoothly and effectively, anxiety is not generated. Instead there is the complex and fluid sensate experience perceived as curiosity, attraction, or avoidance. It is only when these instinctive orientation and defensive resources are interfered with (thwarted) that the experience of anxiety is generated: I am not afraid of snakes or spiders, but of my inability to respond effectively to these creatures. Ultimately we have only one fear, the fear of not being able to cope, of our own un-copability. Without active, available, defensive responses we are unable to deal effectively with danger and so we are, proportionately, anxious.

Orientations, Defense, and Flight

A scene from an uplands meadow helps to illustrate the *motor act* concept. Suppose you are strolling leisurely in an open meadow. A shadow suddenly moves in the periphery of your vision. Instinctively all movement is arrested; reflexively you crouch in a flexed posture; perceptions are "opened" through activation of the parasympathetic autonomic nervous system. After this momen-

© Getty Images/Tim Southall, 2002

tary arrest response your head turns automatically in the direction of the shadow or sound in an attempt to localize and identify it. Your neck, back, legs, and feet muscles coordinate so that your whole body turns and then extends. Your eyes narrow somewhat while your pelvis and head shift horizontally, giving you an optimal view of the surroundings and an ability to focus panoramically. This initial two-phase action pattern is an instinctive orientation preparing you to respond flexibly to many possible contingencies. The initial arrest-crouch flexion response minimizes detection by possible predators and perhaps offers some protection from falling objects. Primarily, though, it provides a convulsive jerk that interrupts any motor patterns that were already in execution and then prepares the you, through scanning, for the fine-tuned behaviors of exploration or defense.

If it had been an eagle taking flight that cast the shadow a further orientation of tracking-pursuit would occur. Adjustment of postural and facial muscles occurs unconsciously. This new "attitude of interest," when integrated with the contour of the rising eagle image, is perceived as the feeling of excitement. This aesthetically pleasing sense, with the meaning of enjoyment, is affected by past experience, but may also be one of the many powerful, archetypal predispositions or undercurrents which each species has developed over millennia of evolutionary time. Most Native Americans, for example, have a very special, spiritual, mythic relationship with the eagle. Is this a coincidence, or is there something imprinted deep with in the structures of the brain, body, and soul of the human species that responds intrinsically to the image of eagle with correlative excitement and awe? Most organisms possess dispositions, if not specific approach/avoidance responses, to moving contours. A baby chick, without learning from its mother, for example, flees from the moving contour of a hawk. If the direction of movement of this silhouette is reversed, however, to simulate a goose, the baby chick shows no such avoidance response.

If the initial shadow in the meadow had been from a raging grizzly bear rather than from a rising eagle, a very different preparedness reaction would have been evoked—the preparation to flee. This is not because we think: "bear," evaluate it as dangerous, and *then* prepare to run. It is because the contours and features of the large, looming, approaching animal cast a particular light pattern upon the retina of the eye. This stimulates a pattern of neural firing that is registered in phylogenetically primitive brain regions. This *pattern recognition* triggers preparation for defensive responding before it is registered in consciousness. These responses derive from genetic predispositions, as well as from the outcomes of previous experiences with similar large animals. Non-conscious circuits are activated, triggering preset patterns or tendencies of defensive posturing. Muscles, viscera, and autonomic nervous system activation cooperate in preparing for escape. This preparation is sensed kinesthetically and is internally joined as a gestalt to the image of the bear. *Movement and image are fused,* registered together, as the *feeling of danger.* Motivated by this feeling we continue to scan for more information—a grove of trees, some rocks—while at the same time drawing on our ancestral and personal memory banks. Probabilities are non-consciously computed, based on such encounters over millions of years of historical evolution, as well as by our own personal experiences. We prepare for the next phase in this unfolding drama. Without thinking we orient toward a large tree with low branches. An *urge* is experienced to flee and climb. If we run, freely oriented toward the tree, it is the feeling of *directed running*. The urge to run is experienced as the feeling of danger, while successful running is experienced as *escape* (and not anxiety!).

If, on the other hand, we chance upon a starved or wounded bear, and moreover find ourselves surrounded on all sides by sheer rock walls, that is, trapped, then the defensive preparedness for flight, concomitant with the feeling of danger, is thwarted and will change abruptly into the fixated emotional states of anxiety. The word *fear*, interestingly enough, comes from the old English term for danger, while *anxious* derives from the Greek root *angst*, meaning to "press tight" or strangle, as conveyed in Edward Munch's riveting painting, *The Scream* (p. vi). Our entire physiology and psyche become precipitously constricted in anxiety. Response is restricted to non-directed desperate flight, to rage, counterattack, or to freeze-collapse. The latter affords the possibility of diminishing the bear's urge to attack. (If it is not cornered or hurt and is able to clearly identify the approaching human being, the bear usually will not attack the intruder. It may even remain and go on with business as usual.)

In summary, when the normal orientation and defensive escape resources have failed to resolve the situation, life hangs in the balance with non-directed flight, rage, freezing, or collapse. Rage and terror-panic are the *secondary* emotional anxiety states that are evoked when the preparatory orientation processes (feelings) of danger-orientation and preparedness to flee are not successful—when they are blocked or inhibited. It is this thwarting that results in freezing and anxiety-panic.

Tonic Immobility—Freezing

Anxiety has often been linked to the physiology and experience of flight. Analyses of animal distress behaviors suggest that this may be quite misleading. Ethology (the study of animals in their natural environment) points to the thwarting of escape as the root of distress-anxiety.[7] When attacked by a cheetah on the African plains, an antelope will first attempt to escape through directed-oriented running. If, however, the fleeing animal is cornered so that escape is diminished, it may run blindly without a directed orientation or it may attempt to fight wildly and desperately against enormous odds. At the moment of physical contact, often before injury is actually inflicted, the antelope abruptly appears to go dead. It not only appears dead, but its autonomic physiology undergoes a widespread alteration and reorganization. The antelope is in fact highly activated internally, even though outward movement is almost nonexistent. Prey animals are immobilized in a sustained (cataleptic-catatonic) pattern of neuromuscular activity and high autonomic and brain wave activity.[8] Sympathetic and parasympathetic responses are also concurrently activated, like brake and accelerator working against each other.[9]

Nancy, in her reexperiencing of the examination room, exhibited this pattern when her heart rate increased sharply and then plummeted abruptly to a very low rate. In tonic immobility, an animal is either frozen stiff in heightened contraction of agonist and antagonist muscle group, or in a continuously balanced, hypnotic, muscular state exhibiting what is called "wavy flexibility." In the hypnotic state, body positions can be molded like clay, as is seen in catatonic schizophrenics. There is also analgesic numbing.[10] Nancy described many of these behaviors as they were happening to her. She wasn't, however, aware of her physical sensations but rather of her self-depreciating and critical judgments about those sensations. It is as though some explanation must be found for profoundly disorganizing forces underlying one's own perceived inadequacy. Psychologist Paul G. Zimbardo has gone so far as to propose that "most mental illness represents not a cognitive impairment, but an (attempted) interpretation of discontinuous or inexplicable internal states."[11] Tonic immobility, murderous rage, and non-directed flight are such examples.

Ethologists have found wide adaptive value in these immobility responses: freezing makes prey less visible and non-movement in prey appears also to be a potent inhibitor of aggression in predators, often aborting attack-kill responses entirely.[12] The park service, for example, advises campers that if they are unable to actively escape an attacking bear they should lie prone and not move. The family cat, seemingly on to nature's game, bats a captured, frozen mouse with its paws hoping to bring it out of shock and continue in the game. Immobility can buy time for prey. The predator may drag frozen prey to its den or lair for later consumption, giving it a second chance to escape.[13] In addition to these aggression-inhibiting responses, freezing by prey animals may provide a signaling and decoy effect, allowing con-specifics, who are farther away, a better chance for escape in certain situations. Loss of blood pressure may also help prevent bleeding when injured. An immobile prey animal is, in sum, less likely to be attacked. Further, if attacked, it is less likely to be killed and eaten, increasing its chances of escape and reproduction. In a world where most animals are both predator and prey at one time or another, analgesia is "humane" biological adaptation.

Tonic immobility demonstrates that anxiety can be both self-perpetuating and self-defeating. Freezing is the last-ditch, cul-de-sac, bodily response where active escape is not possible. Where flight and fight escape have been (or are perceived to be) unlikely, the nervous system reorganizes to tonic immobility. Both flight-or-fight and immobility are adaptive responses. Where the flight-or-fight response is appropriate, freezing will be relatively maladaptive; where freezing is appropriate, attempts to flee or fight are likely to be maladaptive. Biologically, immobility is a potent adaptive strategy where active escape is prevented. When, however, it becomes a preferred response pattern in situations of activation in general, it is profoundly debilitating. Immobility becomes the crippling, fixating experience of traumatic and panic-anxiety. Underlying the freezing response, however, are the flight-or-fight and other defensive and orientation preparations that are activated just prior to the onset of freezing. The "de-potentiation" of anxiety is accomplished by precisely and sequentially restoring the latent flight-or-fight and other active defensive responses that occur at the moment(s) before escape is thwarted.

Uncoupling Fear-Potentiated Immobility: An Example

The key in treating various anxiety and posttraumatic reactions is in principle quite simple: to uncouple the normally acute, time-limited freezing response from fear reactivation. This is accomplished by progressively reestablishing the pre-traumatic defensive and orienting responses, the responses that were in execution just prior to the initiation of immobility. In practice there are many possible strategies that may be utilized to accomplish this uncoupling of the immobility-fear or panic reaction.[14] An example of one type of reworking follows:

Marius Inuusuttoq Kristensen is a native Eskimo, born and raised in a remote village in Greenland. He is a slight, intelligent, boyish-looking young man in his mid-twenties. He is shy but open and available. As a participant in a training class in Copenhagen, Denmark, he asks to work on his tendency toward anxiety and panic, particularly when he is with a man he admires and whose approval he wants. His anxiety is experienced somatically as a weakening in his legs and a stabbing ache on the lateral midline of his right leg. There are also waves of nausea moving from his stomach to his throat, where it then becomes stuck. His head and face feel very warm and he becomes sweaty and flushed. After talking with him and using some exploratory images, he recalls an event that occurred when he was eight. Returning from a walk alone in the mountains he was attacked by a pack of three wild dogs and bitten badly on his right leg. He remembers only feeling the bite and then waking up in the arms of a neighbor. He remembers, too, his father coming to the door and being annoyed with him. Marius still feels bitterly angry and hurt at this rejection. He remembers, particularly, that his new pants were ripped and covered with blood. When he describes this he is visibly upset. I ask him to tell me more about the pants. He tells me that they were a surprise from his mother that morning; she had made them especially for him. He is in a transparent moment, experiencing pleasure, pride, and excitement similar to that day seventeen years ago. Marius holds his arms in front of himself feeling the fur and marveling over his "magic" polar bear fur pants.

"I feel like I want to jump up and down."

"Marius, are these the same kind of pants that the men of the village, the hunters, wear?"

"Yes," he responds.

"Do they wear them when they go out to hunt?"

"Yes." Marius becomes more excited. He describes seeing the pants with clear detail and aliveness. I have him feel the pants now with his hand.

"Now, Marius," I ask, "can you feel your legs inside the pants."

"Yes, I can feel my legs. They feel very strong, like the men when they are hunting." (I am beginning to build, as a resource, a somatic bridge utilizing neuromuscular patterns of the leg.) Marius's walk into the mountains the day of the attack was an initiation, a rite of passage for him; his pants were power objects on this "walkabout." I have him describe the sensations and images of walking up into the mountains. His descriptions are bright, embodied with awareness of detail. The experience he describes is clearly authentic and present. He is also aware of being in a group of students, though without self-consciousness. I would call his state of being primarily a state of presence and retrogression rather than regression. As images and kinesthetic perceptions unfold he sees an expanse of rocks. I ask him to feel his pants and then look at the rocks again.

"My legs want to jump; they feel light, not tight like they usually do. They are like springs, light and strong." He reports seeing a long stick that is lying by a rock and picks it up.

"What is it?" I ask.

"A spear."

"What is it for? What do the men do when they see bear tracks?" (I am hoping that this "play in dream time" will stimulate predatory and counterattack behaviors which were thwarted in being overwhelmed by the attacking dogs. This successive bridging helps to prime required defensive responses that could eventually neutralize the tonic immobility-freeze and collapse which occurred at the time of the attack.)

He goes on, "I am following a large polar bear. I am with the men, but I will make the kill." Micro-flexor extensor movements can be seen in his thigh, pelvic, and trunk muscles as he imagines jumping from rock to rock in following the trail.

"I see him now. I stop and aim my spear."

"Yes, feel that in your whole body, feel your feet on the rocks, the strength in your legs, and the arching in your back and arms. Feel all that power!"

"I see the spear flying," he says. Again, micro-postural adjustments can readily be seen in Marius's body; he is trembling lightly now in his legs and arms. I encourage him to feel these sensations. He reports waves of excitement and pleasure.

"I did it. I hit him with my spear!"

"What do the men do now?" I ask.

"They cut the belly open and take out the insides and then cut the fur off ... to ... make pants and coats. The other men will carry the meat down for the village."

"Feel your pants, Marius, with your hands, and on your legs." Tears form in his eyes. "Can you do this?" I ask.

"I don't know ... I'm scared."

"Feel your legs, feel your pants."

"... Yes, I cut the belly open; there is lots of blood ... I take out the insides. Now I cut the skin. I rip it off, there is glistening and shimmering. It is a beautiful fur, thick and soft. It will be very warm." Marius's body is shaking and tremoring with excitement, strength, and conquest. The activation/arousal is quite intense.

"How do you feel Marius?"

"I'm a little scared ... I don't know if I've ever felt this much strong feeling ... I think it's okay ... really I feel very powerful and filled with an energy. I think I can trust this ... I don't know ... it's strong."

"Feel your legs. Feel your feet. Touch the pants with your hands."

"Yes, I feel calmer now, not so much rush ... it's more like strength now."

"Okay, yes, good. Now start walking down, back toward the village." A few minutes pass, then Marius's trunk flexes and his movements hold as in still-frame arrest. His heart rate accelerates, and his face reddens.

"I see the dogs ... they're coming at me."

"Feel your legs, Marius! Touch your pants," I sharply demand. "Feel your legs and look! What is happening?"

"I am turning, running away. I see the dogs. I see a pole, an electricity pole. I am turning toward it. I didn't know that I remembered this." Marius's pulse starts to drop; he turns pale. "I'm getting weak," he responds.

"Feel the pants, Marius!" I command. "Feel the pants with your hands!"

"I'm running." His heart rate increases. "I can feel my legs ... they're strong, like on the rocks ... " Again he pales. He yells out, "Agh ... my leg, it burns like fire ... I can't move, I'm trying, but I can't move ... I can't move ... I can't move! It's numb now ...

my leg is numb. I can't feel it."

"Turn, Marius. Turn to the dog. Look at it."

This is the critical point. I hand Marius a roll of paper towels. If Marius freezes now he will be retraumatized. (This would occur if somatic bridges were not organized and in place.) He grabs the roll and strangles it. The group members, myself included, look on with utter amazement at his strength as he twists it and tears it in two. (I have asked weightlifting friends to replicate this and only a few have been able to do so.)

"Now the other one, look right at it." This time he lets out screams of rage and triumph. I have him settle with his bodily sensations for a few minutes, integrating this intensity. Then I ask him again to look.

"What do you see?"

"I see them ... they're all bloody and dead."

"Okay, look in the other direction. What do you see?"

"I see the pole ... there are bolts in it."

"Okay, feel your legs, feel your pants." I am about to say, "Run!" (in order to complete the running response). Before I do, he reports, "I am running ... I can feel my legs, they are strong like springs." Rhythmic extensor-flexor undulations are now visible through his pants, and his entire body is trembling and vibrating.

"I'm climbing ... climbing ... I see them below ... they're dead and I'm safe." He starts to sob softly and we wait a few minutes.

"What do you experience now?"

"It feels like I'm being carried by big arms. He's carrying me in his arms. I feel safe." Marius now reports a series of images of fences and houses in the village. Again, he softly and gently sobs. "He's knocking at the door of my family's house. The door opens ... my father ... he's very upset, he runs to get a towel ... my leg is bleeding very badly ... he's very upset ... he's not mad at me. He's worried. It hurts, the soap hurts."

Marius sobs now in waves. "It hurts but I'm crying 'cause he's not angry at me. I can see he was upset and scared."

"What do you feel in your body now?"

"I feel very peaceful now; I feel vibration and tingling all over. It is even and warm. He loves me." Again Marius begins to sob and I ask what happens if he feels that in his body, if he feels that his father loves him. There is a silence. "I feel warm, very warm and peaceful. I don't need to cry now. I'm okay and he was just scared. It's not that he doesn't love me."

In reviewing the session, recall that initially the only image or memory of the event Marius had was the bloody pants, torn flesh, and his father's rejection. Yet here also was the positive seed of the emerging healing nucleus, the "magic pants." The experience of the pants is the thread by which the altered states, related to the traumatic event, were experienced and progressively renegotiated. In working with over a thousand clients I have never found an instance where there was not this dual aspect of a critical image.[15] Within an initial image are the first stirrings of the motoric plan that a person will develop. The renegotiation processes occur stepwise, from periphery to center, toward a destructuring of the particular anxiety response or thwarting pattern, and restructuring of the underlying defensive and orienting responses.

The image of the ripped and bloodied pants was arousing to Marius, but so was the happiness (his legs wanting to jump for joy) he experienced when he saw the same pants for the first time earlier that morning. He was joyful when presented with this first possibility of manhood. In wanting, literally, to "jump for joy" Marius activated motor patterns that were essential in the eventual renegotiation of his freezing response. It is necessary to build just such adaptive motor patterns successively with increasing activation. In moving from the periphery of the experience to the freezing "shock" core one moves away from maladaptive neuromuscular patterns. The latter are neutralized by adaptive, flexible patterns at similar levels of activation.

As I encouraged Marius to track the initial positive pants experience gradually toward the traumatic, freezing shock core, the joyful extensor-dominated pants experience became linked to support, aggression, and competency, that is, when in somatic experiencing Marius sees the image of the rock field, the seed begins to sprout. In jumping from rock to rock and finding and picking up the stick, Marius's dynamic body-unconscious propels the motor plan sharply ahead. He is now prepared to meet the impending challenge. He takes the offensive and moves toward mastery of the previously thwarted situation. Like the hunters, he tracks the polar bear as I track his autonomic and motoric responses. Supported by the magic pants and the village men, he makes the find and the kill in a crescendo of high activation, approaching ecstasy.

In the next sequence of events, the true test will be made. Empowered and triumphant, he heads back down toward the village. There is expansion and awareness. For the first time he sees and describes the road and the dogs. (Previously, these images were constricted as in amnesia.) He senses orientation movements away from the attacking dogs and toward the electric pole. Because he now senses his legs moving the inhibitory freezing response is no longer the exclusive channel of response. The ecstatic trembling for the kill is now bridged into running. This action is, however, only partial; he begins to run but does not escape! I ask him to turn and face his attackers so as not to have him fall back into immobility. This time he counterattacks, first momentarily with rage, then with the same triumph that he experienced in the previous sequence of killing and eviscerating the bear. The motor plan has succeeded. Marius is now victorious; he is no longer the defeated victim.

The event, however, is still not complete. As the sensations and autonomic responses shift from highly activated sympathetic to parasympathetic resolution, the more primary orienting responses can come into play.[16, 17, 18] Marius not only sees the pole, he orients toward the pole and prepares to run. He had begun this maneuver years ago, but until this moment it had not been executed and completed. He consummates this preparation now with the act of running. Since he has already killed his attackers this may not make left brain linear sense, but it is completely logical in the biological, reptilian (body-brain) language of preparation, defense, and orientation. It is that sequence of activity (somatic experiencing) that alters the basic patterns of an individual's adaptive responses. When I returned to Denmark a year later I learned that Marius's anxiety reactions were no longer a problem.

Jody: Case Study

Jody's experience is another example of resolving anxiety states through completing innate defensive responses.

Twenty-five years ago Jody's life was shattered. While walking in the woods near her boyfriend's house a hunter came up to her and began a conversation. It was mid-September. There was a chill in the air. Her boyfriend and others suspected nothing upon seeing a man who was apparently chopping wood. The hunter, however, was a madman who smashed Jody's head again and again with his rifle. Jody's lifeless body was left in the woods, unconscious and violently beaten. Chips from the butt of the rifle lay nearby where they had broken off in the brutal attack.

The only recollection Jody had of the event was scant and confused. She vaguely remembered meeting the man and then waking up in the hospital some days later. Jody had been suffering from anxiety, migraines, concentration and memory problems, depression, chronic fatigue, and chronic pain of the head, back, and neck regions (diagnosed as fibromyalgia). She had been treated by physical therapists, chiropractors, and various physicians.

Jody, like so many head-injured and traumatized individuals, grasped desperately and obsessively in an attempt to retrieve memories of her trauma. When I suggested to Jody that it was possible to experience healing without having to remember the event, I saw a flicker of hope and a momentary look of relief pass across her face. We talked for a while, reviewing her history and struggle to function. Focusing on body sensations, Jody slowly became aware of various tension patterns in her head and neck region. With this focus she began to notice a particular urge to turn and retract her neck. In following this urge in slow gradual "micro movements" she experienced a momentary fear, followed by a strong tingling sensation. Through following these movements, Jody began a journey through the trauma of her assault. In learning to move between flexible control and surrender to these involuntary movements, she began to experience gentle shaking and trembling throughout her body. Thus began, ever so gently, the discharge of her trauma.

In later sessions, Jody experience other spontaneous movements, as well as sounds and impulses to run, bare her teeth, and claw at her assailant. By completing these biological defensive responses Jody was able to construct a sense of how her body prepared to react in that fraction of a second when the hunter raised the rifle butt to strike her. In allowing these movements and sounds to be expressed Jody began to experience a deep organic discharge along with the *experience* of her body's innate capacity to defend and protect itself.

Jody, through her felt sense, was able to follow her body's intentional movement. Intentional movement is non-conscious. It is experienced as if the body is moving of its own volition. Through completing the life-preserving actions that her body had prepared for at the time of her attack she released that bound energy and realized that she had, in fact, attempted to defend herself. Gradually, as more defensive and orienting responses reinstated, her panic-anxiety progressively decreased.

In Somatic Experiencing, traumatic reactions are addressed by a wide variety of strategies. What unifies them is that they are all used in the service of destructuring the thwarted anxiety response and restoring defensive and orienting resources. The overall picture shows how each individual's needs and resources call forth a unique, creatively adaptive solution.[19, 20]

ENDNOTES

1. Peter A. Levine, *Waking the Tiger, Healing Trauma* (Berkeley: North Atlantic Books, 1997).

2. Aaron Beck and Gary Emery, *Anxiety Disorders and Phobias: A Cognitive Perspective* (New York: Basic Books, 1985), 188.

3. Aaron Beck, "Theoretical Perspectives on Clinical Anxiety." In *Anxiety and the Anxiety Disorders,* edited by A. Hussain Tuma and Jack D. Maser (Mahwah, NJ: Lawrence Erlbaum Associated Publishers, 1985), 188. (Italics are the author's emphasis.)

4. This reaction, found in almost all prey animals, will inhibit predatory aggression. See G. Gordon Gallup and Jack Maser, "Human Catalepsy and Catatonia." In *Pyschopathology: Experimental Models,* edited by Jack D. Maser and Martin E.P. Seligman (San Francisco: W.H. Freeman, 1977), 334-57.

5. Aaron Beck (1985), op. cit., 188.

6. Ibid.

7. Desmond Morris, *Primate Ethology* (London: Weidenfield and Nicholson, 1969)

   A. Eric Salzen, "Social Attachment and a Sense of Security," *Social Sciences Information* 12 (1967): 555-627.

8. G. Gallup and J. Maser (1977), op. cit., 345.

9. Ernst Gelhorn, *Autonomic-Somatic Integrations: Physiological Basis and Clinical Implications* (Minneapolis: University of Minnesota Press, 1967).

   Peter A. Levine, "Stress." In *Psychophysiology,* edited by Michael G.H. Coles, Emanual Donchin, and Stephen Porges (New York: Guilford Press, 1986), 331-54.

10. Gallup and Maser, "Catalepsy and Catatonia," 337.

11. Paul G. Zimbardo, "Understanding Madness: A Cognitive-Social Model of Psychopathology," invited address at the annual meeting of the Canadian Psychological Association, Vancouver, B.C., June, 1977.

12. G. Gallup and J. Maser (1977), op. cit., 350-54.

13. Ibid., 354.

14. Peter A. Levine (1997), op. cit.

15. Akhter Ahsen, *Basic Concepts in Eidetic Psychotherapy* (New York: Brandon House, 1972). Refers to this (I believe) as the "Law of Bipolarity."

16. Ernst Gellhorn (1967), op. cit.

17. Peter A. Levine (1986), op. cit., 347-48.

18. The Polyvagal Theory represents a new understanding of the autonomic nervous system (ANS). The theory stems from the research and writings of the psychophysiologist, Stephen Porges, Ph.D. This research has significantly altered the traditional, commonly accepted view of the ANS, which views two component subsystems, the sympathetic and parasympathetic branch. The parasympathetic maintains the essential, homeostatic background operations such as respiration, blood flow, and digestion, those of sustenance, maintenance, and procreation. The sympathetic provides a global stress-response to mobilize vast sources of energy and muscular readiness for fight-or-flight. Ernst Gellhorn and others have suggested that the two branches work in an oppositional, reciprocal manner. It was assumed that anxious states were associated with sympathetic hyperarousal and relaxation with dominance of the parasympathetic branch. The Polyvagal Theory is rooted in comparative neuro-anatomy and autonomic psychophysiology. Porges showed that the ANS has three, rather than two, branches. In addition, their organization is *sequential* rather than reciprocal. (See Porges, *Psychophysiology* 32 (1995): 301-18.)

19. Eugene T. Gendlin, "On Emotion In Therapy." In *Emotions and the Process of Therapeutic Change,* edited by J.D. Safran and L.S. Greenberg (New York: Academic Press).

20. Peter A. Levine (1997), op. cit.

ILONA JERABEK

Etiology of Panic Disorder

Is It Biology or Psychology?

PANIC DISORDER is in fact a perfect illustration for a "Nature or Nurture" debate. Panic attacks and panic disorder present a panoply of symptoms, ranging from somatic complaints, sensory distortions, physiological and neurochemical/hormonal changes to cognitive symptoms and strong emotional responses. There are several theoretical models that aspire to explain the etiology of panic disorder. These theories will be briefly discussed in terms of how they view the etiology of panic disorder, and the main arguments that support them will be presented.

Biological Aspects

The essential assumption of the biomedical model is that mental illness is basically a biological disease. In other words, the etiology of the mental disorder can be explained by physical causes, such as infections, genetics, neuroanatomic pathology, or malfunctioning biochemistry. Evidence has accumulated demonstrating that panic disorder may be viewed as a biological disease.

Panic Symptoms Are Physical in Nature

The onset of symptoms is abrupt, reaching peak within minutes. It rapidly subsides, leaving only residual anxiety. Typically, the panic attacks come out of nowhere, even though some patients experience situationally bound and situationally predisposed panic attacks. Often patients are unable to identify anything that could possibly trigger an attack. They experience panic watching cartoons, playing with their children, resting, etc.—simply put, in situations that do not present any stress or threat to them.

The physical nature of the symptoms of panic attack also provides some reasons for the claim that panic disorder involves biological modifications. The panic symptoms correspond to a great degree to symptoms of acute activation of the sympathetic branch of the autonomous nervous system, typical for the fight-or-flight reaction. Indeed, several authors argue that panic attack is, in fact, a fight-or-flight reaction of the body in absence of a real danger.[1] When confronted with a real or perceived threat, the automatic fight-or-flight response may be triggered to prepare the body for immediate action. This response is accompanied by peripheral secretion of catecholamines, especially epinephrine and norepinephrine, and glucocorticoids.[2] These hormones increase the availability of the body's energy by glycogenolysis in liver and skeletal muscles thus raising the blood glucose and lactate, lipolysis in adipose tissue, mobilization of free fatty acids, and by increasing temperature. Both epinephrine and norepinephrine also dilate coronary blood vessels. As a consequence, the rate and strength of the heartbeat increases to supply more oxygen to the tissues. While norepinephrine produces vasoconstriction in skin, mucosa, skeletal muscles, and most other organs, epinephrine dilates veins in skeletal muscles. These effects result in hypertension and consequently in reflex bradycardia.

Other symptoms of a sympatho-adrenergic stimulation involve modifications of breathing, increased temperature, localized sweating, decreased motility and tone of stomach and intestine, constrictions of sphincters in stomach and intestine, as well as piloerection. Breathing increases in rate and depth to exchange more oxygen to prepare for exertion. Breathlessness, dizziness, and pain or tightness in the chest may be experienced. Sweat glands are stimulated to prevent overheating. The pupils of the eye dilate to admit more light and increase peripheral vision to scan for danger. Sensitivity to bright light and visual disturbances may occur.

The digestive system shuts down to conserve blood for the muscles. Dry mouth, nausea, and constipation may result. Muscles tense to prepare for flight, but may cause spasms and trembling when action is not taken. This complex response was developed through evolution in many organisms and normally serves for survival and protection. As mentioned above, the symptoms of sympathetic activation and panic attack are very similar. Therefore, panic may be viewed as an emergency response which occurs in a situation where it is not appropriate.[3]

Antidepressant and Anti-Panic Drugs Are Efficacious in Treatment of Panic Disorder

Another argument for the biological hypothesis of panic disorder is that pharmacotherapy is efficacious in its treatment. Several classes of drugs are being used in panic disorder patients, namely the benzodiazepines, tricyclic, and heterocyclic antidepressants, monoamine oxidase (MAO) inhibitors, reversible MAO inhibitors, and selective serotonin reuptake inhibitors (SSRI). Except for benzodiazepines, all anti-panic drugs are in fact antidepressants, and act on the aminergic systems(see pp. 284–288).[4] Benzodiazepines act on the GABA-receptors. If panic had no biological bases, its symptoms could not be alleviated by medication. Whatever the type of medication, efficacy of drugs to treat panic disorder implies that the underlying mechanism of development or symptomatology is biological.

Frequency and Intensity of Panic Attacks Vary during Menstrual Cycle and Pregnancy

Clinical and scientific evidence exists demonstrating that gonadal hormones have a strong influence on panic disorder, especially in terms of frequency and intensity of panic attacks. Spontaneous panic attacks rarely start before puberty or after menopause, suggesting that, in women, occurrence of panic may be linked to production of female reproductive hormones.[5] Premenstrual exacerbation of panic symptoms has been documented.[6] Several authors reported that women with PMS are more sensitive to panic-provocation procedures.[7] In addition, the panic rate in women with or without PMS increases when they are challenged during the luteal phase, with PMS patients having a higher rate.[8] This phenomenon is attributed to a drop in progesterone levels before the onset of menses, the women with largest progesterone fluctuation being most vulnerable.[9]

Clinically, a marked decrease of panic has been observed during pregnancy and lactation, with postlactational exacerbation of symptoms. These changes most likely reflect increased levels of progesterone, estrogen, and oxytocin during pregnancy or lactation.[10] The fact that the condition of panic disorder patients improves during this time is a strong argument for the biological view of this disorder. As Klein points out, pregnancy and childbirth present an increased vulnerability, marked by heightened threatening endogenous stimuli. According to cognitive theories, which postulate that panic attacks result from catastrophic interpretation of physiological changes, such states should make patients more prone to panic. Apparently this is not the case.[11]

Experimental Procedures (Challenge) Reproduce Panic Attacks in the Laboratory

For nearly three decades, researchers have been using various procedures in order to reproduce the emotional, cognitive, physiological, and neurochemical changes accompanying panic attacks. Among the first agents used to trigger anxiety-like symptoms were epinephrine and norepinephrine.[12] Cholinergic agents, such as cholinomimetic mecholyl and cholinesterase inhibitor physostigmime, were also used in several studies.[13] One of the most researched panic-provoking pharmacological agents is sodium lactate.[14] Voluntary hyperventilation and carbon dioxide have frequently been used to study the underlying mechanisms of panic attack.[15] Caffeine induces anxiety-like symptoms suggesting a possible implication of the adenosine system in panic-anxiety.[16] The administration of cholecystokinin tetrapeptide (CCK4) has also been used in several recent studies.[17] Several other panic-provocation agents, such as yohimbine, isoproterenol, and piperoxan act on the noradrenergic or adrenergic systems.[18]

These procedures are a valuable tool for the experimental evaluation of neurochemical correlates of panic attack symptoms. They are capable of inducing experiences phenomenologically similar to spontaneous panic attacks, as pointed out by panic patients. Therefore, a phenomenon which can be reproduced by pharmacological means must have biological bases.

Non-Fearful and Limited-Symptom Panic Attacks

Many panic patients report experiencing so called limited-symptom panic attacks, which are characterized by presence of less than four symptoms, and, importantly, absence or low levels of anxiety. Limited-symptom panic is often seen in patients undergoing pharmaco or psychotherapy. Some patients experience panic attacks without fear, which may contain several physical symptoms without the emotional and cognitive components of panic. The mere existence of this phenomenon points to biological bases of panic disorder.

Limited-Symptom Panic

Limited-symptom panic attacks are episodes of less intense anxiety and fewer physical symptoms, such as isolated difficulty breathing and numbness in the hands. Limited-symptom panic attacks may in fact be aborted full-blown panic attacks. They can occur just once, or repeatedly in a person's lifetime. Sometimes they can even progress into full-blown panic attacks. Different treatment methods, like relaxation therapy, can teach people prone to panic attacks to abort their attacks, in essence to limit them. These methods are especially effective when used in conjunction with medication.

Panic Attacks May Be Triggered or Aggravated by Use of Drugs

Many patients can trace the onset of panic attacks to the use of drugs, especially cocaine and amphetamines. Both of these drugs alter the noradrenergic function.[19] The fact that drugs can trigger panic attacks and bring about the onset of panic disorder is yet another argument for the biological bases of panic disorder.

Animal Models of Anxiety and Panic Disorder

The existence and validity of animal models of anxiety and panic form another argument for the biological nature of panic disorder.

These models, mainly using rodents and nonhuman primates, parallel human anxiety. Despite their inherent limitations, animal models of anxiety have been repeatedly proven to be useful in testing of anti-anxiety and anti-panic drugs. They are used to study neurochemical, especially central, changes in anxiety states, taking advantage of techniques such as microdialysis, single neuron recording, electrochemical stimulation of various brain regions, etc.[20]

Specific Brain Regions Are Implicated in Regulation of Panic-Anxiety

The complex nature of symptoms of panic suggests that various brain regions would be implicated. A number of techniques have been used in order to provide an explanation for panic attacks, including brain imaging, staining, electrical and chemical stimulation, as well as electrical recording. Brain-imaging techniques are useful tools that can provide us with information about the brain regions with higher or lower oxygen or glucose metabolism,[21] cerebral blood flow,[22] cerebral blood volume,[23] BBB permeability,[24] and other indices indicating activated areas.[25] Several studies showed apparent region-specific modifications of cerebral blood flow during panic attack.[26] Alterations of the permeability of the blood-brain barrier, which is directly regulated by afferents originating in the locus ceruleus, have been linked to the development and treatment of panic disorder.[27]

The limbic system, especially the amygdala, has long been considered to be directly implicated in anxiety and other emotions. The amygdala receives projections from the frontal cortex, association cortex, temporal lobe, olfactory system, and other parts of the limbic system. It sends its afferents to the frontal and prefrontal cortex, orbitofrontal cortex, hypothalamus, hippocampus, as well as brainstem nuclei, such as the locus ceruleus and raphé nucleus.

The amygdala and its central nucleus thus communicate with many brain regions, including those that control breathing, motor function, autonomic response, and release of hormones, as well as processing of interoceptive and external information.[28] The amygdala is thus in a good position to modulate autonomic responses related to anxiety and panic because of its connections with the brainstem and the reticular formation, both of which control vegetative functions.

Indeed, numerous studies have demonstrated an implication of the limbic system, and the amygdala in particular, in panic disorder. In 1978, Halgren et al. electrically stimulated the amygdala and hippocampus in humans, which resulted in somatic and emotional symptoms of panic attack. In 1987, Iwata et al. observed increases in heart rate and blood pressure in animals, as well as symptoms of sympathetic activation that are also present during a panic attack after injections of excitatory amino acids into the central nucleus of the amygdala. Microinjections of benzodiazepines into the amygdala had "anti-conflict" properties that are correlated with anxiolytic effects in humans.[29] In addition to this, microinjections of CCK8 (both sulfated and non-sulfated) into the amygdaloid nucleus produce fear-motivated behavior in rats, such as facilitation of extinction of active avoidance behavior and retention of passive avoidance.[30]

The locus ceruleus is a particularly important region related to anxiety. This region is a metencephalic nucleus located in the caudal pontine central gray. It contains 50 percent of all brain noradrenergic neurons and is composed almost exclusively of 12,000 noradrenergic neurons on each side of the brain. It also produces a major portion of norepinephrine in the central nervous system. Collateral branches of axons of noradrenergic neurons project to most regions of the brain. Of those numerous projections, there are many that have been associated with panic disorder or panic attacks: with the limbic system, especially the amygdala, hippocampus, septum, and cingulate cortex, all cortices, brainstem, reticular formation, cerebellum, and spinal cord.[31] Evidence from lesion, electrical and chemical stimulation, and single-unit recording studies suggests that the locus ceruleus seems to be implicated in the sleep-wake cycle, arousal, anxiety, and fear.[32] In addition, most agents that alleviate anxiety (benzodiazepines, alcohol, opiates, barbiturates) act also to lower the activity of the locus ceruleus.[33] The locus ceruleus also contains benzodiazepine receptors, as well as receptors for endogenous opiates. During withdrawal from benzodiazepines, opiates, and alcohol, anxiety increases

as does the activity of the locus ceruleus, both lasting as long as the withdrawal symptoms persist.

Other important brain regions appear to be implicated in modulation of anxiety. The hypothalamus and pituitary gland—especially the anterior pituitary gland—are involved in synthesis and release of numerous stress-related hormones. Numerous brainstem regions, namely the pons, medulla oblongata, cerebellum, reticular formation, and periaqueductal gray matter, are also involved, especially in functions such as perception of somatic and sensory stimuli, fear-related reflexes, arousal, and neuro-vegetative functions. The cerebral cortex is implicated in anxiety control and development in terms of storage of memory, cognitive processes, and control of motor movement.[34]

Genetic and Family Studies

Clinical experience with patients revealed that panic disorder seems to run in families and have a genetic component. These findings led to epidemiological studies investigating the incidence of this disorder in families of the patients. Despite methodological differences and variations in the definitions of the disorder, as well as the target population of the anxious patients, the results seem to be relatively consistent. A 1981 study by Carey and Gottsman studied families of probands with anxiety disorders and found that 15 percent of first-degree relatives also suffered from anxiety disorders. A more pertinent 1983 study by Crowe et al. focused on panic disorder. Around 25 percent of first-degree relatives of panic disorder patients received the same diagnosis, as compared to 2.3 percent of relatives of normal controls.

Studies with twins who grew up together can also provide us with useful information. In a 1969 study of monozygotic twins, Slater and Shields had concordance rate of 41 percent for anxiety states, whereas the concordance among dizygotic twins was only 4 percent. Torgersen later investigated concordance rates for anxiety disorders with panic attacks and found that 31 percent of the monozygotic twins had a similar diagnosis compared to 0 percent of the dizygotic twins.[35] When he narrowed down the comparison to panic disorder with agoraphobia, the concordance rate between monozygotic twins was 15 percent. Even though the differences in concordance rates might appear important, they might be misleading. First of all, the number of subjects was small, such that, for example, the concordance rate of 31 percent in monozygotic twins was based on four out of thirteen pairs of twins, which is obviously not enough to generalize. Secondly, the higher concordance in monozygotic twins could be potentially explained by other non-genetic factors. For instance, monozygotic twins may be treated differently by their parents, extended families, and peers. They might have more profound identity crises than most teenagers usually go through. Often they are dealt with as an entity rather than two separate individuals. In addition to this they might tend to develop mutual dependency and have more experiences of separation anxiety, a state that seems to be related to agoraphobia and panic disorder.

Neurochemistry of Panic Disorder

The evidence for neurochemical pathology in panic disorder comes from numerous sources: challenge studies, effects of anti-panic medication, biochemical comparisons of panic disorder population with healthy subjects in terms of reactivity, and basal levels, brain imagery, and animal experiments. Several major hypotheses explaining the neurochemical bases of panic disorder have been formed and supported by evidence.

One of the most intriguing hypotheses postulates an abnormality of the noradrenergic and adrenergic systems. Increased plasmatic and urinary concentrations of epinephrine and norepinephrine in panic disorder patients have been shown in some but not all studies.[36] In addition, augmentations of plasma-3-methoxy-4-hydroxyphenylethylene (MHPG), a metabolite of norepinephrine, have been documented in patients with frequent and severe panic attacks.[37] Panic patients confronted with anxiogenic situations have increased plasma-free MHPG and norepinephrine levels.[38] Stimulation of the noradrenergic system by alpha-2-adrenoceptor antagonist yohimbine and beta-adrenoceptor agonist isoproterenol produces panic-like symptoms in panic disorder patients and some healthy subjects.[39] Pathological changes in the alpha and/or beta-receptors have been demonstrated.[40]

Another plausible hypothesis concerns the serotonergic system, especially in terms of interaction with the noradrenergic system.[41] The raphé nucleus, a midbrain structure with high concentration of serotonergic neurons, projects to the locus ceruleus and has an inhibitory influence on the activity of noradrenergic neurons.[42] Pharmacological agents that decrease serotonergic activity have anxiolytic effects in animals.[43] Serotonin and its metabolite 5-HIAA are reduced in anxious dogs.[44] In humans, alleviation of symptoms is achieved by administration of SSRIs. In 1990, Murphy & Pigott presented evidence suggesting that the anxiolytic effects of benzodiazepines might also be related to serotonergic activity. In addition, panic disorder patients reported an exacerbation of symptoms when they received serotonin precursors tryptophan and 5-HTP, serotonin receptors' agonist m-chlorophenyl-piperazine and flenfluramine, a drug that increases the synaptic availability of serotonin.[45] It is thus possible that an altered serotonergic transmission is one of the elements implicated in anxiety and panic.

Another major hypothesis for panic disorder etiology involves benzodiazepine receptors and their natural ligands. The anxiolytic action of benzodiazepines is mediated through benzodiazepine receptor complex, potentiating the inhibitory effects of GABA.[46] Sensitivity of central and peripheral benzodiazepine receptors have been shown to be modified by aversive life events and social variables.[47] Studies have demonstrated that animals with low exploratory behavior (anxious) have a lower density of brain benzodiazepine receptors.[48] Also, stimulation of benzodiazepine recep-

Getaway
Jack Forbes

Getaway
From one's own paranoia
Are pursuer's real
Really there
Or just demons
Of the dream
Is this my own chase
After myself
Around in circles
Strange neighborhoods
Factory brick walls
And dead ends
Eight-to-five
Streets
Offering no
Getaway.

Getaway
Damn I have to—
Can't stand to be
Murdered
Annihilated
Desecrated
I'm not going to lay there and be
    raped
Over
And
Over
By masked creatures with
    uniforms
of sodden sameness
Leering down at me
No more
No more
Find me
Yes I'll find me a
Getaway.

Getaway
Escape from sanity
What is sane in a
Place where everything
Ends up in a
Sewer
Including one who is
On his
Getaway.

* * *

tors by their inverse agonists, beta-carbolines, produces anxiety and panic-like symptoms in panic disorder patients and healthy subjects.[49]

    The adenosine system also appears to be implicated in panic disorder. Numerous studies have demonstrated that panic disorder patients are hypersensitive to the effects of caffeine, an adenosine antagonist. In large doses, caffeine can produce panic-like symptoms in panic disorder patients and healthy subjects, especially those with low regular consumption of caffeine.[50] Caffeine-induced panic is typically accompanied by increases in plasma lactate, glucose, and cortisol.[51]

    Other neurotransmitters and neuromodulators appear to be implicated in panic disorder. For example, the dopamine-containing mesocorticolimbic system appears to be implicated in anticipation, conditioning, and motivation, and contains neurons with high concentrations of various neuropeptides, including those associated with arousal (enkephalines), anxiogenesis (beta-carbolines), and anxiolysis.[52] Most or some central dopaminergic systems respond to MAO inhibitors, stress, and anxiogenic beta-carbolines.[53] Recently, numerous neuropeptides have been linked to mediation and control of anxiety. Examples include cholecystokinin peptides, neuropeptide Y, beta-carbolines, enkephalines, substance P, and corticotropin releasing factor, which might have modulatory effects on panic and anxiety.[54]

Nocturnal Panic Attacks

Nearly 70 percent of panic disorder patients report experiencing panic in their sleep at some point of their lives, and about one-third experience recurrent sleep panic.[55] Sleep panic attacks appear to emerge from non-REM sleep, especially during the transition to early delta sleep.[56] Therefore, sleep panic does not appear to be provoked by nightmares. Aside from nocturnal panic attacks, insomnia and restless sleep are among common complaints in panic disorder patients. Some studies suggest that panic disorder patients display a moderate reduction in REM latency, decreased REM density, increased eye movement time, and report more frequent awakenings because of their discomfort.[57]

REFERENCES

http://www.queendom.com/articles/mentalhealth/ref_pd.html.

ENDNOTES:

1. D.L. Rosenhan & M.E.P. Seligman, *Abnormal Psychology*, 2nd edition (New York: W.W. Norton, 1989).

2. N.R. Carlson, *Foundations of Physiological Psychology*, 2nd edition (Boston: Allyn and Bacon, 1992).

3. D.H. Barlow & M.G. Craske, *Mastery of Your Anxiety and Panic* (Albany, NY: Graywind Publications, 1994).

4. C.B. Taylor & B. Arnow, *The Nature and Treatment of Anxiety Disorders* (New York: The Free Press, 1988).

5. D.F. Klein et al., "Child Panic Revisited," *J Am Acad Child Adolesc Psychiatry* 31 (1992): 122–16.

6. A. Breier et al., "Agoraphobia with Panic Attacks: Development, Diagnostic Stability and Course of Illness," *Arch Gen Psych* 43 (1986): 1029–36.

   O.G. Cameron et al., "Menstrual Fluctuation in the Symptoms of Panic Anxiety," *J Affect Disord* 15 (1988): 169-74.

7. W.M. Harrison et al., "Provocation of Panic with Carbon Dioxide Inhalation in Patients with Premature Dysphoria," *Psychiatry Res* 27 (1989): 183-92.

8. D. Sandberg et al., "Sodium Lactate Infusion in Late Luteal Phase Dysphoric Disorder," *Psych Res* (1993).

9. U. Halbreich et al., "Premenstrual Changes and Changes in Gonadal Hormones," *Acta Psychiatr Scand* 74 (1986): 576-86.

10. D.F. Klein, "False Suffocation Alarms, Spontaneous Panics, and Related Conditions: An Integrative Hypothesis," *Arch Gen Psychiatry* 50 (1993): 306-17.

11. D.F. Klein, "Testing the Suffocation False Alarm Theory of Panic Disorder," *Anxiety* 1 (1994): 1–7.

12. J.T. Wearn & C. C. Sturgis, "Studies on Epinephrin: Effects on the Injection of Epinephrin in Soldiers with 'Irritable Heart,'" *Arch Intern Med* 24 (1919): 247–68.

    E. Lindemann, "The Psychopathological Effect of Drugs Affecting the Vegetative System," *Am J Psychiat* 91 (1935): 983-1008.

    E. Lindemann & J.E. Finesinger, "The Effect of Adrenalin and Mecholyl in States of Anxiety in Psychoneurotic Patients," *Am J Psychiat* 95 (1938): 353–70.

13. Ibid.

    S.C. Risch et al., "Cholinergic Challenges in Affective Illness: Behavioral and Neuroendocrine Correlates," *J Clin Psychopharmacol* 1 (1981): 186–92.

    S.M. Paul & P. Skolnick, "Benzodiazepine Receptors and Psychopathological States: Towards a Neurobiology of Anxiety." In *Anxiety Research and Changing Concepts,* edited by D. F. Klein and J. Rabkin (New York: Raven Press, 1981).

14. F.N. Pitts & J.N. McClure, "Lactate Metabolism in Anxiety Neurosis," *N Eng J Med* 277 (1967): 1329–36.

   M.T. Haslam, "The Relationship Between the Effect of Lactate Infusion on Anxiety States and Their Amelioration by Carbon Dioxide Inhalation," *Br J Psychiat* 125 (1974): 88–90.

   I.L. Appleby et al., "Biochemical Indices of Lactate-Induced Panic: A Preliminary Report." In *Anxiety: New Research and Changing Concepts,* edited by D. F. Klein and J. Rabkin (New York: Raven Press, 1981), 411–23.

   M.R. Liebowitz et al., "Lactate Provocation of Panic Attacks," *Arch Gen Psychiat* 41 (1984): 164–70.

15. M.A. Van den Hout & E. Griez, "Panic Symptoms After Inhalation of Carbon Dioxide," *Brit J Psychiat* 144 (1984): 503–07.

   J.M. Gorman et al., "Response to Hyperventilation in a Group of Patients with Panic Disorder," *Am J Psychiat* 24 (1984): 857–61.

   L.A. Papp et al., "Hypersensitivity to Carbon Dioxide in Panic Disorder," *Am J Psychiat* 146 (1989): 779–81.

16. D.S. Charney et al., "The Effects of Caffeine on Plasma MHPG, Subjective Anxiety, Autonomic Symptoms and Blood Pressure in Healthy Humans," *Life Sciences* 35 (1984A): 134–44.

   T.W. Uhde, "Caffeine Provocation of Panic: A Focus on Biological Mechanisms." In *Clinical Aspects of Panic Disorder,* edited by J. Ballenger (New York: Alan R. Liss, Inc., 1990).

   J.P. Boulenger et al., "Increased Sensitivity to Caffeine in Patients with Panic Disorders," *Arch Gen Psychiat* 41 (1984): 1067–71.

17. J. Bradwejn & D. Koszycki, "Imipramine Antagonism of the Panicogenic Effects of Cholecystoknin Tetrapeptide in Panic Disorder Patients," *Am J Psychiat* 151 (1994A): 261–63.

   J. Bradwejn & D. Koszycki, "The Cholecystokinin Hypothesis of Anxiety and Panic Disorder," *Annals of the New York Academy of Sciences* 713 (1994b): 273–82.

18. H.R. Olpe et al., "The Locus Coeruleus: Actions of Psychoactive Drugs," *Experientia* 39 (1983): 242-49.

   D. S. Charney et al., "Neurobiological Mechanisms of Panic Anxiety: Biochemical and Behavioral Correlates of Yohimbine-induced Panic Attacks," *Am J Psychiat* 144 (1987): 1030–36.

   D.S. Charney et al., "Nonadrenergic Dysregulation in Panic Disorder." In *Neurobiology of Panic Disorder,* edited by J. C. Ballenger (New York: Wiley-Liss, 1990).

R. Pohl et al., "Isoproterenol-induced Panic: A Beta-adrenergic Model of Panic Anxiety." In *Neurobiology of Panic Disorder*, edited by J. C. Ballenger (New York: Wiley-Liss, 1990).

19. C.B. Taylor & B. Arnow, op. cit., 1988.

20. S. File, "Testing New Antianxiety Agents: Pharmacology and Biochemistry." In *Handbook of Anxiety, Vol. 3*, edited by G. D. Burrows et al. (Amsterdam: Elsevier Science Publishers, 1990).

21. S. Huang et al., "Error Sensitivity of Fluorodeoxyglucose Method for Measurement of Cerebral Metabolic Rate of Glucose," *J Cerebral Blood Flow Metab* 1 (1981): 391–401.

    M.E. Raichle et al., "Correlation Between Regional Cerebral Blood Flow and Oxidative Metabolism: In Vivo Studies in Man," *Archives of Neurology* 33 (1976): 523–26.

22. P. Herscovitch et al., Brain Blood Flow Measured with Intravenous H215O: Theory and Error Analysis, *J Nucl Med* 24 (1983): 782–89.

23. R.L. Grubb et al., "Measurement of Regional Cerebral Blood Volume by Emission Tomography," *Annals of Neurology* 4 (1978): 322–28.

24. P. Herscovitch et al., "Positron Emission Tomographic Measurement of Cerebral Blood Flow and Permeability Surface Area Product of Water using 15O-Water and 11C-Butanol," *J of Cereb Blood Flow and Metab* 7 (1987): 527–42.

25. E.M. Reiman, "PET, Panic Disorder, and Normal Anticipatory Anxiety." In *Neurobiology of Panic Disorder*, edited by J. C. Ballenger (New York: Wiley-Liss, 1990).

26. R.S. Stewart et al., op.cit., 1988.

    E.M. Reiman et al., "The Application of Positron Emission Tomography to the Study of Panic Disorder," *Am J Psychiat* 143 (1986): 469–77.

27. S.H. Preskorn et al., "The Effects of Dibenzazepines (Tricyclic Antidepressants) on Cerebral Capillary Permeability in the Rat In Vivo," *J Pharmacol Exp Ther* 213 (1980): 313–20.

    M.E. Raichle, "Neurogenic Control of Blood-Brain Barrier Permeability," *Acta Neuropathologica*, supplement 8 (1983): 75–79.

28. N.R. Carlson, op. cit., 1992.

29. H. Hodges et al., "Evidence that the Amygdala is Involved in Benzodiazepine and Serotonergic Effects on Punished Responding but not on Discrimination, *Psychopharmacol* 92 (1987): 491–504.

    M.J. Kuhar, "Neuroanatomical Substrates of Anxiety: A Brief Survey," *Trends Neurosci* 9 (1986): 307–11.

30. M. Fekete et al., "Further Analysis of the Effects of Cholecystokinin Octapeptide on Avoidance Behavior in Rats," *Eur J Pharmacol* 98 (1984): 79–91.

31. J.R. Cooper et al., *The Biochemical Bases of Neuropharmacology,* 6th edition (New York: Oxford University Press, 1991).

32. D.E. Redmond, Jr. & Y.H. Huang, "New Evidence for a Locus Coeruleus Norepinephrine Connection with Anxiety," *Life Sciences* 25 (1979): 2149–62.

   D.E. Redmond et al., "Behavioral Effects of Stimulation of the Nucleus Coeruleus in the Stump-tailed Monkey Macaca Arctoides," *Brain Res* 116 (1976): 502–10.

33. H.V. Nybäck et al., "Tricyclic Antidepressants: Effects on the Firing Rate of Brain Noradrenergic Neurons," *Eur J Pharmacol* 32 (1975): 302–12.

   M.A. Geyer & E.H. Lee, "Effects of Clonidine, Piperoxane and Loucs Coeruleus Lesion on the Serotonergic Systems in Raphé and Caudate Nucleus," *Biochem Pharmacol* 33 (1984): 399–404.

   Y. H. Huang, "Net Effect of Acute Administration of Desipramine on the Locus Coeruleus-Hippocampal System," *Life Sciences* 25 (1979): 739–46.

34. N.R. Carlson, op. cit., 1992.

   C.B. Taylor & B. Arnow, op. cit., 1988.

35. S. Torgersen, "Genetic Factors in Anxiety Disorders," *Arch Gen Psychiat* 40 (1983): 1085–89.

   S. Torgersen, "Twin Studies in Panic Disorder." In *Neurobiology of Panic Disorder,* edited by J. C. Ballenger (New York: Wiley-Liss, 1990).

36. S. Braune et al., "Psychological and Biochemical Changes in Patients with Panic Attacks in a Defined Situational Arousal," *Eur Arch of Psychiat and Clin Neurosciences* 244 (1994): 86–92.

   J. Butler et al., "The Galway Study of Panic Disorder," *J of Affective Disorders* 26 (1992): 89–99.

   E.C. Villacres et al., "Sympathetic Nervous System Activity in Panic Disorder," *Psychiat Res* 21 (1987): 313–21.

   R.M. Nesse et al., "Urinary Catecholamines and Mitral Valve Prolapse in Panic-Anxiety Patients," *Psychiat Res* 14 (1985a): 67–75.

   I.L. Appleby et al., op. cit., 1981.

   R.J. Wyatt et al., "Resting Catecholamine Concentrations in Patients with Depression and Anxiety," *Arch Gen Psychiat* 24 (1971): 65–70.

O.G. Cameron et al., "Platelet 2-Andrenergic Receptor Binding and Plasma Catecholamines: Before and During Imipramine Treatment in Patients with Panic Anxiety," *Arch Gen Psychiat* 41 (1984): 1144–48.

37. D.S. Charney et al., "Nonadrenergic Function in Panic Anxiety: Effects of Yohimbine in Healthy Subjects and Patients with Agoraphobia and Panic Disorder," *Arch Gen Psychiat* 41 (1984B): 751–63.

38. S. Braune et al., op. cit., 1994.

G.N. Ko et al., "Panic-induced Elevation of Plasma MHPG Levels in Phobic-anxious patients," *Arch of Gen Psychiat* 40 (1983): 425–30.

T.W. Uhde et al., "The Relationship of Plasma-free MHPG to Anxiety and Psycho-physical Pain in Normal Volunteers," *Psychopharmacology Bulletin* 18 (1982): 129–32.

R.M. Nesse et al., "Endocrine and Cardiovascular Response During Phobic Anxiety," *Psychosomatic Med* 47 (1985b): 320–32.

39. D.S. Charney et al., op. cit., 1987.

D.S. Charney et al., op. cit., 1990.

R. Pohl et al., "Isoproterenol-induced Anxiety States," *Psychopharmacology Bulletin* 21 (1990): 424–27.

40. D.S. Charney & G.R. Heninger, "Abnormal Regulation of Noradrenergic Function in Panic Disorders: Effects of Clondine in Healthy Subjects and Patients with Agoraphobia and Panic Disorder," *Arch Gen Psychiat* 43 (1986): 1042–54.

J.M. Rainey et al., "The Beta-receptor. Isoproteronol Anxiety States," *Psychopharmacology* 17 (1984): 40–51.

R.M. Nesse et al., "Adrenergic Functions in Patients with Panic Anxiety," *Arch Gen Psychiat* 41 (1984): 771–76.

R. Pohl et al., "Isoproterenol-induced Anxiety States," *Psychopharmacology Bulletin* 21 (1985): 424–27.

41. R.M. Zacharko et al., "Behavioral, Nuerochemical, Anatomical and Electrophysiological Correlates of Panic Disorder: Multiple Transmitter Interaction and Neuropeptide Colocalization," *Progress in Neurobiology* 47 (1995): 371–23.

42. H.Y. Meltzer, *Psychopharmacology: The Third Generation of Progress* (New York: Raven Press, 1987).

43. M. Briley et al., "Effect of Serotonergic Lesion on 'Anxious' Behaviour Measured in the Elevated Plus-maze in the Rat," *Psychopharmacology* 101 (1990): 187–89.

44. L.B. Guttmacher et al., "Pharmacologic Models of Anxiety," *Comprehensive Psychiatry* 24 (1983): 312–26.

45. D.L. Murphy & T.A. Pigott, "A Comparative Examination of a Role for Seratonin in Obsessive-compulsive Disorder, Panic Disorder and Anxiety," *J Clin Psychiat* 51, supplement 4 (1990): 53–58.

J.A. Den Boer & H.G.M. Westenberg, "Behavioral, Neuroendocrine and Biochemical Effects of 5-Hydroxytryptophan Administration in Panic Disorder," *Psychiat Res* 31 (1990): 267–78.

S.D. Targum, "Differential Responses to Anxiogenic Challenge Studies in Patients with Major Depressive Disorder and Panic Disorder," *Biol Psychiat* 28 (1990): 21–34

R.S. Kahn & H.M. Van Praag, "A Seratonin Hypothesis of Panic Disorder," *Human Psychopharmacol* 3 (1988): 285–88.

46. L. Lima, "Region-selective Reduction of Brain Serpotonin Turnover Rate and Serotonin Agonist-induced Behavior in Mice Treated with Clonazepam," *Pharmacol Biochem Behav* 39 (1991): 671–76.

S.M. Paul & P. Skolnick, op. cit., 1981.

P. Skolnick & S.M. Paul, "Molecular Pharmacology of the Benzodiazepines," *Int Rev Neurobiol* 23 (1982): 103–40.

47. R. Trullas & P. Skolnick, "Differences in Fear-motivated Behaviors Among Inbred Mouse Strain," *Psychopharmacology* 111 (1993): 323–31.

48. L. Rago et al., "Correlation Between Exploratory Activity in an Elevated Plus Maze and Number of Central and Peripheral Benzodiazepine Binding States," *Arch Pharmacol* 343 (1991): 301–06.

49. R.M. Zacharko et al., op. cit., 1995.

50. J.P. Boulenger et al., op. cit., 1984.

T.W. Uhde, op. cit., 1990.

51. A. Orlikov & I. Ryuzov, "Caffeine-induced Anxiety and increase of Kynurenine Concentration in Plasma of Healthy Subjects: A Pilot Study," *Biol Psychiat* 29 (1991): 391–96.

52. R.M. Zacharko et al., op. cit., 1995.

53. J.R. Cooper et al., op. cit., 1991.

54. R.M. Zacharko et al., op. cit., 1995.

55. T.A. Mellman & T.W. Uhde, "Sleep Panic Attacks: New Clinical Findings and Theoretical Implications," *Am J Psychiat* 146 (1989a): 1204–07.

M.B. Stein et al., "Sleep in Nondepressed Patients with Panic Disorder: Systematic Assessment of Subjective Sleep Quality and Sleep Disturbance," *Sleep* 16 (1993): 724–26.

56. T.A. Mellman & T.W. Uhde, "Electroencephalographic Sleep in Panic Disorder: A Focus on Sleep-related Panic Attacks," *Arch Gen Psychiat* 46 (1989b): 176–84.

T.A. Mellman & T.W. Uhde, "Sleep in Panic and Generalized Anxiety Disorders, in Neurobiological Aspects of Panic Disorder." In *Neurobiological Aspects of Panic Disorder,* edited by J.C. Ballenger (New York: Alan R. Liss, 1989c).

57. M. B. Stein et al., op. cit., 1993.

T.A. Mellman & T.W. Uhde, op. cit., 1989b.

T.W. Uhde et al., "Fear and Anxiety: Relationship to Noradrenergic Function," *Psychopathology* 17, supplement 3 (1984): 8–23.

A Personal Account of Thyroid Disease with Panic Disorder

The Roots of Panic Disorder

MY FIRST FULL-BLOWN PANIC ATTACK occurred when I was barely eleven years old. My father had died six months earlier and my grief was profound. It was my first piano recital and I had chosen to play something special in memory of my father's life. The day he went into the hospital, I came home from my piano lesson and showed him the music. He died less than a week later. I remember becoming very ill a short while later and slept continuously. The doctor came to the house and I eventually got stronger. Most likely, this was my first autoimmune thyroid disease attack, brought to surface by great stress to my heart and soul.

In what I now can describe as stage fright compounded by grief, I was panic-stricken and could not breathe, think, or play my piece as I sat frozen at my recital. My dear piano teacher understood, took me aside, and later let me play my memorized piece with the music after the other children took their turns. Franz Liszt's Hungarian Rhapsody No. 2 is a complex, fast-paced piece of music. This time when I sat down, I played it faster than I had had ever played in my life. Parents and friends cheered as I ran from the room and cried from embarrassment.

My mother remarried a few years later and my stepfather became sexually inappropriate with me. As a budding teenager this terrified me and I was too scared to tell anyone, especially my mother. To the family, he was kind, jovial, and a good substitute father. His fatherly hugs turned into passionate kisses when we were alone, and I couldn't break myself free. Anytime he came near and I was alone with him, I would start to experience the same panic that occurred during the recital. I learned to successfully hide my fears from everyone around me. So often these unspoken fears would lead to arguments and hostility within the family. My only solution was to find a boyfriend bigger than him, six feet, six inches, and handsome. I married him at age nineteen and thought I was free.

We had a difficult marriage from the beginning. As young couples often experience, we had no money, no medical insurance, and struggled to keep afloat. When I was twenty-two, I had my first daughter. The pregnancy and delivery were difficult, compounded by pre-eclampsia, and I bled profusely post-partum. This is called Sheehan's Syndrome and can affect the pituitary gland because of a lack of oxygen to the brain. The pituitary and hypothalamus control all the endocrine hormones. The doctor later said I was fine, but this is when the real physical and anxiety problems began.

Due to post-partum Hashimoto's Thyroiditis, I developed severe insomnia, rapid mood swings, and agoraphobia—unable to leave the house. I would pace from window to window like a caged animal stricken with fear when I was alone, yet would be controlled when others were around. With this unrelenting fear I believed I was going mad, but by this time in my life I had learned to hide my fears quite successfully. I was determined not to show anyone my madness. I cycled between outright courageousness and downright panic. Only my husband witnessed the full extent of my emotions and this put considerable strain on an already failing marriage. Most of our arguments stemmed from my uncontrollable fears. Panic disorder had overtaken my life and mind.

When I was twenty-six, I was pregnant with my second daughter. It was another stressful pregnancy because of what was happening within my marriage and within my body. Five months pregnant with my second child, my daughter and I moved in with my mother, who was recently widowed, and my brothers. My stepfather had died a year earlier, a silent relief for me. My second daughter was two months premature, my marriage was over, and my husband physically and financially abandoned us a month after she was born. I was unable to breast feed because of this undue stress. Within a year I was hospitalized with myxedema coma, diagnosed with severe hypothyroidism, and given medication that I was to take for the rest of my life. My thyroid gland had failed.

Stress and Autoimmune Thyroid Disease

Hashimoto's Thyroiditis is an autoimmune attack on the thyroid gland. It is estimated that 95 percent of thyroid disease prevalence is due to autoimmune thyroid destruction. Antibodies destroy the tissue of the gland, and in the first stages the thyroid gland tries to overcompensate for the lack of hormones by producing more and more T4 (inactive prohormone) and T3 (active hormone). Often the first stage of autoimmune thyroid disease can give hyperthyroid symptoms, but the end result is hypothyroidism. This causes the gland to swell as it tries to compensate by producing excessive hormones. My mother noticed that my neck was swelling soon after the birth of my first daughter. I didn't think anything about it because I had no idea what that thing in my neck had to do with anything I was feeling. Being a new mother was hard enough.

What I did not realize was the nightmare that my life was going to become because of this thyroid imbalance. I would fluctuate from hyper to hypo states depending on the amount of stress I was experiencing in my life. In my first hyperthyroid stage I was anxious and panicked, my heart would pound, and the insomnia and nightmares were frightening. I lost a great deal of weight because my metabolism was skyrocketing. My temper flares were inexplicable. I had no emotional center. My periods were nonexistent for more than a year before I conceived again, another hyperthyroid symptom. The doctor said that sometimes women just don't have periods, so I thought little of it. Here I was, skinny, overly energetic, and living in a constant state of fear and anxiety.

After my second pregnancy and marriage failure, I took a stress index test I found in a magazine. It was the typical stress test with items like: recent death of a family member, divorce, childbirth, severe illness, moving to a new home, and so on. I scored so high on the test that I realized that my life was out of control. I had harrowing nightmares, began to sleep longer, my periods were killers. My emotions were swinging high and low, followed by tears and feelings of abandonment. I sought counseling because I feared a life on tranquilizers. Within months, I was unbearably cold all the time and my hair and eyebrows were falling out. My appetite had diminished considerably but I was gaining weight uncontrollably. My face took on a moon shape and appeared puffy and sleepy, my eyes were like slits. Soon I was sleeping all the hours that my children slept and a half glass of wine had me nodding off at the dinner table. Everything ached, my memory was failing me, and I cried at the drop of a hat. Now I knew I was going mad. Life became more fearful than before and even little noises would startle my weary body. Panic was my existing state of body and mind.

Stress is a major contributor in autoimmune disease. Would I have avoided Hashimoto's Thyroiditis if my life had been calm and peaceful? Perhaps or perhaps not, because the predisposition for autoimmunity is genetically passed down through families. Some family members might get rheumatoid arthritis, some may get lupus, some may have psoriasis, and others may get autoimmune thyroid disease, Hashimoto's Thyroiditis, or Graves' Disease. Some family members may never be affected by any autoimmune disease. There are over a hundred distinct autoimmune diseases, each with their own particular symptomology. It's just the luck of the draw, genetically. Were my early episodes of panic disorder also contributing factors? Most likely they were. Pregnancy, serious illness, traumas, grief, and emotional stress are all contributing factors in thyroid disease.

In the case of pregnancy, the enormous hormonal swings of pregnancy and childbirth can stress the thyroid gland considerably. While pregnant, the thyroid gland puts out extra hormones for the mother and baby. During pregnancy or when the pregnancy ends, the latent antibodies go into full attack mode. The goiter I had after my first pregnancy was a sign that the gland was trying to produce more hormones because it was being attacked by thyroid antibodies. No one is really sure why this happens, but researchers believe that the excessive thyroid hormones, plus the excessive amounts of estrogen and progesterone during pregnancy, are perceived by the body as invaders, a situation akin to that of a viral illness. This is the immune system gone haywire. Stress and high levels of adrenal hormones weaken the immune system. Women are eight times more likely to develop autoimmune thyroid diseases than men and hormones play a key role in autoimmunity.

My Diagnosis and Treatment

By the time I was hospitalized with myxedema (overt hypothyroidism), I was sleeping sixteen hours a day and spent the rest of the day in a physical and mental stupor. I was overwhelmed with exhaustion and the panic attacks caused by a lack of thyroid hormone. In sleep I could escape the waking torture, only to be further terrorized by vivid nightmares. It felt like every effort to think, act, and move made me feel more frightened than I had ever experienced during the traumas of childhood and adolescence.

Once I was medicated a with a T4 preparation called thyroxin, I began to regain my health and strength, but only for a short while. Unknowingly, I was overmedicated and back into the hyper state I had experienced after my first pregnancy. While my life was still stressful, I attributed the panic attacks and high-wired energy to my life situation, not to my medical condition. Now I was experiencing giant hives all over my body. I was the first patient that my doctor ever diagnosed and treated for hypothyroidism and I was never told the signs of overmedication. I just thought it was my particular inherited nature that made me a nervous wreck, so I continued to live with the madness.

I had insomnia and my doctor put me on both antidepressant and anti-anxiety medications. He also tried me on other antidepressants and those proved worthless, making the insomnia worse. Since I lived with my mother, after the children were asleep, I went out walking for hours in the small town where we lived. I walked and walked, hoping that I would become exhausted enough to sleep and burn off the nervous energy. The giant hives came and went with the antihistamines and steroids I was given. I have recently learned that giant hives are a sign of an enormous autoimmune reaction taking place in the body. I also suffered from pneumonia four times in four years. My body was breaking down and my immune system couldn't handle the physical and mental stress.

The Nature of Thyroid Disease

Both hypothyroidism and hyperthyroidism are complex diseases. One of the reasons they go undiagnosed and untreated is that the symptoms can mimic many other diseases from outright mental illness, including panic disorder, psychosis, and depression, to aches, pains, and fatigue. The brain and neurotransmitters are dependent upon having the correct amount of thyroid hormones for proper function. This condition is easily misdiagnosed as fibromyalgia and chronic fatigue syndrome, clinical depression, panic disorder, and other illnesses. Panic disorder occurs in both hypo and hyper conditions. It is the complex of symptoms that should alert a doctor to check thyroid hormone levels first, but all too often this is the last thing they look for. Instead, doctors often use the Band-Aid approach, treating symptoms one by one. Because thyroid hormones affect every cell in the body, every bodily system is compromised.

The endocrine system is complex and includes the pituitary and hypothalamus. The hormones from the endocrine glands work through a complicated feedback system. The endocrine glands include the thyroid, parathyroids, adrenals, ovaries, testes, pancreas, pineal, and thymus. These glands work in harmony, controlled by hormones from the pituitary and hypothalamus, which regulate the output of hormones from the glands. There are other influences as well, but these essential hormones are the chemical messengers that allow our bodies to be healthy and function properly.

Thyroid hormones are needed by every cell in the body to produce ATPs, or energy, and to regulate the metabolism of the individual. Within the metabolism are regulators (through hormonal responses) that maintain the homeostasis, or metabolic balance, of the body. Being in homeostasis is essential for good health and proper bodily function. This is Mother Nature's way of preserving the species in times of famine, illness, and trauma. Thyroid hormones control body temperature, appetite, heart function, fertility, fetal development, brain function, organ function, the muscles, skeleton—everything. Every cell in the body uses thyroid hormones to facilitate normal functioning within the cells.

Hypothyroidism

Weight gain despite dieting

Difficulty remembering things

Mental Confusion

Depression

Unrelenting exhaustion

Chronic constipation

Muscle cramps and weakness

Exercise intolerance, increased fatigue

Infertility, impotence, low libido

Cold intolerance

Slow healing and prolonged illness

Excessive need for sleep, drowsiness

Difficulty breathing with exertion

Numbness and tingling

Carpal tunnel syndrome

Decreased appetite

High cholesterol

Thinning outer third of eyebrows

Hair loss and brittle nails

Dry, cracked skin

Puffy face, hands, and feet

Low or high blood pressure

Slow heart rate (bradycardia)

Enlarged heart

Hoarseness and difficulty swallowing

Heavy menstruation, shorter cycles

Goiter (swelling of thyroid gland)

Low body temperature

Hypothyroidism

Weight loss, but sometimes gain

Nervousness

Restlessness

Irritability

Mood swings

Panic disorder

Anxiety

Increased appetite

Heat intolerance

High body temperature

Increased sweating

Frequent bowel movements

Nausea and vomiting

Rapid heart rate (tachycardia)

Pounding heart

High blood pressure

Exhaustion with exercise

Muscle cramps and muscle wasting

Goiter (swelling of thyroid gland)

Insomnia or little sleep

Hair loss and thin nails

Protruding eyes and tearing

Hives and itching

Excessive energy levels

Absent periods or longer cycles

Infertility

Thyroid Disease and Panic Disorder

HYPERTHYROIDISM

Now, let's get down to the issue of panic attacks and anxiety in thyroid disease. Hyperthyroidism, by speeding up the metabolism to unreal levels, affects the central nervous system, the neurotransmitters in the brain, and the autonomic nervous system. When the body is in a state of hypermetabolism, everything goes at warp speed. People appear nervous, anxious, driven, and often euphoric, manic, and psychotic. Fast talkers, fast thinkers, and fast doers fit the profile when thyroid hormone production goes out of control. Over time, if hyperthyroidism goes untreated, the body begins to breakdown from overuse of resources. A ravenous appetite without gaining weight is a sign, or sudden weight loss. Some people with hyperthyroidism can gain weight by overcompensating with food and a lack of exercise. Hyperthyroid individuals often have higher than normal body temperature, heat intolerance, easy sweating, rapid heart rate, muscle weakness, hair loss, eye problems, digestive problems, and headaches.

The overproduction of thyroid hormones can be maddening and left untreated can cause heart attacks and strokes: the Type A personality! With time, body fat is burned at excessive rates, muscle is wasted, and the lack of sufficient sleep does not allow the body time to heal. Sleep deprivation studies on normal, healthy individuals have confirmed this effect. The physiological symptoms of rapid heart rate, high blood pressure, high body temperature, and disturbed production of neurotransmitters translate into the mental anguish of mania, panic attacks, and anxiety.

HYPOTHYROIDISM

In hypothyroidism, the opposite effects occur. The brain's neurotransmitters are sluggish and there is loss of mental acuity, short-term memory is impaired, depression, and brain fog. The inability to remember the most simple things can make anyone nervous! Bodily functions slow down to a crawl, even to the extent of causing congestive heart failure, coma, and death if left untreated. Everything slows down, from the heart rate to the digestive track to the

DIAGNOSING TIGGER

"We acknowledge that Tigger is gregarious and affectionate, but he has a recurrent pattern of risk-taking behaviors. Look, for example, at his impulsive sampling of unknown substances when he first comes to the Hundred Acre Wood. With the mildest of provocation he tries honey, haycorns, and even thistles. Tigger has no knowledge of the potential outcome of his experimentation. Later we find him climbing tall trees and acting in a way that can only be described as socially intrusive. He leads Roo into danger. Our clinical group has had its own debate about what the best medication might be for tigger. We argue that his behaviors, occurring in a context of obvious hyperactivity and impulsivity, would suggest the need for a stimulant medication. Others wonder whether clonidine might be helpful. Unfortunately, we could not answer the question as scientifically as we would have liked because we could find only human studies in the literature."

—Sarah Shea, Kevin Gordon, Ann Hawkins, and Donna Smith "Pathology in the Hundred Acre Wood: a neurodevelopmental perspective on A.A. Milne," in the Canadian Medical Association Journal, 2000

THE COUNTERDIAGNOSIS

"Tigger is a perfect example of hyperthyroidism. The excessive energy is translated into rapid speech, jerky movements, high-flying stunts, acting before thinking of the consequences of the action. A true hyperthyroid state can lead to euphoric episodes as seen in mania. Rapid heart rate, little need for sleep, panic attacks, nervous gestures, mental confusion, even megalomania. His throat has an enlarged profile and his eyes are always bugging out. I imagine he sweats a lot and has diarrhea. Many disorders like panic attacks, nervous disorders, nightmares, visible shaking, hot flashes and such are seen even in subclinical hyperthyroidism. Someone give Tigger a beta blocker!"

—Leslie Blumenberg, in response to the above diagnosis

production of neurotransmitters in the brain. Muscles become weak and cramp because of the lack of sufficient oxygen and essential nutrients to the cells. The essential organs become unable to handle the normal workload of the body and this cascades off into a long list of symptoms that include weight gain despite low appetite and low caloric intake even while exercising, high cholesterol levels, hair loss, profound fatigue, exercise intolerance, dry skin, constipation, muscle cramps, and joint pain. Reproductive problems include shorter menstrual cycles, infertility, heavy, painful menstruation, and loss of libido. Subclinical hypothyroidism is often ignored and not treated, except by the Band-Aid approach.

Adrenal Hormones

The adrenal hormones, most notably cortisol, adrenalin, and noradrenalin, are also adversely affected in both hyper and hypo states. The workload on the adrenals in both hypo and hyper conditions can cause adrenal burnout or mild adrenal insufficiency. The adrenals were designed not only for flight-or-fight, a natural human response to danger, but to quell infections, inflammations, and to deal with stress. Sufficient cortisol is needed to keep the immune system working in a healthy manner and can substitute, short-term, for low thyroid hormones. Adrenalin and noradrenalin are the flight-or-fight hormones and cortisol is the feedback control. More stress requires more adrenal hormones. Adrenalin and noradrenalin are considered short acting hormones, needed for specific situations of stress, injury, or illness to keep the homeostasis of the body. Cortisol keeps them from getting out of hand when the stressors are gone.

In thyroid disease, the adrenal hormones are called upon to take over the function of the missing thyroid hormones (hypo) or to calm the excess thyroid hormones (hyper). The adrenals can only do so much to keep the body in homeostasis and are soon depleted if the thyroid condition is not addressed. This constant overuse of adrenal hormones to counter the effects of too much or too little thyroid hormones results in panic disorders and anxiety. When diagnosing thyroid disease, the state of the adrenals must always be taken into consideration. In fact, the manufacturers of thyroid medications recommend treating adrenal insufficiency before treating the thyroid, if deemed necessary by blood tests and symptoms.

Life Moves On

Hyperthyroidism

In my overmedicated state, I managed to burn the candle at both ends. With my newfound freedom, I explored love and life. I worked during the day, spent wonderful times with my children, and partied at night. I began to drink to soothe my nerves, a form of self-medication. From my perspective this seemed to keep my life in balance because I had no idea I was overmedicated with thyroid hormones. I learned to turn panic and anxiety into courageousness and fun. I was overextended on every level and the young woman my doctor saw so frequently was smart, energetic, and enjoying life—but had giant hives covering her body. If only I could have explained the fear in my heart from moment to moment. I knew that I was still grieving my past mistakes, so again, it all just amounted to the stress in my life and emotional imbalance. I covered up my fears too well, so the emotional distress was never easily seen. The physical and mental symptoms of being hyperthyroid are akin to being on amphetamines.

To put it simply, too much thyroid hormone speeds up the metabolism and too little thyroid hormone slows down the process. This is a normal occurrence in everyday life. Metabolic cycles are under the governance of circadian rhythms that control the rise and fall of hormones throughout the day and night. When more energy is needed, more thyroid hormone is produced and visa versa when less energy is needed.

When the desire to sleep is constant, either your thyroid gland is putting out too little thyroid hormone because of an autoimmune destruction of the gland from Hashimoto's Thyroiditis, or you're undermedicated with thyroid hormones. Other conditions causing hypothyroidism include congenital hypothyroidism and surgery or radioactive iodine treatment for Graves' or thyroid cancer, as well as iodine deficiency or excess. If the pituitary gland is damaged, secondary hypothyroidism can occur where the gland functions normally but the signals from the pituitary aren't working correctly. Thyroid hormones are made from iodine and tyrosine, an amino acid found in food. In these conditions, medical attention is needed and proper treatment and medication suited to individual needs is essential. A good lifestyle, diet, and exercise also benefits all of the endocrine glands.

When my daughters were nine and five years old, I decided to go back to college at Lesley College in Cambridge, Massachusetts. I found an apartment I could afford in the city, and had student loans and help from my mother. I had a year of college behind me before my first marriage and found that the small town I was living in was not going to fulfill my intellectual needs. I often wonder if I hadn't been an overmedicated Supermom, would I otherwise have attempted going to school full-time, working part-time, and raising two children? Getting less sleep and being constantly energized gave me more time to do it all. The panic attacks were just a part of life now, an everyday occurrence that drove me to exceed my natural limits. I had an euphoric feeling that is often associated with excess thyroid hormones and I was slim because my metabolism was accelerated. With no car in the city, once again I walked and walked to burn the excess energy.

HYPOTHYROIDISM

While in college I met my present husband, who was certainly attracted to my vitality. After graduating, I moved to his suburban home with my girls and we began life together. In a year we were married, and I cooking more and walking less than my hectic city life. During the year before my marriage, things began to change, which I attributed to the slower pace and security of having a wonderful man in our lives. I gained more than thirty pounds rather quickly, and much to my dismay, my skin broke out with acne. The fatigue I was experiencing was embarrassing. I became depressed and moody, interspersed with panic episodes from nowhere. Once again, I questioned my sanity. Eventually, I went to a doctor who raised my thyroid medication. I was better but still tired and PMSing all the time. Another doctor raised my medication again, only this time I became slightly hyper. The insomnia rebounded, my appetite increased, I continued to gain weight, and the panic attacks resumed with a vengeance. I had periods of six months to a year where I felt reasonably well, and then without warning the symptoms began to return. Soon they were constant. Autoimmune thyroid disease is noted for causing fluctuations in function and needs for dose changes when medicated. My doctors were only testing my TSH once a year and anywhere within the range was fine with them.

Anxiety and panic attacks in thyroid disease come from this hormonal and physiological stress. When we're tired, we like a little adrenal rush, but we don't want it to continue forever. When we're stressed, the cortisol is there to calm us down. The most important thing to consider is that sufficient cortisol is needed to convert the inactive thyroid hormone (T4) into the active hormone (T3). In hypothyroidism, this low level of cortisol doesn't allow for sufficient conversion and at the same time there isn't enough cortisol to control the surges of adrenalin and noradrenalin that are trying to get the body into homeostasis. This is also true in hyperthyroidism, in that the depleted cortisol levels allow the adrenalin and noradrenalin to run amuck. Hence, the sensations of anxiety and panic.

As humans, we are ruled by how our minds perceive the physiological signals of the body. Unfounded anxiety, which has no obvious mental or emotional cause, is a result of surging adrenalin and noradrenalin without sufficient cortisol to balance the levels. Add in real life stressors and the panic accelerates. Many other conditions can also cause this adrenal imbalance. For example, low blood sugar in hypoglycemia and diabetes will cause symptoms of nervousness and anxiety because the body is looking for glucose, which happens to be essential for brain and nerve function. When someone has low blood sugar, they search for food to satisfy the need and if food is not available, panic can set in and behavior is altered. It's not so easy to get sufficient thyroid hormones if the gland is malfunctioning or if you are undermedicated. Hypoglycemia and insulin resistance are recognized symptoms of both hyper- and hypothyroidism.

Decades of Ups and Downs

I am fortunate to have married a kind, gentle, and understanding man. Because of his background in the sciences, he understood that my excess or lack of thyroid hormones were causing my uncomfortable panic disorder. The problem was, I took the hormones prescribed for me and we didn't understand the fluctuations that an autoimmune disorder causes. He also helped me to resolve many of my childhood fears and find new paths for understanding the nature of what I had experienced for so many years. This is not to say we didn't have difficulties; my mood swings and panic attacks, while of an organic nature, naturally spilled over into our daily life. I was also experiencing severe PMS that could last three weeks a month with excruciating menstrual cramps. I often wonder if I could have survived without his help and understanding.

I started seeing doctors to address the physical problems and time and again was told that my thyroid was fine—it must be something else. I even had a female doctor tell me that my menstrual cramps were "all in my head." At the root of this continuous misdiagnosis by gynecologists, endocrinologists, and internists is the "gold standard" TSH test. TSH is thyroid stimulating hormone that is produced by the pituitary gland in response to the need for thyroid hormones in the body. In general, the range that is used to measure TSH is broad, from hyperthyroid to hypothyroid. When the number goes below the range, you're considered hyperthyroid. When it goes above the range, you're considered hypothyroid. Most doctors, even today, will test only TSH and if the number falls anywhere within the range it is considered normal. Only recently did the American Association of Clinical Endocrinologists declare that for thyroid function to be considered normal a TSH that falls in the lower part of the reference range is best, for most individuals with and without thyroid disease.

When testing for hypothyroidism, if TSH is in the upper part of the range or higher, you may technically have subclinical or overt hypothyroidism. In most cases, a high TSH indicates that the pituitary gland is asking for more thyroid hormones (T_4 and

T3) from the gland. This is a feedback system whereby higher levels of TSH indicate that the body needs more thyroid hormones. Ideally, a low TSH with above midrange levels of T4 and T3 is best—for people with and without thyroid disease. To know how poorly or well your body is reacting to thyroid hormones, the actual thyroid hormones levels of T4 and T3 must be measured. The optimal range for T4 and T3 levels is in the upper half of the range, sufficient to resolve the bodily symptoms that accompany hypothyroidism. Too much T4 and T3 with an extremely low TSH is a sign of excessive thyroid hormones, hyperthyroidism.

Subclinical hypothyroidism is not as severe as the myxedema I had experienced years before, but for most people it is a debilitating state. How unfortunate that many doctors are not aware of this and only use the TSH test for screening and monitoring medication when it's the T4 and T3 levels that are most important. Hypothyroidism caused by pituitary damage often presents with low TSH levels, but also low T4 and T3 levels. This is because pituitary damage doesn't allow the TSH to rise and fall naturally.

Using TSH alone can be misleading in cases of secondary hypothyroidism caused by pituitary malfunction and many patients can remain undiagnosed and untreated for years.

Eventually I found a doctor willing to increase my thyroid medication. After some time, I again found myself experiencing the insomnia, wired brain, and panic associated with hyperthyroidism. This time my TSH was in the lowest part of the range and still the doctor said my thyroid was normal. What then, was causing the cascades of symptoms? While I felt more energetic, it was like I couldn't turn off the switch. Sleep became short and unrefreshing, I gained weight because I was constantly hungry. I found exercise to be increasingly difficult. I was even given a five-hour glucose tolerance test and diagnosed with reactive hypoglycemia, which I now know is caused by excessive or deficient thyroid hormones. This was the roller coaster ride of my life. One day my test results actually showed me in the hyperthyroid range and something clicked in. The amount of medication can be *slightly* wrong and cause a whole lot of symptoms.

A Personal Account of Thyroid Disease with Panic Disorder

Research and Understanding

I was baffled and I naively trusted my doctors' judgment and authority. How much am I supposed to know about how my body works? I had read articles about thyroid disease in magazines and science books. Something just wasn't right and my husband knew it too. I was in my forties and all my symptoms seemed to be pointing toward perimenopause, so I began researching. I also went to various alternative practitioners to find solutions for my mysterious symptoms. I embarked on a diet and exercise program that helped me lose forty pounds in six months. Because I was experiencing some of what I guessed were perimenopausal symptoms, I started adding soy to my diet. For three years, I continued the diet and exercise but was no longer losing weight. My muscles ached terribly when walking, especially up hills or stairs, enough to make me cry. The most severe hypothyroid symptoms appeared and I thought I would soon die.

The panic and anxiety elevated to frightening levels. I had difficulty with mental acuity, attention span, and even expressing myself verbally. Often I would stare off into space in the middle of a sentence without a clue as to what I was discussing. I was constantly exhausted, my body hurt to even touch it, and my days and nights were spent in misery. I was so cold that my body would shiver violently and uncontrollably. While heating up the water for an instant shower, I would take my temperature. I felt like I was having controlled convulsions, with just enough presence of mind to know what to do. My temperature would be as low as 95.5 and I'd jump in the shower to raise my core body temperature. Keeping warm was a daily and nightly struggle. These are clinical symptoms of hypothyroidism. Chronic hypothermia is the result of too little thyroid hormone, causing the metabolic processes to slow down, which can eventually cause organ failure if not treated.

I was diagnosed as having fibromyalgia. Because my TSH levels were within the normal range, although much higher than previously, again four doctors said those normal TSH levels weren't related to my thyroid medications or my symptoms. These doctors were an osteopath, two endocrinologists, and a rheumatologist.

I had also sought treatment from a chiropractor and two acupuncturists. Extremely frustrated, I began to search the internet for answers. I researched my menstrual disorders, fibromyalgia, thyroid disease, and adrenal issues and eventually found articles on the dangers of soy for thyroid patients. Soy interferes with the absorption and utilization of thyroid medications. I immediately removed the soy from my diet and within weeks, the symptoms began to melt away—most miraculously!

I am still astonished that media and healthcare professionals, backed by the soy industry, are promoting the consumption of a goitrogenic substance, which causes the elevation of thyroid antibodies and blocks thyroid hormone absorption and release for metabolic purposes. Goitrogenic foods include soy, the cabbage family, broccoli, brussel sprouts, rutabaga, turnips, cauliflower, African cassava, millet, kale, mustard, rapeseed, peaches, pears, pine nuts, peanuts, walnuts, and many others. These foods can act like the antithyroid drugs propylthiouracil and methimazole in disabling thyroid function, so they should not be eaten in large amounts by someone with hypothyroidism and on medication. It's thought that enzymes involved in the formation of goitrogenic materials in plants can be destroyed by cooking. Thorough cooking may minimize goitrogenic potential, except in millet where it increases with cooking.

Armed with this information and my personal experience of having removed soy from my diet, I finally began to understand what the doctors had neglected to tell me about thyroid disease for more than a quarter century. Thyroid disease is complex and not easily treated, although most doctors would like you to believe it's as easy as "one little pill a day." I learned about the importance of testing Free T4 and Free T3 levels along with the TSH. The Free tests tell how much usable thyroid hormone your body has, whereas other measures of T4 and T3 include hormones that are bound by proteins and not available for use, thus giving an inaccurate blood profile. I also learned the importance of taking my medication on an empty stomach, an hour before eating and waiting at least four hours before eating foods or supplements that contain iron, calcium, or fiber. Such nutrients block the absorption of the medication. For years I took my thyroid hormones along with my supplements and a big bowl of iron fortified, high-fiber cereal with milk. No wonder my medications weren't regulated! The doctors said it was fine to take meds with breakfast.

My current doctor is listening. I provided research to show that low levels of T3, the active thyroid hormone, were contributing to many of my unresolved symptoms. As a trial, we tested medications that contained both T4 and T3 hormones and I have thrived taking this combination. I now use a natural thyroid hormone made from a pig's thyroid gland along with synthetic T4 to replicate the approximately 90 percent T4 and 10 percent T3 a normally functioning thyroid gland makes. There have been many dose adjustments but I can easily say that now I'm medicated correctly because of the absence of symptoms, including panic disorder. I still have my aches and pains from years of hyper- and hypothyroid mistreatment, but I am improving. The journey continues.

Panic Disorder and Thyroid Disease

I write daily on a thyroid internet forum and still continue to research the fine details of proper medication, diet, and exercise and how other hormones are influenced by the proper balance of thyroid hormones. I have become knowledgeable enough to help others with thyroid disease explore their medication options, how to approach their doctors with this information, and how to meet their individual needs. Many of these individuals have been given antidepressants, anti-anxiety medications, cholesterol lowering drugs, pain killers, sleeping pills, diet pills, and other drugs to alleviate symptoms that could be easily addressed with the proper combination of T4 and T3 medications. Many have spent years in psychotherapy trying to deal with the anxiety, panic disorder, and depression that accompany thyroid disease.

In reading the personal experiences of fellow thyroid sufferers for close to three years, I have learned something of the universal human sufferings that accompanies thyroid disease. As people have related their stories, some common factors are seen that relate panic disorder to thyroid disease. This is certainly not the only reason for panic disorder, but one to be considered seriously in the diagnosis and treatment of panic disorder and/or other hormonal imbalances. Once properly medicated, many have been completely cured of anxiety and panic disorder.

Often the symptoms of being under or overmedicated with thyroid hormones are seen by doctors as having nothing to do with thyroid disease when they have everything to do with thyroid disease. These individuals are suffering, yet their doctors refuse to see the connections. Most often they are told that they are simply clinically depressed, stressed and anxious, overweight and out of shape, and frankly, hypochondriacs. They wander from doctor to doctor without resolution and in frustration of never finding a practitioner who will see the symptoms for what they are: manifestations of thyroid disease. While a patient should be well informed, the patient also needs to be assertive in seeking quality care.

There are clinical signs of thyroid disease that are easily confused with other disease conditions. Panic disorder is most always seen as a psychological aberration and rarely as a malfunctioning of endocrine hormones. The physical symptoms of panic disorder are many, but what the patient and doctor alike often see is the inability to deal with stress and psychological trauma that hasn't been resolved. A reasonably calm person suddenly shifts gears into a mode of fear and panic, and stands dazed and confused by the process.

Hyperthyroidism

In hyperthyroid conditions, symptoms associated with panic disorder are: visibly trembling hands, easy sweating, compulsive behaviors, fidgeting, excessive talking and moving, rapid heart rate, elevated blood pressure, diarrhea, stomach cramps or irritable bowel syndrome, nausea, staring eyes, dizziness, and often migraine headaches. People appear nervous, anxious, high-wired, overly energetic, driven, elated, or depressed, even psychotic.

If anything deserves a panic disorder label, hyperthyroidism does. It is a very difficult state to live in. You get taken over by a racing mind that won't quit: too many thoughts, too many actions in a given day. Even when someone with hyperthyroidism tries to relax or sleep, it seems impossible. Many hyperthyroid individuals are often exhausted because in advanced stages, the muscles are weakened and the rapid heart rate and high metabolism make them candidates for heart attacks and strokes. Hyperthyroid people often have low cholesterol levels, low body fat (but the opposite is true as well, from overeating), and a high risk of osteoporosis from rapid excretion of calcium, magnesium, sodium, and potassium.

The resting heart rate is high (tachycardia) and often the heart is pounding—aren't these the same physiological reactions that we feel when hit by life events that are difficult and overwhelming? When a person is hyperthyroid, the body wastes essential minerals, vitamins, and nutrients. Magnesium deficiency exhibits many of the same symptoms as hyperthyroidism, namely muscle spasms, weakness, anxiety, tachycardia, asthma, headaches, high blood pressure, and heart problems. Potassium deficiency causes pain and weakness in the muscles, a nervous behavior pattern, rapid heart rate, and many symptoms associated with panic disorder. An interesting thing is that magnesium and potassium deficiency is also found in hypothyroid conditions.

In either situation—a thyroid gland that overproduces hormone or a patient overmedicated for thyroid disease—the body is screaming for help. Our minds are screaming for help as well, as the body interprets these sensations as if it were faced with a serious trauma or emotional situation. When these sensations are ongoing for months and years, long after the original trauma took place, we can either go to a doctor or learn to live with it. It is unfortunate that the medical profession so easily overlooks hormones and nutrients in cases of panic disorder and other diagnoses in the mental health field.

Hypothyroidism

When a person has a lack of sufficient thyroid hormones, panic disorder displays itself in a different fashion. The body is struggling to keep warm, shunting the blood from the extremities and brain to the central core of the body. It takes a lot of adrenalin to compensate for the lack of sufficient thyroid hormones. The reason that hypothyroids so easily gain weight is to insulate their vital organs. This is essential for the minimal functioning of the vital organs, which must maintain a constant core temperature. This causes the extremities to be cold and shivering. There is a sensation that is difficult to describe except as your organs being cold with internal shivering that is only relieved by applying direct heat. A hot water bottle or a hot bath can raise the temperature enough to be comfortable, but it doesn't last. This shivering might easily be perceived as nervousness and will cause the sufferer to over-dress, move very little, and feel anxious and depressed. This person pushes to get things done but all too often fails because the effort feels overwhelming.

When such individuals do what most would consider a normal amount of work or recreation, they are exhausted for days afterwards, having depleted the available stores of thyroid hormones, and possibly adrenal hormones. It is often said that a great need for sleep is a sign of depression, but it can also stem from low levels of thyroid hormone. Depression is a clinical symptom of hypothyroidism and can take on the form of apathy and disassociation. Often in hypothyroidism the adrenal hormone cortisol is deficient. One of the roles of the adrenals is to take over the metabolic functions that are normally the role of the thyroid hormones.

This means that more fight-or-flight hormones, adrenalin and noradrenalin, are produced to compensate for the lack of thyroid hormones with less cortisol as the feedback mechanism. If there isn't sufficient thyroxine or cortisol, these short-acting

Panic attacks can occur as the result of changes in hormones, especially during the perimenopause phase. As a result, the timing mechanism in your heart gets hypersensitive to other hormones which can irritate it. A simple way to calm down this timing mechanism is through the use of baking soda. By mixing just one-fourth tablespoon of baking soda in a glass of water and drinking it, you can shift the pH balance in your body, neutralizing the effect of these hormones on the sinus node, which sends electrochemical signals to the heart muscle. In addition, baking soda slows down the stomach's ability to compress a ganglion, a switching station for nerves, behind the duodenum, which also sends signals to the sinus node and on to the heart.

If you find yourself experiencing panic attacks during a particular recurring time during your menstrual cycle, you may need a low dose of 17-beta estradiol, a natural form of estrogen, to help restore your hormone balance.

—Dr. Larrian Gillespie, retired assistant clinical professor of urology and urogynecology

hormones will be continuously produced to keep the blood flowing and the body functioning. This is a precarious position to be in, a step away from developing high cholesterol, heart disease, and weight gain despite a low-calorie diet. The compounding factor here is that if you eat less than 1,200 calories a day, your body thinks it's starving and slows the metabolism further. It's a dieter's dilemma, believe me.

In hypothyroidism, panic disorder may come forth in the form of worry and self-doubt. We worry that we can't keep up with life and the demands feel burdensome. We feel that we are failing our partners and families, losing our grip, struggling to be our old selves. For most, self-esteem is first to go. A look in the mirror tells you something is radically wrong—puffy eyelids, missing eyebrows, hair falling out, and a swollen body. Not only that, you ache so badly that you think you'll soon be in a wheelchair.

At this point the nerves are shot. Every environmental stimulus known to man is just too much for the system to handle. This is also true in hyperthyroidism. Noises, sudden movements, brightness, tactile sensitivities, tastes, and smells are all on overload as the central nervous system tries to compensate. Some days it feels like being pierced by pins and arrows on a continual basis, day and night. There is also inescapable pain at times from muscle cramps, easy bruising, swollen joints, carpal tunnel syndrome, numbness, and tingling of the extremities. Often chronic heart failure and heart attacks are signals that indicate the thyroid may be the cause. Hypothyroidism represents the breakdown of the physical and mental processes. It's interesting that these symptoms are the same as seen in fibromyalgia, a disease with supposedly no cure.

Resolutions

Who wouldn't think you have panic disorder, clinical depression, psychosomatic symptoms, and hypochondria with all these symptoms? You go to the doctor and complain of aches and pains, weight gain, depression, needing naps, forgetfulness, and brain fog. You look like a couch potato and are told to exercise and diet. Exercise hurts and you're already on a diet—and have been for years! Autoimmune thyroid disease has a timetable of its own. Often the amount of thyroid hormone produced is just enough to get by, but not enough to flourish. Thyroid hormones also fluctuate depending on a myriad of things, from the disease process itself to other hormone imbalances and dietary nutrients.

Selenium is a mineral that is essential for the conversion of the inactive T4 to the active T3 molecules. Modern farming techniques of the past century have depleted our food supply of this and other important minerals. Magnesium is a very important mineral that calms the nervous system and heart, as well as making strong bones. Bone loss is high in individuals with excessive thyroid hormones.

Thyroid disease is far more prevalent in women because of hormonal fluctuations and different needs for thyroid hormones, such as in pregnancy and childbirth and the hormonal fluctuations of the menstrual cycle. The demands of a woman's body with a normally functioning thyroid gland would be met with increased or decreased hormonal output, only as needed. In someone with thyroid disease, hyper or hypo, the level of thyroid hormones determines the levels of reproductive hormones, male or female. Both of these conditions can produce infertility and sexual dysfunction in both sexes.

Taking the right dosage of thyroid hormones, both T4 and T3, has made my life a joy again. During the three years that I suffered the worst hypo symptoms since my diagnosis twenty-five years ago—when I ate soy because both the doctors and media were telling me to—I was taught a strict lesson in what to do, and what not to do, to preserve my health and sanity. What I have learned so startlingly is that doctors just don't understand the nature of thyroid disease. I am still appalled when I read about patients who have endured years of being misdiagnosed and drugged with the Band-Aid approach. They have suffered physically and mentally, emotionally and spiritually, because their doctors say "it's something else" or "it's all in your head."

It is estimated that 3–5 percent of the population at large has thyroid disease and an equal number are approaching the statistical levels seen in blood test diagnostics for thyroid disease. In the United States alone, 13 million are diagnosed with thyroid disease and an equal number remain undiagnosed or misdiagnosed. This translates into 180 to 300 million people worldwide estimated to have thyroid disease that is diagnosed. The rest remain undiagnosed and in poor health. Much thyroid disease in low-iodine areas, especially in developing nations, is due to iodine deficient soil and low-iodine foods that can easily be supplemented with iodized salt.

© Getty Images/Tim Southall, 2002

This is why proper testing with TSH, Free T4, Free T3, and a thyroid antibody test is so important to the diagnosis and treatment of thyroid disease. Iodine deficiency or excess can cause autoimmune thyroid disease. By carefully scrutinizing the early signs of thyroid disease, more progress will be seen in mending the spider's web of the endocrine system.

My life feels very good right now. As I enter menopause, my hormones feel balanced. My effort to lose the accumulated weight is ever in progress. I can now walk further with less tiredness and maintain energy throughout the day. My sleep is good with only occasional interruptions compared with the horrible nights I have endured throughout this journey. I'm losing weight slowly but my muscles are building strength. What once was exhausting is now manageable. My mood is light and my emotions feel stable. Even during the most grievous days of the recent terrorist attacks and ensuring war, I experienced no panic attacks. I haven't experienced a panic attack in the last year since getting my thyroid medications suited to my personal needs. I may need dose adjustments in the future, but at least I now know what to look for.

Things to Consider

There are far more facts to learn and understand about the nature of thyroid disease than I can present here, and a list of recommended books and websites can be found in the reference section (pp. 400–01). If you or anyone you know exhibits clusters of symptoms that resemble the hyper or hypo conditions I have presented, educate them about this poorly recognized disease. While thyroid disease is complex and has many components, there are some simple recommendations I would like to include.

Everyone over the age of thirty-five should have a baseline thyroid screening. I personally recommend that the screening be done earlier, especially for women of childbearing age, which includes teenagers. Thyroid disease can occur from birth onward, but is most often found in women of childbearing age, during menopause, and in the elderly. In fact, 17 percent of men and women over the age of sixty-five are diagnosed with thyroid disease. Men do get thyroid disease and should be routinely checked as well, especially those with a history of heart disease. If other autoimmune disorders are prevalent in the family and symptoms of thyroid disease are present, ask for TSH, Free T4, Free T3, and a thyroid antibody test. If you have high cholesterol, weight gain despite dieting, and unfounded depression and anxiety, thyroid levels should be checked. Attention Deficit Hyperactivity Disorder may well be closely related to unstable thyroid levels, as the scientific literature is now showing.

If you've had a head or neck trauma or experienced excessive bleeding at anytime in your life, look into the pituitary involvement in thyroid and adrenal disorders. Secondary hypothyroidism is due to the pituitary not being able to control the function of the thyroid gland. Adrenals need to be checked with same-day morning and afternoon cortisol tests to determine if you have overworked these life-sustaining glands. Lifestyle should be taken into consideration, including diet, exercise, medications, vitamins and minerals, and other factors such as family and work stress. Stress-reduction exercises and meditation, yoga, and alternative therapies are also beneficial during the healing process. Search until you find a healthcare practitioner who is willing to listen and not dismiss this condition simply as a mental health issue.

Some Thoughts

Part of what makes us human is our diversity of size, shape, and kind. Something as seemingly simple as thyroid hormones can alter the physical, mental, emotional, and spiritual cores of our being.

The quality of our lives depends on the proper amount of this hormone coursing through our blood. It is intimately connected with the neurotransmitters, the central nervous system, and the thoughts we think. How we perceive our body's reactions to the world around us is tied into how we perceive our bodies in our most private and intimate worlds. Panic disorder and the symptoms that surround it are linked to hormonal fluctuations gone wrong. Modern medicine is capable of restoring that balance, if the imbalance is correctly identified and fine tuned to individual needs.

As so many of my thyroid friends are quick to say, "It's in my neck, Stupid! Not all in my head!" My butterfly-shaped thyroid gland, just below my Adam's apple, has shriveled to nothing. The quality of my life is totally dependent upon the proper medications and lifestyle. What I learn about this disease daily, in my own life and the lives of others, is that by understanding the nature of this disease, I have conquered my mental demons. Fear and panic have melted away. I understand well the effects of too much or too little thyroid hormone on my emotional life, how it has affected my family and friends, and most importantly, how it has affected me. Never again will I allow hyper or hypo states to exist within my body. Life's too precious for that.

A Phenomenology of Panic

I.

PANIC IS AN EXISTENTIAL STATE. No matter how its attributes are squeezed into diagnostic criteria and medicalized, it remains an irreducible condition of being.

Our basic situation in this realm is profoundly terrifying. We simply appear here, helpless in bodies; we are given no instructions, no explanation; at our demise, we face extinction, or worse. The Yaqui sorcerer Don Juan Matus warned his disciple Carlos that an insatiable eagle-like spirit awaits our deaths to pounce, tear apart, and devour our souls. The Russian esoteric philosopher George Ivanovitch Gurdjieff preached that, unless we transmute our essence into a higher compound during life, the Moon will swallow us at our end, igniting our remains; our pyres will then light the universe as suns. Not comforting propositions.

The modern astrophysical realm, now in full ascendancy, has proven no more assuring. Its universe is so banal, antipathetic, and nonhuman that our world, its entire history, and all its creatures might be annihilated on any given day by a stray asteroid or comet; it will ultimately be obliterated, along with all mammalian and other vestiges, by the explosive death of the Sun.

This portends no moral order anywhere—nothing except an unreliably thin veneer of symbols to protect us from not only Nazis, comets, and al Qaeda, but the enigma of nature itself, coiled around our heart.

Gurdjieff declared, in effect, that anyone who wasn't freaking out wasn't aware of his or her predicament. He said that if any of us could at any instant be shown our actual situation, we would find existence intolerable.

The psychoanalytic establishment has its own "Oedipal" version of the same crisis:

> Caught between the harshness of the world and the urgency of his or her instincts, the child is born with a readiness for terror. Psychoanalysis affirms that there is something unmanageable about being a person … : the demonic—possession by alien meanings—starts at home. Fear is always familiar.[1]

The only reason we are not all in states of constant panic is that, to one degree or another, we are buffered from raw existence. A flow of hormones and the hum of our nervous system reassure us and make life even exhilarating (sometimes).

Biochemical and autonomic cycles set in motion at our birth and during early infancy apparently dissolve or convert the terrors of incarnation. Our natural condition is to be comforted and invigorated by our bodies and the belief systems that our minds generate. We enjoy being here—existence better than nonexistence—and are not undermined by the nakedness and vulnerability of the human plight (which is the plight of all animals).

Nonetheless, people panic. They become terrified to the point of incapacity. They do not panic (usually) because of a vulture spirit or lunar cauldron; they are haunted by more mundane fears, and sometimes they panic with no discernible cause.

Panic is a universal experience, transcending class, gender, culture and, likely, species. Animal panics are concrete and crisis-based—i.e., the frantic scurry of prey from predator—but not only do they resemble human panics, they are probably their direct antecedents in the emergent nerve nets and ganglia that coalesced long ago into the primate proprioceptive field.

Animal terror is the archetypal experience to which all modern panics refer. Human panics may be abstract and ambivalent by comparison to animal ones, but they are biologically and phenomenologically rooted in primal mechanisms of fright and flight.

Our courage and calm are also animal.

The existential experience of panic is nonverbal, but among words that capture aspects of it are: dread, terror, hopelessness, hollowness, sterile grief, joylessness, restlessness, frigidity, obsession, paranoia, inconsolableness, desperation, shock. Panic is inconsolable because no one can help; obsessive because you can never take your mind off it; restless because, with your mind on it constantly, you flee from place to place, seeking oases of respite, and cannot think of doing anything else. Panic is paranoid because it suspects others of trying to harm you or of falsely reassuring you, of humoring you to exploit you through your fear. Because it is paranoid, it is isolate, cut off from human contact, the opposite of eros.

Anxiety is the standing condition out of which clinically defined panic detonates in its acute forms. Most people who panic for systemic (as opposed to external) reasons experience low-to-medium levels of anxiety all of the time. Since full-on attacks are unpredictable, chronic foreboding contributes to persistent states of worry. People who experience panics are forever in incipient panic.

A "normal" person mediates the dangers of everyday life by continuously and semi-consciously inventing ways of reducing tension and potential anxiety without escalating fear. A neurotically anxious person protects himself or herself with exaggerated prudence and superstitious rituals. Phobias and kindred compulsive responses to perceived threats help ward off anxiety and keep full-blown panics at bay, so they are integrated into a person's character structure where they shape who he is and how he acts on a daily basis. What look like intentionally controlling and motivated behaviors are artifacts of anxiety control, masking the real individual, though they chronically deteriorate into anxiety. Rudiments of caution and fright are also converted into mounting states of hypervigilance, tension, alarm, tantrum, and, if the limits of compensation and emotional endurance are crossed, abject terror.

Acute anxiety and panics may express themselves in mild, temporary disorientation, some loss of coordination, and confused thought and speech; they can also be as physically disabling as a stroke or heart attack. In fact, panics are phantom somatic attacks, their symptoms mimicking those of many life-threatening diseases. As anxiety escalates toward red alert, perception and rational thinking become increasingly distorted; delusions and hallucinations arise spontaneously, converting sensations into "diseases" and phobias and superstitions into self-fulfilling prophecies.

Panic is a self-perpetuating, naturally erupting state. The more anxiety increases, the greater the somatic discharge, and vice versa, until blind terror becomes inevitable. The actual attack merely relieves a contemporary build-up of cathexis and tension. Then innate anxiety reasserts itself and begins recruiting toward the next attack.

Degrees and durations of panics vary. Episodes may last for moments, hours, days, or months, though their levels of intensity will fluctuate during that time from moderate anxiety to unbearable fright. A person may imagine she is under magical assault, is losing her mind, or is suffering from a terminal illness. Her psychic integration on the verge of being overwhelmed, the victim responds by wild alarm that may seem irrational and counterproductive but in truth is a last-ditch attempt to prevent her sanity from disintegrating altogether.

The somaticization of terror is how the unconscious finally gets the attention of the ego. Something even more unbearable is converted to "mere" panic and given an alias. It must be more unbearable because panics are extremely painful conditions in themselves.

Panic is loss of meaning pretending to *mean* everything. People panicking "behave as if they know what they are frightened of; if they did not believe they knew this, there would be no solution available: their fear is an act of faith."[2] Without it, they face a quite different moment of truth, formless and nameless, with real monsters where they actually dwell.

The Jungian psychologist Edward Whitmont once told me: "You cannot keep panic out. It knocks at the front door; you bolt it shut. It is at the back door; you bar that; it is at the front door again. You put chairs and tables at both doors; it is at the windows. You cover the windows; it comes through the roof."

Panic is like Pandora's box; once opened, it can never be closed. The ancient story-tellers knew this well: once the Medusa has been viewed, once the Sirens have been heard, once the fruit of the tree has been tasted, the experience will never leave the mind. Once certain boundaries have breached, the safety they govern can never be fully restored:

"There may, sometimes, be a cure for symptoms, but there is no cure for the unconscious, no solution for unconscious desire. Knowledge can't put a stop to that, only death can."[3]

Or cure must come from somewhere other than undoing. Desire itself must change. Undoing (unknowing) is impossible.

2.

The modern neo-Freudian etiology of panic views it not as a self-originating state with its own meaning but a clinical condition, a last-ditch psychosomatic coping mechanism. Panic is given a narrative and derivation as compelling as any Greek myth: the imperiled psyche under siege by discharges from unresolved infantile conflicts defends itself by chameleon feats of emotional decompensation and displacement.

A panicking person has unknowingly regressed and is reexperiencing infantile crises and rages that could not be worked out in their time. Unresolved primal events invariably leave behind defective ego boundaries through which they later break to reassert themselves in apocryphal and terrifying guises. As contradictory demands on the psyche put it at risk, the ego goes into overdrive to preserve its integrity; it resolves surges of conflicting and unconscious impulses, providing them with immediate somatobehavioral outlets.

Early conflicts that persist unconsciously in adult life include: projections from an anxious and tense mother, disillusionments and frustrations ambient in a home, apprehensive childhood training, parental neglect, undeserved punishments, projection of a bad conscience, hyper-perfectionism, excessive teasing, sexual seduction, physical abuse, and the like. Unconscious urges spawned by these and similar conditions impose themselves undyingly through the rest of life, projecting the wounds and frustration of the past into a future which can only replicate them forever as long as no other future is imaginable.

Eros deviates from its ordinary goals toward redemption of old sorrows and insults because nothing else feels good or right. Life becomes its own eternal return. "Fear ... confronts the child with desire as contradiction, the to and fro of emptiness and plenitude; with emptiness always defined by the shape that will fill it...."

In fear, and perhaps out of fear, we make a future we also cannot afford to believe in."4

A child cannot create his or her own ego boundaries or confident personality structures in the context of adult uncertainty and blame. An ego maturing in an environment of apprehension, guilt, and abuse is marred and deformed in peculiar ways. Later adult situations "arouse infantile object relationships and experiences" which have been kept alive "in both manifest dreams and neurotic symptoms [and] which correspond emotionally to the adult ones."5 Infantile needs imperfectly translated into adult regressed states can never be fulfilled. The guilt and anxiety provoked by their rearousal are infantile too—timeless and global.

When adult and infantile object relations, needs, and longings mingle with one another in an adult context, the person tries futilely to placate ancient urges that are incompatible with present life goals and with one another. He maintains dysfunctional behavior partly because there is no emotional substitute and partly because dysfunctionality has properties that are unexpectedly comforting.

Phobias, compulsions, and the like are "indirect derivatives of ... unconscious processes ... [including] defenses and the superego."6 Fascinated by and drawn to anxiety-provoking situations, the neurotic person finds himself "repeatedly doing things which he thinks he does not want to do, things that defeat his adult ends."7 He is "pursuing something by running away from it. (The neurotic is always arriving at the place he is running away from.)"8

Ignorant of the true source of anxiety and blaming a proximate threat, he seeks protection or release from primal retributions and may even attempt to punish himself. Each of these misplaced impulses augments and abets an already panicked response. Yet, for the psyche, this ritual is the only way in which ancient conflicts can be activated, made lucid, and provisionally resolved.

When panic is understood as a circumstantial sociopsychological response to indeterminate conflict, it becomes clear that the true object of its terror is less the ostensible and immediate cause of fear than the psychosomatic discharge provoked by irreconcilably ambivalent emotions. The discharge is in fact the last line of defense against a very different threat—the impending breakdown of meaning.

As we have seen, the dynamic purpose of chronic anxiety, however temporarily maladaptive, is to prevent full-scale disorganization and hallucination. Anxiety itself is painful and debilitating, but it exempts the ego from being taken over by more dire unconscious material. It is a way of staying afloat in a stormy sea—often the only means by which the ego can handle primitive, highly charged needs and fears while also maintaining its adult configuration.

Panics are propitiatory enactments aimed at making existence bearable and letting the ego survive to fight another day. There is always blind hope that victory can finally be achieved.

3.

Whatever the unconscious, infantile basis of terror, projections of danger in the West tend toward machine phobias, existential alienations, mega-paranoid inflations, and Kafkaesque dread of being trapped in one or another maze. Western society provides plenty of anxiety-provoking situations for unconscious conflicts. Travelling in a metal can shooting flames 35,000 feet up in the air, being trapped at a steering wheel bumper to bumper in a traffic jam, being stuck at a crowded party of loud, unpleasant strangers, being forced to work on the ninetieth floor of a skyscraper all elicit phobias that are panic-provoking: agoraphobia, claustrophobia, acrophobia, and their kin.

Fear objects in tribal cultures tend more toward directly malign agencies such as curses, spirits, and charms. In Westernized Asia, Africa, indigenous America, and the native Pacific, individuals may atavistically finger some form of totemic invasion, often in the guise of superstitions and hexes.

Children raised in non-Western contexts but conducting otherwise-ordinary Western lives grow up to see ghosts. Westerners probably see ghosts too, but they are social or mechanical projections. The threat we intuit is more diffuse, less personal. Sometimes it is an irrational fear without an object or a dread of being overwhelmed by the vastness of the civilization itself, its relentless social and economic demands. Primitive magical portents are, paradoxically, more concrete and less global and cosmic than the limitless paranoias unleashed by nihilistic materialism.

4.

Generally panic is a false imagination of an overwhelming, subliminal threat, but that is not always so. Some sources of anxiety (like forces of nature) are quite real and legitimate—bombardments from war, tornados, floods, home invasions, gang violence, murder of a family member—but their being real does not preclude them from becoming the raw material of childhood projections that gradually turn into undifferentiated adult traumas.

It is not the force of the events themselves that becomes the source of anxiety (and guilt); it is how adults handle the crises and the climate they create around them. The intimate moods and unexpressed anxiety of grown-ups generally penetrate far deeper into children than actual wars, hurricanes, deaths, and fires, for psychological projections make these into more than just hostile events; they acquire a twilight life as malicious agencies—fiends, ghouls, and vampires—and, in those guises, sap courage.

Peril from an unconscious realm is far more threatening than immediate danger from a blatant and identifiable one. Projected unhappiness compounds a malignancy beyond actual violence. Bombs dropped on a neighborhood and bullets fired through windows, strewing plaster and glass, will usually be less traumatic than parental disappointments if the parents in a war zone protect their children and do not foist their own anxiety onto them, ask them to carry it for them, or blame them somehow for it. The children may even become courageous:

"The war inside is always worse than the war outside. The war inside is ahistorical and beyond contingency; the war inside is the truth of our being; the war outside is merely history. The enemy outside is a weak impersonation—an accident of history—compared with the enemy within."[9]

A child's constitution and raw personality also play a role in determining his or her adult fate. Virtually identical events can mold a neurotic, a warrior, a president, a serial murderer, a punk musician, or even a healer and compassionate therapist. Some marginal personalities who thrive in tribal cultures as sages and warriors are destined to be mental patients in Western civilization. Still others with defective ego structures become political and military tyrants when opportunity presents itself; they impose their skewed views on their victims. Adolf Hitler, Osama bin Laden, and Idi Amin all could have been institutionalized if they didn't first seize power and "normalize" their realities.

But that doesn't make their acts any less real.

The psychosocial explanation of panic follows the dictum of anthropologist Claude Lévi-Strauss, who proposed that what was truly frightening to men and women in tribes was not lightning, floods, or wild animals, but the ambiguities generated by each individual's fragile identity and the emergent symbolic order around him.[10] Violent, life-threatening agencies of nature may scare people transitorily and superficially, but nature is finally not the problem; it is an honest adversary. It is in language and the devious structure of cultural things that true anxieties are incubated.

Totems exist in equivalent form today as the needs and demands of the modern nuclear family, the repressive rules of bureaucracies, morality cults, and hungry ghosts generated by technology.

5.

The neo-Freudian treatment for anxiety and panic is to educate the person about the infantile cause of his or her terror and alienation and, with the therapist playing the role of a parent or other formative figure, to reenact a primal event in a supportive way that leads to emotional clarity. Suffering and pain are not eliminated, but they are keyed to appropriate objects.

This method of treating panic is now antiquated to the point of appearing almost prescientific in many professional circles. During our post-Freudian psychotropic era, panic has been redefined as a chemical, often genetically inherited defect or imbalance. Traumatic context, while not ignored altogether, is regarded as secondary and circumstantial. Historicodynamic events are presumed not to cause panics so much as to push people with marginal biochemistry over the edge.

A majority of medical professionals today believe unqualifiedly that panic and other psychopathological disorders can be treated successfully only by drugs. Transference-based interactions between patients and therapists are seen as imprecise, termless, indulgent, and a waste of human resources. In fact, they have been either mocked or vilified (depending on the ideological perspective of the critic) as pseudo-confession, spiritual materialism, or bourgeois decadence.

The dramatic, Jekyll-into-Hyde success of Prozac and other serotonin-uptake inhibitors in treating primarily depression (but anxiety and panic too) has tended to reinforce the biological prejudice, contributing to a paradigm shift in which most psychiatrists prefer to prescribe drugs. This upholds the current molecular bias of medicine and evolutionary philosophy and fits well into the modes of socialized and institutionalized medicine being practiced. In a profit-oriented healthcare market, there are simply not the budgets, facilities, or personnel to treat so-called pathologies with long psychotherapies, so these methods have become the vestige of a kinder, gentler time.

In any case, if large numbers of people whose behavior was self-destructive and neurotic suddenly become mellow and well-adapted from merely a new pharmaceutical regime, there is a tendency to presume (and hope) that a high percentage of psychological disorders are chemical at core, and can ultimately be traced to genetic, environmental, or other proximal causes.

Psychopharmacologists generally dispute that traumatic events can *ever* be actual (even if unconscious) motives of persistent pathological behavior—but if we fuse a molecular model with a classical Freudian one, the operative question becomes whether psychochemical adjustments alter existential conflicts at the basis of panic by mutating their meaning (all memory presumably chemical at base) or whether they merely divert chemical distress signals imposed by an epibiological urgency at the core. The former has an Orwellian overtone of replacing a lived life with an artificial one in order to sedate an aggravated person, and the latter intimates symptomatic regulation of a problem without addressing its roots.

At least traditional psychotherapy, whatever its lacks from a hard-science standpoint, attempts to get at a phenomenological core. Pharmaceutical reductionism makes panic (and depression) into commodities. Once simplified to undesirable chemical states, they can be transformed into more desirable ones by other commodities. Thus, the entire predefined panic structure is passed into an economy that readily envelops it correlative to the entertainment, communications, and even automotive industries: life enhancement attained by a customized, mass-produced product.

6.

Either a purely clinical or biological approach to panic breeds many epistemological problems. After all, where can a definitive line be drawn between a pathological, ontologically deviant state and ordinary life itself? If some of our thoughts and behaviors are merely tropismic, chemical activities, are not the rest more subtle and complex reactions of the same order? If so, we have no free will or creative potential. Human civilization with its progressive credo is not only a fraud but an illusion, and we populate little more than a glorified ant village.

Although psychopharmacologists do not intend this implication (and usually do not apply it to their own mind-states), they pay no heed to the social and symbolic consequences of a purely medical approach to mental illness, promoting a tacit double standard—the acts of sick people are hereditary, chemically based, or psychosomatic delusions; the acts of healthy people somehow transcend their chemical and psychic constituents.

But of course, there is no dividing line, even in rigorous psychological diagnostic systems, between madness and sanity. As Lévi-Strauss wrote at the beginning of his genre-defining work on totemism, "... there is no essential difference between states of mental health and mental illness.... [T]he passage from one to the other involves at most a modification in certain general operations which everyone may see in himself; ... consequently the mental patient is our brother, since he is distinguished from us in nothing more than by an involution—minor in nature, contingent in form, arbitrary in definition, and temporary—of a historical development which is fundamentally that of every individual existence."[11]

We all panic, but panic takes on a temporary, societally circumstantial form in some of us.

7.

The name "panic" falsely suggests that one kind of phenomenon on one level is involved. The prominent clinical treatments for panic (whether behavior modification or drugs) also approach it as pretty much a single-vector target. But panic is not a uniform modality, etiologically, behaviorally, or phenomenologically; people experience things that they each call "panic" having quite disparate expressions and meanings.

Panics only seem to fit diagnostic paradigms when victims are taught to homogenize their experiences and, reinforced by stock language and terminology, to name their unaccountable states. Much as Eskimos have a variety of snow words, we need a spectrum of nouns for panics.

Panic is not an explicit medical or psychopathological condition. It is not even a thing; it is a process, a shifting phase-state of events and experiences which, if sharing symptoms and themes, nonetheless mutates constantly in relation to its own phenomenology and the meanings each person inside it assigns. It continually generates new realities and choices.

The eidetic aspects of panic certainly rebel against reductionism. Not only levels of panic but all modalities of being are experienced profoundly and existentially; they are more than "real" to the individual encountering them inside himself (herself), they are the very marrow of being. Someone undergoing clinically predetermined psychopathological states is experiencing and internalizing those states and signifying them in unique ways. Her nature and destiny, her life goals, are defined by that awareness.

So-called mental effects ("normal" or "pathological") are the sole basis from which we muster our truths, our institutions, our conduct, and our identities.

From a subjective viewpoint, it appears that many panickers would be better off if they were chemically deeded a different anatomical and phenomenological basis on which to feel and act—though this presumes that the goals of life are adaptation and purges of unpleasant sensations. In truth, it is impossible to know in advance which experiences and states of being are symptomatic displacements that block expression of a person's true nature (however this might be defined) and which experiences, while debilitating, uncomfortable, and terrifying, are crucibles through which the person is transformed and made more conscious and whole.

To believe in panic and depression as beneficial, creative states, one has to accept that some aspect of being is not merely chemicodynamic or, if life is only molecular, that we transcend our molecularity in a fundamental way. For instance, one could adopt a Jungian position which thirty years ago didn't seem so outlandish—human beings have an archetypal, transpersonal, individuating dimension and a soul.

Whatever belief system about the source of psychopathologies is applied, people have two choices (either from their own impetus or as a result of the decisions made around them): to live through spontaneously arising phenomenological states or to have those states mutated psychosocially or pharmaceutically such that their experience of them and consequent behavior proceed medically.

8.

A purely clinical approach to panic becomes especially provincial when terror is addressed from a cross-cultural perspective. Although the biochemical basis of panic and depression may be universal for *Homo sapiens* (and primordial for other mammals), the ranges of sensations kindled by hormones and synapses and the social and symbolic contexts in which they occur, are interpreted, and used differ widely from culture to culture.

Other societies have recognized terror, evil spirits, possession, and various altered states of being without considering these as diseases or diagnostic categories. The Greeks assigned certain effects to the god Pan, but they did not deem panic a clinical event.* During vision quests some tribal peoples incite Pan-like terror; the goal of such an artificial neurosis is to bring the person into contact with the transpersonal aspects of his or her own personality—to make a civilian into a healer.

Even psychopharmacology varies from culture to culture. Where panic and other extraordinary mental states are regarded as

---

*Carl Jung proposed that we have turned gods of Olympus and Valhalla into our neuroses and diseases, in which state they are far more dangerous.

opportunities and bridges to separate realms of reality, people take drugs to *increase* the level of "madness." The tendency is to use herbs and potions to encourage and, in many cases, enhance symptoms—precisely the opposite of the goal of Western psychopharmacology, which is to calm a person down and get him into a more moderate range of experience and behavior, even if such a change means turning him into an automaton and making his life less rich.

An Amazonian indigenous "doctor" would not alleviate the negative symptoms of panic or depression by dampening or eliminating sensations, since excited states are prized as gateways to supernatural realms that offer insight and transformation. To heighten dissonant sensations is to ride them into new realizations of the universe. Indigenous healing ceremonies in the Amazon and elsewhere (e.g., ayahuasca-induced trances) seek to establish contact with disembodied spirits and demons in hopes of not only bringing a crisis to a head but transforming it into knowledge and power.

The strategy of appropriateness, normalization, and coping is paramount in our society because our stratification of roles is fragile enough to require conformity. The point of life in our cultural context is not so much to individuate as to graft oneself and one's experiences into sanctioned acts.

Many potential shamans, poets, and political leaders end up in mental hospitals, living on the streets, or impressed into service as office workers and bureaucrats. The visionary poet Allen Ginsberg started a career in the advertising business and, only by rebuffing socialization, turned himself into an avatar. While he realized his shamanic potential, how many artists and healers have remained in public relations or other office pools? How much creativity has Western society forfeited in its goals of goods, comfort, consensus, and technological progress?

Our experience of panic arises from the belief system and lifestyle that our society attempts to impose on states of being, reducing them to simpler and more orthodox phenomena than they are. Once panic is secularized, it attracts other meanings and acts that tend to reinforce this definition. It builds its own iconography from there. This leads to humane, progressive treatment of some forms of mental illness that otherwise would cause immense, sterile suffering, but it also subjects all phenomenological states, including many divine panics and depressions, to decompensation, trivialization, and authoritarian compliance.

Medicalizing panic is a way of getting numinous experiences down to a level where a community can understand and tolerate them.

9.

Throughout my life, I have experienced two types of panics. One is concrete, with a clear focus, and is usually alleviated by withdrawal of the objective occasion of fear. The other is cosmic, undifferentiated, and nihilistic, and it cannot be reassured. It feeds off a terror that the universe itself is essentially warped or malevolent, that existence is hopeless, and that there is nothing to be done or anywhere to hide. Death is no solace either because it will land one in a hell realm among cruel, antipathetic monsters.

An objective form of panic can evolve into this state if it goes on unrelieved for too long. Its focus deepens and changes; the fear of a disease or other disaster becomes globalized; body chemistry learns to answer and support anxiety; nothing feels safe.

A number of times before the age of twelve I thought I had mistakenly eaten or drunk a poison. When, as a child digging vanilla ice cream out of a Dixie Cup with a wooden spoon, I noticed tiny black spots, I thought some toxic soot had gotten inside me. Once at summer camp a weird boy gave me an orange and then, after I had swallowed a section, he told me he found it in the woods and it was cursed. A couple of years later I bit off a piece of bread on which I then saw fungus. In each of these instances, icy pangs throbbed inside me into a panicked state that was a totally convincing replica of poison spreading.

At other times I imagined I detected a deadly disease on my body. A large pimple or a muscle felt in an unaccustomed way became a tumor. A rash foreshadowed fatal pox. An upset stomach, lingering pain, or intense headache portended total deterioration somewhere inside me. Once fear took over, no ailment was innocent or minor; I had no faith I would ever get better, even though I had recovered from similar symptoms innumerable times.

When I was either reassured by a doctor or enough time had

elapsed that I realized I couldn't be poisoned or terminally ill, I would emerge from the panic state as spontaneously as I entered it.

In adult life I have also experienced this sort of panic, for instance on a plane during turbulence. I won't eat, talk, or watch the movie and, if possible, I will check the flight crew, stare out the window incessantly, listen for the health of the engines, look ahead to make sure that we are clear of objects. When the flight ends, I find myself returned to normal.

I have always acted on planes the way a lot of fliers have come to behave since 9-11-2001, i.e., scanning fellow passengers for hijackers. Vigilance itself is not mad; it is an exaggeration of what people do briefly or are compelled to do in extraordinary times. 9-11 provided an opportunity for society's ordinary vigilance to catch up to my own projections.

I have had a similar panic at times when my wife has gone out for the evening and not returned at the expected time. During the hour when she is, to my mind, unaccounted for, a sense of hopeless desperation and panic begins to set in. "It's not that dangerous out there, you know," she said once. "You act as though I'm going into a country at war." Of course, that country is inside me, not beyond the door.

The terror ends when she returns.

During the bigger kind of panic it seems as though the universe has always been malefic and I have been in denial and not recognized the obvious. The only imaginable remedy is to be totally expunged from existence with all my thoughts and memories, my past and my future—just not to be, never to have been. It is a desperate sensation that nothing could be more painful than what I feel. When I am in this state, I totally understand my mother's suicide which, at other times, seems maudlin and narcissistic to me.

A cosmic panic elicits a different vocabulary from the object-based kind. It is feelingless, sterile, alienated, pessimistic, beyond hope, robotic, cosmic paranoid, intellectually and emotionally vacuous, eviscerating, even tedious. Its span can be quite brief, but on a few occasions one of mine has persisted for months. Five or ten years may also pass between occurrences.

While the sensations of my "big panic" have changed over time, its essential content has not. In early childhood I lay in my crib and stared at a dark window overlooking a courtyard reverberating with the sound of an opera singer practicing. My imagination, while encompassing her, went beyond to diabolical creatures staring coldly at me from the vistas of deepest space. I imagined a dungeon at the bottom of stone stairs on another world into which prisoners were cast forever. I imagined that my brain could be stolen and put in an insect or another body.

As an adult, I have experienced this panic as an existential emptiness, the oppression of a demonic or spiritless universe.

Cosmic panic permeates my dreams to the degree that I wake terrified, often with a start, feeling as though I am in the wrong body in the wrong universe. "Being" itself is agonizing. I dread going back to sleep because it will plunge me deeper into an antipathetic void.

My nightmares then are not classic nightmares; no terrifying things happen in them—I am not chased, threatened, drowned, pushed over a cliff, jailed, or dismembered in any way. The dreams contain hauntingly ordinary events from which I awaken, more frightened than from any "real" nightmare. They are nightmares only because they feel like nightmares.

Getting up from affectless dreams, I walk frantically through the house, looking for anywhere to alight. I stare out the window at lights and buildings, but they all seem flat and inappropriate, incapable of eliciting connection or rescuing me. I am doomed to a sentence of mere existence.

The sensation is that time has stopped, that I have moved outside of time into a place where nothing can live—a state expressed in the song "I Can't Stop Loving You": *"They say that time heals a broken heart,/But time has stood still...."*

My intimation is that, if only I could get time moving again, I could arouse a flicker of hope. Yet monumental effort is required to push a single moment forward; each second takes forever to elapse, and there is another, and then another.

Two journal notes from 1992 speak to this:

Time was my enemy because it rolled on forever, forcing me to dwell in it like a conveyor belt of torture moving always infinitesimally slower because my thought tracking it and trying to escape it slowed it down even more like the degrees of Zeno's paradox.

Its spell is like a clock that breaks the relationship to time. Without panic, oneself and time move fluidly in concurrent streams that resonate each other's presence. In panic one is suddenly not moving at all but is drowning in the pool of time.

No viable experience lies outside of time, no feeling, no solace. Outside of time is a vacuum in which the sensuous, joyful aspects of life cannot blossom. Such a state, wrote Samuel Taylor Coleridge, "rob(s) me of my mirth;/ ... Suspends what nature gave me at my birth...." He calls out to "viper thoughts that coil around my mind,/Reality's dark dream!" then observes the wind "[w]hich has long raved unnoticed. What a scream/of agony by torture lengthened out...!/Bare crag, or mountain-tairn, or blasted tree...,/Or lonely house, long held the witches' home...."[12]

This is depression so deep and profound that it cannot wallow in itself—depression with an agitated, restless disposition. Coleridge's name for his state on April 4, 1802, is preserved in his title: "Dejection: An Ode."

Perhaps panic and depression are faces of the same coin, biologically, phenomenologically, or both: "A grief without a pang, void, dark, and drear,/ ... stifled, drowsy, unimpassioned...,/Which finds no natural outlet, no relief,/In word, or sigh, or tear...." It is little wonder that drugs used to treat depression have been surprisingly successful in experiments on panic. Panic-depression is a dull, blank mega-terror suppressing a grief so overwhelming it cannot be allowed to surface. It flees itself in dread of what it is. In such a form panic is not only terror, dejection, and despair; it is unconscious avoidance of mourning—an unwillingness to feel both the joy and loss implicit in every human life. It is fallow, arid dread.

Watching the crescent moon rise among stars set into motion by thin flakes and bars of clouds, Coleridge laments, "I see them all so excellently fair,/I see, not feel, how beautiful they are!"

It takes an internal shift to end this kind of panic. For one reason or another, time starts moving again. The dark vision detaches itself and slides away. The panic is still there, but it is outside; I am allowed to live. Clouds travelling across a blue sky, a flock of geese, or some other simple natural event can suddenly reconnect me to the living world.

One time, I escaped a long panic by dreaming of a terrific wind blowing debris through an empty city. Coleridge himself longed for such a release: "And oh! that even now the gust were swelling,/And the slant night-shower driving loud and fast!/Those sounds which oft have raised me, whilst they awed,/And sent my soul abroad,/Might now perhaps their wonted impulse give,/Might startle this dull pain, and make it move and live!"

Living is like flying. People don't know how they fly, but soar they do, almost miraculously, through difficult events, experiencing things which make their life pleasurable and meaningful. If they quit flying, if motion stops for them, they can't fly, and they can't live. Life scrutinized at a standstill doesn't happen at all, for there is no transformation, no basis for the simple courage of everyday acts—the faith that keeps all human beings out of despair.

10.

Because of my panics, bed-wetting, and general anti-social behavior, I was put into psychoanalysis on my eighth birthday in the fall of 1952. I spent the next ten years through high school in therapy with two renowned Freudians, first Abraham Fabian (who died when I was thirteen) and then Maurice Friend (who, I later learned, was an associate of the renowned French child analyst, Jean Piaget).

Both of these men treated my panics in traditional fashion. I remember Dr. Fabian's approach better because I did not have any big panics during the period I saw Dr. Friend—I was mostly a sullen teenager. Dr. Fabian summed up my panics by a single epigraph: "You are afraid something terrible is going to happen to you." He repeated it so often that it came to sound like the lyrics of a popular song or the proverb at the end of one of Aesop's fables. By this yardstick he proceeded to explore, using symbolic free connection, my stories, dreams, accounts of my relationship with my family—all aspects of my life—trying to elicit the breakthrough clue to what had traumatized me originally. He gave me the impres-

CHILDHOOD

One evening the radio was left on in an empty room. A voice said: "Yet another one fell down the stairs, into the dungeon ... forever!"

"... forever ...!"

My life sank into infinity against this other—obscure, expanding, hostile.

It wouldn't listen. It had never listened. It could do anything to me it wanted, and there was no one to protect me.

Frosty the Snowman sang his jingle in the back of my mind, a mere rattle against the resonance of existence.

Since I couldn't hide I stood in the hallway, screaming, making fists, tearing away, refusing their consolation. They had no idea what I was confronting. My mother, however ominous, was just a lady. The danger wasn't an irregular heartbeat or a spot in my chest. It wasn't polio. It was so much worse than they could imagine. Their shrieks and histrionics were almost comical against such an intruder.

It was my destiny to stand alone in the watchtower.

*

Fear remained my closest companion, unconnected either to family strife or daydreaming. It was the dungeon stairs, the hospital, the invisible executioners—and something else again. It was the color of light, the persistence of morning, afternoon, and nightfall, one after another, those same streets, shop windows, shop insides, day after day, hour by hour, relentless, profound—these people, this family, our carpets and furniture, plates and cups, meal after meal, the sound of the carpet sweeper, these same rooms, the rattling elevator up and down and up and down, the black front door. No single thing was that disturbing, but all these things together, unbroken and unending as light seeped and changed, dividing day from night, night from morning, were a march into oblivion.

I woke shivering in the middle of a sleep and staggered into their room, willing to ask even them for help, their husks heaped in murk, Daddy snoring. Alarmed by me standing there whimpering, Mommy jumped out of bed, put on a bathrobe, and hastened me down the hall, turning on lights as we went.

She opened a wooden cabinet and found unfamiliar objects. Out of an ornamental bottle she poured a wee glass of brandy. I didn't want to drink it, but she helped my hand and the bitter gave me such a jolt I stopped shaking and sat down. She was so relieved she began laughing. She laughed so hard tears ran down her face.

I wanted to stay with her there in the light forever.

*

Behind the scattered memories of childhood, a vast memoryless curtain covers my life. I can create names for that curtain, but they are intellectual constructs. The original sadness was an ocean. It wasn't even "sad"; it was sensual and rich, and I swam in its eternity—a planet of waters as large, in scale, as the lake into which *The African Queen* plunged in the movie. It too had lightning and demon cruisers. There was no opposite shore to that lake, but childhood was the process of sailing there anyway. Fear was my guardian, but fear was the same as timelessness—unrelinquishable, impenetrable.

Games kept me busy—toys, comic books, movies, waterguns—so that a yellow plastic Sorry token or a green Pennsylvania Avenue card brings back the whole enchantment.

*

Sometimes the haunting in me softened into a sadness, a sense of being lost and forlorn (resonating in an image

sion that there was a single event which, if I could remember it, would have its spell broken by the knowledge, and I would be freed from fear forever.

of Heidi's grandfather searching frantically for her through wintry villages). It was more than a sadness. It was a shadowing of limitless depth, of layers parting to reveal other layers themselves parting, like the leaves of maples in an autumn breeze. In this form sadness was not only not sorrow; it was secretly the most joyful thing I knew. Not joyful like Grossinger's but joyful like experiencing loss and then recovery, leaving home and coming home at the same time.

The songs of the play *Finian's Rainbow* (performed by the older kids at Chipinaw) bore shards of this sensation. I tried singing but couldn't keep a real tune. Upon request (and with a little help on the lyrics) Bridey reproduced them in her brogue: *"How are things in Glocca Morra ... Does that leapin' brook still...."* Words and melody put their spell over me; the world itself seemed to drop a chord into slow motion and swim by in solemn, stately fashion. Yes, it was sad and fearful, but it was beautiful—shockingly beautiful. Then she sang, *"Look, look, look to the rainbow...."* I had no words to match it, but I leaned into the song like a sunflower into sun.

Jonny and I would run along the Nevele solarium, building little piles of snow on the railings in an effort to thaw some of the winter away in March. Debby splattered in puddles at our feet. Mommy sat on a lawn chair, her eyes closed, a silver reflector about her neck. Clump after clump of puffy cold was placed on rusty ledges as Jon and I called to each other to check the progress of melting at either end. This industriousness would arouse a sense of the profoundest well-being in me. I'd be thinking about where I was in my latest science-fiction book and how later I'd lie toasty by the radiator and read it— then we'd eat dinner; afterwards, chocolate horseshoe cookies ... and the song would seep through my veins: *"Follow it over the hi-ill and stream...."* I twisted the

vowels in "follow" and "stream" until they were barely English in the back of my throat. There was a tenuous point, before they became ridiculous, at which they held the whole mystery, the fairy tale, Bridey's Ireland.

It was a book I read, maybe; a dream I had; or it was something else entirely, vast and incomprehensible. All the time, this mood dogged me, conveying secrets and masks—and also that strangely immense joy. *("So I ask each weeping willow, and each brook along the way ... ")* Jon and I would buy candy bars and comics at Ivy's Store, go pinball bowling, and then sit in the lobby engrossed in Almond Joy and Porky Pig while languid crowds swept past. Smell, color, and mood combined in a wonder that we existed at all. Gradually the mood would fade, or it might call to me from the faint center of a dream.

Its nether side was sheer blind terror. The less there was to cause it, the more powerful its claim on me. It happened one night, as I came into the dining room for supper. I looked at everyone seated there at the table— Mommy, Daddy, Jonny, Debby. Bridey was serving halved grapefruits. The reflected ambiance of the walls was too pale. I thought, 'This is it, forever—no!' I couldn't relent to it, so I ran into my bedroom, hurled myself onto blankets, and dug my fingers into them. A black invisible light shot through my forehead.

I could tell later, from their judging looks, they thought it was that I'd rather be at Grossinger's, but it was more a feeling of having come into the wrong century altogether.

—Selections are taken from Grossinger's nonfiction novel *New Moon*

My mother also panicked, and her sieges were chilling to me. She alternately cried hysterically, screamed that she was dying, attacked us, threw things, and lay semi-comatose in her bed with only a dim candle-shaped bulb lighting her room. Her panics dominated the mood of our household. But she would have nothing to do with psychoanalysis and even opposed my going. I was sent by my father from a different family.

Through my time with Dr. Fabian I came to associate panics with not only my mother's moods and my Nanny's witchlikeness but some lost event inside me and a whole realm of arcane spells. Intellectually I believed him when he said that everything would be solved by his divination, but at heart I could not imagine being without my fears. After all, what was going to change the universe? Who was going to take away evil people and A-bombs?

This all became moot after Dr. Fabian died and I began seeing Dr. Friend.

Psychoanalyst Adam Phillips summarizes the classic method of therapy from the perspective of almost half a century:

> [A]s each theorist offers us a new redescription of the unacceptable—of what we are suffering from, of what we have to fear—they become, by the same token, the masters of our suffering. By punctuating our unhappiness, they make it legible. Like religious or political leaders, they tell us persuasive stories about where the misery comes from, and hence, by implication, what we might do about it. They want to change our (and their) relationship to the fear they have formulated for us. The expert constructs the terror, and then the terror makes the expert.... Experts, in other words, can give us descriptions that allow us to be unhappy in new ways.[13]

Dr. Fabian took my unhappiness from the inner world I inhabited and attached it to an indeterminate psychological attack arising from a riddle. I needn't blame interstellar outlaws and ghosts any longer. Things had merely gotten tangled and dangerous inside me, inside language, and their calling card was panic.

It is quite possible that I would not even use the word "panic" for my own experiences if I had not been deeded it by Dr. Fabian in childhood, at the same time that I was initiated into reading and arithmetic. My subsequent behavior and experiences were colored by both his interpretation of what I was undergoing and my extrapolations of his oracles. Once named, my experiences obeyed their definition, which also provided an acceptable terminology for discussing my "condition" with others and socially navigating its shoals and crises. The word "panic" became as prescribed as the letter "a" or the number 4. The story of my panic evolved into adult guises which I inherited and performed like clockwork. I had a repertoire of behavior and explanation called "panic," a sanctioned, set series of causes and meanings assigned a name by Western psychiatry.

The phenomenological experience of panic is organized in part by the secondary benefits of a clinical definition. At least panic is "something"; it is a sword to hold over others: "Be careful with him; he's crazy; he loses it!" or "You can't ask him to do that because he might not be able to handle it." Panic excused me from unpleasant responsibilities and elicited instant attention and help. A physician's letter was all that I needed to present to the draft board in 1968 to escape the Vietnam War, but no doubt there were many other people who could not clinically define or certify their fear at getting dragged into that morass, so they had to find other ways of getting out—or not.

The diagnosis also kept wild and troubling sensations within known boundaries and allowed me to discount the extent of their actual danger and act bravely in spite of it. When I felt scared or inadequate or even depressed, I became anxious and called it panic; in truth, I was already waiting for, expecting, a familiar state, however uncomfortable and unlucky my susceptibility. It would have been much more frightening for something else to happen instead. "Panic" gave me an identity, a reason for being terrified when others weren't, and a way to communicate my difference to them. I could say, "I am having a panic," and it would draw instant recognition and relief inside me while resonating for others. Any variant of that phrase would redeem my restless terror and wildness, making it merely and apologetically clinical, though it would also preclude me from exploring it in its own terms.

I began to valorize and appreciate panic. It made me special, if star-crossed, like someone from another, better world. I could reclaim my identity someday if I didn't allow myself to get sucked into this place so deeply that I forgot who I was. In that sense panic was better than submission to authorities or norms. It kept the drama going, the ball in play, except (of course) I *did* forget who else I was. Panic became a self-fulfilling prophecy, a gift that was also an addiction and a curse. What my bare experience might have evolved into otherwise is unknown.

Phillips notes: "Psychoanalysis starts with the story that we are too much for ourselves; that we are, in a sense, terrorized by an excess of feeling, by an impossibility of desire." Fear drains off passion even as it generates a new excitement; it "turns panic into meaning. It makes fear bearable by making it interesting."[14] It even makes panic into a love story, albeit a narcissistic one.

To a certain degree, I was inventing panic from outside-in, scaring myself in order to escape an impossibility of desire, a vision quest I wasn't ready for, to replace it by festive dialogues with Dr. Fabian. This unintentional plan then gathered its own momentum, making panics a requisite of intellectual curiosity (the only dream that deciphered itself), a birthright (an entitlement to act crazily as if authentically), a way to squirm through life's many ambushes and hazards—a note to hand to the Martians, if they came to kill all Earthlings, that said: "I'm not part of this. I don't count." A note to hand to panic: "Don't hurt me. I know your name. And, anyway, I'm not really me; I'm just panicking."

II.

I had my first significant panic as an adult in the spring of 1964 (see pages 122–23), about eight years after my last childhood one and shortly after I began going out with the woman who was to become my wife. I navigated this and ensuing panics mostly on my own steam for about eleven years, except for three crises—one around the draft physical and the birth of my son, another around a violent act of my brother, and a third shortly after beginning to teach at an experimental college in Vermont. During each of these I saw a psychiatrist or counselor on a short-term basis.

In the summer of 1975 on a trip to Berkeley, two years removed from the last of those three panics, I found a bioenergetic therapist, and my work with him commenced an odyssey of engaging my own states of being, including panics, somatically and energetically rather than psychotherapeutically. This journey came to include (after I moved to Berkeley) not only Reichian-based bioenergetics (1975 to 1978) but t'ai chi ch'uan (1975–1997); Lomi breathwork with Gestalt therapy and shiatsu (1977–1992); craniosacral therapy, visceral manipulation, somatoemotional release, and Feldenkrais Method (1990 on); Cheng Hsin martial-arts mindwork, boxing, and hsing-i (1991–1997); acupuncture and Chinese herbs (1992 on); rebirthing (1992–1994); Rolfing (1994–2000); plus briefer stints of Breema, Polarity Therapy, alchemical hypnosis, chi gung, Alexander Technique, Bates Method, Body-Mind Centering, Continuum, Reiki, homeopathy, and Integrated Manual Therapy. I have trained in many of these and treated myself and others.

During the same twenty-year period I also participated in Jungian dreamwork (1980–1982), Zen meditation (1987–1993), and Tibetan visualization (1992).

All of the above share the premise that the psychohistorical and emotional components of panics (as well as other neuroses and blocked states) are not as imperative as their immediate dynamic, somatic aspects. The former are interned in the past, their truth concealed by false memory, their effects amplified by habit, whereas the latter are present in the body and can be contacted directly in the energetic form in which they are organized.

If a deep-seated trauma or anxiety is lodged in neuromusculature, viscera, breath, eye movements, and behavioral patterns (e.g., as fear during martial encounters or rage and sadness elicited by Gestalt exercises), then it can be addressed on the spot, without an archaeological quest. It can be literally touched, eased, and unwound by palpation, breath, visualization, push hands, and yoga. If its psychosomatic component can be identified and released, then the habitual anxiety underlying it will also dissipate. The story underlying the trauma can be liberated too, although since it is part myth/part true memory, what actually happened is not as important as how it is presently maintained and revalidated in the telling.

My journey through these psychospiritual modalities deepened my experience of the universe immeasurably. I made space in my body and learned to transform anxiety and tension into energy.

12.

Body-oriented therapies, rebirthing, martial arts, Zen meditation, and other practices are practicable means of lessening anxiety and its symptoms. I have visited Robert Zeiger, an acupuncturist and Chinese herbalist, at the height of a panic attack with no hope that his needles placed into my body could undercut the icy waves of fear. Yet each time their stings and jolts penetrated directly into the core, both physically and psychically, of my panic. They touched the energetic grid of the actual thing. Nothing in the external world changed; the objects under vigilance remained. But a new combination of energy and sensation began to flow through my being, altering its pitch and making the world normal again.

Combinations of craniosacral therapy and visceral manipulation have put me into trance states in which not only did I participate with a therapist in untangling blocks and letting go of rigid neuromuscular patterns but I learned how, practicing on myself, to project my intention through my tissue and subtly follow tension lines to anxiety cysts without imposing vectors of oversimplified will.

Somatic and breath-oriented therapies have given me an array of new sensations and meanings to work with and considerably more physical and phenomenological compass in which to handle terrifying upsurges of thoughts and sensations. I now accept these as messages from the unconscious, sacred lessons from the dark spirits of the universe.

Yet I have not affected the inner core of my panics. Despite interludes of remarkable insight and epiphany, I am surprised—or actually not surprised—to find that the background level of anxiety I have known my whole life has been essentially unaltered. The emotional structure underlying my anxiety seems to be "me" in some fundamentally unchangeable way. After twenty-six years of practicing somatic techniques successfully, I can use them for chronic relief and personal growth, but my panics themselves are as primitive, infantile, and intractable as they always were—and vast and cosmic in new, more terrifying ways.

It seems that, while developing abilities to heal, I have also given myself greater resources to scare. I would imagine that this is the shaman's eternal dilemma at the crossroads of transmutation.

13.

The reason certain problems seem vast and insoluble is that they begin before we have language and they arrange themselves outside of language. Any attempt to heal them must also go outside language. Unquestionably, somatic modalities such as craniosacral therapy and acupuncture do this—that is their natural trajectory. But their dilemma is that the way in which they go outside language (using energy channels, palpation, stillpoints, visceral release, and the like) is not necessarily the way in which a neurosis or other emotional pathology was structured primally (or the way in which it maintains its stasis subliminally and transformationally).

The manner in which somatic and spiritually oriented therapists voice or otherwise portray primal landscapes to their clients requires a fully adult level of conceptualization, albeit the hypothetical adult reconceptualization of an abused or wounded infant. But this is not the language or system of expression either a soul between bardos or a newborn uses.

Unless one breaks into the true precognitive self, the best alternative treatments are usurped into other ancient dialogues such that, as they improve some visceral, neuromuscular, or psychospiritual condition, they also amplify core neurosis—the gap between the languaging self that is mature and cerebral and the primitive self that is still thrashing about in conflict. The greater this gap becomes, the more serious its consequences. A rebirther once warned me that the gap between who I was when I was panicking and who I was otherwise "is big enough to kill you."

Somatic therapies and Westernized shamanisms often propose unrealistic requirements of self-improvement. Healers who think they can cure anything are like corrupt gurus, seizing psychospiritual power for themselves at the expense of unresolved emotional conflicts in the patient. The energetic components applied by such healers become incorporated into detracting and inflationary voices of tyrannical authority in the mind of their recipient because the instinct of the psyche is to resist orders, while the nature of resist-

COLLEGE

On a Saturday morning in mid-May I was sitting in a cloister of sun in the Phi Psi stairwell, reading *The New York Times* and eating by hand from a box of Corn Kix into which I had poured half a carton of currants. There were complete Yankee and Met articles to devour, plus seasonal averages. Lindy and I were going out that night.

Suddenly the ocher hue on the rug seemed to flicker and change. The world deepened by a layer, and I felt something oppressive inside me. I took a quick breath and put my interest back into details of box scores.

There was a brief hiatus; then the deepening came again—a tremor followed by a series of tremors. Their sheer output was incredible. I felt disoriented.

I bolted from the stairwell and took an immediate protective stance on the floor of my room—feet up, arms around my knees. The biggest one yet swelled ... right out of my center, visceral, primeval, bottomless.

I told myself that nothing was happening; it was some sort of passing sensation like heartburn or a headache. It would subside.

I was astonished how solid and fixed it was. Everywhere I turned I felt it coming at me, nameless, remorseless, looming up from the background of existence —neither simple nor manipulable.

I reached behind and around my neck ... and contacted a string of odd lumps. Had I developed tumors overnight? In alarm I jumped to my feet and grabbed for the top of my backbone. It was hard as stone!

Racing to the bathroom mirror, I ran my fingers frantically up and down my skeleton. I had always had a backbone, but what was that floating bump above it? It throbbed, as I twisted and pressed it.

*

Lindy and I met for dinner in Northampton and afterwards sat on a Smith lawn; she stroked my suspect backbone, felt nothing odd, and reassured me. The anticipation of seeing her—and then the logistics of getting there—had sustained the day till then. In her presence the world was soft, sensuous, just a fraction out

of orbit. I thought maybe I could outrun it and live.

But panic came the next morning, synonymous with my awareness of waking; its dread waves rolled through the overbrightness of sun. I heard a distant radio, like a foghorn. Getting dressed, I caught a glimmer of spring outside, guys beyond the window in tee shirts and shorts—so much easy-going activity it was intolerable. Just two days ago I was one of them—baseball, banter, classes. I was normal, a bit of a rebel and a nut but an okay guy. Now I walked like a zombie, going through a pretense of conversation and meals.

Why was this happening? I searched inside me for anything that felt mutable, capable of humor. Instead I recalled the lobby of the Y with its fruit machines, as real as yesterday, more real for its mucid gloominess. I saw the natal sun come up through swamp vines from a whining train. Those images were lethal, cold as radiation. I thought: I can wait this one out.

I couldn't. For it wasn't just a matter of minutes, or hours. Every second, my heart beat ... and I took another breath.

It would have been manageable (I thought) if the panic were the trauma of my wound from my mother, but once again she seemed a pathetic accomplice to forces beyond my lifetime. This must have been the evil my parents saw and feared in me—that I was the carrier of darkness. I might contaminate others. I should be quarantined from the whole human race. Even as I thought that, I thought, 'Down the dungeon stairs, into the darkness, forever.' The threat was a million times worse than the Cuban Missile Crisis, for nuclear war would incinerate all life and thought. I would be blasted into nothing. This, on the other hand, would go on forever, waking me up from every life and every death, to experience it again. I was truly and utterly terrified.

How did *anyone* live?

*

For lack of another option I kept going to class, almost losing hold of Geology because I didn't have the patience to sit through labs with rocks all over the floor imitating a landscape. I wrote my term paper as a script, with the monadnocks and mountains and rivers announcing their roles aloud. At least I got a bemused C.

Abnormal Psych was my one solace, for I could pore over the textbook for disorders that seemed to apply to me. I wanted to be an episode like an oxbow lake or continental drift, something explicable that Dr. Friend could cite from years of work with me. But I sensed the reticence in his response, his unwillingness even to admit that we were the blind being led by the blind.

I had fallen down the dungeon stairs, past Nanny's ancient grasp, into the darkness, forever. But now—I understood—it wasn't a dungeon of granite or stone. It had nothing to do with matter. Yet even the wildest volcano had a cause, a force behind it:

"Anxiety attacks are acute episodes of emotional decompensation usually appearing in a setting of chronic anxiety, and exhibiting to an exaggerated degree the characteristics of normal fright. The fright usually comes from within, from a sudden upsurge of unconscious material that threatens to disrupt ego integration. The anxiety attack often climaxes a long period of mounting tension to which the anxious person has been progressively adapting, but with ever-increasing difficulty. Finally the limits of tolerance are reached, he can compensate no further, and the continued stress precipitates a sudden discharge into all available channels."

"… into all available channels!"

My diagnosis was that I was plummeting through the entirety of my unconscious childhood, recapitulated as blind terror at this turning-point in my life. On the path to my freedom, I had met my shadow head on. And it was bigger than the whole universe!

"Whether or not the patient is able to verbalize what he is doing and what attracts him, the basic situation is the same. He is impelled to repeat his futile, frustrating behavior—in overt action or in fantasy or daydream—because of the relentless pressure of unconscious infantile urges, fears, temptations and conflicts."

The next time a wave of panic came I ran to Roy Heath's house. He was hurrying down the front stairs to class. He looked at me.

I tried to explain, clenching my fists, running fingers through my hair down over my face, grabbing my arms.

"What affect!" he noted instructively, never breaking stride. His observation cast a quick mirror; I saw myself absurdly in our textbook, then laughed at both of us and accompanied him to class.

The next night I dreamed of an unexpectedly immense wind. It blew across the darkness, carrying images, image fragments, scraps of paper down avenues of the City. Fierce, unformed animals—wolves and cats and curs—tore off the dream shroud, led me through its scar into a hollow, a true void. There, UFOs patrolled an outer sky of too many planets and moons.

This counted. This was real too. This was an actual place—always had been.

They never spotted me as I ran through high grass and hid in vines. The wind was frantic, bracing. Everything that needed to be changed it ripped apart, swallowed into its momentum without distraction or regard.

In the morning I felt both better and worse. I was dizzy and hung-over but, paradoxically, not as afraid. I went to geology class without fully appreciating the change. I had a spark; I felt normal!

—Selections are taken from Grossinger's nonfiction novel *New Moon*

ance is to inveigle everything into its service. The attempted taming of resistance yields only greater truancy. The therapist makes the treatment into an epiphany. The epiphany of the so-called cure then operates like a corrupt guru within the patient.

An inner voice tells you that you are not improving because of some ancient malady, some inherent lack, or some inattention to the healer's instructions, whereas you are partly not improving because of the voice itself, because the voice allies with the pathology, because the voice is actually its own opposite, because the voice does not want you to improve, because the voice is expressing loyalty as well as self-protection, because the voice is enlisting and corrupting the external therapeutic aspect for its own design, because the voice has all the danger of the devouring and critical parent combined with the uniquely devastating probity of oneself to know one's own true weaknesses (as a parent never could).

The actual horror or trauma, primal and indifferent to language, no longer looks like itself anymore. Too painful to be viewed in its primordial aspect, it cannot be recognized in any adult vista or by any imposed symbolic system either. This is why bodywork that succeeds at a visceral level often does not translate to an emotional level, why the most powerful mantras may not represent one's true self.

No amount of Feldenkrais work, rebirthing, deep-tissue Rolfing, or craniosacral/visceral release can affect primal patterns in a fundamental way. One has first even to know they are "thinking" dangerous things unconsciously and without words or they will forever subvert the curative material of any modality into its deadly opposite as well. In fact, the very act of retrieving mythologized traumatic events may supply one's own inner voice with the contemporary material it needs to build new baleful kingdoms.

Stated differently, none of the conventional processes of "going back" actually go back (of "going in" actually go in). Instead they invent a drama or figment of going back; they spin a false past that looks the way the past might look without any epistemological gap or transition in consciousness. They don't take into account how strange the past or the unconscious would actually look if exposed by an unravelling of each of its torques and metamorphoses back to the drama of birth or beyond. Compared to adult mytho-inflation and embroidering of it, the domain of bewitching might actually be numb, sterile, and landscapeless.

A butterfly doesn't remember the wingless state of its grub, and it certainly doesn't know who it truly is.

A neurosis forms intractably not because its initiating trauma was so devastating but because it provided a structure, and that structure served as the basis for an ensuing structure which served as a basis for another structure, and so on.

Anxiety attacks begin incrementally, first for the infant, then the child, the adolescent, the adult, etc. Small panics creep into chronic states of panic; chronic panics evoke big panics, much as local weather systems set off typhoons. By the time mature stages of life are reached, an impulse of distress rather than comfort has been biologically built into the body's homeostases to the point where panic becomes its own rationale.

This chain of events only worked its way into language as a subconscious event far removed from the actual originating experience, causing everything to grow even more crooked from there.

The neurosis gestates and hides as it melds with the personality; thus it matures with the organism in every way, becomes integrated with its healthy functioning as well, becomes part of its character structure and adaptation to a social order. It is an obstacle solely because of its obfuscation and repeated cathexes over a long period of time, each of which shroud an immediately prior form and thus reactivate more primal dysfunctional behavior and disguise.

Even psychoanalysis fools itself on its capacity to excavate causes and meanings, to snare and pluck ghosts; it "can show us, from developmental theory and reconstruction, how we construct our fears (like precious artifacts), but it cannot always show us, though it usually wants to, what it is that we are really frightened of. What it can do, at its worst, is persuade someone of the source or object of their fears."[15] And this is perilously like inventing new fears, new camouflages, new deceits.

An allegiance to a fear or other neurosis is finally an allegiance to oneself. For every impulse to give it up, one faces the loss of something valuable and nostalgic, even something essential. Mere recognition of its negative aspect doesn't encourage letting go, because negative and positive aspects are fused prior to personality formation and function symbiotically. At its formative stage the trauma was larger than the ego. It continues to be larger than the ego because it dilates with the organism, taking on aspects of all its functions, even its successes.

A combination of loyalty and compulsive attachment gives panic attacks their mettle. On one side, there is an exogenous force demanding compliance with its regime, even against desire, even against logic. On the other side, desire has been created artificially by the attempt to steep a sense of loss: "[O]ur fears [are] the clue to our desires"[16]; they are our desires suffocated by their own excitation. True emotion is drained out of relationships and replaced by an artificial set of feelings and acts loosely simulating emotional life. Fear and anxiety—or in other cases depression, past-life fantasies, and low self-esteem—replace the actual emotions generated by loss, betrayal, and abuse. They form an affective ring mirroring a somatic ring. Each reinforces the other phenomenologically, giving the person a sense that his or her behavior is honestly motivated and expresses actual goals and desires. One thinks she is paralyzed by real impediments and inadequacies, whereas she is actually paralyzed by the false belief that she *must be paralyzed.*

Thus, a mature personality may engender a profound neurosis even while neutralizing it superficially and polishing it into something polite and even admirable. This is how spiritual practice and psychoanalysis, once subverted by an ego, become inflationary.

Neurotic attachment to fear is different from foreshadowings of karma. Actual bardo realms are not the same as what one creates from terrifying images of Buddhist iconography to make oneself afraid in order to fulfill a primordial injunction; the mythic destinies we invent to serve a neurosis are a different hex. Their *modus operandi* is to think up the most frightening possibility and, if that doesn't work, to make it even more frightening ... yet presuming each instance to be coming from an authentic cosmic place.

The ghosts of other lives (if they exist)—even of witch burnings, quarterings, drownings, and other terrors—are not the same as ghosts fabricated through compulsive dicta to fear, though their grim images can be used to give teeth to such neurotic impersonators. Put otherwise, our false ghosts are a horror film, compulsively played and replayed, but meager preparation for the actual transitions and requirements, even the hell realms, of a universe that is. They are certainly not preparation for the emotional and energetic requirements of this world across which they cast their ritualized shadow. They are one-dimensional objects pretending to be livable processes.

Don Juan's story about an eagle is not an effective way to prepare most people for an encounter with a voracious spirit bird. The actual eagle is probably more like the circumstance of being born into a devouring family in a violent city. It is escaped the same way any carnivore is, blindly and instinctively. Focusing on a pop-shamanized totem merely disables oneself or incites one to extravagant preparation for the wrong thing.

The divine punishments to which infidels and sinners are sentenced in some religious traditions as well as Endtimes and apocalypses may in fact be projections of infantile fantasies onto the vastness of the universe, which has the capacity to make them appear infinitely huge and threatening, as though based in God's actual persona. Meanwhile true bardos and hell realms are missed because they (like the core neurosis) are real only in some totally other emotional way—some way that has little or nothing to do with what we tell ourselves they are. They also have little to do with how we tell ourselves we are healed or have visions.

Only after the fact and years later did I realize that much of my occult and spiritual thinking provided an ideal framework for my neurosis to grow as large as the cosmos, where it could be fused with a landscape on a tarot card or Tibetan funerary instructions, to become an utterly terrifying destiny.

14.

In 1994, after decades of dealing with panic somatically and archetypally, I began seeing a psychotherapist for the first time as an adult. I chose Gene Abbot (the name I will give him in this piece) because I intuited from the beginning that he had a remarkable capacity to feel and talk to my states of panic.

Over the years Gene has provided a host of new insights into both the nature of panic and possible ways for handling anxiety. As a rule, his analyses and methods turned out to be simpler and more straightforward than anything I had previously considered.

It took him about six months to get past my predilection for showing off old-time psychotherapeutic acumen while adding astute somatic observations. ("You can spin circles intellectually around me, Richard," he said, "but that's not what this is about.")

He told me that Drs. Fabian and Friend, though no doubt meaning well, took the wrong approach. "What you needed," he said, "was someone to put their arm around you and say, 'You're a great kid.' Or 'let's go out and have a catch.' What you didn't need was to have your panics made into mysteries with clues; that trapped you in the labyrinths of your own fantasies and fears by making them so complicated and important. You also didn't need your mother represented as the guardian of your secret. That unduly inflated her at your expense and, instead of making her less important, elevated her to mythic heights. You became part of her story, which was already your problem."

He considered that the somatic and psychospiritual therapies in which I had been involved were similarly inflationary. While reducing certain aspects of anxiety, they increased others by making it seem as though either a therapist or I myself could take responsibility for changing my body or psyche. The quest for an etiology of panic wound in craniosacral cycles and torqued viscera became an extension of Dr. Fabian's oneirophanic grail, which was resurrected and projected into a somatoemotional sphere and onto avatars of alternative-medicine and Buddhist pantheons. What couldn't be solved by the symbols of everyday life was now set at the altar of koans, conscious breaths, and palpations.

A number of issues were brought to the fore by an unexpected juxtaposition of events during the second year I saw Gene. When I had a severe panic in between weekly visits, I called him (as he had recommended) and we talked twice on the phone for over an hour combined.

By the time I arrived for my next session, the panic had subsided but, before I could say anything, Gene told me that we had spent so much time talking he had to charge me for an additional session.

I immediately bristled, so he changed it to "any future conversations."

We continued then without revisiting money until, at the end of our hour, I realized the matter had been dormant but unresolved in my thoughts the whole time. "This isn't quite right," I offered, "but it's the best I can do with so little time. It's sort of like, you shouldn't charge me at all. You should be honored to have the famous patient of the great Doctors Fabian and Friend. You're the one who gets to solve the mystery where they failed."

"That's just the point," he said; "you never wanted to be the famous patient of the great Doctors Fabian and Friend."

So long had those two seers been valorized in my mind, I had neglected to question their simple story, even this late in the game. Tears rolled from the corners of my eyes, and I understood I was just a kid then, and it was all too much. A part of me was still just a kid, and it could finally give up the weight of the vast symbolic universe. It was sad; no more, no less.

15.

Gene commented that it was astonishing how, over a lifetime, I had battled such intense states of panic to a standstill. "No one handles that level of panic in this day and age," he said, "without drugs or hospitalization." I heard what he was saying, but in fact I took my battling panic to a standstill as the single major accomplishment of my life.

I will sometimes make a list of my landmarks: my relationship with my wife is second, my kids third, my writing fourth, my friends fifth, my spiritual practice sixth, North Atlantic Books (my job) seventh, and so on. Fighting panic without props is number one. It is my way of declaring that my life is an existential condition, a karmic opportunity, not a clinical, remediable state. I sometimes forget the price I have paid because I have never known or permitted it any other way.

An important aspect of this stand is the fact that Gene's "no one" does not include those in developing countries, indigenous peoples, refugees, or the dirt-poor in the West—cumulatively far and away the majority of people in the world. If they suffer panic attacks, it is like all the rest they handle. They have to survive to feed themselves and their children. They do not get removed from the battlefield, rehabilitated (or sedated), and then returned. They do not get letters from physicians to keep them out of armies.

I am uncomfortable in making my panic anything different from that or valorizing my condition to a level at which I merit special dispensation or medical treatment.

I have never let "panics" deter me from basically living my life and, unlike some people who panic, I am generally cheerful (the rest of the time) and feel I can attempt and accomplish anything. I may carry a constant quantum of anxiety, but real panics (of both varieties) are relatively rare.

Yes, holding them at bay does consume a lot of time and energy. There are experiences I haven't had because of not so much the panics themselves as my fear of them happening without warning. I dread being in a situation where I might panic and not know what to do (Gene has argued that this too is a projection and I probably *would* know what to do). I haven't travelled on my own to countries where I would like otherwise to go. That is a big concession, a limitation not so much unique as personal.

Without panic as a reminder, other people move through many situations of potential danger, often unaware of them. They do not plan in terms of them; they do not experience their own vulnerability to dangers that are simultaneously within and without and beyond their capacity to neutralize. Sometimes their optimism and bravado lead them into jams—physical and emotional—at least as painful as any panic and more dangerous. Yet, in most ways, theirs is a happier lot because their life is lived more naturally and, when surprises occur, they are dealt with at the time. This recalls the adage: "Heroes die once, while cowards die a thousand deaths."

Anxiety doesn't give me that option. I generally choose not to take certain kinds of chances because panic has made me appreciate the slippery slope of these risks. Being cautious tends to take precedent over any imagined pleasure or ambition that might engender psychic peril.

Part of the problem with panics, Gene taught me, is the very sense that *there is a problem.* This creates a bogus responsibility for either oneself or someone else to solve it. If one can't solve it, he is not only panicking, he is a failure. If he is a failure, then he has good reason to be terrified and daunted. If he passes the responsibility for his care to a clinician, he loses power and gives up the right to direct his own life.

I had been told so relentlessly throughout childhood that I was sick, damaged, couldn't function, and was unable to take care of myself that, whether I accepted this prognosis or not, I behaved as though my "being" intrinsically contained something irreparable that was evident to all. It never occurred to me that everyone is broken and struggling in some way. I lost empathy for other people and, unless they were evidently "sick" too, I continued to imagine their experiences as fundamentally different from my own, their sanity and capacities greater. I gave my panic an almost supernatural power and inflated it to cosmic and demonic levels that would have overwhelmed and astonished not only Dr. Fabian, the person who taught me to inflate, but many advanced spiritual practitioners as well.

Gene proposed that some of the ways in which I defined and dealt with my panics increased my fears, even to the point of being cumulatively more frightening and debilitating than the forgotten sources of the anxiety itself. He realized, for instance, that he experienced equivalent terrors to mine, but they were brief, and he always recovered. Once while camping with his son he felt an incapacitating fear of the dark; then he thought, "That's what it must be like for Richard." Another time, while in his car, he had an inexplicable premonition that something horrible had happened to his son. He pulled over and acknowledged his empathy with me to himself. When he told me about these episodes, I understood that my experience wasn't separated from that of the rest of humanity. His act of "therapy" substituted for assurances not given in my childhood.

The difference between Gene and me was that my states mushroomed and globalized rather than dissolved from their sudden ignitions of fear; instead of going away, they fed off themselves. My basic mind-set included so many precautions and litanies that

I tended to examine every subtle prodrome with such vigilance that I provoked onsets of panic from mere hints of danger. I did not trust either my imagination or my history. I cast events purposely in a negative light and then harangued myself relentlessly with questions about what I was going to do if something dire happened. No past resolution or precedent gave me solace.

Why did Gene not stay scared? How could he be so sure that something terrible wouldn't happen?

"I have good defenses," he said. "I just know things will work out."

But that seemed a *non sequitur.* His internal defenses hardly afforded protection against disasters from without.

"Defenses aren't rational," he explained. "In fact, a rational defense is not a defense at all. Defenses must be irrational if they are to work. Rationality as a defense would be neurosis or madness."

Defenses are forged and set in place when a child is young enough to accept a parent's irrational assurances. For some reason, the defense mechanism instilled by a good parent stays in place throughout a lifetime—unless something as big as a holocaust overwhelms it.

"When a mother goes out for the day and the child says, 'Will I see you later?' the mother doesn't answer, 'If I don't get hit by a car—'"

"Or, nowadays," I interjected, "'if terrorists don't fly a plane into my building.'"

"The mother says, 'Of course.'"

And the person with a good defense mechanism keeps saying, "Of course" to himself at a subliminal level forever, even through interludes of worry and grief.

16.

Gene was finally led to ask himself why that was: "Why would someone scare themselves so badly?"

Most people who panic are generally not as counterphobic as I am. They prefer not to look out the plane window or check the wings and the engine. They usually pick the middle or aisle seat, away from the objective reminder of fear. Something in me took the opposite tack, at least in part because I had a second voice, also representing something very old and who was not playing along with the panic story. During bumpy plane flights, "he" initially felt other things beside fear—pleasure, excitement, challenge, a "kid on a roller coaster"—but that was so blasphemous that I instantly reterrified myself. The voice said: "This is terrible! Get scared at once!" And, since my lack of fear seemed so dangerous in itself, I did. "This is the dungeon stairs, and there is no way out; the moment of the terrible thing has finally come, for real."

Unless I freaked out, I wasn't safe. In fact, I was asking for divine punishment.

Whether paranoid logic is a psychological response to a biological imbalance or an addiction to obsessive-compulsive harping for infantile reasons (and lack of a defense mechanism) is not a resolvable question, since it is merely a choice between two hypothetical paradigms that may work interchangeably as cause and effect for each other.

An artificial panic can be borrowed or invented from motives and acts independent of the seemingly immediate source of fear. Such a panic resembles obsessive-compulsive behavior as a secondary artifact of a mind unable to satisfy itself in the context of *any worry at all*.

A voice was ever warning me of the disastrous things that would happen if I did not immediately get afraid in a big way. So I did. I was closeted on an ongoing basis with a sadistic, relentless drill sergeant. He was always there, pretending to be me, terrifying me, demanding compliance.

There is little justification in concluding that someone who is an hour late is lying murdered in a parking structure. Turbulence during a flight is not wind vortices of which the pilot is unaware; how many planes have been flung out of the sky? People get sick all the time without being terminally ill.

Why would one continuously and compulsively rag on oneself with forebodings? Mild concern may be elicited by certain circumstances, but usually panic is not the appropriate response. It is a super-rational surrogate for the normal, moderately rational reaction.

After listening to repeated accounts that sounded to him like scaring myself, Gene began to question how much I actually panicked and how much I reenacted a learned performance from my childhood. He thought that my panic could be a vestige of an ideology, an unspoken oath. Maybe I was honoring a primitive, forgotten loyalty that combined a superstition (to think something is to make it happen) with a fear of hubris and punishment if I "pretended" I didn't have to think it.

Panic-fear assumes that its own past (the past of previous incidences of the fear) must be repeated. On the surface, it may be a fear of loss (of one's life, of a loved one), but it is also a statement that loss can be prevented *only by fear* (in part since previous fears never came to fruition, as though dread itself was a charm against catastrophe). Such a state becomes panic when the unresolved tension is indefinitely prolonged, because the internal battle between the imaginary and the actual, the historic weight of superstition and the ordinariness of history itself, becomes untenable. Panic thus fuels itself by its own loyal history of fear set against a counter-history of regular events (which most people use for solace). When I panic, I have literally no other use (except panic) for my time.

When we were children, my brother used to place his hand on a light bulb to try to make it burn; he would also re-read the same page of a book over and over again to see if he could force himself never to stop. On more than one occasion, he had to call me to rescue him by taking the book away. This was his notion of courage, of defying those who dared him, who said he couldn't. To fail was to be a coward, to lose everything. But what was "everything"? The joke was that "everything" was really "nothing," was really *loss* of everything human.

I could not remove my own figurative hand because I had no other place to put it. The fact that most fears are baseless and, even when they aren't, people manage to survive tragedies and find ways to live, gave me no relief. Everything had to be at stake always.

Something stubborn and proud inside me insisted on inventing life over each time from scratch, as though there was both honor and renunciation of *false* pride in this act. I was profoundly loyal to my superstitions, to a fabricated past that proposed itself as my future, so much so that I did not develop any other options. I was loyal because it alone felt perversely safe.

Compulsion is a strange beast. It speaks in concatenations of riddles. It tells you, superstitiously, if you think "it," it will happen, so you try very hard not to think it, which is impossible. It also tells you if you don't think "it" (if you fail to be vigilant), it will happen, so you try to think it without letting thought blaze out of control. You end up fleeing your own jinxes and prophecies. You become afraid of the psychic capacity of your own mind to harm. Every thought turns into Nostradamus. But it is just as dangerous not to think "it" (not to prepare yourself) because then it could come unannounced from everywhere and anywhere.

Such omnipotent grandiosity is a structure of a failed defense mechanism, and, sadly, it marks the way people have come to conceive of comets, predictions of cataclysm and pole shift, Armageddon, etc. It functions on an individual level by channeling men and women into narrow agoraphobic patterns, and it functions on a societal level creating cults in which the members provide transference for one another in collective delusions. People start out defending themselves against a real threat; then their method of defense becomes far more dangerous (and primal) than the threat, their loyalty to it far more urgent. The passage from the sacred to the sociopathic is evident in the declension of a single root word:

Vigil: As in the Osage Rite of Vigil, a trained watchfulness over the spirit realm, or the night-long chanting over a sick patient during a Navaho sandpainting.

Vigilance: Compulsive surveillance against both imaginary and real threats; the rigidified inability to drop one's guard; sterile alertness.

Vigilantes: A group united in vigilance, come together to strike out at their consensus projection.

17.

My mother had dramatically empowered her own fear rituals, but they could not hold a candle to mine at the scale at which I (ultimately) embellished and darkened them by projecting my own infantile and magical belief system onto them. Add the Freudian grail quest imposed by Dr. Fabian, and I was facing an opponent as cosmic and complex as any in the possible universe. Then, as an adolescent and adult, I fused this terrifying enigma with other esoteric belief systems. Eventually I found myself in a realm where only warrior lamas and Yaqui sorcerers belong. You don't want to summon ghosts unless you are trained to receive them, unless you also know how and when to banish and protect.

Panic became my sacrament and guide, the profane equivalent of individuation. It not only linked me back to my mother but the original lama-sorcerer, Fabian himself. "Into the dungeon with you" was the same—at a totally other, contradictory level—as fellowship with the gods. This is the way in which panic can be another form of epiphany, a means of gaining access to higher levels of enlightenment and power for which one is not ready: enlightenment without enlightenment. At least it gets you there; at least you have a moment with the ascended lamas and primal forces of creation, dire and horrific as it is.

Perhaps infantile crises, over time in the unconscious, come to feel like ethereal darkness. Panic becomes a way to make the world mythical, dramatic, fresh, childlike, and euphoric. What operates as panic and suffering at one level sponsors a kind of proxy vision quest at another.

Ecstasy can likewise be a state of terror turned (as it were) inside-out and illuminated by positive energy and infantile complexity. As long as one is excited, exhilaration dynamically displaces panic, wave by literal wave.

When I showed up at his office on a morning in the early '80s after having momentarily mistaken red drops from an overzealous toothbrush as spitting up blood, and then, in the rush of relief after realizing my mistake, saw San Francisco from the Bay Bridge as an extraterrestrial metropolis, the Jungian therapist Charles Poncé remarked, "You're having a better day than I am so far. Sacred blood! Luminous cities!"

That was a good low-key way to draw my attention to what I was (also) doing—as well as panicking.

Gene speculated about a unique benefit of growing a terrible fear inside oneself: if one had a mother who intentionally used scaring a child as a way of controlling him, the best protection against such a parent would be to become more effective at scaring oneself. Though I might be opening myself to a cosmos of adult terrors, I was making myself immune to assault by someone who was more intimately ever-present and omniscient than the gods—watching me like a hawk, owning my acts as her possessions.

Perhaps panic was the original state of personal, solitary magic with which I repelled my mother and her spooks, plus the demons and ghosts of the milieu to which she belonged. Panic was my art, my treason, my guerrilla tactic, my proof of difference: it was *my* panic, not hers. It could not be renounced thereafter because it became the original basis of my mature intellect and grail quest, my complexity and magic, my identity as a capable person (a partner, a father, a writer), and my means of escape from her milieu, though it bound me to it forever on another, infantile level.

People forget that there was a time when they were a child and had no power or magic at all, when they had to create spells and ordain guardians, to make art out of the rough material at hand, whatever it was. It would be hard not to stay loyal to such a project, no matter the consequences, for what else was there; what other way was there to avoid going back and having to do it all over again?

What option had I but to be afraid? Desire without fear was a precarious gamble; it risked everything. It meant having to "just live," despite the risks, the indignities, the self-righteous glory of rebellion and subversion.

I created a vast algorithmic universe, much like the actual universe, but with no parental protection. It was a black qabala *sans* God or angels, without grace or beneficence, without anyone having died for our sins. I manufactured it whole-cloth, a child's science-fiction and horror tale, out of the raw material of pop culture (Flash Gordon, the Lone Ranger, Superman, Grimms' fairy tales, *The Wizard of Oz*, the torments and hazings of fellow kids, the Korean War torture stories of Bert the school-van driver) as well as the limitless darkness of my own mind. Dr. Fabian was its satanic priest.

Panic was the primordial, supernatural epic inside me, my source of wizardry, eros, and creation, even the intensity I put into rooting for my sports teams (the terror-relief I experienced during their cliff-hanging games). My mother was a petty provocateur by comparison.

With Gene's help I began to perceive that, though the originary aspect of my panics was arguably real ineffable terrors from beyond birth and true enactments of them by me, their secondary aspect was an infantile performance to which I had addicted myself in a child's futile effort to connect with a remote, punishing mother whose only empathic mode of being was her desperate anxiety and desire to escape her own panic by insisting her children carry it for her, then projecting as much of it as she could onto them. My early panics belonged to her or were appropriated by her, but later they became ambitious and self-glorious forays, initially to meet Dr. Fabian on his own hallowed ground—to prove that I could play his game—but later to join other poets and magicians. They functioned not only as psychodynamic acts, but enantiodromias and ceremonies, counterfeit omens masquerading in distortions of others' voices. They gave me heroic roles at school and in summer camp: the embodier of terrors, the interpreter of everyone else's dreams and fears, the speaker of *Catcher in the Rye* truths, the sorcerer's apprentice, the only one who could tell the Martians they were Martians and order them away.

I didn't learn any other role or model any other behavior. I not only refused; I stubbornly held my ground, in school and at camp, disdaining activities (like basketball and sailing) in which everyone else dutifully participated. I wanted to dribble and race too, but I couldn't allow myself.

I acted my part so well, my virtual self, I forgot how to do anything else, how to be brave and honorable in simple ways, how to shoot hoops and pick up a breeze, how to be me. I lost my real joy and gumption even as I tried (like my brother with his hand on the light bulb) to be complicated, to be everyone else's hero—even making it to a podium with Allen Ginsberg and Robert Duncan, two of the great poet-magicians of my time, at Kent State University (1971) a year after the shootings, reading our work to thousands. I knew I was a fraud, but I didn't tell anyone (except Duncan), even myself. "We're all frauds" was his immediate answer.

LATER ADULT LIFE

One night I awoke and stared into the "thing" again. It was all it ever was, even vaster than I remembered. How could I have deemed it a mere "spook"? It was bigger than the whole universe.

I had no ploy, no identity against it. I existed either by its grace or its negligence. My mother had jumped into it.

I struggled for its boundary, its name. It felt like raw wind, carnivorous stars (without the decorative span and twinkle of the night sky). But even these were just words and what pressed against me was incarnation itself, in all its boundaryless vertigo, its tenacity to declare itself over the entire labyrinth of life and death as something else again.

I sat riveted against the headboard, praying it would pass. I tried to pretend innocence, to appease it with my terror, but these were also words or—at best—concepts. I knew beyond a doubt that death would not end this. Death was a concept too.

It ended by itself. It didn't actually end; it stopped noticing me and merged back with night.

"You met the big one," Richard* said. "We don't try to handle that wave; none of us do. Too much energy, too much sorrow, and probably—if we could ever allow it—too much joy. So we stay in place, pray quietly, and let it pass through."

* my martial arts teacher

—Selection is taken from Grossinger's nonfiction novel *Out of Babylon*

On the other hand, paradoxically, I insisted on being me. That was how I could be happy and productive most of the time; that was how I played centerfield and left wing (games I chose) and earned my way to the podium. My native pluck would come out at moments when I wasn't panicking or resisting the authorities, e.g., in craving the plane's bounces or just being carefree. At other times I was too scared even to want to exist.

Misguided loyalty to the old law was a way of keeping some version of my mother alive, maintaining her as my alter ego and gadfly. But it was not my mother I was keeping alive; it was my own ancient warrior existence that had battled with her, mirrored her, created her as a ghost, and framed my identity as her adversary, her confidante in panic. As long as I honored that internal echo, there was the eternal hope of return and reconciliation, something that could not happen with a long-dead figure.

This is how a panic attack might not be a panic but an obsessive compulsion, made up of loyalty, guilt, protection, and habit, and containing the seeds of primal tantrums and orthodoxies that will simply not let go until their impossible needs are met.

Even if my panics did eventually take on some conventional psychological guise and resolution, their core deviancy could not be solved simply by straightening it out, for it understood itself as crooked and always adjusted back to its axiom.

Years later, if my kids were late from school and I wasn't immediately scared, I felt a flutter of both worry and guilt. I had to get scared, for I was risking their fate by the arrogance of my confidence, by being me instead of looking out for them according to the old law (which was the truest one). Ultimately I was not so much intrinsically susceptible to terror as desperately protecting something tabooed long ago, perverse yet precious.

Gradually I began to intrude upon my internal dialogue, to catch the slight but palpable gap between my natural, more mild response to panic-evoking events and the injunction (like a voice from on high) to be afraid. What I had always experienced as homogenous fear had a component that was more like a prescription to think a certain way (or else!). Otherwise, I even tended to handle crises calmly, not freaking out when others did. I led frightened bunkmates through the dark and removed insects (both flying and crawling) by hand. I was not afraid (at various opportunities over the years) of suspension bridges, snakes, spiders, lightning, arguments, financial gambles, money crises, emotional conflicts, boxing with advanced opponents and getting smashed. My problem wasn't real danger. It was thought itself which sabotaged me. A near miss on the highway or physical confrontation didn't faze me, but I was helpless before superstition and prophecy. Someone claiming that the planets of the Solar System were lining up to cause an earthquake or al Qaeda was striking on a given day would elicit frantic, irrational behavior; my own bodily signs and portents were even more terrifying.

I had long conducted dialogues of voices in my mind without realizing they were unconsciously staged. I thought there was just one voice (my own), that "being afraid" was being afraid. Likewise, I assumed that when I behaved (to my judgment) badly it was a character flaw. I never stopped to think that self-accusation might itself originate within the dynamics of compulsion, ensuring that I continued to behave badly and thus never developed my full complement of courage and compassion, having rigidified long ago into thinking I was incapable of them.

I began to hear whose voice was speaking to me, but even before that I began to hear that it wasn't my voice. Of course, at the same time, it was no one else's.

Many years later when my wife was away travelling, I awoke in the middle of the night to terror and a simultaneous awareness my pajamas were soaked with sweat.* Unable to imagine what to do, I soon became desperate that there was no way out of this state, that it was the base condition that defined everything else.

I had embarrassingly maudlin fantasies of self-immolation, sabotage, revenge, vindication through destruction. I blamed her for not being there (as though my partner was always supposed to be at my side to help because I was defective). I was in the throes of a combination rage, tantrum, panic, agitation, paralysis. I could not slow down. I could not settle. I could not find myself.

I knew I was alone and I had to handle this. Sliding across the bed to the cold pillow on the other side, I shot straight to the core, or where I imagined the core to be. The question I asked myself was: "Why can't I just drop this and be okay."

Instantly I was back in childhood in a *déjà vu* that transcended any psychological conceit.

The answer was obvious: "If I am normal, nothing will happen; no one will hear me. *It won't even count.*"

Being okay was not allowed. It wasn't an option for me in my mother's gaze (for it would have removed me from my role in her crisis); it wasn't an option because it wasn't who we were. "Freaking out" was my assigned role in our play. Only by disrupting could I have an impact, could I feel real to myself. In fact, it was my panics (or pseudo-panics) that brought my father back into my life and forced my mother to take me to Dr. Fabian.

All through childhood I was goaded by her to be eccentric, abnormal, incapable, in need of protection, to not be me or believe

---

*This is the most recent incident in this piece, added a month after I finished writing it. It occurred a year later than any other part of the narrative.

in my own clarity and goodness … until I was goading myself, right up to the present moment, fifty years later.

The moment I saw it I dropped it. The state evaporated. I *was* normal. I felt utter relief. The night breeze turned pleasant; out the window the stars were a wonder again. "This is the way it's supposed to happen," I thought. "This is therapeutic insight. Maybe it was never panic at all."

But that was dangerous too; it would not only disqualify this from being a piece on panic; it would make me have to live a different life. It would force me out of my drama into the awesome responsibility of being myself. Not just as a naracisisstic *tour de force,* but every moment as a legitimate life commitment.

I awoke again three hours later, before dawn, with a different version of the same terror—less rage and tantrum, more a sense of nonexistence and abandonment. I thought, "She will never come back." After pacing for about a minute, I made a choice: I sat on the zafu by the bed and began meditating. At three breaths, the fear began to dissolve. After an hour, I was deeply and totally normal and committed to staying that way.

18.

Gene next explored with me the possibility that the etiology of my panics might reenact the original state of separation from human contact I experienced in my family. Because my mother made intimacy with other people too dangerous, I trusted no one (while imagining myself contradictorily both affable and receptive), thus engendered a proxy world in which I alone was responsible for my safety. By fiat I could not risk deep connection with others (except, at some price to all of us, my wife and kids).

No matter how intense the unconscious conflicts and irruptions of panic attacks, no matter how frightened I got, the real terror, Gene guessed, was a sensation of inescapable alienation from everyone else—a state imposed on me in an infantile setting, internalized unintentionally, and gradually instituted as a world-view.

He thought that our goal should not be to try to get rid of my anxiety-vigilance, which had pretty much alloyed itself into my personality, but to establish a new trust of human contact so that the interpersonal effects of panic would be minimized. To get rid of only the symptomatic aspects of panic—presuming that was even possible—would (after all) still leave me in a state of separation from people.

Contact with another person has often mitigated a panic and taken me out of its isolation. Panic itself is dry, sterile, tight. Real empathy with someone during its spell feels like rain on a desert.

Like most things in the mind, panic maintains contradictory purposes; it works in opposite ways. I was receptive to company because I longed for relief from anxiety. Panicking impelled me to seek help, to be candid and open, to trust people. While its state is intrinsically and trenchantly anti-social and isolating, its terror also undermines aloofness and a stance of impenetrability. A panicking person cannot be a lordly and isolate satyr, a sullen recluse. Panic is essentially humanizing, a foolproof means of rescuing a neurotic from what otherwise would be a vapid, lonely existence. A person running from a lion will accept any help he can get, even love.

While intimacy relieves terror, it makes one more vulnerable to the unconscious conflicts that underlie it. That is why Gene thought I had my first big adult panic after finding someone I could love. He surmised that whenever I allowed other people into my feelings, the jagged edge of my panic evaporated. On the other hand, love provoked fresh anxiety about betrayal and loss.

A portion of the guilt that arises in people and serves as an obstacle to change is not actual guilt for real crimes but guilt as an adjunct to false self-judgment in the same punishing way that the ghosts of projected hell realms are masquerade ghosts. Trauma wallows in its own negative expression, so even the most devout spiritual or therapeutic practice, the most heartfelt self-critique and good intention, can develop a negative aspect.

Real compassion emerges in a place different from where we are looking for it. We try to be better people than we are, but neither role exists nor could exist. The people we think we are are projections, and the "better person" is a guilt-propagated fantasy, a compulsive judgment.

When we worry that we are incapable of emotional connection, we place unrealistic demands on ourselves to make contact in ways that are actually impossible. Required to love and tolerate others while suppressing our secret repulsions, repugnances, enmities, jealousies, resentments, and the like, we end up secretly despising them and projecting onto them our own authoritarian perfectionism.

When people are not allowed to be normal, to smell, embarrass, and offend (for instance in the nuclear family), then everything about them, particularly their humanity, is lost; their foibles and farts and ugly fashions become reasons not to love them. Their beliefs that do not accord with ours make them noxious, even abominable. This is one source of religious fundamentalism and ethnic cleansing, also of the misogyny of the narcissist who, while desiring women in an artificial, alienated way, comes to hate their actual carnality. False religion and eroticism can mutate marginal people into sociopathic killers.

19.

We live in a "panic culture," though its signs are usually missed, attributed to other things. The restless, desperate, counter-phobic quality of Pan manifests in drug use, street violence, road rage, anonymous sex, shopping sprees, and the like. When an estranged husband or ex-husband stalks and murders his wife and children, when a fired worker returns to his office or factory to gun down his former bosses and co-workers, this is panic.

Panic is childhood rage that has no outlet, that can no longer find the ones "who did this to me," i.e., who made me emotionally incapable, so instead feeds off a paranoid frenzy against immediate tormenters who can be gotten at. The suicide bomber may be a legitimate martyr, a selfless and audacious soldier for his own oppressed people, but he or she is also both acting out and evading (in an ultimate way) the panic-rage of occupation, marginalization, and erotic denial.

The problem is not victimization; the problem is having no options, for a long time. The problem is "a grief without a pang, void, dark, and drear … no natural outlet, no relief" and not even knowing that such a thing could exist or what it is. When sterile panic offers no place to go, in total flight and incognizance one rushes to the only place he can't be.

Listen to the words of a former county sheriff's deputy, a law-enforcement officer, before slaying his daughter, his three step-children, and himself, words he put on the answering machine of a friend at the sheriff's office before setting out on his deed:

"I love you guys. I'm bankrupt morally, physically, emotionally. I have nothing left. I can't stand what she does to me. I'm sorry, I don't know what else to do. God bless and take care."[17]

Love is invoked, God too. But, amazing as it sounds: "I don't know what else to do."

Panic is a condition of being overwhelmed suddenly by the impossible and having no resources except to do the unthinkable, not only to destroy the people one loves and take one's own life but to attack the world itself, to attack life. This is the double-meaning of terror. So terrified is one that he becomes a terrorist in a last-ditch attempt to survive. In truth, this person was morally, physically, and emotionally bankrupt long before he decided his wife was doing "it" to him, as are so many others who would not deign to panic until, in their very denial, they become the god Pan.

If we could simply drop the schizophrenic charade—the internal fascistic dialogue—then we might find we already had the very capacities we were trying to cultivate and we would no longer be caught up in a rigid enactment of an ancient conflict in place of the actual world at hand. We might find we knew exactly what to do, always, no matter how dire the situation.

Healing and intimacy require not complexification, iconography, heroism, martyrdom, or past lives, but honesty and emotional simplicity.

The only antidote to panic phenomenologically, the only cure, is love—not romantic love or erotic love (though encompassing these sometimes), but selfless, unequivocal love. The sole basis of faith to live in a universe of hemorrhaging stars, predatory demons, occupying armies, and inevitable loss and grief is connection to other human beings, real connection. Otherwise, life is a march of zombis. "There is a land of the living and a land of the dead," Thornton Wilder wrote, "and the bridge is love, the only survival, the only meaning."[18]

20.

When I was a child, my stepfather provided no protection in the household against my mother's torments. He usually fled. After I went to college, she convinced him I was an enemy of the family, so he and I were estranged to one degree or another for over thirty years, though coming together briefly around her suicide. He seemed to want to have nothing to do with me, otherwise. I thought he knew nothing about my real adult life.

I always liked him, so I persisted in attempts at reconciliation. Only months before his ultimately fatal stroke we met for two lunches on consecutive days at an Italian restaurant for which he did advertising and promotion, the second inspired by the success of the first meeting.

We talked about our shared history and, at the end of the last lunch, I finally got to the family "spook"—an interpretation of us he had never embraced, even with his wife having jumped out the window and his son sleeping in Central Park. When he resisted, I told him that it was in me the same as in my brother and sister and mother.

"Not in you," he protested. "All I see is a capable man with a family. I see someone who's giving me more pleasure yesterday and today than I could have imagined. Richard, I hope these meetings mean as much to you as they do to me."

Tears surged up in me. We had reached the climax, of everything. "They do. They definitely do."

Now both the pitch and volume of his voice rose. "If I were you I'd say, 'Why don't you get the hell off me, you sonofabitch spook! Get the hell off me!'" He waved his right hand in such a striking gesture that the tables around us grew momentarily silent. And I realized, 'This is it. Profundity itself has come to its most profound moment.'

His words struck at my heart because he alone was the father and could speak such a thing, could threaten the profane spirit, could give me the reassurance, not now, when I didn't need it anymore, but back then when his voice echoed throughout our tiny flat, *"Old man river, that old man river...."* Such a message resounded in the remote dark and came flowing back through my whole life so that by his very voice again I felt released, if only for a moment. He stood between me and my oppressor and, if it was too late to rescue the haunted child, it was not too late to meet in the world as men.

"The spook is me," I said.

"The spook isn't you. Kick the bastard out and be done with it."[19]

There is an irrational moment in childhood, when one is taught to swim, to fly. It shouldn't work, but it does. If it is done then and done right, the child finds himself magically endowed with courage, capable of everything. If it is done wrong or not done, the child seeks it his whole life and wavers before the demons in his own mind.

Both children live in the same world. Both children, like all the rest of us, are afraid. But one child knows he will be okay and the other knows he won't. Both are right; both are wrong; but one gets to pretend to be invulnerable; the other suffers every imagined vulnerability for both of them.

Only certain people are privileged to release each of us from fear. They all become proxy fathers, surrogate mothers.

During five years in the mid '90s I worked on a book project with a former baseball pitcher whose career I had followed: Terry Leach. Although he is more than ten years younger than me, I am the eternal child and he is the Major Leaguer. Thus, as we became friendly and he heard about my panics, he took it upon himself to encourage and reassure me, even calling to check in. When my wife and I were travelling to England and I was anxious about the long flight, Terry told me to have a beer for him on the plane. "I'll be with you, buddy." Somehow he knew that that was the right thing to say.

When I was freaking out about other stuff, he'd sigh, "Oh man, I get like that too. My wife would like me to disappear. I just have to go somewhere else, a ballfield, maybe watch a game, any game. Some days it just seems like I can't do life."

His pep talks had the amazing effect of snapping me out of whatever funk I was in and making the world normal again.

No one can enable the child to be here the way a parent can, but through our lives, many people get to play that role. We know instinctively who is allowed to do it, and they know who they are and, as best as they can, they do it.

One afternoon I climbed the stairs to Gene's office in a state of full-blown panic and despair. Having suffered silently for five excruciating and sleepless days and nights, I announced theatrically—and with bashful relief at getting to display my open wound—"I'm defective. They should throw me in and get another model."

"You're not defective," he said, "you're not even weak; in fact, you're my hero. I can't imagine anyone else standing up to this kind of onslaught as honorably and courageously as you have for so long. You're one of the strongest people I know."

He didn't have to tell me that if someone had said those words to me during childhood instead of telling me all the time I was sick or searching for the great trauma, I might not have created a monster.

21.

In 1998 I took Gene's advice and made an appointment with a psychiatrist in San Francisco (whom I will call Roger Houseman) because, as an M.D., he could prescribe drugs that Gene could not. I had been experiencing a month-long panic at the time with only momentary refuges. Gene's recommendation was that I try a psychotropic drug for six months to break the momentum and establish a new chemical-neurological base. With that as a frame of reference, I might not need to keep taking the drug.

Terror is habit-forming. As noted earlier, its neurohormonal and behavioral effects feed it and feed off it. Panicking makes the body susceptible to more and greater panics. Fear of panic becomes the chemicodynamic fuse for each fresh panic. Breaking this cycle requires introducing a different experience and phenomenology into the nervous system.

The first time I tried to see Houseman I was so dismayed by the other patients in his waiting room, many with bandages on their heads, that I nearly left before my appointment; it looked like a mental hospital. I had spent my whole life not being one of them. My stepmother had lost years of her youth being them, and my brother had been incarcerated with them for eighteen months that changed his destiny, pushing him over the edge irretrievably. I was more in empathy with my mother who, one year older than I was then, simply jumped out the window.

The choice was made *for* me. Apparently I had sounded so tentative on the phone that Houseman thought he had told me to call back to confirm my appointment, whereas I remembered only that he told me to call if I changed my mind. The upshot was that I wasn't on his schedule. For all the gumption it took me to get there, the hour drive, the additional time looking for a parking space, the effort to keep from bolting, I doggedly retraced my steps, feeling more reprieve than regret. I didn't try again for a year.

The second time, my wife came along. The brunt of my panics had been falling on her over the years, and she felt I needed to take more responsibility for my behavior and it wasn't fair to reject a possibly elegant solution out of hand.

Houseman began our meeting by stating his fee, more than twice what I paid to see Gene who at least had an emotional grasp of what I was undergoing. Houseman didn't have a clue. He was concerned with sets of diagnostic criteria for different drugs. I had experiences that, in his reckoning, were not panic but something else—maybe obsessive compulsive disorder, maybe phobic reactions, maybe manic depression. He was not interested in delving into their infrastructure; he wanted to identify the right drug. I tried to help him; that's what I was there for.

At the same time, my sense was that I had been panicking (or doing something I called panic) for so many years with so many layers of paradox and shifting meanings that I was unwilling to have the whole series of events pasteurized to a set of linear criteria.

For instance, I lacked many of the key physiological traces of panic—irregular heartbeat, nausea, hot flashes, dry mouth, sweat, shortness of breath, urinary urgency, weakness of knees. My red-letter symptoms included "chilly creeps" (pangs originating around my atlas bone and spreading viscerally through my gut), an irrational sense of impending doom, and vigilance to the point of exhaustion.

A Phenomenology of Panic

Houseman decided, primarily on the basis of those symptoms and my mother's suicide, to recommend a selection of medications. Succinctly yet thoroughly he described their uses (mostly for depression) and their side effects. I thanked him, wrote out his check, and we left.

Once out of the office, my wife said that he was uninspiring. She had gone with the plan of enlisting him as her ally, but, before I could give my opinion of the visit, she declared that his lists of side effects were so scary and his conviction so lacking that she did not want me to take any of the drugs. I didn't.

Several years later, I was headed home after driving my daughter to an early flight at the Oakland Airport, and I inadvertently made a wrong turn along a stretch of highway rebuilt since the 1989 earthquake. This took me right into rush-hour traffic crossing the Bay Bridge to San Francisco—a place I had no intention of going.

I had planned a busy morning and was in a hurry to get home and off to work. Now it was obvious that I faced at least a two-hour delay, probably longer. Plus, the only way to get out of the labyrinth was to creep in traffic, reach the toll booth, pay $2, cross half the bridge, exit at Treasure Island, turn around, and come back.

Movement was almost undetectable, as streams from different highways merged into lines at the toll booths. Fumes from the stalled traffic made me nauseous. I was not supposed to be there, but I had no way to turn around.

Then, one by one, I realized I was experiencing Houseman's keynote symptoms: heart pounding, dry mouth, difficulty breathing, hyperventilation, trouble focusing my vision, cold sweats, hot flashes, a terrible urgency to pee. I had been thrown into a state of garden-variety panic—the first time, as far as I could recall.

I started a rebirthing breathing cycle in which I initially increased the hyperventilation while integrating it by accepting it as a positive sensation. Rebirthing is a technique for encountering trauma and pain through deep breathing. One affirms unpleasant bodily sensations and anxiety patterns while conducting breath through their blocked emotions and memories. Whereas psychoanalysis asks one to verbalize feelings and communicate them as discourse, rebirthing requires only that one inhale in a rapid (but relaxed) cycle, emphasizing sucking in while eliding the pause before releasing the breath. From breath to breath the "patient" embraces each sensation and mood as a gift of the universe and considers himself fortunate for being able to live and experience it. He transforms waves of anxiety into waves of healing.

After modified rebirthing, I used Zen breathing and clear-mind meditation to slow myself down and become an observer-witness rather than a victim. The traffic jam was merely another bardo, and it required acceptance, respect.

The physical symptoms suddenly were gone. If it hadn't been for the fact that the fumes (and initial anxiety) gave me a splitting headache, I would have been triumphant. The panic itself was a piece of cake.

22.

At about the time I saw Houseman, a friend who is a trauma expert, Peter Levine, advised me not even to consider trying the usual psychotropic drugs; he considered them useless and dangerous. Instead, he mentioned a "new" medication called Neurontin. Generically Gabapentin, Neurontin has actually been around for quite a while, but was used primarily for epilepsy and a range of other neurological disorders. Peter said that in low, almost homeopathic amounts (100 mg. or less, a fraction of its epilepsy dosage), Neurontin had inexplicably dramatic success in relieving certain kinds of panic.

He ventured that, when the mother fails at being a protective presence, the hormonal, autonomic clock—a neuroendocrine cycle functioning as a natural homeostatic buffer to fright—never starts. The person becomes like a car without lubricants or shock absorbers: its parts grind; everything hurts. Constant wear without relief creates biological susceptibility to panic.

Neurontin works, Peter proposed, because it ostensibly restores the missing chemistry of the feedback loop.

Terrors occur for everyone, but in people who do not panic, instead of becoming fixated, these are met and dealt with in the terms in which they arise because they have to be. As Annie Proulx put it, "If you can't fix it, you've got to stand it."[20] People learn to stand grief, loss, disappointment, disease, a life of slavery, etc., without being thrown into panicked states; this is because of a healthy biochemical system, in part set into motion by transference from the "good mother" or her equivalent in early infancy. They live through fear and horror because that is their situation.

Conversely, when that psychosomatic system is not set in motion, loss and disappointment, instead of being normal (even if agonizing) life processes, also reinvoke infantile needs and preconscious fantasies that can never be satisfied.

Gurdjieff's assessment of our situation was that if any one of us could experience the universe as it is, he would be unable to bear it. But we don't experience it, in part because our body provides assurance, a natural enzymatic, electromagnetic antidote that makes being here okay. Since its effects start early in infancy, most people don't ever know what unfettered panic feels like. They get momentarily frightened, paranoid, even terrified, but it does not progress into a sterile, vigilant state or become restless frenzy; the body will not allow it.

If a plane flies into the office building, the result may be mass panic, but that is not clinical or existential panic, panic from within. It is a transient, external agitation. In fact, in the face of a real threat, most people behave with surprising courage (not only those in the World Trade Center and Pentagon but others aboard the planes used in the 9-11 attacks). Acts of bravery and selfless heroism were performed, probably even by people who suffer panic attacks—because danger from outside is *real* and does not stir the secondarily terrifying aspects of panics that arise autonomously. Remember: "… the war inside is the truth of our being; the war outside is merely history.…"

Peter Levine's infantile hormonal feedback system is different from Gurdjieff's trance that prevents people from experiencing their cosmic situation, for it is less a conformist coping mechanism than a natural chemicohomeostatic mechanism that converts moments of fright and phobia—however intense—back into sensations of normal life by dissolving them into the natural phenomenology of existence. It does this even for enlightened spiritual teachers who would seem to have transcended such a need. Not even a lama can function if he cannot liberate his body's fears and excitations.

This may be a return to neurobiological reductionism, but our entire existence is biologically derived; thus, the innate chemical mechanisms we are born with may have an existential validity that more linear and literal pharmaceutical intrusions do not.

American soldiers in the Pacific during World War II suffered as horrible conditions as imaginable on Earth. They were constantly under fire. In unrelieved heat of 110 degrees "excrement was flung from where it was evacuated, its stench mixing with the putrefaction of the dead."[21] Bodies of fellow soldiers were decapitated, butchered, and otherwise mutilated, their genitals stuffed in their mouths. Prisoners, only partly dead, had their cheeks slashed open and their gold teeth pried out. Eighty-five percent of some regiments were killed. Not surprisingly, one combatant reports "shock, horror, fear, and fatigue.... My body shuddered and shook. I was sickened and revolted.... I felt I couldn't take any more.... To be shelled in the open is terror compounded beyond the belief of anyone who hasn't experienced it."[22]

Yet, for the most part, they did not panic. They experienced all sorts of other terrible feelings, including preference to die ("the dead were safe"[23]), but they continued at their military duties, minute by minute, hour after hour, waking and sleeping, day by day, for months at a time. They carried out acts of almost unimaginable courage. Something basic inside them made it bearable, endurable.*

The rule of thumb is this: when the body itself is comforting, no outside threat, however severe, goes deep enough to incite a generic panic attack. When the body is not comforting, even the slightest disturbance, or premonition of a disturbance, can throw a person into a response worthy of a battle in World War II.

Panic is the failure of the body to soothe.

---

*For the sake of this argument, I am ignoring Post-Traumatic Stress Disorder, which is a form of delayed panic reaction to traumatic situations like battles and physical attacks. Terror can also get lodged in the body and erupt later when the person is out of immediate danger.

23.

During my session with him I asked Houseman if he knew about Neurontin. He looked baffled; then he said, "If that's what you want, I'm not your man."

It was hard to pin down who "my man" was. I tried my GP; acupuncturist Robert Zeiger (who used to be a pharmacist); a friend M.D.; and Gene, but they were all unfamiliar with this use of the drug (or not licensed to prescribe it).

My search went on a back burner until a year or so later when, at my mother-in-law's funeral, I became reacquainted with a member of my wife's family, Leonard J. Schmidt. In telling him about my recent problems with panic, I mentioned Neurontin out of curiosity. I did not expect him to know about it because he is a mainstream psychiatrist. But not only was he familiar with Neurontin; he had used it regularly with success. Soon after our meeting he sent my GP an explanatory email, and I was able to get a prescription.

I too was impressed by Neurontin. It produced a wonderful laid-back buzz that told me: no matter how things are, they are okay. That buzz may have been partly a self-induced high because I seemed to get it instantaneously upon taking a pill, before its ingredients could have travelled through my bloodstream. Perhaps in low dosages it works by a homeopathic transcendence of ordinary physical laws.

I found that Neurontin dissipated some of the spooky aura of my panics, especially at the nightmare stage. One pill would take the rough edge off the state and reduce it to mere anxiety with a subcurrent of euphoria and relief. After Neurontin I often felt the way I did before I went to bed, though when I fell back asleep, the terror often returned.

I also found Neurontin to lessen the anxiety of plane flights.

It had no impact at all on most of the other situational panics I experienced, so it is two years since I have taken a pill.

24.

It is not my intention to adopt a doctrinaire position; i.e., that panic is existential and phenomenological rather than medical and clinical, that it is cultural more than biological. In fact, the point is that it is all these. Panic involves a phenomenology that is heavily influenced by cultural context. Panic also entails a biochemical event, even though that event—like all other lived events—is experienced, interpreted, and given meaning phenomenologically and psychodynamically.

The biochemical component of panic cannot be overlooked, yet cannot be valorized as the sole cause, meaning, and vector of cure. When panic is seen only as a biological and/or genetic defect, without social and phenomenological components, its social and phenomenological components are imposed (anyway) by a reductive psychopharmacology. Whatever people experience, they are encouraged to define and invalidate it as sickness, thus to interpret their altered state of reality as an aberration or intrusion. They lose the shamanic and archetypal benefits of strange energy, the opportunity to draw meaning and individuate from it.

When panic is over-medicalized, cultural factors are also minimized, and various marginalizations and injustices of the society that induce panic-like states are vindicated without a trial. A homeless person panicking has an existential basis for sensations of high anxiety, even though these may also express biochemical imbalance and possibly could be alleviated by psychotropic drugs. As noted earlier, since all meanings in life forms are processed along neurohormonal vectors, it makes little sense ontologically to medicalize some and not others.

Conversely, when an otherwise devoted mother drowns her five children in the bathtub because of the effects of post-partum depression, likewise when an adopted son (unknown to his parents to be the product of a rape between two patients in a mental hospital) develops violent paranoid schizophrenia and commits suicide in late adolescence after a happy, normal childhood, we appreciate the implacability of biological destiny.

Every chemical imbalance cannot be made right by beneficial social conditions or transformative phenomenology. Some represent serious lesions in reality itself, distortions of such a nature as to render their bearer incapable of normal growth and individuation as much as genetic brain damage would. With our pharmacotechnology, there is no option but to regard these as diseases and attempt to cure them by drugs. This is both humane and a necessary precaution (to protect others) in society.

The goal should be not to confuse such biologically damaged individuals with those undergoing extraordinary experiences, perhaps with a biochemical vector, that can be reinterpreted and used for psychospiritual growth.

Panic is (like war or crime) simply energy in the wrong place. It is not the "wrong" place because there are "right" or "wrong" places in nature or psyche. It is the wrong place because it gives rise to profoundly painful, destructive behavior and because it is repetitive, sterile, and narcissistic and impedes its own metamorphosis into different energy and new acts.

All of us have to run energy; the current flowing through our metabolism and nervous systems is a biological, genetic endowment. It may be identified to a certain extent with Freud's id or its pagan forerunner, the "it." Some people just inherit more intense and unruly manifestations of it than others.

How we handle our own charge determines who we are and what we give to others. In order to love or create, we tap and control excitation. Yet energy is not only harmonious and benign. As the ego-self continually tries to settle into a comfort zone, the "it" arouses and disturbs it. The priest and magistrate equally battle this unsettling force. In response, some people adopt wild, free lives, identifying with their own excitement, but this can elicit its own range of shallow, rigid personality structures: from playboys and flamboyant artists to gluttons and orgiasts.

How we experience our energy determines how we run it. If our energy snarls and constantly stimulates us to acts of which we are guilty or fearful (whether we enact them or not), anxiety and panic are an inevitable consequence. If, in order to be protected against our own energy, we undermine the way we perceive the world (gradually and unconsciously), we forfeit natural ease and erode the phenomenology of daily life. Everything then subtly develops an alien edge and becomes threatening. The beautiful, the ugly, the pleasant, the unplesant turn indiscriminately bleak and are mindlessly pushed away. Existence becomes depleted.

In normal life, one is sustained by sounds of vehicles and habitation, hues of light and color, smells and tastes. Ordinary humanity with its flow of deeds and images, even when tragic or horrific, is intrinsically comforting. Everyday events keep one connected at core.

When energy cannot be run comfortably, we change the way we perceive the world. Guilt, perverse loyalty, fear, and counter-phobia take away the comfort of ordinary things. We reject gifts of images and sensations. The world turns against us—that is, our excitement opposes and torments us. The sound of tires on the pavement or the sight of a mother and her child become enemies rather than solaces. This is the start of the phenomenology of panic.

When we do not feel connected, we cannot serve others or ourselves. The very current which should be our elixir and joy is converted into a poison: first, because the id is dangerously potent—it is what roots us in our bodies; second, because when energy that is meant to give us pleasure and hope turns against us, we are at war with the only thing that can rescue, heal, and redeem us.

A vicious cycle follows. Potential acts of a compassionate Buddha become petty tyranny, road rage, greed, sadism, and often (under the weight of ambivalence and shame) terror/panic—which is also the last best hope of rupturing a rigid, narcissistic structure and liberating a real human being.

When society breaks down and dissonance prevails, more and more people lose the ability to run their energy. Violence excites and arouses, provoking acts familiar to Pan. It is in war that the old insatiable, deranging boy god meets his modern counterpart face to face. Witness the panic attacks of Rwanda, the Balkans, Afghanistan, Chechnya, and greater Palestine. Panic can flee in blind terror, but it can also lead people to kill their neighbors, adopt fierce, counter-phobic personae, massacre their ostensible enemies with tanks and planes, cut open live captives, and blow themselves up in the discos and plazas of their enemy's cities. All are acts of Pan gone wild, which is a tautology: Pan is always wild.

When one becomes overly frantic, fierce, or vengeful, he becomes Pan. In the Middle East, where pride, vengeance, frenzy, counter-phobia, Semitic metabolism, and a collective mythology of disaspora, Crusades, concentration camps, economic enslavement, and colonialism run into one another, it is no wonder that Pan becomes a religious fanatic and a suicide bomber. The Dalai

Lama is trying to prevent a similar cycle from erupting fifty generations hence in Tibet.

Some Fresh Approaches

Raw panic is a guide. It may be a symptom of emotional decompensation, but it is also the shortest path back to the etiology underlying its own intense states. If I want to understand panic, I have to confront it on its own terms.

"Talk to it," martial artist Peter Ralston told me. "Say, 'Is that all you've got to offer? Let's see your real stuff!' Challenge it. Tell it to fuck off. Say, 'I've seen tougher opponents in assisted living.'"

On the day I was finishing this essay, a therapist friend at a party told me about a system he was practicing. It divided anxiety into three categories of defense: telling ourselves scary things, fear from feelings, and fear at the edge of the unknown. For each of these, there was a slightly different treatment strategy.

For thoughts that generate fear, the antidote is to unravel the fear with equally devious ideas that make its arguments less convincing. For fears that come from denying feelings, the goal is to create space for anger, sexuality, and the like, then to practice containing them emotionally. The therapist also teaches the patient that exploring feelings is different from acting them out.

For fears at the edge of the unknown, the remedy is to mobilize natural curiosity and make the unknown into a benign source of new energy.[24]

In recent years I have had some success applying Dzogchen Buddhist practices to panic states. Meditating directly on thought processes during panics, I open myself moment by moment to the profound questions about existence they ask. I treat them as not only iconographic maps of hell realms but the fluctuating razor's edge at which my incarnation touches the material, manifest world. Rooted in exactly and only what is happening, I am accelerated toward understanding and acceptance:

"The awareness arising at the first sudden instant of sense contact is indeed that pure presence which arises without correction or modification and which is uncreated by causes. This very condition of existence which transcends the limitations of both subject and object is the authentic self-originated primal awareness of pure presence....

"Looking directly into the face of that state of pure presence, we observe with bare attention who it is that is meditating. Not finding anything recognizable or confirmable there, a lucid and naked self-originated primal awareness self-liberates as it arises."[25]

Taking life and the world one breath at a time, we slow our energy cycle down and detach ourselves from the frenzy, restlessness, and narcissistic drama of panic. We become the wiser, calmer being we truly are. But only breath by breath by breath ... no furloughs....

At moments of deep clarity, panic can seem laughable. From a Buddhist viewpoint, all states are imaginary and passing. Since everything is conditional, temporary, and uncontrollable, and since decay and death are inexorable, we might as well enjoy the unlikely gift of our lives. It's a free ride; we are risking nothing except the temporary illusion of being real.

The goal of existence should be simply to observe, experience, and not react. A person developing a practice of meditation cultivates the capacity to watch neutrally all desires, anxieties, emotions, and fears as they pass through states of becoming and dissolution. Stages of perfecting this process lead to a reduction of anxiety, not in spite of our social and cosmic situation, but because of it—because of full appreciation of its larger context.

We might then accomplish through meditation what psychotropic drugs attempt through chemical change. The difference seems to be whether the control is internal (active) or external (passive), whether it is rooted in a person's essential being or must be derived from the cultural storehouse of goods being tendered to each of us. Learning to modulate our unconscious delusions through a practice of understanding our bodies and minds and our actual condition is far preferable to medications, for it allows us to develop as individuals. It is also cheaper and more efficient than having to import a solution or therapist for every irruption. It attempts to get to the source of the problem rather than merely its symptoms. Whether a person with intense unconscious conflicts, urges, and anxiety can relieve them through meditation is uncertain, but it would at least be a useful alternate course in a society addicted to chemical solutions and quick fixes.

It is not a matter of inflatedly applying enlightenment principles to pathologies, for all mind states have both pathological and liberating elements. One moves not toward an epiphany but toward thoughts themselves, their components and putative, transitory meanings in becoming thoughts. The beginning point (panic or calm, misery or joy) little matters as long as one sticks to the process. The high energy of panic may actually serve to sharpen attention and make focus more intrinsic and imperative.

Making panics real while assigning them to an iconography and spiritual inquiry ultimately renders them less threatening, for they become not so much "everything from everywhere" as explicit information needing a response. If we honor the spirit of panic and treat it with respect, it likewise treats us with respect and makes us stronger. In confronting panic, we also confront our destiny.

NOTES

The pessimistic narrative that begins this essay presents a view of the darkness of our condition expressed absolutely. It is a vision of the cosmos that opens historically (perhaps) with the seventeenth-century mathematician Blaise Pascal and surely has not been alleviated in modern times. But it is a vision, a view; it is an ontological commitment, and yet it is never in itself sufficiently challenged in the intellectual itinerary that follows. The consideration and exploration of what might be alternative to or at least confront this possibility is never quite dealt with at the level of the ontological commitment that the first page delivers. I always come back to the raw terror and my root cognitive engagement with it, something that dissipation by later energetic means does not address.

The narrative formations of the ontology of darkness, though neither discouraging nor deterring exploratory techniques as such, are also not addressed by them. Practices and ideological stances which might—and even *do*—alleviate suffering are not taken seriously as ways to to dispel or refute this ontology. They remain methods only, subsidiary to the dark plan. Likewise, intuitions arising from my experiences in therapies, meditations, and daily life are not allowed to mature as ontological possibilities in their own right. Even though I entertain the serious option of the existence of other frames and let them, for instance, portend something worse than or different from death itself, these and other possibilities of an enlightened state or process—of an actual condition of liberation from the domination of the unconscious and the machinations of the being-projecting mind—are never authorized to confront the original theme of primordial darkness. They are always managed psychologically, while the stark vision itself is projected everywhere ontologically.

The primordial, pre-linguistic, pre-cognitive registrations of terror, filtered through early cognitive and emotional conditioning and developed through concepts and narratives available to me, become fixed in the dark story of Being that the first page knows. The narrative then continues to filter the primordial horror but is at the same time projected backwards onto it as a representation of it in such a way that other possibilities are explored not only as defenses against the horror, but as defenses against this narrative, this description, which then have to be deconstructed so that the pure ontology of darkness can once again affirm itself. Yet the *characterization* of "our basic situation" in the ontological realm where panic has always shown itself is *itself* matter for exploration—not just for attempts to transform its residual or recurring dread energies through bioenergetics, imagery, or whatever.

Of course, my plan in this piece is to address the Freudian premise behind—let alone panic—psychoanalysis itself and the modern paradoxical circumstance of desire, a circumstance which fuses negative capability and guilt into both eros and so-called anti-eros (i.e., eros) at every level. I can't simply bail out of Oedipal karma because some other postmodernism or psychospiritual practice offers new identities and escape from a tragic destiny.

But there could also be ways of locating this story elsewhere than the primordial darkness. Dzogchen is not, after all, a "practice"—it is a view, a working ontological intuition. It could arise completely outside the dark view and its presumption of raw terror.

*

This work is mostly original; however, approximately three pages were grafted from an already published essay of mine into an early draft of this one and then rewritten. That essay, "Why Somatic Therapies Deserve As Much Attention as Psychoanalysis in *The New York Review of Books,* and Why Body-workers Treating Neuroses Should Study Psychoanalysis," appeared in an anthology entitled *The Body in Psychotherapy: Inquiries in Somatic Psychology,* edited by Don Hanlon Johnson and Ian J. Grand (Berkeley: North Atlantic Books, 1998, pp. 85–106). Both the essay and the book address the relationship between somatics and psychotherapy and provide further discussion of the issues in this piece.

My book *Planet Medicine: Origins* (North Atlantic Books, 1995, 2000) explores Freudian psychology in depth; the second volume, *Planet Medicine: Modalities* (North Atlantic Books, 1995, 2002) describes many of the leading somatic therapies and their psychotherapeutic applications.

My memoir *New Moon* (Berkeley: Frog, Ltd., 1996) includes long narratives describing Drs. Fabian and Friend and briefer ones on Charles Ponce. A second memoir, *Out of Babylon* (Frog, Ltd., 1997), includes additional narrative material about those therapists and personal accounts of the psychotherapeutic application of bodywork.

ENDNOTES

For information on G. I. Gurdjieff's cosmology, see P. D. Ouspensky, *In Search of the Miraculous: Fragments of an Unknown Teaching* (New York: Harcourt, Brace and World, 1949) and G. I. Gurdjieff, *Views from the Real World: Early Talks of Gurdjieff* (New York: E. P. Dutton & Co., Inc., 1973). For an account of the spirit eagle, see Carlos Castaneda, *The Eagle's Gift* (New York: Pocket Books, 1981).

1. Adam Phillips, *Terrors and Experts* (Cambridge, MA: Harvard University Press, 1995), xi.

2. Ibid., 58.

3. Ibid., 7.

4. Ibid., 52–53.

5. Norman Cameron, *Personality Development and Psychopathology: A Dynamic Approach* (Boston: Houghton Mifflin Company, 1963), 263.

6. Ibid.

7. Ibid., 264.

8. Phillips, op. cit., 48.

9. Adam Phillips, *Promises, Promises: Essays on Psychoanalysis and Literature* (New York: Basic Books, 2001), 52.

10. Claude Lévi-Strauss, *The Savage Mind,* translated from the French anonymously (Chicago: University of Chicago Press, 1966), 95.

11. Claude Lévi-Strauss, *Totemism,* translated from the French by Rodney Needham (Boston: Beacon Press, 1963), 1.

12. "Dejection: An Ode" appears in Samuel Taylor Coleridge, *Selected Poetry and Prose,* edited by Elisabeth Schneider (New York: Rinehart & Co., Inc., 1951), 127–31.

13. Phillips, op. cit., 1995; 14.

14. Ibid., xii.

15. Ibid, 48–49.

16. Ibid., 48.

17. Suzanne Herel, "I think my ex-husband has killed my children," *San Francisco Chronicle,* March 29, 2002, A4.

18. Thornton Wilder, *The Bridge of San Luis Rey* (New York: Albert & Charles Boni, 1928), 235.

19. Richard Grossinger, *Out of Babylon* (Berkeley: Frog, Ltd., 1997), 549-550. (Excerpted in slightly different form.)

20. E. Annie Proulx, *Close Range: Wyoming Stories* (New York: Simon & Schuster, 1999), 285.

21. E. B. Sledge, *With the Old Breed: At Peleliu and Okinawa* (Oxford: Oxford University Press, 1981); quoted in John Gregory Dunne, "The Hardest War" (*The New York Review of Books,* Volume XLVIII, Number 20, December 20, 2001), 52.

22. Ibid., 52, 51.

23. Ibid., 52.

24. Peter Bernhardt is my source for this; he said the system should be attributed to Yvonne Agazarian.

25. Namkhai Norbu, *The Cycle of Day and Night: An Essential Tibetan Text on the Practice of Contemplation,* translated and edited by John Reynolds (Barrytown, NY: Station Hill Press, 1987), 45, 51.

INSIGHT

MARSHALL ALCORN

A Lacanian Perspective on Panic and Fragmentation

P ANIC-ANXIETY, more so than other forms of anxiety, puzzles attempts to make sense of its sheer senselessness. Considerable work done by clinicians and theoreticians seeks to understand the mysterious cause of panic. Many explanations of panic have proved useful, but many questions persist: What is it exactly that is feared in panic? How do harmless objects and situations give rise to panic?

According to the DSM-IV (p. v), there are two kinds of panic disorder. There is panic disorder without agoraphobia and panic disorder with agoraphobia. The term *agoraphobia* was coined by German psychiatrist C.F.O. Westphal in 1871 as a first attempt to name the object feared by three men who complained of high anxiety. These men feared a set of common public situations, such as crossing broad urban squares and walking empty streets. The word *agora*, from Greek, means marketplace or crowd of people. In contemporary psychiatric usage, agoraphobia has a broader frame of reference. Agoraphobia is an anxiety "about being in places or situations from which escape might be difficult (or embarrassing) or in which it may not be available."[1]

Even for Westphal, though, the term agoraphobia (the principal effect of panic) was a confusing name for a confusing object of fear. Westphal cited in one of his agoraphobia cases a man who fears being alone in city squares. This man was calmed when people were present with him in those same squares; but in another situation, in churches and theaters, the presence of people added to his fear. In one instance the presence of other people helped to reduce the panic, while the presence of people in the other seemed to contribute to the panic. Why are the objects that generate panic so senseless in their pattern?

In the case of panic with agoraphobia, the victim of the attack recognizes something specific as a signal of danger in the perceptual field. This signal, be it an empty square without people or a church full of people, triggers fear and panic. In cases of panic without agoraphobia, there is panic and even fear of panic, but there is no recognizable situation that works as a signal for the panic. Panic apparently comes from nowhere and it causes extreme anxiety. Here then, the object cause of panic is even more puzzling.

This diagnostic gesture of the DSM-IV to distinguish between two forms of panic reveals a primary desire to understand the nature of panic. What does panic respond to? What is the cause of panic? The attempt to understand this cause has led to a careful examination of how the mind works and how objects of the world, interpreted by the mind, trigger anxiety. Clearly people can suddenly come to develop some terrible fear when the object that triggers this fear poses no real danger. The problem, we say, is "all in the mind."

Before Freud formulated an understanding of anxiety, a number of European doctors examined cases that suggested interesting relationships between panic and memory. In one case, published by a student of Auguste Forel, a pre-Freudian psychiatrist at the University of Zurich, a man experienced a panic or profound anxiety attack as the result of learning some forgotten truth about himself:

> In August of 1895, a thirty-two-year-old man, sitting in a Zurich café, was startled by a news item he read in a newspaper. It was reported that a certain Mr. N. who, a few months earlier, had left Switzerland for Australia, had disappeared and was feared dead as a victim of murder or of an epidemic infection. Stirred by this news, the man rushed to his boarding house, searched anxiously through the pockets of his clothes, and found a passport bearing the name of Mr. N. The idea that he himself was Mr. N. preyed on his mind, but he wasn't quite sure of it; there was a wide gap in his memory.[2]

Two factors here will become central to all subsequent development of psychoanalytic thought. First there is an encounter with a powerful sense of anxiety. This man is first "startled" by a bit of information and this startle response leads him to search "anxiously" for something that is lost or hidden. What is lost is in a literal sense a passport with his name on it. Figuratively what is lost is his memory; a "wide gap" appears that clearly at some earlier point in time contained something important. In this example the man has literally lost his own memory of "himself." What is particularly interesting here is that anxiety is produced not in the loss of self, but in the recovery of it.

If we work on the logic of this example we can begin to posit certain logical relationships between the objects in the world that trigger panic and the objects of the mind that connect to or stand behind these more visible objects of the world. The newspaper article causes the panic, but only because it is linked to a loss of memory, and the loss of memory contributes to panic only because it is linked to a certain fundamental loss of self. The remainder of this chapter is dedicated to explaining how Lacanian theory argues that anxiety is always and necessarily linked to a loss of self and to the unstable fictional structures the mind uses to establish a sense of self and reality.

In most of Freud's case histories, and in his later theoretical work, anxiety seems triggered by the recovery or attempted recovery of what is lost to memory. This observation raises the questions: Why should what is lost to memory be recovered only in a moment of profound anxiety? If memory is a place where something can be missing, why should the recovery of that which is missing generate anxiety? To understand these questions with proper depth we must examine what it is that becomes lost and then, by way of return, threatens the self, not with happy completion, but with fragmentation and death.

Freud, like Florel, began to approach the problem of anxiety in relation to the complex character of memory. In his analysis of the simple phobia of "Little Hans," who develops an "unaccountable fear of horses," Freud argues that memory is tied to unconscious desires and fears. According to Freud, the anxiety of the phobia develops as repressed material seeks to emerge in consciousness:

> The instinctual impulse which underwent repression in Little Hans was a hostile one against his father. Proof of this was obtained in his analysis while the idea of the biting horse was being followed up. He had seen a horse fall down and he had also seen a playmate, with whom he was playing at horses, fall down and hurt himself. Analysis justified the inference that he had a wishful impulse that his father should fall down and hurt himself as his playmate and the horse had done. Moreover, his attitude toward someone's departure on a certain occasion makes it probable that his wish that his father should be out of the way also found less hesitating expression. But a wish of this sort is tantamount to an intention of putting one's father out of the way oneself, that is, to the murderous impulse of the Oedipus complex.[3]

As Freud sees it, anxiety emerges from a conflict between desire and guilt. Desire for Freud is "instinctual," the presence of the id, and guilt is the effect of the presence of the super-ego, that faculty within the self that sets itself up in order to judge the ego. This conflict generates an impossible dilemma for the self because there is great fear on both sides of the conflict. There is the "instinctual" wish of the id, feared for its innate power, and there is fear of the super-ego, for its threat of punishment. The Third Edition of the Psychiatric Dictionary describes anxiety hysteria thus: "The thing that is feared may be feared because it represents a temptation, or it may be feared because it represents the punishment for the forbidden impulse."[4]

Contemporary diagnostic criteria distinguishes between panic disorders and simple phobias such as that of Little Hans. This distinction has not always been clearly marked, but a variety of anxiety phenomena can become imbedded in the resultant form that panic may assume. While the DSM manuals describes more profound bodily effects of panic, it is essential to consider the broader field of anxiety as a whole.

Freud's account of conflict between id and super-ego as generative of anxiety offers clinicians a useful interpretive tool, but it

is not a helpful theoretical model in all cases. In the case of multiple personality disorder, for example, panic and anxiety do not seem readily connected to a conflict between the id and the super-ego threat. Consider the famous case of Sybil, the woman who allegedly harbored sixteen different personalities; panic developed in relation to the separated understandings of the different inner selves that inhabited the one woman. In the biography written by Flora Schreiber, Sybil discovers a key to a room that she has in her purse, but can't remember having picked up. The narrator says: "The key to room 1113 was the engine that drove her, the motor on which her panic turned."[5] The key is a real, powerful object, with a real connection to Sybil's other selves. But as a metaphor the key also offers several layers of meaning. It is an object that opens doors, that promises answers to questions that have not yet been formulated in the thinking mind that experiences the panic. Unlike Freud's example, the key does not represent a conflict between desire and guilt; it is, for Sybil, the memory of another self that is not connected to the self named Sybil. It suggests, with feelings of terror, that the self is a fiction, a construction formulated precisely to hold anxiety at some comfortable distance from experience.

What then is this thing, this ordinary object from an ordinary world that triggers panic and self-fragmentation? To understand the more profound anxiety of panic, and to understand the emphasis of the Lacanian account of anxiety, it will be useful to begin with some claims made by the American psychiatrist Harry Stack Sullivan. Sullivan used the term anxiety to describe all forms of emotional pain, but he used the word panic to describe the "utmost state of terror and emotional paralysis that a person can experience. Sullivan saw panic as most closely tied to schizophrenic illness, but his insight into the disintegration of the self, which panic threatens in schizophrenia, provides a useful orientation to Lacanian theories of anxiety and self-fragmentation.

In Freudian and post-Freudian theory, anxiety emerges from the ego in relation to the other structures of the self. Lacanian theory asks us to consider the most basic dynamics of the self's cohesion. If anxiety emerges from the ego for Freud, it is the reverse for Lacan. The self emerges from, and is always threatened by, a primordial anxiety that churns like a vortex at the core of the self.

Lacanians believe that people are very real, but that the ego is an imaginary structure. If we think of anxiety as a kind of undifferentiated energy that drives human action, this energy must be given form in order for human behavior to have organization, purpose, and direction. When anxiety is given direction and representation it becomes desire. When this primordial energy has no structure to work with it becomes oppressive in the form of anxiety. In Lacan's well-known essay on the Mirror Stage, the child, seeing its own image in the mirror, constructs an imaginary self-

"...the ego is the actual seat of anxiety. There is no reason to assign any manifestation of anxiety to the super-ego; while the expression 'anxiety of the id' would stand in need of correction, though rather as to its form than its substance. Anxiety is an affective state and as such can, of course, only be felt by the ego. The id cannot have anxiety as the ego can; for it is not an organization and cannot make a judgement about situations of danger. On the other hand it very often happens that processes take place or begin to take place in the id which cause the ego to produce anxiety. Indeed, it is probable that the earliest repressions as well as most of the later ones are motivated by an ego-anxiety of this sort in regard to particular processes in the id."

—Sigmund Freud, *Inhibitions, Symptoms and Anxiety*

image on the basis of a real reflective image. Before the child constructs this image of itself as a whole being, it is a fragmented body driven by need and demand and tormented by anxiety. In Lacanian theory, humans operate in three different registers termed the Real, the Imaginary, and the Symbolic. The Real signifies the object of anxiety. Dylan Evans quotes from an early seminar by Lacan:

> The Real is the object of anxiety; it lacks any possible mediation, and is thus 'the essential object' which isn't an object any longer, but something faced with which all words cease and all categories fail, the object of anxiety par excellence.[6]

In response to a primordial object of anxiety, humans begin to structure a world and a self. The first significant structure is the formation of a self through an identification with a reflected image. This is the imaginary dimension Lacan describes in his essay on the Mirror Phase, where the child, "unable yet to walk or stand up" responds to an image of itself in the mirror. The child, unlike an animal that examines its image, responds with wonder, power, and fascination. This wonder, power, and fascination, Lacan claims, demonstrates a transformation that takes place in the child. It is no longer a fragmented collection of body parts. It sees itself, in a momentary triumph of fantasy, as a whole, in control of itself. This control is not quite an accurate experience of the self; it is instead a narcissistic ideal that the child seeks but does not have. Self-representation, or the ego, is thus a representation, much like a dream. The child does not have control of itself, but imagines that it does. According to Lacan, the child imagines, in an uncontrolled "flutter of jubilant activity," a self-control that she does not have. This new identification, an imaginary ego, then accompanies the child in all acts of self-knowledge and self-reflection. By means of this fantasy of control, the anxiety of non-control is held at bay.

In suggesting anxiety as primordial, Lacan, in a small way, follows Melanie Klein, who argued in *Envy and Gratitude:*

> The threat of annihilation by the death instinct within is, in my view—which differs from that Freud—the primordial anxiety, and it is the ego which, in the service of the life instinct—deflects to some extent that threat outwards.[7]

Rather than seeing anxiety generated by conflicts between the ego and the super-ego, as did Freud, Klein, like Lacan, saw anxiety as fundamental to self-experience. Lacan differs from Klein, however, in viewing the ego as having no ability to significantly manage anxiety. Roberto Harari, in Lacan's seminar on Anxiety, points out the difference between post-Freudian and Lacanian thinking:

> The post-Freudians argue that anxiety is a kind of wisdom of the ego, which chooses it among the defenses available against panic-anxiety, which is what one is trying to avoid. Lacan answers by saying that anxiety is a defense independent from the fatuous designs of the ego.[8]

Harari is making several points here. First he is saying that we should not imagine significantly different varieties of anxiety; anxiety proper, for example, is not a defense against panic-anxiety. Second, in making anxiety independent of the ego, Harrari emphasizes the primordial nature of anxiety. It is the disorganized, fragmentary, emotionally chaotic ground from which the ego develops. If, for Freud, the inner structures of the mind generate anxiety, Lacan reverses this claim. It is not that the structures of the mind generate anxiety; it is that anxiety generates the structures of the mind. To put the matter more precisely, the structures of subjectivity emerge so that anxiety can be contained. The whole person, therfore, evolves so that anxiety can be managed or defended against. This means that panic-anxiety threatens the person with wholesale disintegration.

If subjectivity emerges as a fiction to contain anxiety, subjectivity is never fully protected from the anxiety it seeks to contain. Arnold Modell, in *The Private Self,* offers a good example of what he terms "annihilation anxiety—a fear of losing the continuity and coherence of the self."[9] Modell's example comes from William James, who experiences a life-changing experience while going through a period of depression. James writes:

> Suddenly there fell upon me without any warning, just as if it came out of the darkness, a horrible fear of my own existence. Simultaneously there arose in my mind the image of an epileptic patient whom I had seen in the asylum, a black-

haired youth with greenish skin, entirely idiotic, who used to sit all day on one of the benches, or rather shelves against the wall, with his knees drawn up against his chin, and the coarse gray undershirt, which was his only garment, drawn over them inclosing his entire figure.... This image and my fear entered into a species of combination with each other. That shape am I, I felt potentially. Nothing that I possess can defend me against that fate, if the hour for it should strike me as it struck him.[10]

When James writes that "nothing that I possess can defend me against that fate," he makes a testimony to the fragile nature of selfhood. We construct selves to hold the awesome power of anxiety at bay. But we are always threatened, and at some moments we experience this threat with palpable fear.

Panic speaks to the failure of the connection between the self and its lived world. What emerges in these objects that cause panic is the empty core of the self, what some Lacanians term the Real, the pure anxiety that signals the self's fundamental lack of cohesion. In panic, it is precisely the body that fails to operate as it should. In the case of James, our familiar self-image vanishes, and we find ourselves "not that" identified with some other image of ourselves. In other instances of panic, our bodies break into component parts that do not operate in harmony. The heart loses its rhythm; breathing may become difficult; there may be intense sweating on a cold day.

This chapter is a reflection upon the various objects that trigger anxiety and an exploration of the mysterious nature of these objects. The DSM-IV notes that panic-anxiety can be triggered by clearly recognized situations, but in other cases it can be triggered by nothing obvious. In the case of William James, panic is triggered by a memory of a person that James is not, but fears that he may become. Here it is as if panic, whether triggered by keys, passports, or city streets, can fix to a single memory-image to introduce almost unimaginable anxiety into the self. Objects of anxiety can also be things discovered by art, and further, that art can engage in an attempt to contain and manage the anxiety that it encounters. Lacanian cultural critic Slavoj Zizek shows how an artist can confront his anxiety and self-fragmentation in the pure medium of art. Zizek describes the final anxious suicide of the abstract painter, Mark Rothko:

> Rothko pictures this struggle [between the Real and reality] as a tension between a gray background and the central black spot that spreads menacingly from one painting to another (in the late 1960s, the vivacity of red and yellow in Rothko's canvases is increasingly replaced by the minimal opposition between black and gray). If we look at these paintings in a "cinematic" way (i.e. if we put the reproductions one above the other and then turn them quickly to get the impression of continuous movement), we can almost draw a line to the inevitable end, as if Rothko were driven by some unavoidable fatal necessity. In the canvases immediately preceding his death, the minimal tension between black and gray changes for the last time into the burning conflict between voracious red and yellow, witnessing the last desperate attempt at redemption and at the same time confirming unmistakably that the end is imminent.[11]

What we can see in the development of Rothko's abstracts, Zizek argues, is an increasing recognition of the object of panic and anxiety. Where James spontaneously fixes upon a memory-image that haunts the self, Rothko discovered his anxiety through art, in an image. Rothko's case shows the complete plasticity of the object of anxiety. In agoraphobia there is some suggestion that the phobic object "makes sense" in some way. We are prompted to think that it may be "only natural" for shy people to fear crowds, and so the crowd "makes sense" as a object of panic. In the case of James's memory of the epileptic patient, it may seem more difficult to make sense of the object of panic. After all, James is not the patient but the doctor. He should not fear such an outcome, or be haunted by such a memory-image. And yet Lacanian theory suggests that whatever we are, we are always threatened by anxiety because we are a product of imagination constantly threatened by anxiety. We are the stuff dreams are made of. We can see this most clearly in Rothko's case. The panic object is something encountered purely in an imaginative act. But this object, too, threatens the self, and in the end, for Rothko, the force of the imaginary object, as a pure energy of anxiety, overcomes the seemingly real and stable self. Rothko, as if attacked by his own art image, kills himself.

ENDNOTES

1. *Diagnostic and Statistical Manual of Mental Disorders, Fourth Edition.* Washington, DC, American Psychiatric Association, 1994.

2. Henri Elenberger, *The Discovery of the Unconscious* (New York: Basic Books, 1970).

3. Sigmund Freud, *Inhibitions, Symptoms and Anxiety* (London: Hogarth Press, 1936).

4. Leland E. Hinsie and Robert Campbell, eds., *Psychiatric Dictionary, 3rd ed.* (Oxford: Oxford University Press, 1985).

5. Flora Schreiber, *Sybil* (New York: Warner Books, 1995).

6. Dylan Evans, *An Introductory Dictionary of Lacanian Psychoanalysis* (London: Routledge, 1996).

7. Melanie Klein, *Envy and Gratitude* (London: Karnac Books, 1997).

8. Roberto Harari, *Lacan's Seminar On "Anxiety"* (New York: Other Press, 2001).

9. Arnold H. Modell, *The Private Self* (Cambridge, Harvard University Press, 1993).

10. Ibid.

11. Slavoj Zizek, *Looking Awry: An Introduction to Jacques Lacan Through Culture* (Cambridge, MIT Press, 1993).

COLIN CLARKE

The Isolation of Panic and the Panic of Isolation in the Poetry of Sylvia Plath and Anne Sexton

I T WOULD BE FLATLY MISLEADING to say that panic is the major theme in the poetry of Sylvia Plath and Anne Sexton. To do so would be to misrepresent the variety of their work, to attribute, as has been too often done, too much of their poetry to their bouts with mental illness. Similarly, it would be misleading to say that the topic of panic deserves no attention as a presence in their work. For even though panic as a theme in their poetry is sometimes elusive, its appearance in Plath's and Sexton's writing is inherently bound with issues of hospitalization, mania, depression, and confinement, all of which were factors in these poets' work and in their determination to write.

Although never diagnosed with panic or anxiety disorder, both Plath and Sexton exhibited symptoms which were consistent with those illnesses. Both poets experienced episodes of fear and anxiety, both experienced severe depression in conjunction with their attacks,[1] and both poets at times suffered from sleep disorders and agoraphobia as a result of their anxiety: before her first suicide attempt in August of 1953, Plath "rarely stirred from the house and complained that she could not sleep."[2] Sexton, by all accounts, feared leaving her home, would often insist on having a companion just to cross the street, and, during periods when she was off her medication, found that she had difficulty eating or sleeping.[3]

While these symptoms are consistent with panic disorder, they are not offered here as a suggestion that Plath and Sexton necessarily suffered from such a disorder. Ultimately, such a suggestion would be difficult to prove and would offer little additional insight into the poets' lives. Rather, the appearance of panic in the lives

"disappointments," 2001. **Anthony Lukens**

and works of these two poets is suggestive of what the craft of poetry meant to them. Both poets struggled with the difficulty of understanding their illnesses as part of their lives and as part of their creative urges. It can be a dangerous business to confuse a poet's work with her life, although critics of Sexton and Plath have done so often enough. It is never easy or certain to say that a poet's work is specifically about her own life and experiences. Even in the cases of Sexton and Plath, where the biographical evidence can sometimes be very neatly matched to the events depicted in a particular poem, it is best to be cautious. Although the reader recognizes the frequently autobiographical origins of many of their poems, it would be a mistake to take everything Plath or Sexton wrote as fact. In an interview with Patricia Marx, when asked if she ever distorted the facts to get at some underlying truth, Sexton replied:

> Well, I think this is necessary. It's something that an artist must do [. . .] To have that effect you must distort some of these facts to give them their own clarity. [. . .] So you don't have to include everything to tell the truth. You can exclude many things. You can even lie (one can confess and lie forever) as I did in the poem of the illegitimate child that girl had to give up. It hadn't happened to me. It wasn't true, and yet it was indeed the truth.4

Ultimately, then, whether or not these poems reflect actual events, or whether or not the emotions expressed within are based on an actual and identifiable disorder, is less important than that these poems are informed by, as Sexton puts it, "the truth."

For both Sexton and Plath, the truth was that they suffered periodically from debilitating bouts of anxiety and depression, which eventually led to their suicides. For both, their illnesses were intimately entwined with their drive and desire to write. Plath's journals reveal a young writer who was desperate to write accomplished and meaningful poetry and prose, and who despaired when she found that something prevented her from doing so. In a summer 1951 journal entry, Plath wrote:

> There comes a time when all your outlets are blocked, as with wax. You sit in your room, feeling the prickling ache in your body which constricts your throat, tightens dangerously in little tear pockets behind your eyes [. . .] in your new and horrible independence you feel the dangerous premonitory ache, arising from little sleep and taut strung nerves, and a feeling that the cards have been stacked high against you this once, and that they are still being heaped up. An outlet you need, and they are sealed. You live day and night in the dark cramped prison you have made for yourself.[5]

Similarly, approximately one month before her first suicide attempt in 1953, Plath wrote in desperation of her condition and her increasing thoughts of suicide:

> Read a story: Think. You can. You must, moreover, not continually run away while asleep—forget the details—ignore problems—shut walls up between you & the world & all the gay bright girls—: please, think—snap out of this. Believe in some beneficent force beyond your own limited self. God, god, god: where are you? I want you, need you: the belief in you and love and mankind. You must not seek escape like this. You must think.[6]

The panic which can be discerned in Plath's writing here is based partially on her fear of being cut off from words, a fear obviously and immediately connected to her writing, her fear of depression, her fear of her own suicidal impulses, and her fear of the electroconvulsive therapy she was about to undergo. In June of 1953, Plath was in New York City as a guest editor for *Mademoiselle*'s college issue, and soon after returning to her mother's house in Wellesley, Massachusetts in July found herself in a deepening depression.[7] Looking for something to occupy her time, Plath worked briefly as a nurse's aid at nearby Newton-Wellesley Hospital, "[b]ut she did not stay long [. . .]; she was herself too ill," experiencing at this point lethargy, insomnia, and depression.[8] Distressed at her daughter's behavior, Aurelia Plath took Sylvia to see Dr. J. Peter Thornton on July 18, 1953; his diagnosis a week later was that:

> Sylvia suffered from a severe depression that would leave her hovering on the brink of nervous collapse unless she received the medical treatment believed at that time to intervene most dramatically with emotional distress—electroshock therapy.[9]

Two days after his diagnosis, Dr. Thornton gave Plath her first round of electroconvulsive therapy; in *The Bell Jar*, Esther Greenwood, suffering from the same symptoms as Plath, undergoes electroconvulsive therapy at the hands of a Dr. Gordon:

> Doctor Gordon was unlocking the closet. He dragged out a table on wheels with a machine on it and rolled it behind the head of the bed. The nurse started swabbing my temples with a smelly grease. [. . .]
>
> "Don't worry," the nurse grinned down at me. "Their first time everybody's scared to death."
>
> I tried to smile, but my skin had gone stiff, like parchment.
>
> Doctor Gordon was fitting two metal plates on either side of my head. He buckled them into place with a strap that dented my forehead, and gave me a wire to bite.
>
> I shut my eyes.
>
> There was a brief silence, like an indrawn breath.
>
> Then something bent down and took hold of me and shook me like the end of the world. Whee-ee-ee-ee-ee, it

Apprehensions
Sylvia Plath

There is this white wall, above which the sky creates itself—
Infinite, green, utterly untouchable.
Angels swim in it, and the stars, in indifference also.
They are my medium.
The sun dissolves on this wall, bleeding its lights.

A gray wall now, clawed and bloody.
Is there no way out of the mind?
Steps at my back spiral into a well.
There are no trees or birds in this world,
There is only a sourness.

This red wall winces continually:
A red fist, opening and closing,
Two gray, papery bags—
This is what I am made of, this and a terror
Of being wheeled off under crosses and a rain of pietàs.

On a black wall, unidentifiable birds
Swivel their heads and cry.
There is no talk of immortality among these!
Cold blanks approach us:
They move in a hurry.

* * *

shrilled, through an air crackling with blue light, and with
each flash a great jolt drubbed me till I thought my bones
would break and the sap fly out of me like a split plant.
   I wondered what terrible thing it was I had done.[10]

Plath's experience was much the same, and it is not surprising
that she had a lingering fear of hospitals long after this experience.
Alexander claims that this treatment "caused her to cease communication with other people almost entirely," further imposing
on Plath the verbal repression which she feared.[11] Plath underwent at least six similar electroconvulsive sessions during the month
before her suicide attempt, procedures which could have been a
factor in her attempt to commit suicide.[12]

For Plath, as for Sexton, panic was twofold, and never easily negotiated. On the one hand, Plath feared being cut off from words, being unable to write and express herself, a problem which fed off of her depression and anxiety. On the other hand, however, Plath had an equal fear of the treatment which had been recommended for her illness. This dual anxiety can be witnessed in "Johnny Panic and the Bible of Dreams," a 1958 story for which Plath drew heavily from her own experience with mental institutions and electroconvulsive therapy. The narrator in "Johnny Panic" is "Assistant to the Secretary of the Out-Patient Departments of the Clinics Building of the City Hospital," a lengthy title which entirely masks her sole duty: to transcribe patients' dreams.[13] It is through these dream transcriptions, which she pursues in her free time and in moments stolen from her work, that she dedicates herself to "Johnny Panic," the "dog-face, devil-face, hag-face, whore-face" god of insanity who, according to the narrator, runs the world.[14] The narrator's obsession with these dream transcriptions becomes increasingly obvious during the story, until she is discovered early one morning in a hospital restroom, where she has spent the night transcribing dreams from old hospital records. Although Plath develops this subtly throughout the story, the line between worker and patient gradually dissipates, as it becomes increasingly likely that our narrator, while a worker for the outpatient service of the hospital, is likely to be, or have been, a patient as well. As she is led by hospital orderlies into the electroshock room, the narrator triumphantly presents the "Bible of Dreams" in a gesture of benediction to her captors: "Peace! I bring to you … " but is cut off by the head nurse, who cautions, "None of that old stuff, sweetie."[15] The narrator's pursuit of these dreams, and her devotion to their preservation, is an attempt to return to Johnny Panic; as so often in Plath's writing, official standards of health are dubious. The narrator longs for a return to that which Johnny Panic represents, and as the story draws to its conclusion, it becomes clear that her devotion to the Bible of Dreams has led her back to him, as she is crucified for her faith: "The crown of wire is placed on my head, the wafer of forgetfulness on my tongue."[16] Although the electroconvulsive treatment is meant to relieve the patient of her suffering, it is also evidence of Johnny Panic's presence. In the midst of the treatment,

"Johnny Panic appears in a nimbus of arc lights on the ceiling overhead," and the narrator, far from being shocked from her obsession, is driven into Johnny Panic's arms:

> The air crackles with his blue-tongued lightning haloed
>   angels.
> His love is the twenty-story leap, the rope at the throat,
>   the knife at the heart.
> He forgets not his own.[17]

Despite the force, violence, and pain of the treatment, the narrator welcomes the return of panic, almost seizes it as her right. In Plath's and Sexton's writing, this is the consolation the hospital often provides; it allows the patient a relatively safe environment in which to nurture her illness. The institution can either exclude panic or protect it.

Although "Johnny Panic" reveals a woman desperate to reclaim her illness, Plath's 1956 poem "Miss Drake Proceeds to Supper" presents a woman who struggles to negotiate the inherently threatening nature of the environment within the institution.

> No novice
> In those elaborate rituals
> Which allay the malice
> Of knotted table and crooked chair,
> The new woman in the ward
> Wears purple, steps carefully
> Among her secret combinations of eggshells
> And breakable hummingbirds,
> Footing sallow as a mouse
> Between the cabbage-roses
> Which are slowly opening their furred petals
> To devour and drag her down
> Into the carpet's design.[18]

While the environment of the institution is inherently threatening in Plath's description, it is also negotiable given the knowledge which Miss Drake possesses. "No novice," although new to this particular ward, Miss Drake carefully negotiates the simultaneously delicate and dangerous environment. The "elaborate rituals" and "secret combinations of eggshells" implies that Miss Drake is paranoid and possibly obsessive compulsive, but they also reveal her to be an initiate in the ways of the ward; insanity is also privileged knowledge. Lacan writes that in order to establish the relation between the real and fantasy, "there is only one method of knowing that one is there, namely, to map the network. And how is a network mapped? One goes back and forth over one's ground, one crosses one's path, one cross-checks it always in the same way [. . .]."[19] Miss Drake may very well be engaged in this act of mapping in order to confirm her presence. Yet this notion of mapping is also applicable to Plath's tendency to continually return to and reexamine panic, anxiety, and the institution in her poetry. In doing so, she maps and re-maps the spaces of her illness, simultaneously exercising control over those spaces and charting her current movements away from or toward the institution.

As "Miss Drake" proceeds, however, her movements are designed to chart a specific course through the increasingly dangerous space of the ward:

> With bird-quick eye cocked askew
> She can see in the nick of time
> How perilous needles grain the floorboards
> And outwit their brambled plan;
> Now through her ambushed air,
> Adazzle with bright shards
> Of broken glass,
> She edges with wary breath,
> Fending off jag and tooth,
> Until, turning sideways,
> She lifts one webbed foot after the other
> Into the still, sultry weather
> Of the patients' dining room.[20]

Miss Drake's animal identification changes in this second stanza, from mouse to bird, which is finally identified as a duck. Her name is clarified, although given her careful and triumphant navigation of the ward, Plath may also be implying a connection with the British navigator. The shift from mouse to bird is a necessary adaptation, allowing Miss Drake, "in the nick of time," to better negotiate her environment: first the voracious pattern of the rug, then the needles in the floorboards, until finally the air itself threatens to capture or cut her. It is an exhausting process, and although Miss Drake is successful, one is reminded that it begins again after dinner, and is repeated daily. In "Miss Drake Proceeds to Supper," the ward does little to dispel panic, paranoia, and obsession; it only offers new challenges. According to Ted Hughes in his introduction to the *Collected Poems,* "Miss Drake Proceeds to Supper" was written "on a parapet over the Seine on 21 June 1956," a further reminder that, although Plath certainly employs her 1953 hospitalization in this poem, she continued to reexamine the presence of panic, obsession, and confinement throughout her life.[21] "Miss Drake" is a particularly apt companion piece for "Johnny Panic," revealing the institution as a site of both panic and consolation. Plath continued to examine such issues in other poems, such as "Tulips" (1961), which was based on a surgical procedure Plath underwent in 1961. The poem's speaker, lying in her hospital bed, sees the flowers sent by her husband and children and which, far from offering consolation, seem to promise suffering:

> The tulips are too red in the first place, they hurt me.
> Even through the gift paper I could hear them breathe
> Lightly, through their white swaddlings, like an awful
>   baby.
> Their redness talks to my wound, it corresponds.
> They are subtle: they seem to float, though they weigh me
>   down,
> Upsetting me with their sudden tongue and their color,
> A dozen red lead sinkers round my neck.[22]

As the tulips assume the place of children, who become weights which pull at the hooks imbedded in the speaker's skin, it becomes clear that the panic the speaker experiences in this poem is not due to the hospital, but to the idea of returning to her domestic life. "In Plaster," written on the same day as "Tulips," shows a woman on the mend who finds herself at once dependent upon and resentful of the plaster cast which envelops her. Her grim determination to overcome her cast is tempered by her fear that the cast is stronger, and will never let her escape. In these poems, Plath gradually develops a picture of the hospital as a place of healing and a place of suffering; the hospital can drive out panic, it can nurture it, or it can protect the patient from the sources of panic in the outside world. For Plath, in her life and her work, anxiety can result from being in the hospital or *not* being in the hospital, from being on the mend or being separated from illness. With such a complex and conflicting relation to health, the hospital, and the world, it is difficult to imagine a life *without* anxiety. It is no coincidence that the narrator in "Johnny Panic" strives to reclaim panic through words; in writing that story, and poems like "Miss Drake" and "Tulips," Plath examined how the expression of her experiences through the written word could allow her to reclaim and master those experiences, to take the presence of anxiety and panic in her life and turn it to something useful.

Writing served a similar purpose for Anne Sexton. Approximately a year after the birth of her second child in August 1955, Sexton began seeing Dr. Martin Orne for treatment for suicidal urges, depression, and an uncontrollable anger toward her children, for which she was "prescribed vitamins and various psychoactive medications."[23] Her relationship with Dr. Orne quickly became an important part of Sexton's life: in November of 1956, Sexton overdosed on Nembutal (a barbiturate). She was admitted to Glenside Hospital outside of Boston, where her main treatment was psychotherapy with Dr. Orne, which apparently saved her from undergoing the electroconvulsive therapy recommended by Glenside's staff.[24] As was the case with Plath and other poets of their generation,* Sexton suffered not only from her disease but also from the lack of medical and social understanding of her problem, which was certainly both chemical and psychological in origin. Her overdose of Nembutal was just the first of many such incidents she would live through, as she self-medicated throughout her life, sometimes with random combinations of drugs and often recklessly in combination with alcohol.

---

*Robert Lowell, John Berryman, and Theodore Roethke, among others, were all hospitalized multiple times during their lives for treatment for bipolar disorders.

Orne held frequent sessions with Sexton in his office, and in January 1957 began asking her to write poetry as part of her therapy.[25] Orne's goal in this was not to find in Sexton's poetry some insight into her problems, but rather Orne wanted Sexton to write poetry primarily "as a means to dispel her sense of worthlessness."[26] While this project was not immediately successful (Sexton attempted suicide in May 1957), Orne persisted in his encouragement of Sexton's writing to show her that she had a talent, that she had in her something to give, and something of worth.[27] It was not long before Sexton was writing almost compulsively, and although her therapist encouraged her writing, Sexton certainly did not accept it as having only therapeutic value. In January 1957, Sexton began attending a poetry workshop led by John Holmes at the Boston Center for Adult Education; in the summer of 1958, she attended a writer's conference at Antioch College; and in September 1958, she enrolled in Robert Lowell's poetry seminar at Boston University.[28] She had also begun to publish; in 1958, she published six poems in two journals, while the following year she published twenty-five poems in nine journals.[29] In 1960, less than four years after she had started writing poetry, Sexton's first book was published. As is fitting, given the origins of Sexton's writing, much of *To Bedlam and Part Way Back* is devoted to Sexton's experiences with mental illness and the hospital. For if poetry proved to Sexton her own self-worth, it was also a way for her to comprehend and validate the experiences embedded therein.

As with Plath, panic as a theme in Sexton's poetry is never constant, and it is often bound up with the institution as a simultaneously protective and threatening presence. In "Music Swims Back to Me" from *To Bedlam and Part Way Back,* Sexton portrays the first few hours of confinement, before the bipolar attack has fully passed. In this case, the patient is pleased to be in the institution, as it allows her free rein to indulge in the manic phase of her attack. Yet these are the first few hours of confinement, and while Sexton as the lucid poet, writing the poem in retrospect, is clearly aware of her setting, Sexton as the patient only partially comprehends her situation.

Wait Mister. Which way is home?
They turned the light out
and the dark is moving in the corner.
There are no sign posts in this room,
four ladies, over eighty,
in diapers every one of them.
La la la, Oh music swims back to me
and I can feel the tune they played
the night they left me
in this private institution on a hill.[30]

Unlike some of the other hospital poems from *Bedlam,* such as "You, Doctor Martin" and "Unknown Girl in the Maternity Ward," which employ a more consistent formal and rhythmic approach to reflect the confinement of the patient in the hospital, the absence of a regular form in "Music Swims Back to Me" allows Sexton to better express the sense of freedom she found in these last hours of her bipolar episode. Yet Sexton's joy at this moment is out of step with the darkness and complete enclosure of the room and the physical conditions of her fellow patients. The alterations in tense in this poem are important; Sexton moves from past to present, reminding the audience that some of this is felt or realized only in retrospect. That she repeats "here" implies that she is still confined, but, in the passing of her initial attack, has come to see the reality of her confinement.

Imagine it. A radio playing
and everyone here was crazy.
I liked it and dance in a circle.
music pours over the sense
and in a funny way
music sees more than I.
I mean it remembers better;
remembers the first night here.
It was the strangled cold of November;
even the stars were strapped in the sky
and that moon too bright
forking through the bars to stick me
with a singing in the head.
I have forgotten the rest.[31]

Sexton, hearing the music in the present, which evokes this moment in her past, recalls the freedom she felt at the time as well as the confinement to which she was oblivious. Yet a great deal of that confinement exists outside of the ward, in the weather and the night sky; inside, Sexton dances. In Sexton's description, the bars on the window were designed to keep danger out. Only the moonlight, in a clear reference to lunacy, reaches her; the attack continues, but now in the safety of the ward, isolated from the "strangled cold" of the outside world. But as the episode passes, the patient emerges into a greater awareness of her situation. The poem concludes:

> They lock me in this chair at eight a.m.
> and there are no signs to tell the way,
> just the radio beating to itself
> and the song that remembers
> more than I. Oh, la la la,
> this music swims back to me.
> The night I came I danced in a circle
> and was not afraid.
> Mister?[32]

Mary Ann Frese Witt, in her study of captivity in French Literature, contends:

> [T]he depr ivation of physical liberty opens the way to a spiritual freedom. Enclosure in its literary forms, as in ritual and psychology, means anxiety and isolation but also may mean protection and restoration.[33]

In "Music Swims Back to Me," it means all of those things. Following the manic freedom of her first night in the institution, Sexton is strapped in a chair, and while the effect of the music may still allow her some psychological freedom, her body is clearly confined. Middlebrook sees this poem as Sexton's desire for "the security of complete delusion,"[34] and there is no denying the comfort Sexton takes in the unfettered madness she is allowed to express during her first night. Yet, as Witt indicates, confinement can also imply isolation. "Music Swims Back to Me" begins and ends with Sexton speaking to a "mister," probably the orderly who brings her to the ward, and whom she does not want to leave. In the first

Imitations of Drowning

Anne Sexton

Fear
of drowning,
fear of being that alone,
kept me busy making a deal
as if I could buy
my way out of it
and it worked for two years
and all of July.

This August I began to dream of drowning. The dying
went on and on in water as white and clear
as the gin I drink each day at half-past five.
Going down for the last time, the last breath lying,
I grapple with eels like ropes—it's ether, it's queer
and then, at last, it's done. Now the scavengers arrive,
the hard crawlers who come to clean up the ocean floor.
And death, that old butcher, will bother me no more.

I
had never
had this dream before
except twice when my parents
clung to rafts
and sat together for death,
frozen
like lewd photographs.

Who listens to dreams? Only symbols for something—
like money for the analyst or your mother's wig,

* * *

stanza she wants to ask him how to get home; this question, coupled with her twice mentioning the lack of signposts in the room,
points to her complete disorientation. The question also implies
that she has had enough of this fun, and would like to go home
now. Confinement allows her the freedom and security to revel in
her attack, but once she enters the institution she has relinquished

the arm I almost lost in the washroom wringer,
following fear to its core, tugging the old string.
But real drowning is for someone else. It's too big
to put in your mouth on purpose, it puts hot stingers
in your tongue and vomit in your nose as your lungs break.
Tossed like a wet dog by that juggler, you die awake.

Fear,
a motor,
pumps me around and around
until I fade slowly
and the crowd laughs.
I fade out, an old bicycle rider
whose odds are measured
in actuary graphs.

This weekend the papers were black with the new highway
fatalities and in Boston the strangler found another victim
and we were all in Truro drinking beer and writing checks.
The others rode the surf, commanding rafts like sleighs.
I swam—but the tide came in like ten thousand orgasms.
I swam—but the waves were higher than horses' necks.
I was shut up in that closet, until, biting the door,
they dragged me out, dribbling urine on the gritty shore.

Breathe!
And you'll know...
an ant in a pot of chocolate,
it boils
and surrounds you.
There is no news in fear
but in the end it's fear
that drowns you.

* * *

any claim to the freedoms she enjoyed outside. "Music Swims Back
to Me" presents this duality beautifully, yet also implies in its ending that eventually the attack passes and confinement wins out.
The initial mania is followed by a more subtle yet pervasive anxiety that expresses the patient's increasing uncertainty. In the final
stanza, the present tense is more prominent than the past; what-

ever pleasant recollections the patient may have of that first night are slowly being subsumed to her present confinement. This matter of tense is significant because it can reveal how quickly the bargain Sexton originally struck can fall apart. Sexton can accept her isolation in exchange for the freedom and security the ward provides; the next morning, locked in a chair, that freedom is gone, but the isolation remains. It is fair to say that Sexton found different forms of freedom and confinement both inside and outside of the institution. But as in "Music Swims Back to Me," the constant sense of isolation should remind the reader that neither the institution nor the outside world provided sufficient response to Sexton's problems.

If "Music Swims Back to Me" reveals the protective role of the institution, and the way in which the institution can allow, even if briefly, the patient to revel in her attack, Sexton's "Noon Walk on the Asylum Lawn," another poem from *To Beldam and Part Way Back*, displays how very threatening the institution can be. In "Noon Walk on the Asylum Lawn" what should be a rare moment of freedom within confinement becomes a dangerous and threatening journey into the outside world.

> The summer sun ray
> shifts through a suspicious tree.
> *though I walk through the valley of the shadow*
> It sucks the air
> and looks around for me.
>
> The grass speaks.
> I hear green chanting all day.
> *I will fear no evil, fear no evil.*
> The blades extend
> and reach my way.
>
> The sky breaks.
> It sags and breathes upon my face.
> *in the presence of mine enemies, mine enemies*
> The world is full of enemies.
> There is no safe place.[35]

As the speaker walks further and further into the asylum lawn, the sense of anxiety increases. Danger is present everywhere; sun, trees, grass, and sky are all threatening and conspiratorial forces, and this moment of freedom, of being let out onto the grounds for a walk, quickly turns into a confinement as complete and frightening as anything offered by the ward. As the speaker leaves the institution, though only temporarily, her need for guidance and protection suggests Psalm 23, which begins, "The Lord is my shepherd; I shall not want." Yet the constant intrusion of the environment distracts her from her recitation. As each aspect of the environment in its turn becomes threatening, the speaker stalls, unfortunately, on the part of the psalm that mentions "enemies." And though that line continues "thou anointest my head with oil; my cup runneth over," the speaker never makes it past her "enemies." Looking around her and seeing nothing but danger and threat, even within the official bounds of the asylum, the speaker sees no possibility for safety or protection. Though unspoken in the poem, this puts a dark emphasis on the conclusion of the psalm: "[. . .] and I will dwell in the house of the Lord forever." Finding no protection or solace outside of the ward, the speaker may never leave again.

For both Plath and Sexton, panic was a contradictory and difficult presence in lives filled with uncertainty and conflict. In their poetry, panic is sometimes denied, sometimes confined, sometimes deified, and sometimes claimed as a right. Plath, especially in the poems written during the last year of her life, almost embraced panic and mania, writing from their sources in what has been seen by some as poems of empowerment, and by others as poems of desperation. For Sexton, as she fought through year after year of attacks, treatments, and suicidal depression, her response to panic became flight. In "Flee on Your Donkey" (1966), Sexton's flight is from the institution, which has lost any quality of charm or protection with which she endows it in earlier poems, toward an uncertain and undefined freedom. In *The Awful Rowing Toward God*, the last book she saw through publication,[36] Sexton's flight is toward God, whom she desperately hopes will offer refuge and consolation. Although both women eventually committed suicide, their poems significantly reflect many of the forces which inspired and perhaps required their writing. The cumulative effect of those poems reveals that there are no easy answers to what their illnesses meant to their lives or their work. Nowhere do they present a final, coherent, and definitive answer to what panic, illness, and depression meant to them. Rather, their poetry reveals those issues in all of their complexity, as things to be hated, feared, protected, nurtured, and sometimes even desired. In "Flee on Your Donkey," Anne Sexton defined mental illness as a mouth talking to itself. It is through these poets' interpretation of that interior dialogue that they began to both translate and control the sometimes chaotic experiences which inhabit their work.

Endnotes

1. National Institute of Mental Health, *Panic Disorder* (Rockville, MD: National Institute of Mental Health, 1999), 1.

2. Edward Butscher, *Sylvia Plath: Method and Madness* (New York: Seabury Press, 1976), 112.

3. Diane Wood Middlebrook, *Anne Sexton: A Biography* (Boston: Houghton Mifflin, 1991), 210.

4. Anne Sexton, *No Evil Star: Selected Essays, Interviews, and Prose,* edited by Steven E. Colburn (Ann Arbor, MI.: University of Michigan Press, 1985), 75.

5. Sylvia Plath, *The Unabridged Journals of Sylvia Plath,* edited by Karen V. Kukil (New York: Anchor Books, 2000), 84–85.

6. Ibid., 187.

7. Linda Wagner-Martin, *Sylvia Plath: A Biography* (New York: Simon & Schuster, 1987), 99–101.

8. Ibid., 105.

9. Paul Alexander, *Rough Magic: A Biography of Sylvia Plath* (New York: Viking Press, 1991), 119.

10. Sylvia Plath, *The Bell Jar* (New York: Bantam Books, 1971), 117–18.

11. Paul Alexander, op. cit.

12. Ibid., 120.

13. Sylvia Plath, "Johnny Panic and the Bible of Dreams." In *Johnny Panic and the Bible of Dreams* (New York: Harper and Row, 1978), 152–53.

14. Ibid., 152.

15. Ibid., 165.

16. Ibid., 166.

17. Ibid.

18. Sylvia Plath, *Sylvia Plath: Collected Poems,* edited by Ted Hughes (New York: HarperCollins, 1992), 41.

19. Jacques Lacan, *The Four Fundamental Concepts of Psycho-Analysis,* translated by Alan Sheridan and edited by Jacques-Alain Miller (London: The Hogart Press, 1977), 45.

20. Sylvia Plath (1992), op. cit., 41.

21. Ted Hughes, Introduction to *Sylvia Plath: Collected Poems* (New York: HarperCollins, 1992), 17.

22. Sylvia Plath (1992), op. cit., 160.

23. Diane Wood Middlebrook (1991), op. cit., 33–34.

24. Ibid., 34.

25. Ibid., 42.

26. Peter Davison, *The Fading Smile: Poets in Boston from Robert Lowell to Sylvia Plath* (New York: W.W. Norton, 1994), 133.

27. Diane Wood Middlebrook (1991), op. cit., 42–43.

28. Peter Davison (1994), op. cit., 134–38.

29. Cameron Northouse and Thomas P. Walsh, *Sylvia Plath and Anne Sexton: A Reference Guide* (Boston: G.K. Hall, 1974), 89–91.

30. Anne Sexton, *The Complete Poems* (Boston: Houghton Mifflin, 1982), 6.

31. Ibid., 6-7.

32. Ibid., 7.

33. Mary Anne Frese Witt, *Existential Prisons: Captivity in Mid-Twentieth-Century French Literature* (Durham, NC: Duke University Press, 1985), 4.

34. Diane Wood Middlebrook (1991), op. cit., 70.

35. Anne Sexton (1982), op. cit., 27–8.

36. Diane Wood Middlebrook (1991), op. cit., 366, 371.

INSIGHT

ROBERT COMBS

The Short Story in the Age of Anxiety

W. H. AUDEN STRUCK A CHORD with the title of his Pulitzer-prize-winning poetry collection of 1947. His phrase "The Age of Anxiety" has echoed through the century with its suggestion that the vague, objectless state of fear or dread that we call anxiety is somehow inescapable in our time. In an essay mostly about operas and why there are not many new ones, Auden characterizes the literary response to what writers—and dramatists, visual artists, and composers—experience as a collective sense of powerlessness.

> The rapidity of historical change and the apparent powerlessness of the individual to affect Collective History has led in literature to a retreat from history. Instead of tracing the history of an individual who is born, grows old and dies, many writers, beginning with Poe, have devoted their attention to timeless passionate moments of life, to states of being.[1]

It is interesting that Auden selects Edgar Allan Poe—whose tales more often than not tap into the fear and anxiety of the reader—as touchstone for the kind of writing he is describing. This trend toward personal psychological apocalypse, when witnessed in writing, can reach into the depth of the collective human experience. Anxiety is a stranger to no one. The masters, Poe among them, can bring a reader to the verge of panic. John Cheever makes a case for the short story as the literary form *par excellence* of the age of anxiety, for it may well be that the short story at its best consistently exemplifies the soul on edge:

INSIGHT

(The short story is) what you tell yourself in a dentist's office while you're waiting for an appointment. The short story has a great function, it seems to me, in life. Also, it's the appeasement of pain, in a very special sense, in a stuck ski lift, a sinking boat, a dentist's office, or a doctor's office— where we're waiting for a death warrant. Where you don't really have long enough for a novel, you do the short story. I'm very sure that, at the point of death, one tells oneself a short story—not a novel.[2]

And Nadine Gordimer essentially agrees. In her elegant essay, "The Flash of Fireflies," Gordimer declares the short story well suited to "convey the quality of human life, where contact ... is like the flash of fireflies, in and out, now here, now there, in darkness." The short story, she claims, conveys the "only thing one can be sure of—the present moment.... The short story is a fragmented and restless form, a matter of hit or miss, and it is perhaps for this reason that it suits modern consciousness—which seems best expressed as flashes of fearful insight alternating with near-hypnotic states of indifference."[3] The short story, these writers suggest, draws upon its audience's willingness to see life microscopically, within a sharply focused narrative of subjective crisis. Whether Romantic—warm, wet, and dark—like stories by Poe or D. H. Lawrence, or Realistic—cool, dry, and clear—like those of Flaubert or Joyce, a short story at its best offers a revelation of some sort, not as mere literary novelty, but as representative truth. It offers a glimpse into the soul so true that it evokes a jolt, an awareness that someone else is articulating, relating an experience we've all known and feared.

What writers and critics call "short stories" are not simply narratives of a certain limited length. Tolstoy's "The Death of Ivan Ilych" and James's "The Beast in the Jungle" are routinely included in short story anthologies, although they take hours to read, while selections from Boccacio's *Decameron* and Chaucer's *Canterbury Tales* and most chapters from modern novels are not. What seems to define a short story is its satisfying rendering of a moment of truth, a fleeting connection, a momentary insight that makes us tighten our stomachs, clench our jaws, wait to exhale. Whether experienced as closure or the withholding of closure, the short story achieves an exquisite balance of perilous opposites—form and content, disclosure and concealment, thought and feeling, reality and dream. This rather precious standard of aesthetic excellence—first formulated by Poe as "unity of effect"—has held the short story as a literary form aloof from merely cute, anecdotal magazine fiction, creating over the years a canon of masterpieces in miniature. Practitioners of this art as diverse as Poe, Maupassant, James, Kafka, Hemingway, O'Connor, and Paley demonstrate the range of expression possible within an aesthetic of psychological discovery both feared and desired.

The short story was originally a Romantic form that developed out of the dramatic monologue of Browning and Tennyson, described well by Robert Langbaum as a "poetry of experience." Like the German idealists, Browning and Tennyson celebrated robust life as it is, which requires knowledge of evil for the development of the soul. Both poets see acceptance of the world, including evil that inspires terror, as a triumph of the spirit. The aristocratic narrator of Robert Browning's "My Last Duchess" fascinates and repels us as he arrogantly reveals, without caring whether he does or not, that he has had his previous wife murdered as he now prepares to take another—all the while extolling the virtues of a portrait of his murdered wife:

> That's my last Duchess painted on the wall,
> Looking as if she were alive;[4]

The poem evokes a sympathetic curiosity about the narrator's psychology, requiring the reader to develop a "role-playing or projective attitude of mind"[5] in order to comprehend the narrator in spite of his repugnance. Langbaum correctly identifies this seeking after dangerous truth as Faustian. Goethe's Faust desires to experience what any and every person experiences, even if this process of sympathetic identification eventually wrecks him.

> Let me suffer in my inmost being
> Whatever is the destiny of man!
> Let me seize the deepest and the highest,
> Heap on my breast man's weal, man's woe,
> Include in myself the self of all mankind—
> And, like it, be obliterated in the end![6]

Browning's dramatic monologue allows the reader to see the speaker's mask of sanity in his coherent rhetoric, and at the same time infer the madness in the speaker's soul. The reader is engaged; empathy is combined with anxiety as Faust proclaims his desire to know what many of us suppress and control. It is only the *appearance* of sanity that is conveyed by the objectification of human life.

It is a small step from a poem like Browning's "My Last Duchess" to "The Tell-Tale Heart," by Edgar Allan Poe. The narrator of this story insists upon his own sanity as he describes in meticulous detail his obsession with the cloudy eye of an old man, how he murdered him, dismembered the corpse, buried it under the floorboards, then invited the police to sit in the very room of the murder while he tried to calmly answer their questions. The climax of the story comes when the murderer thinks he hears the beating of the old man's heart—actually his own auditory heartbeat, a symptom of extreme anxiety. Poe is a master of suspense, tantalizing the reader with anticipation. Throughout the story, Poe foregrounds the murderer's nervous, self-conscious narrative voice as he insists that he suffers not from madness but from "over-acuteness of the senses." Ironically, his efforts to appear sane only convince the reader, addressed directly throughout the story as "you," of the narrator's madness. Yet the overall effect of this tale, like that of Browning's poem, is to hold up for the reader's consideration a state of soul everyone might have the capacity to experience. Evoking anxious tension and panic states connect the reader to primal fear. Browning reveals inhuman coldness in a person easily capable of murder.

Poe reveals terror of an obsession no rational explanation can account for. Poe's narrator says, "It is impossible to say how first the idea [of murdering the old man] entered my brain; but once conceived, it haunted me day and night." He finally hits upon the eye with its cataract as a possible cause of his obsession. "I think it was his eye! Yes, it was this!"[7] But the reader understands, if the narrator does not, that this image, an eye that cannot see, represents not so much a rational motive for murder as a projective symbol of the narrator's perplexity. Perplexity and lack of rationale contribute to the element of unpredictability, lack of control, and chaos—precursors to panic states. The beating heart likewise expresses the narrator's merciless experience of ongoing time within this state of panic. It simply will not end until he makes it end by giving himself away. When the murderer reveals the corpse to the police and tells the story we are reading in which he insists upon his sanity, he no longer inhabits the unbearable condition of his compulsion. Now he resides in the false consciousness of his explanation to the reader of how and why he committed the murder. The reader sees through the explanation but understands the compulsion no more than the narrator does. In this way the reality of the terror that has no rational cause is expressed.

Poe was one of the first to discuss the aesthetics of the short story, and his emphasis is clearly psychological. In a review in which he praises the tales of Hawthorne, Poe argues that a story should be short enough to be read in one sitting so that the story's effect upon the reader may derive from the story's *totality*. He also says that a skillful writer will first determine the effect he wishes to achieve upon his reader, then fashion incidents and details that bring about this effect. Such deliberate labor ultimately serves the purpose of what he calls the "exaltation of the soul."[8] In other words, Poe understands the short story to be an occasion for experiencing states of intense mental or spiritual subjectivity. Although the story must be carefully crafted, it is not an end in itself. Nor does it explain itself as the sum of its parts. A story facilitates the reader's encounter with quasi-religious psychological processes that are convincing not because they are named, but because they are experienced in the process of reading the story, and these processes verge upon rapture because they press up against something absolute, infinite, or ultimately mysterious.

In the 1840s, when Poe, Hawthorne, Gogol, and others were creating the Romantic short story, Danish theologian Soren Kierkegaard was formulating his psychology of existentialism, in which anxiety plays a crucial role. In *The Concept of Anxiety* (1844), Kierkegaard says, "Anxiety is freedom's possibility, and only such anxiety is through faith absolutely educative, because it consumes all finite ends and discovers all their deceptiveness."[9] For Kierkegaard, anxiety, understood in light of faith in God, delivers modern people from an impoverishment of spirit in which life is imagined only literally in terms of specific fears and desires. Possibility for Kierkegaard is a qualitative, not an incremental leap of existence. Anxiety, therefore, is an inevitable, sane, and potentially constructive reaction to all that it is possible for human beings to experience. Kierkegaard's view of anxiety has been very influential in humanistic, analytical psychologies. Theologian Paul Tillich, like Kierkegaard and the Romantics, sees anxiety as an encounter with nonbeing. The terror of anxiety derives from the discovery that "nonbeing is a part of one's own being."[10] And such a close, inescapable terror has an equally impressive positive corollary, stated in the provocative last line of his book, *The Courage To Be* (1950): "The courage to be is rooted in the God who appears when God has disappeared in the anxiety of doubt."[11] Rollo May, in *The Meaning of Anxiety* (1950), puts it more pragmatically, but still echoes Kierkegaard: "the positive aspects of selfhood develop as the individual confronts, moves through, and overcomes anxiety-creating experiences."[12] These three thinkers share a view of anxiety as ontological, as rooted in the way a subject experiences himself as existing. Freedom is the good and the bad news of anxiety. It may be creatively liberating or simply overwhelming.

A romantic story by Poe uses the materials of story—character, action, setting, etc.—to create an almost solipsistic dreamscape. We cannot discover in what city "The Tell-Tale Heart" takes place or what the relationship is between the murderer and the old man. These details do not matter. In a realistic story by Guy de Maupassant, on the other hand, the author strives to "show how minds are modified under the influence of environmental circumstances."[13] Maupassant emphasizes that the effect an author creates is an "*illusion* of reality." And there can be as many fictional universes as there are writers, for "each of us makes, individually, a personal illusion of the world. It may be a poetic, sentimental, joyful, melancholy, sordid, or dismal one, according to our nature."[14] Maupassant selects those details which dramatize the clash between his characters' temperaments and the environments in which fate has placed them. This clash results in a revelation accompanied by panic as does a story by Poe, but the fictional illusion created is one of an entirely particular time and place. In classic Maupassant stories, like "The Neckless" and "A Piece of String," ordinary men and women experience chance happenings that cause their lives to come apart at the seams. Panic, for Maupassant, always lies just below the surface of realistic, everyday life, residing in simple objects like jewelry and string. Maupassant, master psychologist and storyteller, makes clear that it is not catastrophes that cause his characters to come undone, but their own inability to imagine themselves except exactly as they always have.

"The Necklace" is a typical Maupassant story. The first sentence really tells us everything: Mathilde Loisel "was one of those pretty and charming girls who are sometimes, as if by a mistake of destiny, born in a family of clerks."[15] Ashamed to be seen at the ball without some token of finery, she borrows a diamond necklace from a wealthy friend, only to lose it after her one night of fulfillment in which she cheats fate for a while. She and her husband borrow the money to replace the necklace, still too ashamed to admit what has happened. After ten years of scrubbing floors to pay off her debt, Mathilde meets the wealthy friend who loaned the necklace to her and, no longer ashamed, proudly tells her of the ordeal she has been through and her triumph over destiny. Then her wealthy friend informs her that the necklace was only paste. Readers can argue about the "moral" of this story. Does it express sympathy for the cruelties of class or worldly cynicism in the face of these cruelties? Is Mathilde ultimately heroic or foolish? Is her life a triumph or a disaster? Regardless of which interpretation one chooses, it is the psychology of the story that makes it powerful. The central character cannot become conscious enough of her mode of existence to develop a sense of irony. In this way she is like a child. She cannot distance herself from the panic of her reversal of fortune. But the reader grows in consciousness and in appreciation of how necessary irony is as a means of dealing with panic so that life can be understood and endured. Maupassant puts it best: "How life is strange and changeful? How little a thing is needed for us to be lost or to be saved!"[16] Typically, a Maupassant story turns on one trivial object—a paste necklace, a piece of string, a lost Roman coin. And Maupassant's trademark surprise-ending twists life into a caricature of itself, so that no one wins; the author's irony prevails. In "The Necklace," he gives Mathilde Loisel every chance to embrace her freedom, yet her true self shines through only in the paradoxical way she defeats herself. When she discovers that she has lost what she assumes to be a valuable necklace, she panics and spends the next twenty years paying for her mistake. Yet ultimately, because of her suffering, she becomes a woman she never thought she could be, a common woman who can stand proudly and speak honestly to a woman of "quality." In the treacherous, very secular world of Maupassant's fiction, we see a kind of wisdom similar to that described by Kierkegaard as anxiety's education toward faith. Reading the fiction is an education in irony and patience, which can transform anxiety into wisdom.

In the psychological realism of Henry James we see the fulfillment of the narrative possibilities explored by Poe, Hawthorne, and Maupassant. In "The Beast in the Jungle," James places a character in a world that is, to some extent, like Poe's, a projection of the character's anxieties. James approaches the story, following Hawthorne, as a study in moral ambiguities that he renders allegorically. And like Maupassant, James leaves us with a sense that, although circumstances often trap people, character determines fate. Such a view offers the reader freedom both from a narrow sense of historical determinism and from a naïve sense of personal empowerment. In the Jamesian definition of experience as "a kind of huge spider-web of the finest silken threads suspended in the chamber of consciousness"[17] we see a sophisticated appropriation of anxiety to literary sensibility. For James, a writer's greatest talent is "the power to guess the unseen from the seen, to trace the implications of things."[18] Experience, James tells us, consists of impressions. But it would be a mistake to think of James's fiction as an explicit account of authorial perceptions. James teases and challenges the reader to explore his material along with him. His famous admonition is also a dare: "Try to be one of the people on whom nothing is lost."[19]

"The Beast in the Jungle" begins *in medias res,* when John Marcher, age thirty-five, and May Bartram, age thirty, take up a conversation they began ten years earlier in which John confided to May "the deepest thing within [him], the sense of being kept for something rare and strange, possibly prodigious and terrible, that was sooner or later to happen to [him], that [he] had in [his] bones the foreboding and the conviction of, and that would perhaps overwhelm [him]."[20] May vows to watch with John for the beast in the jungle of his life, which she does until her death. She seems to discover near the end of this long story—or John believes she does—what John's beast all along has really been, but she refuses to tell him what she sees, only that he will not suffer. After her death, John visits May's grave where a chance encounter with a stranger in mourning reveals to John—or John believes it does— the mystery he has desired and feared to know his whole life. In the grief visible on the other man's face John sees the love he never allowed himself to feel for May Bartram or for anyone. His own self-absorption had paradoxically robbed him of his own life. John formulates his view of himself very exactly and with typical self-aggrandizement: "he had been the man of his time, the man to whom nothing on earth was to have happened."[21] This statement implies that the life John Marcher led, although it was completely unfulfilling to him, did have in its way an ironical world-historical significance. He was the man of his time, The Man of the Age of Anxiety.

John Marcher's struggle is explicable in terms of the views of psychiatrist Harry Stack Sullivan on the function of anxiety in the personality as a whole. Sullivan thought that anxiety, along with pain and fear, served as necessary restraints to freedom in the acculturation of the child. Anxiety allows the self, the "custodian of awareness," to maintain its all-important isolation in the personality. Experiencing anxiety is the price the self pays for remaining sovereign so that it can decide how best to employ the energies available in the personality as a whole. Limiting freedom paradoxically preserves freedom. Interestingly, Sullivan likens the experience of anxiety to peering into a microscope. "As (the self-dynamism) develops, it becomes more and more related to a microscope in its function," he says. But also like a microscope, the self as it develops "interferes with noticing the rest of the world."[22] For James and for Sullivan, one could say, there is something problematical about the self in the Age of Anxiety. Consciousness threatens it absolutely. In order to understand how this might be so, we turn to an intriguing reading of "The Beast in the Jungle" by gender critic Eve Sedgwick. In her essay, "The Beast in the Closet," Sedgwick suggests that what John Marcher is hiding from in the jungle of polite society, with its hypocritical "compulsory heterosexuality," is his own potential for homosexual desire. John is experiencing barely repressed "homosexual panic,"[23] which he needs May Bartram's companionship to contain. When he "sees" at the graveyard that loving her would have saved him, he is entering into a kind of false consciousness or rationalization like that of Poe's murderer in "The Tell-Tale Heart" when he explains why he killed the old man. Now John can be a would-be widower in spite of himself. From this position he is safe the rest of his life from knowing why he was really afraid. Whether or not one accepts such a specific reading of "The Beast in the Jungle," Sedgwick demonstrates how the self can be threatened by consciousness in The Age of Anxiety. In an age characterized as one of freedom and discovery, the self can be simultaneously attacked from within and without. Race, class, gender, sexual orientation—all these categories can be experienced as jungles in which a modern person wanders, threatened by beasts of prejudice, the self-interests of others, and one's own self-doubts. Freedom means the possibility of "visions and revisions" in which one's identity can vanish, or seem to. Perhaps John Marcher, like T. S. Eliot's J. Alfred Prufrock, experienced himself more fully than most people do in that he realized his own non-being.

Franz Kafka represented the trials of the self in all its comic/grotesque futility, imagining it in terms of his own dreamlike inner life. Yet he was a very reluctant prophet. In a reported interview with Gustav Janouch, Kafka rejected his devoted friend's adulation: "Your trust oppresses me," he said.[24] Kafka seems to have realized how closely his writings reflected the present, the future, and, at the same time, what he understood to be his own personal inadequacy in life. "One must be silent, if one can't give any help. No one, through his own lack of hope, should make the condition of the patient worse. For that reason, all my scribbling is to be destroyed. I am no light. I have merely lost my way among my own thorns. I'm a dead end."[25] Max Brod, Kafka's literary executor, refused to destroy Kafka's manuscripts. And so Kafka and the Kafkaesque have come to stand, in the words of Milan Kundera, for "the bureaucratization of social activity that turns all institutions into boundless labyrinths; and the resulting depersonalization of the individual."[26] Kafka's psychological paralysis (his inability to marry and escape oppressive mutual dependencies with his parents), his sense of what the world was moving toward socially and politically, his dedication to his own insomniac version of the Flaubertian religion of writing, and the death sentence of his tuberculosis—all combined to form works of literary art uniquely terrifying in their relevance and yet comically self-effacing.

"The Metamorphosis," one of the few stories Kafka allowed to be published in his lifetime, begins with the deadpan sentence, "As Gregor Samsa awoke one morning from uneasy dreams he found himself transformed in his bed into a gigantic insect."[27] One wonders what "uneasy dreams" could compete with Gregor Samsa's waking reality, which he accepts with patient equanimity. The long story recounts his apologetic self-presentation to his family, *their* gradual transformations into self-sufficient citizens, no longer dependent upon him for their livelihoods, and his acceptance, "with tenderness and love,"[28] of the necessity of his own disappearance. As John Updike points out, Kafka's story resembles "The Death of Ivan Ilych," by Tolstoy, conveying the unspeakable truth that could be anyone's story: "Ivan Ilych's life had been most simple and most ordinary and therefore most terrible."[29] And Updike grasps the significance of Kafka's repugnance at his editor's suggestion that "The Metamorphosis" be illustrated with a drawing of a large insect. The combination of horror and irony that constitutes Kafka's style cannot be rendered visually, but exists only "where language and the mind's hazy wealth of imagery intersect."[30] Kafka illustrates quite well with words the close association of anxiety and despair. As Kierkegaard scholar Gregory Beabout says, "anxiety precedes despair and is the condi-

INSIGHT

tion for the possibility of despair."[31] In Kierkegaard's view, modern spiritless people react to anxiety as a signal to abandon freedom for entrenchment within power schemes. This is self-defeating in that the self will ultimately disappear in an inhuman world. In Kierkegaard's reading, the wiser path would be to follow Socrates, who "raise(s) the poisoned cup,... shuts himself up with it and says to the surgeon when the painful operation is about to begin: Now I am ready. Then anxiety enters into his soul and searches out everything and anxiously torments everything finite and petty out of him, and then it leads him where he wants to go."[32] But when Gregor Samsa awakes to the condition of the self in his time and place, he can only live it out to the bitter end.

Hemingway, one of the most admired stylists of the short story, writes a kind of posttraumatic realism in which the reticence of his characters conveys angst and despair, almost magically. Hemingway does not need to define the violence that his tortured souls have survived or the violence toward which they are moving in order to charge their conversations with implications of life and death. "Hills Like White Elephants" reads like a four-page overheard conversation between a man and a woman waiting at a railway station. The drama underneath their glib banter is unmistakable, like any intimately private argument transpiring in a public space. Yet no third consciousness intervenes, so the conflict moves along to its conclusion. The location of the couple, somewhere between Barcelona and Madrid, is as foreign to the reader as it is to them: the story is written in English with occasional Spanish phrases. And Hemingway uses few dialogue tags so the reader has to practically lean forward to peer into this conversation. The effect created is one of absolute vulnerability and isolation. The man wants the woman to have an abortion, although this word never appears in the story. Indeed no word accurately names any emotion of significance. When the man says, "I'll go with you and stay with you all the time,"[33] he is actually being oblivious to the woman's needs. When the woman says, "Then I'll do it. Because I don't care about me,"[34] she is actually parodying the man's unacknowledged indifference, mirroring it back to him angrily or helplessly. As Charles E. May points out, Hemingway uses the pronoun "it" in a shifting way to point to an underlying gender-based conflict, characterized by masculine logic and reason versus feminine metaphor and simile.[35] The reader sees the story's real issues in the psychological projections of the characters upon the environment. She says that the hills look like white elephants: in the language of alienation, something rare and strange, possibly of religious significance; yet in the language of domestic familiarity, something of dubious value. After the woman begs the man to stop talking—the climax of the story—he looks at their suitcases with "labels on them from all the hotels where they had spent nights."[36] Are their lives, separately and together, transcendent or accidental, significant or trivial? Should their relationship continue or not?

The anxiety at the heart of this story relates to the transition the couple is undergoing. She is pregnant. Things will never be the same again regardless of which decision is made about the abortion. He denies the anxiety of their transition. She faces into it, but feels abandoned. When the man says, "But I don't want anybody but you. I don't want anyone else,"[37] he is referring to the possible birth of a child. But his words clearly say that he fails to grasp her otherness. She *is* "someone else," not simply an extension of his experience. So his words also say that he does not want *her*. Her sense of abandonment is justified. Similarly, the woman's final words have a double meaning. She says, "I feel fine.... There's nothing wrong with me. I feel fine."[38] On one level she is simply indicating her readiness to go on with their train journey. On another, she is expressing her new sense of well-being within the accepted truth, as painful as it is, that he does not love her. Hemingway's style is just as many-layered in its way as that of Henry James. Both writers locate the energy of fiction within the anxiety generated by a penetrating consciousness that looks behind appearances to find what should have been obvious all along to someone "on whom nothing is lost."

Flannery O'Connor, a writer of great influence to this day, boldly reiterated the short story's commitment to psychological apocalypse when she declared herself a Catholic writer in revolt against adultery-in-the-suburbs realism. She was not so much flaunting a parochial temperament as asserting a voice that could cut through what she saw as collusion between contemporary readers and writers. For O'Connor, it is as though readers and their favorite authors enter into conspiracies with each other to deny that there is anything to be afraid of in life. Readers in a consumer culture expected to have their needs met on demand in terms of instant titillation or instant uplift, "mock damnation or mock innocence."39 In other words, anxiety and panic—like religion—are simply unnecessary in the modern world. She wanted to tell her readers, in her words, to "go jump in the lake."40 O'Connor's approach to fiction is consistent with the practice of short story writers examined thus far. She is not concerned with "abstract meaning but experienced meaning,"41 which to her means an attempt to "reveal as much of the mystery of existence as possible."42 And the mystery of existence cannot be experienced without anxiety that often verges on panic. The "almost imperceptible intrusions of grace" in her stories are preceded and followed by violence, which is "the only thing capable of returning [her] characters to reality" and to themselves.43 Mystery is the one thing everyone has in common, she felt, because of the human conditions of mortality and insufficient knowledge. It made communication instead of collusion possible with her audience.

"A Good Man Is Hard To Find" tells the story of a Georgia family who decide to drive to Florida on vacation in spite of newspaper accounts that a dangerous criminal called The Misfit has escaped from federal prison and is headed to that very state. The Grandmother is a Southern Lady who holds her head high in spite of disappointing fortunes, vulgar surroundings, and the general state of the world before, during, and after World War II, for which Europe and Communism are mostly to blame. Unfortunately she gets the family off on a country road where they have an accident and encounter, of course, The Misfit. A man of exquisite manners, he nevertheless has his accomplice take them into the woods and murder them one by one, except for the Grandmother whom he shoots three times in the chest himself. Before doing so, however, he gives her an account of his life with his numerous imprisonments: "I call myself The Misfit ... because I can't make what all I done wrong fit what all I gone through in punishment." He is particularly resentful toward Jesus, who "threw everything off balance."44 There is so much crime in the world and so much punishment, so much random, meaningless suffering: it seems particularly cruel for a savior to hold out hope in such a world. When the Grandmother realizes she is going to die despite her efforts to bribe The Misfit ("Lady, there never was a body that give the undertaker a tip."), she has the hallucinatory insight in a moment of sheer panic that The Misfit is "one of her babies ... one of (her) own children!"[45] She reaches out and touches him on the shoulder, and he shoots her. Her experience of compassion for her killer is the story's "almost imperceptible moment of grace." The violence speaks for itself.

The heirs of O'Connor are fortunately many. One short story renaissance of the late 1970s and 1980s particularly bears her stamp, so-called minimalism or neo-realism, heralded by *Matters of Life and Death* (1983), an anthology compiled by Tobias Wolff. Raymond Carver, an apocalyptic writer of the first order, deserves special mention, while fine writers in this school also include Richard Ford, Bobbie Ann Mason, Ann Beattie, Joy Williams, and many others. What is minimal about minimalism is not so much the narrative compression of its style, after the manner of Hemingway, as the spiritual barrenness of the world of its characters. Minimalism confirms the well-known theory of Frank O'Connor that characters in short stories tend to be members of "submerged population groups"[46] and that the short story's dominant theme is simply loneliness. Whether their lives transpire in the affluent suburbs or in broken down automobiles, minimalist characters inhabit a spiritual wasteland of almost psychotic limitations. Sometimes their anxieties are their only friends. But it is the anxieties of the characters, bordering on revelation, and not the impoverished settings themselves, that minimalist writers explore.

Writers of another school of fiction, including John Barth, Donald Barthelme, and Robert Coover, to name a few, use metafiction to examine language for its role in constructing reality. Their postmodern stories place critical and analytical discourse on the same plane as storytelling, creating cerebral, indeterminate narrative spaces. Life in such stories is irremediably both fact and fiction; it is represented as a disjunctive collage that can never be seen completely as one or the other. I would like to close by discussing a writer who tempers realism with postmodern insights, in effect bridging the gap between them. Grace Paley writes down-to-earth stories that express sympathy for the human condition not so much by posing philosophical questions, as by reminding us that life is not art, nor should we wish it were. Panic, she suggests, lies in the ways we imagine life. If we can find the faith to trust life itself to provide alternatives, we may not have to get trapped in those seductive tragic scenarios that terrify us—those which literature tends to perpetuate. Art can remind us of our human freedom by critiquing, and no longer repeating, the fictional formulae used by authors of the past to represent life.

"The open destiny of life" is exactly, in Kierkegaard's view, what anxiety properly maintains. It is "freedom's possibility." One could even draw a parallel, perhaps, between meta-fiction and anxiety as a meta-emotional state of being. Reading meta-fiction, one soon learns to stop wondering how the story will turn out in favor of wondering what kind of story this narrative is evolving toward or revealing itself to be or to have been all along. Even beyond that, the reader finally understands that the narrative is not evolving at all, but continuously exposing and sometimes debunking the protean forms of fictional consciousness we need in order to imagine life. Similarly, theorists of anxiety tend to distinguish between anxiety and fear.[47] Fear has an identifiable object; anxiety does not. The fearful person knows what he or she is afraid of and reacts accordingly. The terribly anxious or panicky person, on the other hand, experiences a far worse terror. It feels like immanent insanity or death. A person in such a state feels that abstractions of consciousness are useless and regards herself with intense self-consciousness, like a person in a fictional universe in which the terms of being are no longer clear.

Psychoanalysis attempts to configure anxiety within psychic structure; it thus places anxiety or panic beyond the grasp of ordinary consciousness. Freud, equating anxiety with fear, nevertheless describes forms of anxiety that are subjectively bewildering without psychoanalytic hypotheses. For Freud "reality anxiety" is a response to some threat from the external world. But "moral anxiety" represents a threat from the super-ego, and therefore cannot be averted through flight. And worse still, "neurotic anxiety," resulting from threatening impulses from the id, can be avoided only through the formation of symptoms.[48] Otto Rank believed that all anxieties derive from the trauma of birth, an experience obviously inaccessible to consciousness.[49] Although Jung did not formulate a theory of anxiety as such, his views on the ego's relation to the archetypes of the collective unconscious have implications for a general theory of anxiety and for this study of the short story. Jung believed that people are afraid of becoming conscious, usually with good reason. When archetypal contents of the unconscious press toward consciousness, anxiety naturally results.[50] Nevertheless, personal psychological growth—perhaps even survival—requires that awareness be "let in," so to speak. If the anxiety of such an experience is great enough, we call it panic, the domain of Pan.

James Hillman builds upon Jung's idea that the gods of yesterday are very much alive in the psyches of people today, especially in their psychopathology. For Hillman, the study of mythology sometimes surpasses laboratory investigation in illuminating the phenomenology of psychic distress. He puts it boldly: "psychopathology is the enactment of myth."[51] Pan, the goat-footed god of all nature was the beloved of all the gods. He inhabited the uncultivated landscapes of shepherds, and his stories recount his pursuit of nymphs, who are transformed into pine trees, echoes, and shepherds' pipes. In Pan, Hillman sees human behavior that is nature-bound and yet divine in the sense that it is "transcendent to the human yoke of purposes, wholly impersonal, objective, ruthless."[52] In the echoes and flute music of Pan's transformed nymphs, Hillman hears reflection or consciousness in the form of immediate bodily awareness. Pan enacts the "strongest longing of nature": the "union with itself in awareness."[53] Instinct unites with soul and soul with instinct. Reflection removed too far from instinct becomes sterile, but keeping reflection close to fear reminds us "we reflect in order to survive."[54] It is often said that civilization has killed Pan, that it has transformed him and his nymphs into devil and witches, thus accounting for the terror natural experiences such as sex can have for some people. But Hillman suggests that the nightmare aspect of Pan is implicit in his archetypal nature. All know him, inescapably, as part of the destiny of being earthly creatures.

Nadine Gordimer's metaphor for the epiphanies of short stories, "the flash of fireflies," points to an Arcadian eruption of light within nature. The short story is close to Pan's world, partaking of the energies of anxiety, nightmare, and panic. Far all its shocks, gentle and not so gentle, the modern short story is ultimately a comfort and a guide in an age of anxiety, reuniting us with ourselves as simultaneously natural and spiritual beings.

ENDNOTES

1. W.H. Auden, *The Age of Anxiety: A Baroque Ecologue* (New York: Random House, 1947).

2. John Cheever, "Is the Short Story Necessary?" In *Short Story Theories,* edited by Charles E. May (Athens: Ohio University Press, 1976), 94–106.

3. Nadine Gordimer, "The Flash of Fireflies." In *Short Story Theories,* edited by Charles E. May (Athens: Ohio University Press, 1976), 178–81.

4. Robert Browning, "My Last Duchess." In *Literature of the Western World, Volume II,* by Wilkie and Hurt (Upper Saddle River, NJ: Prentice Hall Press, 2001), 983–84.

5. Robert Langbaum, *The Poetry of Experience: The Dramatic Monologue in Modern Literary Tradition* (New York: Random House, 1957), 25.

6. Ibid., 516.

7. Edgar Allan Poe, "The Tell-Tale Heart." In *The Short Story and Its Writer, An Introduction to Short Fiction,* 5th edition, edited by Ann Charters (Boston: Bedford/St. Martin's, 1999), 1151–54.

8. Ibid., "The Importance of the Single Effect in a Prose Tale," 1531–33.

9. Soren Kierkegaard, *The Concept of Anxiety: A Simple Psychologically Orienting Deliberation on the Dogmatic Issue of Hereditary Sin,* edited and translated by Reidar Thomte in collaboration with Albert B. Anderson (Princeton: Princeton University Press, 1980).

10. Paul Tillich, *The Courage to Be* (New Haven: Yale University Press, 1952), 35.

11. Ibid., 190.

12. Rollo May, *The Meaning of Anxiety, revised edition* (New York: W.W. Norton, 1977), 393.

13. Guy de Maupassant, "The Writer's Goal." In *The Short Story and Its Writer, An Introduction to Short Fiction,* 5th edition, 1504.

14. Ibid., 1505.

15. Ibid., "The Necklace," 976.

16. Ibid., 981.

17. Henry James, "The Art of Fiction." In *The Short Story and Its Writer, An Introduction to Short Fiction,* 5th edition, 1485.

18. Ibid., 1485.

19. Ibid.

20. Ibid., "The Beast in the Jungle." In *The Short Story and Its Writer, An Introduction to Short Fiction,* 4th edition, edited by Ann Charters (Boston: Bedford/St. Martin's Press, 1995), 647.

21. Ibid., 672.

22. Harry Stack Sullivan, *Conceptions of Modern Psychiatry* (New York: W.W. Norton, 1953), 21.

23. Eve Kosofsky Sedgwick, "The Beast in the Closet: A Gender Critic Reads James's 'The Beast in the Jungle.'" In *The Short Story and Its Writer, An Introduction to Short Fiction,* 4th edition, 1492.

24. Gustav Janouch, "Kafka's View of 'The Metamorphosis.'" In *The Short Story and Its Writer, An Introduction to Short Fiction,* 5th edition, 1486.

25. Ibid., 1487.

26. Ibid., 1491.

27. Franz Kafka, "The Metamorphosis." In *The Short Story and Its Writer, An Introduction to Short Fiction,* 5th edition, 794.

28. Ibid., 825.

29. Leo Tolstoy, "The Death of Ivan Ilych." In *The Short Story and Its Writer, An Introduction to Short Fiction,* 5th edition, 1285.

30. John Updike, "Kafka and 'The Metamorphosis.'" In *The Short Story and Its Writer, An Introduction to Short Fiction,* 5th edition, 1563.

31. Gregory R. Beabout, *Freedom and Its Misuses: Kierkegaard on Anxiety and Despair* (Milwaukee: Marquette University Press, 1996), 127.

32. Soren Kierkegaard, op. cit., 159.

33. Ernest Hemingway, "Hills Like White Elephants." In *The Short Story and Its Writer, An Introduction to Short Fiction,* 5th edition, 654.

34. Ibid., 655.

35. Charles E. May, *The Short Story: The Reality of Artifice* (London: Twayne Publishers, 1995), 65.

36. Ernest Hemingway, op. cit., 656.

37. Ibid., 656.

38. Ibid.

INSIGHT

39. Robert H. Brinkmeyer, Jr., "Flannery O'Connor and Her Readers." In *The Short Story and Its Writer, An Introduction to Short Fiction,* 5th edition, 1629.

40. Ibid., 1626.

41. Ibid., 1617.

42. Ibid., 1617.

43. Flannery O'Connor, "A Reasonable Use of the Unreasonable." In *The Short Story and Its Writer, An Introduction to Short Fiction,* 5th edition, 1622.

44. Ibid., *"The Fiction Writer & His Country."* In *Mystery and Manners: Occasional Prose,* edited by Sally and Robert Fitzgerald (New York: Farrar, Strauss & Giroux, 1970), 25–35.

45. Ibid.

46. Frank O'Connor, *The Lonely Voice: A Study of the Short Story* (Cleveland: The World Press, 1962), 18.

47. William F. Fischer, *Theories of Anxiety* (New York: Harper & Row, 1959), 165–67.

   Herbert H. Krauss and Beatrice J. Krauss, "Anxiety and the Experience of Time." In *Anxiety and Related Disorders: A Handbook,* edited by Wolman and Stricker (New York: John Wiley & Sons, 1994), 132–57.

   Charles E. May, op. cit., 63.

   Paul Tillich, *The Courage to Be* (New Haven: Yale University Press, 1952), 35.

   Benjamin B. Wolman, "Defining Anxiety." In *Anxiety and Related Disorders: A Handbook,* edited by Wolman and Stricker (New York: John Wiley & Sons, 1994), 3-10.

48. William F. Fischer, op. cit., 140–44.

   Lawrence Josephs, "Psychoanalytic and Related Interpretations." In *Anxiety and Related Disorders: A Handbook,* edited by Wolman and Stricker (New York: John Wiley & Sons, 1994), 12–21.

49. William F. Fischer, op. cit., 140–44.

   Sigmund Freud, *Inhibitions, Symptoms and Anxiety,* translated by Alix Strachey; revised and newly edited by James Strachey (New York: W.W. Norton, 1977), 87.

50. C.G. Jung, *The Structure and Dynamics of the Psyche,* 2nd edition, translated by R. F. C. Hull (Princeton: Princeton University Press, 1975), 131, 133–35.

51. James Hillman, *Pan and the Nightmare,* from the German by A. V. O'Brien, M. D. of *Ephialtes: A Pathological-Mythological Treatist on the Nightmare in Classical Antiquity,* by Wilhelm Heinrich Roscher, together with *An Essay on Pan,* serving as a psychological introduction to Roscher's *Ephialtes* (Zurich: Spring Publications, 1974), xxxvii.

52. Ibid., xix.

53. Ibid., xlix.

54. Ibid., liv.

INSIGHT

KIM NEWMAN

Panic in the Cinema

THE HISTORY OF PANIC IN THE CINEMA began, and perhaps ended, on December 28, 1895, at the Grand Café on the Boulevard des Capucines in Paris, where—after some months of demonstrating their cinematographic projections before learned scientific groups in France—the brothers Louis and Auguste Lumière essentially invented the art, entertainment, and commercial forms of cinema by screening films for members of the public who had paid for their tickets. Though the brothers would eventually invent the fiction film by staging a child's prank with a garden hose in order to capture it on film *(L'Arroseur Arrosé)*, the Grand Café screening was held when filmmakers spoke of *taking* films rather than *making* them, and all the subjects on view were in effect mobile snapshots of the staff leaving the Lumière factory or a couple feeding a baby.

The sensation of the evening, a film whose impact on the medium is still being felt, was *L'arrivée d'un Train,* a snippet shot at the railway station of La Ciotât in which a steam engine thunders up to the platform. The brothers, who famously stated "the cinema is an invention without any future," initially saw moving pictures as simply an extension of still photography, chiefly of scientific and technical interest. They did not consider that the non-scientific, ticket-buying curiosity-seekers of 1895 would have only the vaguest idea of the novelty they had come to see and that the crowds would interpret the soundless, black and white image of a train arriving as an actual thing, and flee in panic on the assumption that the express was about to emerge from the screen and grind the first few rows of seats under its wheels. It was a brief, but genuine terror, repeated

Still from "L'Arrivée d'un Train," 1895. **Louis and Auguste Lumière**

as the Lumières exhibited their films throughout France in the next months; but it was also tinged with excitement, fascination, and wonder. The reaction may well have puzzled the brothers, so focused on the gadgetry of the cinema (their specific advance was the patenting of sprocket-holes) that they had never considered how an uneducated eye (and in 1895, all eyes were uneducated to the movies) would respond to their projections. The next great advance in the medium came from the brothers' French contemporary, Georges Méliès, a stage magician whose initial experiments were in Lumière-like documentary fragments but who soon hit upon the idea of trading in the astonishment factor of the medium by using the cinema to create illusions—the transformation of a Moulin Rouge dancer into a skeleton or his own head swelling until it exploded.

By then, mere months after the dawn of cinema, the scramble for the exits had stopped, and that first shock would never be recaptured, not even by such 1950s crazes as 3-D ("a lion in your lap!")

or Cinerama ("you see it without special glasses!"), though the gimmicks of showmeister William Castle for his flamboyant horror films came close. At the climax of *The House on Haunted Hill* (1958), a living skeleton arises from an acid bath on screen, and - thanks to the miracle of *emergo*—a glowing fake skeleton is supposed to be winched across the heads of the audience. In *The Tingler* (1959), a rubber lobster monster gets loose in a cinema, and Vincent Price addresses the on-screen and actual audiences with an exhortation to scream for their lives (the noise incapacitates the creature). An alternate version was prepared for drive-in theatres, as in selected cinemas during the first run, a vibrating device *(percepto)* under some chairs in the audience gave patrons genuine tingles.

The horror movies of the 1950s and 60s often staged scenes like this, even without the gimmicks, in which audiences were exposed to the spectacle of audiences like themselves being assaulted by a monster—like the creeping red jelly that invades a cinema in *The Blob* (1958), or the sniper who picks off drive-in patrons at the end of *Targets* (1968). In every case, we have a reprise of the scenes of 1895, as we see patrons rapt by the on-screen spectacle they are enjoying—the silent *Tol'able David* (1921) in *The Tingler,* the obscure *Daughter of Horror* (1955) in *The Blob,* the Karloff vehicle *The Terror* (1963) in *Targets*—while we are aware of the danger to them. Then, the terror strikes and we get shots of screaming women, men trampling each other to get to the exits, spilled popcorn, patrons dying and, most terrifying of all, the burning or interruption of the film on-screen (the monsters *always* get the projectionist first). Joe Dante's winning *Matinee* (1992), set during a Florida screening of a William Castle-like gimmicked monster movie *(Mant!)* during the Cuban missile crisis, winds up with an *atomo-vision* effect that convinces the audience that World War III has started and that they're seeing a mushroom cloud rising through the shattered cinema screen. Here, the panic is shown to be a good thing—not just part of the fun of a horror movie, but in narrative terms, since it makes most of the audience flee just before the unsound balcony collapses.

Gimmick merchants without the budget to rig up emergo, skeletons, or percepto seat-buzzers resorted to a far cheaper, and arguably more effective—depending on the enthusiasm of any given cinema staff—method also parodied in *Matinee*, of pausing the film at a strategic moment to send monster-costumed ushers into the auditorium to menace, harass, or assault random patrons. The archetype of this is Ray Dennis Steckler's remarkable *The Incredibly Strange Creatures Who Stopped Living and Became Mixed-Up Zombies!!?* (1963)—on its initial run, the committed director-star dressed up in his own zombie costume and ran out among the audience himself. This was a risky venture in some venues; anyone whose reaction to Castle's glowing skeleton was to reach for a zip-gun had few qualms about roughing up a guy in a monster suit. Far more obscure is the short *Monsters Crash Pajama Party* (1964), which was often seen—like Méliès's films—as part of a vaudeville-style evening of entertainment, especially around Halloween, with sinister magicians and costumed terrorizers. Here, as in the early cinema, film content meant very little, as the cinematographic equipment was just one of a variety of trick devices in use, creating an attraction more akin to a ghost train ride than a scary movie.

Regular horror movies often depict panic but rarely try to cause it. Think of the citizenry fleeing Godzilla in numerous Japanese monster movies or the many heroines reduced to quivering wrecks in nightmare movies—Judith O'Dea in *Night of the Living Dead* (1968), Marilyn Burns in *The Texas Chain Saw Massacre* (1973), Jamie Lee Curtis in *Halloween* (1978), Heather Donoghue in *The Blair Witch Project* (1999). In theory, patrons have already paid for their seats and so there's no financial loss if they run screaming from the cinema, but in practice filmmakers want them at least to sit still, even if frozen in terror, until the end credits. In *Boogie Nights* (1996), porno director Jack Horner (Burt Reynolds) muses that he wants to make films so compelling that his ideal masturbating patron will stay in the theatre after he has come to see how the story plays out; William Castle, and all his successors in the fright business, feel the same way, accepting the tiny percentage of walk-outs from people who somehow didn't expect something called *The Texas Chain Saw Massacre* to be so upsetting, as an indication that they're more or less doing their job. If a screen comedy can't be too funny or a porno movie too arousing, then it follows that a screen horror can't be too frightening—though, in all cases, the limits of physiological response to external stimulation might perhaps be a factor in determining how far a film should go.

Though effective screen horror depends on identification—we *feel* for the heroines cited above or such rare male equivalents as Bruce Campbell in the *Evil Dead* films—there is also a distance: what we see can't hurt us. Even if and when interactive virtual reality technology allows us to star in our own versions of *The Hills Have Eyes* (1977) or *A Nightmare on Elm Street* (1984), there is likely to be only the slimmest market for hardcore versions in

which we feel the pain or risk the loss of life and limb suffered by our on-screen avatars. The terror-in-the-cinema films manage to be subtly more disturbing than the average horror film because they play a sneakier game—in *The Blob* and *The Tingler*, we seem to be in the usual horror business, with characters we like and identify with or dislike and want to see suffer (*The Tingler*, apart from everything else, is an unusually nasty movie in that the supposed hero and heroine are almost invisible and everyone else is murderously horrid). When we get to the scenes in cinemas, our usual identification process shifts—suddenly, we're not playing at being Steve McQueen or Vincent Price because we have a far closer on-screen equivalent, the mass of extras playing an audience much like the one we're a part of. Suddenly, we're more deeply implicated in the spectacle and seem more liable to suffer the consequences. That's *us* up there getting killed.

Peter Bogdanovich's *Targets* is a sophisticated analysis of the horror film and its relationship with real-life horror, making all manner of parallels and oppositions between old-time monster star Boris Karloff and a Charles Whitman-like sniper, but most of these films are just out to *get* us. William Castle titled his autobiography *Step Right Up: or: How I Scared the Pants Off America*, and that's what these various violations of the barrier between the movie and us are all about. Later, more intricately referential films like

Lamberto Bava's *Demons* (1985) and Bigas Luna's *Anguish* (1987) take the *Monsters Crash Pajama Party* aesthetic more literally. In *Demons,* the monsters from a horror movie explode out of the screen during a midnight premiere and possess or murder audience members, eventually taking over the whole city; while the insanely-intricate Quaker Oats box-top model horror *Anguish* has a mad slasher in a cinema picking off patrons who are watching a horror movie *(The Mommy)* in which a more flamboyant madman eventually goes to a cinema and kills people watching the silent version of *The Lost World* (1925). After that, the cinema opening of *Scary Movie 2* (1999) seems simplistic.

The cinema can still cause panic, especially on first exposure. An anecdote from my own childhood: my first experience with the cinema came at the age of five, when my parents took me and my three-year-old sister Sasha to see *The First Men in the Moon* (1964). After a few minutes, I had discovered what would eventually become a lifelong set of interests in the medium, several genres (science fiction, horror, steampunk, literary adaptation, social satire), and some key creative participants (H.G. Wells, Nigel Kneale, Ray Harryhausen); my sister, however, was terrified to the point of throwing a tantrum that forced my parents to leave the cinema, which prompted me to a display of sulky resentment that forced them to take me back a few nights later (without Sasha) to see the whole program—which also included the forgotten B movie, *A Twist of Sand* (1963). It is important to understand that my sister was not driven to a panic by anything specific to *The First Men in the Moon* like a monster on screen (we had to leave before the space travelers reached the moon), but to the whole *experience* of cinema: the big dark space of the auditorium, the press of a crowd of strangers, the shock of looking at what seemed a colored window into another world, the break from routine of being in an unfamiliar place, the stress of a young family tackling the business of *going out.* I remember that, as was common then, we arrived in the middle of the program and so did not go through the airlock-like experience of sitting in the cinema as the lights went down—it was a sudden immersion effect.

Talking about this incident, I learned that my sister's initial reaction to the movies was not uncommon. Both my parents

The Panic Bird
Myra Schneider

That moment
when the mattress splits
and seeps its stuffing
when floors crack, roads
break up, ground gapes

that moment
when the breathstream
dries, the belly ceases
to exist and the self
can no longer hold on

that moment
when reason bolts
and six obsessive words
pound pound on the shell
of the emptied brain

is the moment
the wingspan spreads.
The predator descends,
traps hair, neck—
I am eclipsed.

I try to yell
for someone to put out
the rock-blue eyes,
smash the razor beak,
crush the claws,

Only a child
looms. Weightless as a leaf
she's crouched on a mountain ledge
whimpering: 'I can't bear
blood, illness, change.'

I want to
take her in my arms, struggle
to a safe place, outstare
the bird, seize it by the neck
pull the gaudy feathers.

I want to
call out, voice belled
by fierce red joy, to alight,
toes touching waterbird
rings on lake calm.

* * *

remember similar experiences with their own first experiences of going to the pictures, which frightened them so much that they made their parents take them out of the cinema: my father citing *Hound of the Baskervilles* (1939) and my mother an early 1940s Tarzan film. The story varies as to how much of the film they saw before reaching panic and as to whether there was a specific on-screen trigger (my mother remembers an unspecified violent incident upsetting her) for the tantrum. But three members of my close family all reacted on first exposure to the movies in exactly the way that the more impressionable patrons of the Grand Café in 1895 did. It may be that this is no longer likely: children of the early 2000s will certainly have experienced a lot of moving pictures on television or computer screens before their first visit to the cinema (a semi-ceremonial communion with the mediated spirit of Walt Disney, most likely). More than earlier generations, they are innoculated to the effect of cinema. Having learned a visual language analagous to the movies exactly as they have learned a spoken language, and (thanks to video, DVD, remote controls, channel-changers, etc.) having taken for granted their *control* over visual media (though today's children may be disturbed to find that they cannot pause, replay, or turn off a film in a cinema).

The current direction of new technology in the cinema and related media is toward so-called "interactivity," which essentially gives the viewer—an individual, rather than a collective audience—more control over what she sees and hears. This should make the experience *safer,* less panic-inducing, than *L'arrivée d'un Train* in 1895, *The Tingler* in 1959, or *The First Men in the Moon* in 1964. But it is possible that complete safety will mean complete tedium (paradoxically, we become more involved in play but less likely to be affected). Giving an audience control may be seen as a cop-out by patrons who want to be told a story rather than forced to make up their own. We may demand *more* panic, and want our films to turn round and bite us again.

DEVON HINTON

Munch, Agoraphobia, and the Terrors of the Modernizing Urban Landscape

Munch, the Symbolist

EDVARD MUNCH was born in Christiana (now Oslo), Norway in 1863. 1889 to 1892 marked marked the transition from Impressionist to Symbolist expression in Europe.[1] Munch followed this trend with his art, playing a vital role in the development of German expressionism as well. He is most famous for his portrayal of psychological and emotional themes, many painful and morose. He lived for years in France and Germany, but always returned to Norway. Later in life he began to take an interest in nature, finding a way to express his intense emotion through landscapes. Munch died peacefully in 1944 in his beloved homeland.

> For Munch nature became a metaphor for interior emotions, and the landscape came to symbolize a state of mind.... Munch's figural landscapes became metaphors for his emotionally charged subjects: anxiety, despair, melancholy. His boldly expressive brushstrokes projected his own inner turmoil as much upon nature's elements as upon the figures that inhabit his landscapes.[2]

One contemporary commentator remarked of Munch's symbolist works:

> It follows that nature and the motif cannot resemble nature, because this or that changes according to mood. He is not a "mood painter" but a "painter of mood."[3]

A key image in the founding of the symbolist agenda was Gauguin's *Jacob's Struggle with the Angel* (1888).[4] In the painting, Gauguin depicts various women attentively listening to a preacher

INSIGHT

sermonizing; and, additionally, in the center of the canvas, he paints the woman's mental imagining of Jacob's battle. Going yet one step further, Munch emphasized the sensory experience—not only the mental visual imagery—of the viewer. Thus, in certain of Munch's canvases, as in *The Scream,* we see what the experiencer views (a precipice and a bridge), the experiencer (the central figure in *The Scream*), the experiencer's emotional state (a figure covering the ears to avoid sound and a frightened face), and how the experiencer feels in the body and through the senses, represented through the use of symbolist methods (the legs in an "s" shape conveying the central figure's sense of instability, and the swirls in the sky showing how, in a state of vertigo, the central figure sensorially experiences his surroundings).[5]

Munch's Childhood and Youth: A Predisposition to Panic

Munch's mother died of tuberculosis when he was five years of age; he had to watch his mother spit forth blood, grow paler and weaker, and slowly asphyxiate. Several of his paintings depict the anguish of that death *(The Dead Mother and the Child, The Death Chamber, Death in the Sickroom).* After the death of his beloved mother, Munch could not always find solace from his father:

> … father had a difficult temper, inherited nervousness with periods of religious anxiety which could reach the borders of insanity as he paced back and forth in his room praying to God. When anxiety did not possess him, he could be like a child and joke and play with us…. When he punished us … he could be almost insane in his violence.[6]

At age thirteen, Munch himself coughed up blood, announcing the onset of a tubercular condition and instilling the fear of death in him all over again. Munch describes the experience in the following way:

> Daddy it is so dark the stuff I am spitting—
> It is my boy—
> He took the light and looked at it—

I saw he was hiding something—
The next time he spit on the sheet and he saw it was
    blood—
It is bloody Daddy—
He stroked my head—don't be afraid my boy
I was going to die from consumption—he had heard so
    much about it that when one spits blood then one got
    consumption—
I am walking to you—his heart beat—
He crawled out to his father if to seek protection—
Don't be afraid my body said the father once more—
His voice was choking with tears—
When you spit blood then you get consumption said
    Karl—
He coughed again and more blood came up—
Turn yourself to the Lord my boy
Then his father put his hand on his head—and I shall
Bless you my boy—
The Lord bless you—may the Lord let His face shine
    upon you—
May the Lord give you peace—
During the day he had to lay still—not talk—
He stared quietly into space—He knew one could live
    several
Years with consumption—But he couldn't run down on
    the street—couldn't play "Einar Tambarskjaelve"
    with Thoralf—Toward evening he had a higher
    temperature—and more coughing—Then he got a
    mouthful of blood which he spit into the
    handkerchief—it became dark red in color—he held
    it up in front of him and looked at it—look father and
    he showed it to his sister—
She rushed terrified and brought back the aunt—
There is more coming—they shouted for the doctor—
He ordered ice "don't be afraid boy".
But he was afraid.7

A year later, when Munch was fourteen, his sister came down
with the same symptoms; she would soon die of tuberculosis just

like their mother. Munch watched as Sophie periodically spat up blood, grew physically weaker, and ultimately asphyxiated.

At the end of the nineteenth century, tuberculosis and mental illness were considered hereditary, some families said to experience a progressive deterioration. Summing up his childhood, Munch states:

> I inherited two of humanity's most dreaded enemies—consumption and mental illness. Sickness, madness and death were the black angels that surrounded my crib.
>
> My mother died prematurely—from her I inherited the seeds of consumption. My father was obsessively nervous and obsessively religious—to the point of madness. This had been the fate of his family for generations. From him I inherited the seeds of madness.
>
> The angels of fear—sorrow and death—had stood by my side since the day I was born. They followed me when I played—followed me everywhere. Followed me in the spring sun and the glory of summer.
>
> They stood by my side at bedtime when I shut my eyes—they threatened me with death, hell and eternal damnation.
>
> Often I awoke in the middle of the night—I gazed around the room in wild fear—was I in Hell?
>
> Illness was a constant factor all through my childhood and youth. The tuberculosis bacteria turned my white handkerchief into its victorious, blood-red banner. The members of my dear family died, one after another.
>
> I remember one Christmas Eve when I was thirteen years old. I was lying in bed—blood trickling from my mouth—fever raging in my body—fear seething inside me.
>
> I believed that the moment had come for me to be judged—and that I would be condemned to eternity.
>
> He was saved—but his entire youth was worm-eaten. He was tormented by doubt—fear and illness.
>
> He was almost alone in life—his vitality was broken. He had accustomed himself to the idea that he was unsuited to marriage. That it would be wrong of him to start a family—his children would certainly inherit the same seeds of ill-

ness. Should they follow his footsteps and experience the same terrible childhood and youth?[8]

Research demonstrates that illness experiences may set the stage for later panic. Such a panic predisposition may result from either observed or experienced illness.[9] A strong panic predisposition ensues from illnesses that cause fear of symptoms that were present during a panic attack. For example, respiratory illness in childhood is associated with suffering from panic later in life.[10] Those later panic attacks were seemingly focused upon—and triggered by—feelings of shortness of breath.[11] Research also reveals that suffering the death of a parent before the age of seventeen strongly predisposes to agoraphobia and panic;[12] Munch lost not only his mother at an early age but also his sister. Hence, according to recent psychological research, Munch's childhood traumas—observing the slow death by asphyxiation of his mother and sister, and his own serious illness as a child—would predispose him to later experience panic.

From Impressionism to Symbolism and The Scream and Anxiety

The Sick Child (1885–1886)

One of Munch's most well-known images, *The Sick Child,* depicts his sister's illness; in the picture, the pale sister lies reclined against a large white pillow. On the table beside her we see a glass of a bright red color containing the scarlet blood she continually coughed forth, draining her body, bringing a ghostly pallor. This painting was Munch's first great symbolist work. Munch recreated a key aspect of his embodied viewing of that very moment of his sister's illness—the vertical lines created by his cast-down eyelids portray his own melancholy, tearful view of the scene:

> I tried numerous times to recreate the first impression—the transparent pale skin against the canvas—the trembling mouth—the trembling hands ... I scraped about half, but I left some paint. I thus discovered that my eyelashes took

part in my first impression. I suggested them as shadows on the painting.[13]

Rue Lafayette (1891) and Rue Rivoli (1891)

Munch traveled to Paris in 1885. From 1889 to 1892 Munch lived in France, returning home for the summers to Oslo. During this period he was strongly influenced by French painters, first the Impressionists, and then the post-impressionists. In 1882, Munch's close friend Werenskiold had published an article attempting to articulate the main principles of the new art form called Impressionism: "when a wheel turns, each spoke is not depicted, rather it is indicated, trying to render a sense of vibration, blurriness, fugacity, that is to say, all that which is characteristic of movement."[14] Munch considered the depiction of movement to be a key aspect of his art, an art he called *modern:* "for realism it was the façade that counted, for Impressionism the character. Now it is the shadows and movements ..." [15] Werenskiold's article articulated the impressionist motif that depicted the busy boulevards viewed from balconies, as seen in Caillebotte's many images. In a new version of one of Caillebotte's balcony scenes, Munch tried to go beyond what Werenskiold laid out and detail the intricate motion of movement and speed.[16] "Munch continued this tradition, but while the previous painters had, like a photograph, transformed the urban motion into frozen still-life, Munch retained the city's visual life."[17] Munch's portrayal of motion can be seen by comparing two paintings, *Rue de Rivoli* and *Rue Lafayette* with Caillebotte's rendering of a balcony viewing. Heller comments that Munch's *Rue Lafayette* combines Caillebotte's balcony image with the strong sense of a rushing of traffic, using in particular the technique of blurring the images of carts and horses in order to convey a sense of linear speed, just as the newly invented camera, having slow shutter speeds, caused a moving object to blur.[18]

Completed before Munch returned to Norway on May 29th, ... [*Rue Lafayette*] demonstrates other impressions he received of contemporary French painting and his ability to adapt its techniques to his own purposes. The broken, blurring brushstrokes of the painting derive directly from the numerous neo-impressionists works displayed at the Independents by Seurat and his followers, but Munch used pointillist technique not to gain greater luminosity or color harmony, but rather to lend the scene the subjective impression of the speed and motion proper to a city street. The moving blurs of horse-drawn carriages and taxis, the rushing movement of crowds of people ... perspective line of the balcony railing, and the single isolated stable figure of the man leaning on the railing acting as a contrast and accent to the movement in the street: all devices and elements of the composition serve the single purpose of rendering the mobile life of the modern city.[19]

The image was painted when Munch rented a room at 49 *Rue Lafeyette* in Paris. "Its structure, with the balcony railing in perspective and the figure of the observer, prefigures the layout of works like *The Scream* and *Despair.*"[20]

Evening on Karl Johan Street (1893–1894)

Munch experienced agoraphobia, noticeably in his fear of crowds, throughout his life.[21] The first documented episode of Munch's agoraphobia transpired during the time of his break-up with Mrs. Heidberg. In 1885, Munch fell in love with a married woman after his return from a three-week stay in France; she soon left him and went on to have other lovers, causing him great anguish. Munch would consider this one of the most painful experiences of life, the trauma of the separation resulting in the creation of his later angst-full art.[22] Munch wrote in his diary of walking on Johan Street (the main avenue in Oslo, a broad Parisian-type Boulevard, along which large numbers of people strolled), hoping to meet Mrs. Heidberg, and then, his great anxiety as she passed by him.

> At the University clock, he turned around and crossed the street, intently looking ahead.—There she comes.—He felt something like an electric shock pass through him.
> —How much like her this one looked from the distance.—
> ... And then finally she came. He felt long before that she had to come ... He saw only her pale, slightly plump face,

horribly pale in the yellow reflections from the horizon and against the blue [sky] behind her.

Never before had he seen her so beautiful. How lovely was the bearing of her head, a bit sorrowful.

She greeted him with a weak smile and went on ... He felt so empty and so alone. Why did he not stop her and tell her she was the only one—that he deserved no love, that he never appreciated her enough, that everything was his fault. She looked so sad. Perhaps she is unhappy. Maybe she is the one who believes that he does not care for her, and that it was his own fault. What a spineless wretch you are, a yellow coward, a yellow yellow yellow yellow coward.

He worked himself into a frenzy. Suddenly everything seemed strangely quiet. The noise from the street seemed far away, as if coming from somewhere above. He no longer felt his legs. They no longer wanted to carry him.

All the people passing by looked so strange and odd, and he felt as if they were all staring at him, all these faces pale in the evening light.[23]

Munch writes of his feelings as Mrs. Heidberg did not stop but continued walking on:

Everyone who passed looked at him, stared at him, all those faces, pallid in the evening light. He tried to concentrate on some thought, but he could not. All he felt was emptiness in his head ... His whole body trembled, and sweat ran down him. He staggered, and I am falling too. People stop, more and more people, a frightening number of people.[24]

Elsewhere he emphasized that the faces of the approaching persons caused him fear, skull-like images announcing the inevitability of death: "I saw all the people behind their masks—smiling, phlegmatic—composed faces—I saw them through them and there was suffering—in them all—pale corpses—who without rest ran around—along a twisted road—at the end of which was the grave."[25]

As described by these diary entries, Munch began to suffer multiple panic attack symptoms, constituting full-blown panic attacks:[26] fear, derealization (all seems strange), a fear of insanity (an inability to keep his mind on one thought, resorting to just looking at a window to try and maintain his grip on reality), faintness (a sense of his legs giving way), sweating, and trembling. This image and the others were painted when he was experiencing agoraphobic fears in the metropolis of Paris and Berlin, both cities where he lived and painted.[27] The image's emotionality combines his original street panic with his later agoraphobic experiences in the bustling metropolitan cities of Paris and Berlin.

In *Evening on Karl Johan Street,* the oncoming figures are cut off at the bust or waist to give an unsettling effect of nearness which emotionally involves the viewer (note that this is how a walker visually experiences the scene);[28] by choosing his angle of vision so as to crop the people walking along the pavement at waist or chest height, Munch gives us a sense of the crowd's oppressive proximity.[29] This cropping of bodies, creating a sense of rush, was a new pictorial device that came into great fashion with the Impressionists, used to render a sense of excitement. In Munch's image, however, the effect is one of discomforting proximity, dizzying confusion, and excessive speed.[30] Additionally, multiple parallel lines that rapidly recede give a sense of a chaotic rush: the line of buildings to the right, the line of persons, and the lines of the road and opposite sidewalk. The oncoming crowd seems to pour down on the viewer, an asphyxiating and imposing avalanche of people.

And there is an extreme emphasis on circles—seemingly profusive, an art nouveau turned sinister: round hat brims, cylindri-

INSIGHT

"Anxiety [*Angst*] has an unmistakable relation to *expectation*; it is anxiety *about* something. It has a quality of *indefiniteness and lack of object.* In precise speech we use the word 'fear' [*Furcht*] rather than 'anxiety' if it has found an object. Moreover, in addition to its relation to danger, anxiety has a relation to neurosis we have long been trying to elucidate. The question arises: why are not all reactions of anxiety neurotic—why do we accept so many of them as normal? And finally the problem of the difference between realistic anxiety and neurotic anxiety awaits a thorough examination.

The advance we have made is that we have gone behind reactions of anxiety to situations of danger. If we do the same thing with realistic anxiety we shall have no difficulty in solving the question. Real danger is a danger that is known, and realistic anxiety is anxiety about a known danger of this sort. Neurotic anxiety is anxiety about unknown danger. Neurotic danger is thus a danger that has still to be discovered. Analysis has shown that it is an instinctual danger. By bringing this danger which is not known to the ego into consciousness, the analyst makes neurotic anxiety no different from realistic anxiety, so that it can be dealt with in the same way."

—Sigmund Freud, *Inhibitions, Symptoms and Anxiety*

cal hats, circular hat tops, tubular ribbons tied at the top of the hats; ring-shaped eyes; spherical pupils; semi-circles for eyebrows; circles for nostrils; everything is depicted by round curves—the noses, the faces, the necks, the shoulders, and even the great mass to the right of the picture.[31] The multiple oncoming circles combined with the sense of the onrush of the crowd and a feeling of oppressive proximity induce a sense of dizziness and vertigo. In *The Scream,* the various swirling lines work to induce a state of vertigo, and in *Anxiety* the same onslaught of circles draws the viewer into a state of discomfort.[32]

Munch brilliantly captures a key aspect of the psychological experiencing of the modern cityscape in *Evening on Karl Johan Street*—the contradictions between physical proximity and psychological remoteness in an urban environment.[33] Torjusen[34] states of *Evening on Karl Johan Street:* "The contrast between the crowd of people and the lonely individual is important in both the text and the image." The figure seen from the back, walking against the flow and ignored by all, represents a state of loneliness and isolation.[35] The figure against a cold blue background, hunched over, seems to stagger forward—compare this lone walker's bent posture to the upright stance of the approaching figures. The figure recalls Westphal's description of the agoraphobic's fear of open city spaces.[36]

Thus, several dimensions of the terror of the cityscape are depicted: a dizzying onrush of persons, a bouncing, oncoming torrent of round objects, loneliness (a sort of lightness and cold), and anonymity. Through symbolist technique and compositional choice, Munch pictorially represents not only the smothering closeness but also loneliness, isolation, and alienation.

Despair (1892)

Munch spent time in Nice, often without food or money or friends. The death of his father in 1889 had a deeply disturbing effect.[37] Too, Munch continued to remember his broken relationship with Mrs. Heidberg with bitterness and obsessively revisited his feelings for her.

> I met a worldly-wise woman, and she was responsible for
> my baptism by fire. Through her I came to know the heated

misfortunes of love—and for several years I was almost mad. That was when the fearful, grimacing mask of madness appeared.

You are acquainted with my painting *The Scream?* I was at the end of my tether—completely exhausted. Nature screamed through my veins—I was falling apart....[38]

While in Nice, Munch wrote: "I live with the dead and every memory, event, the most insignificant one, comes back to me.... As my only friend, I have the fire in the fireplace."[39] During the time he painted *Despair,* Munch compulsively gambled in Monte Carlo, taking a three-hour train ride back and forth almost daily— he called this period a *hell.*[40] In 1892, on return from France for short sojourn in Oslo, Munch witnessed a bright red sunset while walking along a bridge overlooking a fjord. He recorded his moment of intense anxiety:

One evening I walk down a hillside path near Kristiana [Oslo]—together with two comrades. It was a time during which life had ripped open my soul. The sun went down. The sea dipped quickly under the horizon. It was if a flaming sword of blood cut open the firmament. The air turned to blood—with cutting veins of flame. The hillsides became a deep blue. The fjord—cut in a cold blue—amongst yellow and red colors. That shrill, blood red. On the road and the fence. The faces of my comrades became a garish yellow-white. I felt a huge scream welling up inside me—and I really did hear a huge scream. The colors in nature—broke the lines in nature. The lines and colors quivered with movement. These vibrations of light caused not only the oscillations of my eyes. My ears were also affected and began to vibrate. So I actually heard a scream.

I was walking along the road with two friends—then the sun set. The heavens suddenly turned a bloody red and I felt a shiver of sadness. A clutching pain in my chest. I stopped— leaned against the fence, for I was deathly tired. Over the blue-black fjord and town lay blood in tongues of flame. My friends continued walking—and I was left trembling in fear. And I felt a huge endless scream course through nature.

It felt as if a scream was coursing through nature—I seemed to hear a scream.[41]

Munch clearly experienced a panic attack on that bridge overlooking the fjord. As his revelation clearly express, Munch saw the heavens turn an intense red color;[42] next, as the sun set, a cold descended at the passing of the last rays of light, and he felt a shiver of sadness, a sort of simultaneous chill and dysphoria. Munch also endured a pain in his chest. Unable to walk, unsteady on his feet, he leaned against a fence. Next, feeling afraid, he began to tremble, and subsequently, seemingly at the height of anxiety, a buzzing in his ears created the sensation of screaming. Munch's symptoms included the typical DSM-IV symptoms:[43] chest pain, trembling, fear of insanity, dizziness ("oscillations of the eyes"), and faintness. Other symptoms experienced in his attack are also typical of panic attacks: blurry vision, tinnitus, wobbly legs, and a sense of fatigue.[44] Munch mentions hearing a sound like a scream. Often, in panic attacks, patients experience tinnitus, a ringing in the ears. This aural perception then serves as a sort of Rorschach. Cambodians frequently endure tinnitus during panic attacks,[45] said to be due to "wind shooting out the ear," comparing the sound to the lugubrious song of a cicada or an insect—or now, in a more modern image, to the bruit of an idling car engine.[46]

But what would cause Munch to experience the tinnitus as a "scream?" Were there cultural precedents? There were. For one, while working on *The Scream,* Munch help edit a journal called *Pan;*[47] Munch was no doubt aware of the origin of the word "panic:" according to Greek legend, the god Pan would periodically surprise wanderers with a scream, causing them to have a feeling of terror, of "panic." In his diaries, written while ill with rheumatic fever in Nice, and before he created *Despair,* Munch wrote of an unending scream pervading nature,[48] the phrase most likely a loose quotation from a Heinrich Heine's *Twilight of the Gods* (1888)—"the great scream running through nature"—Munch inscribing the title of Heine's book on one of the versions of *The Scream.*[49]

But what triggered Munch's panic on the bridge overlooking the Oslo fjord? The reddening sky, a sunset, would evoke many experiences for Munch. Red is the first sign of tuberculosis: the scarlet streak of blood viewed on a handkerchief, the red clot in the glass at the bedside, the heralding of death. One of the main traumas for Munch was the death of his mother when he was just five. Munch would take walks with his mother along a bridge overlooking an Oslo fjord, a location like that depicted in *Despair;*[50] she would have been coughing red blood, her face pale, walking slowly and out of breath. A red sunset evokes an earthly existence of hell; Munch greatly feared burning in sulfurous flames, his father a highly religious man; Munch drew himself once, naked, surrounded by red and orange flames (*Self-Portrait in Hell,* 1902). Also, the drop off at the side of the bridge, a vast void, and the linear hurtling perspective of the railing and road, would create a sense of dizziness; and adding to this vertigo-inducing effect, the round shape of the lake, the undulation of the sky and horizon, and the ships rocking on the distant sea. As Munch slumps to the rail to brace himself, his friends walk on, leaving him behind. He stops a second, frightened; then the others, unaware of his state, move forward. Munch is left alone, heightening the impression of abandonment and isolation, intensifying his state of terror. This sense of abandonment would resonate throughout his life: the death of his mother, sister, the separation from Mrs. Heidberg, and the recent death of his father. Lastly, the oncoming of night—the descending chill as the sun sets—symbolizes death.

The Scream (1895)

In *The Scream,* Munch tries to express the same experience depicted in *Despair* through the utilization of Symbolist means.

Rosenbaum places *The Scream* in the context of the late nineteenth-century art, of the speed and chaos of the rapidly modernizing world.

> In at least one case, the *Rue Lafayette* of 1891, Munch painted, as Kirk Varnedoe has shown, what is virtually a reprise of vertiginous balcony view by Caillebotte. And given such clues, it becomes easier to understand how decisive for Munch was this new pictorial image of modern, Haussmannized Paris, in which regimented city boulevards, stretching infinitely from near to far, tilt up and down at angles of breathtaking velocity; in which large foreground

"The Scream," 1895.
Edvard Munch

figures abruptly clash with glimpses of tiny pedestrians at a distant crossing; in which anonymous faces suddenly loom past us as in a phantom promenade. Looking at Munch's successive interpretation of Oslo's main thoroughfare, Karl Johan Street—first on a spring day in 1891 and then, in the following year, during an evening walk (cat. No. 28)—makes us realize how he used the human and spatial premises of Parisian urban images of the 1870s as the foundation for his rapid shift from the external to the internal world of the modern city-dweller. The funneling perspective of lines of an urban axis suddenly move, as they threaten to do in Caillebotte's painting, from reason to feeling, from the measurement of city spaces to a suicidal plunge; and the anonymous pedestrians constantly encountered singly, in pairs, or in crowds in the city streets are swiftly transformed into the immediate terror of a confrontation with skull-like, menacing faces in the foreground or the potential terror on an encounter with tiny, shadowy figures lurking in the remote distance. Pressing further Caillebotte's images of the new rectilinear facts of Paris city-planning and the new human facts of crowds of strolling, middle-class strangers, Munch turned these urban truths of the late nineteenth century into a private nightmare that accelerated dizzyingly in *The Scream* (1893; cat. No. 29) and *Anxiety* (1894; cat, no. 34). To be sure, this rush from the brink of objectivity to the depths of private fear had to be the product of Munch's personal turmoil and, as such, inaugurates a new world of psychological responses to the city, from the feverish pitch of swarming crowds and agitated spaces in Kirchner's Berlin scenes to the paralyzing strangeness of distant cast shadows and irrationally inverted perspective systems in de Chirico's dreamlike resurrection of Italian Renaissance city spaces. Yet it should not be forgotten that Munch's art, in turn, turns backward to Parisian urban painting of the 1870s, where that tension between the individual and the modern city was first defined.[51]

Linear elements are prominent in *The Scream*. The three courses of the railing shoot into the distance, each slat actually forming two diagonals, which are the sunlit top and the side in shadow. The three railing slats converge together rapidly, creating the perspective of extensiveness and expanse, a trainlike speed of motion. And the many lines in the surface of the bridge move in parallel with the rails. Amplifying the sense of directionality, the figures plunge into the depths,[52] down a downward slope. As an art critic comments on the sense of rush created in the *The Scream*:

Caillebotte used rapidly receding orthogonals to suggest the rush, speed, exhilaration—but also alienation—of modern life. Munch pushes this point further. The near vertigo-inducing diagonals collapse onto the figures, creating a feeling of claustrophobia commensurate with the subject.[53]

In *The Scream,* as yet another device to create a sense of rushing speed, Munch juxtaposed the looming central figure with the small figures of the two friends walking away,[54] creating the optical illusion of a great distance traversed in a short time.

The two men mark a harsh vertical end to the intensified rush of the street and the railing into depth, a movement which now begins at the lower right of the painting, not modified by the stable mass of the man's figure as in the previous painting [*Despair*]. The dizzying perspective generation of space and movement in straight lines ...[55]

Another commentator remarks: "The bridge and railing, instead, are indicated with straight lines in perspectives which penetrate the landscape, leading the eye into the painting's depths, where two figures with their backs turned, who do not hear or turn toward the screaming man, testify to the measure of his heartbreaking loneliness."[56] The figures are blurred, giving the impressing of rapid movement,[57] a rapid abandonment, the figures quickly receding into the distance. In the late nineteenth century, a linear path, hurtling along, would evoke congested sidewalks and boulevards, as well as the railroad: a dangerous speed, the blur of the landscape out the window, the impossibility of stopping, and danger—the era expressed this terror of speed by the phenomenon of *railroad spine,*[58] a trauma ontology of a body destroyed by rapidity, the late nineteenth-century equivalent of posttraumatic stress disorder, and the emergence of agoraphobia in the same period (railroad spine emerged in 1866, gaining increasing popularity after that date;[59] agoraphobia was first mentioned in 1871, the diagnosis not becoming popular until the mid 1880s).[60]

As in *Evening on Karl Johan Street,* Munch used multiple circles. There are sinuous lines in the environment of the painting: the swirlings of the red sunset sky, the roundness of lake, the circular, colorful waves in the lake, and the curving landscape. These swirls and circles all render the central figure's sensorial experience: vertigo, a turning and swirling—an onslaught of circularities, a whirling sky and ambient world. The central figure manifests multiple undulations, circles, and semi-circles: the roundness of the screaming mouth, nostrils, eye sockets, eye whites, pupils, head, and jaw; the curves of the hands around the face, the shoulders, and the elbows; and undulations of the body itself—in chaotic motion, the central figure seems to disintegrate within the spirals.

Circles also symbolize sound, waves of sound: "The colors of the landscape are spread on the canvas like sound waves moving from the back of the painting toward the viewer."[61] Synesthesia is the result:

> Synesthesia occurs as waves of color evoke an auditory experience. The oscillation of matter are no longer optical illusions but the acoustic figures of the scream.[62]

In Munch's hands, the decorative line becomes a powerful synesthetic equivalent for the reverberating scream that slices through the landscape;[63] this was a conscious action by Munch, according to "... contemporary theories of synesthesia, where light and color impulses can produce an impression of sound, and visa versa."[64]

A sense of dizziness is heightened by several further devices. The severe drop-off creates a sense of falling amplified by the downwardly leading road and the seeming precariousness of the bridge itself. The boats in the distance suggest the voyage of life, a metaphor richly used in the Norwegian context, a land bordered by sea; and the boats in the scene evoke images of rocking and swelling seas and feelings of loss of control and danger. The s-shaped legs of the central figure depict the sensorial experience of wobbly or rubber legs—this a common complaint of panic patients[65]—a sense of imminent collapse; and this impression of instability is amplified by the ramrod uprightness of the two figures in the background.[66] The head of the central figure is contortedly twisted to one side, conveying sudden muscular tension (of note, greatly heightened muscular tension commonly occurs in panic attacks[67]). The head casually turned appears much differently than the head turned in rage or fear[68]—and given the face of terror, the position of the head in *The Scream* conveys a sense of crisis and muscular tension in the neck and head. The mere existence of the head turning, a cephalic swivel, a kind of spin-inducer, the kinesthetic drawing of a circle, increases the impression of dizziness. This effect is greatly amplified by the eyes and pupils that roll to one side, creating a triple turning of body, head, and eyes.

The ears are covered by the hands, emphasizing the experiencing of distressing sound. At the same time, the mouth opens as if to yell forth a sound, a scream of insanity. The ambiguity of the title, *The Scream,* leaves the viewer wondering whether the figure hears a scream or is screaming.

Anxiety (1896)

The scene is a bridge near Oslo, the same setting as in *Despair* and *The Scream.* In *Anxiety,* the viewer sees a repetition of much of the composition of *Evening on Karl Johan Street.* However, there is no solitary figure, only the onslaught of the crowd. Also absent is the linear perspective provided by buildings, sidewalks, and streets, giving less a sense of speed, though the handrail—and the line of persons—does provide a cutting diagonal. But new dizzying elements are added. There is the drop-off from the bridge and a wide vista. Circular elements are even more emphasized. Other than the circles found in *Evening on Karl Johan Street,* the following elements are included: the round of the cravat, a stylization of some faces to pure circles, the first figure whose hand forms a circle below the chin, with bangs that form a similar shape; and a landscape that undulates and swirls—the sky, horizon, lake, and land itself. As in *Evening on Karl Johan Street,* the lack of control of being hurtled at a frightening speed is felt by the viewer, the lightheaded spinning sensation of velocity, the blur of the passing objects, the vertigo as the head turns from side to side to identify oncoming threat. Munch revisits the theme of red tints in the sky that create a sense of heightened emotionality.

The Scream and *Anxiety* each elaborate themes present in *Evening on Johan Street. The Scream* represents the emotion of loneliness and angst, the void, and being hurtled along a path, a feeling of near collapse that was also conveyed by the bent over figure of the solitary walker in *Evening on Johan Street. Anxiety* symbolizes a sentiment of being overwhelmed by the onrushing crowd, a chaos of rushing persons, forcing a bodily avoidant shift from this place to that, a vigilant turn of the head to the face of one and yet another oncomer, as well as the avalanche of dizzying circles also rendered in *Evening on Johan Street.*

In 1908, acute anxiety led to an emotional and mental breakdown, followed by Munch's in hospitalization and subsequent return to Norway. This event initiated a major turning point in Munch's art and style. The melancholy and anxiety-ridden images of his early paintings, spurred by childhood trauma, rejection in love, and overpowering agoraphobia were replaced with paintings of nature and portraits, including self-portraits.

Munch lived out the rest of his life, until his death in Oslo on January 23, 1944, in relative tranquility. This is reflected in his artwork—

"Anxiety," 1896. **Edvard Munch**

murals for the University of Oslo from 1910-1916 and his brightly colored landscapes. Visibly absent are many of the tortured portrayals of sickness and desolation. Although it is said that Munch lost much of his passion and vigor, there is notable introspection in his late self-portraits. Few of Munch's paintings are found outside of Norway, as he dedicated his collection to the city of Oslo upon his death.

ENDNOTES

1. O.S. Bjerke, *Edvard Munch, Harald Sohlberg: Landscapes of the Mind* (New York: National Academy of Design, 1995), 19.

2. Ibid., 15.

3. Krohg, 1902 appears in Bjerke, op. cit., 85.

4. Bjerke, op. cit., 34.

INSIGHT

5. "... pivoted figure turning the structure of the landscape inside out, and changing all perspective in our world, ordering it from the privileged position of the other" (Prelinger, 1995), 201.

6. Munch, quoted in F. Deknatel, *Edvard Munch* (Boston: Institute of Contemporary Art, 1950), 10.

7. Munch, quoted in B. Torjusen, *Words and Images of Edvard Munch* (White River Junction, VT: Chelsea Green Publishing, 1986), 58.

In this and other passages, Munch speaks of himself often in the third person as "he."

8. Munch, quoted in P.E. Tojner, *Munch, Edvard: In His Own Words* (Munich: Prestel, 2001), 204.

9. M. Craske, "Phobic Fear and Panic Attacks: The Same Emotional States Triggered by Different Cues?" *Clinical Psychology Review* 11 (1991): 91.

10. For a review, see D. Hinton et al., "Panic Disorder, Somatization, and the 'New Cross-Cultural Psychiatry,'" *Culture, Medicine, and Psychiatry,* special issue (forthcoming).

11. One would speculate that panic states tend to occur in those with a history of severe illness for two reasons: 1) when a somatic symptom present in that original illness event is encountered, all the fear and anxiety of that illness is recalled, a sort of conditioning of the sensation to terror, evoking the original traumatic event; and 2) the patient fears that death will occur, worrying that sensation may mediate a catastrophic event, maybe the same illness, this being a cognitively mediated fear of the symptom (see Hinton et. al., 2000, 2001a, b, c).

12. G. Brown and T. Harris, "Aetiology of Anxiety and Depressive Disorders in an Inner-City Population in Early Adversity." *Psychological Medicine* 23 (1993).

Tweed et. al., "The Effects of Childhood Parental Death and Divorce on the Six-Month History of Anxiety Disorders," *British Journal of Psychiatry* 154 (1989).

13. Munch, quoted in F. Zeri, *Munch: The Scream* (Ontario: NDE Publishing, 2000).

14. Werenskiold (1882), quoted in A. Eggum and R.M. Rapett, *Munch et la France* (Paris: Spadem, 1991), 102.

15. Munch, quoted in A.O. Benesch, *Edvard Munch* (New York: Phaidon, 1960), 9.

16. Werenskiold (1882), quoted in A. Eggum and R.M. Rappet, op. cit., 103.

17. R. Heller, *Edvard Munch: The Scream* (New York: Viking Press, 1972), 62.

18. R. Brettell, *Impressionism, Painting Quickly in France 1860–1890* (New Haven and London: Yale University Press, 2001), 57.

19. R. Heller, op. cit., 62.

20. F. Zeri, op. cit., 44.

21. Later in life, Munch told one of his patrons that at the time he heard "the scream" (that inspired his painting *The Scream*) he felt a great fear of open places, found it difficult to cross the street, and developed a great dizziness at the slightest height (Heller 1976: 67). Munch often described his fear of crowds and his perception of other walkers as specters. "I was on the *Boulevard des Italiens*. with thousands of unfamiliar faces who in the electric light looked like ghosts" (Munch, quoted in Zeri, 2000: 12). "The people, ant-like, crawl along, banging one against the other. The omnibus transports a mass of walking of human insects—they all seem indifferent and happy" (Munch, quoted in Eggum and Rapetti, 1991: 347). "I stopped going out in the places of entertainment—each time I did, I had a crisis of nerves" (Munch, quoted in Eggum and Rapett, 1991: 348). Later Munch confided how before turning to alcohol, his agoraphobia was severe; and that later in life the fear worsened yet more. He was unable to visit large cities, finding even the thought of them to be intolerable, avoiding even the markets of small towns (Bjornstad, 2001: 5).

22. J. Perron, *Between Fear and Sex: The Odyssey of Edvard Munch* (Montreal: Montreal Museum of Fine Arts, 1995), 2000.

23. Munch, quoted in R. Heller, *Munch: His Life and Work* (London: Murray, 1984), 40. In this and other passages, Munch speaks of himself often in the third person as "he."

24. Munch, quoted in J. Howe, *Edvard Munch*, op. cit.

25. Munch, quoted in M.H. Wood, ed., *The Frieze of Life* (New York: National Gallery Publications, 1992), 98.

26. American Psychiatric Association: Diagnostic and Statistical Manual of Mental Disorders, Fourth Edition. Washington, DC, American Psychiatric Association, 1994.

27. J. Hodin, *Edvard Munch* (London: Thames and Hudson, Ltd., 1972).

28. F. Zeri, op. cit., 44.

29. U. Bischoff, *Edvard Munch 1863–1944* (New York: Barnes & Noble, 2001), 51.

30. L. Nochlin, *The Body in Pieces: The Fragment as a Metaphor of Modernity* (New York: Thames and Hudson, 1994), 25–26.

31. Also note the multiple square windows, seemingly amplify a sense of being watched, bring greater attention to the eyes of the oncoming crowd,

Munch, Agoraphobia, and the Terrors of the Modernizing Urban Landscape round eyes, pupils, and eyebrows, contrasting with the square window frames and the bright rectangular windows.

32. In *Evening on Karl Johan Street* we have swirling whirlpools of a river, a swirling flow, but composed of persons; here we are reminded of Galen's and Arataeus's description of the vertigo-inducing spinnings (Arataeus; translation by Adams, 1856). Also, as the walker turns the head from side to side, bobs up and down, the feeling of dizziness and spinning would be yet further amplified. Of note, in his original formulation of "place dizziness," Benedict (Knapp and Schumacher, 1988: 25) stated that the cause of dizziness and fear of outdoor spaces was a blurriness of vision as the eyes turned to one side, resulting from an inability to converge the eyes, from a sort of ocular weakness. According to this model, when walking through the crowd, the agoraphobic has a sense of blurriness and dizziness, turning the head from side to side, negotiating a way in the midst of the onward coming pedestrian flow—and turning the head back and forth to cross a street and faster walkers and carts moving past one from behind.

33. Nergaard (1978: 138) describes this aspect of the modern cityscape, as depicted by Munch, in the following manner:

Fellowship on the public level is revealed as an empty ritual. The mass of people have no contact with each other. Even in the midst of public intercourse, individuals are bringing their private loneliness to a public gathering. The intercourse merely consists of everybody passing one another in the same public space. Companionship is only experiences as momentary instants of contact within prescribed rituals of recognition and acknowledgment.

34. P.E. Torjusen, op. cit., 39.

35. F. Zeri, op. cit., 4.

36. T. Knapp and M. Schumacher, *Westphal's "Die Agoraphobie" with Commentary* (London: University Press of America, 1988), 25.

37. J. Hodin, op. cit.

38. Munch, quoted in P.E. Tojner, op. cit., 204.

39. Munch, quoted in R. Heller, op. cit. (1984), 55.

40. A. Eggum and R.M. Rapett, op. cit., 341-64.

41. All three selections from Munch, quoted in P.E. Tojner, op. cit., 96.

42. A friend (Skredsvig (1892), quoted in Heller, 1972: 66) said of Munch's *Desperation:*

For some time Munch had been wanting to paint the memory of a sunset. Red as blood. No, it actually *was* coagulated blood. But not a single other person would see it as he had; they would all see nothing but clouds. He talked himself sick about that sunset and how it had filled him with great anxiety. He was in despair because the miserable means available to painting never went far enough. 'He is trying to do what is impossible, and hi s religion is despair,' I thought to myself but still advised him to try to paint it—and that is how he came to paint his remarkable *Scream.*"

43. American Psychiatric Association, op. cit.

44. For a discussion of typical panic attack symptoms that are nonetheless not included in DSM-IV, see Hinton and Hinton, 2002; also see Clum et al., 1990.

45. See Hinton et al., 2001a, b, c.

46. Ibid. Also of note, Tinnitus as cultural Rorschach is well evidenced by the description of the physician Aretaeus, writing in Greek in the A.D. In terms of the metaphors used, recall that dizziness was thought to be caused by the spirits, a substance viewed as both a wind and fluid, that was thought to roil in the head or shoot out of the ears; too, since tinnitus (i.e., the fluids roiling in the head or shooting out the ears) and dizziness were thought to have a similar source, the two conditions are considered a syndrome: "If darkness possesses the eyes, and the ears ringing as from the sound of rivers rolling along with a great noise, or like the wind when it roars among the sails, or like the clang of pipes or reeds, or like the rattling of a carriage, we call the affection *Scotoma* (or *Vertigo*)" (Aretaeus; translation by Adams 1856: 295).

47. F. Zeri, op. cit., 47.

48. Ibid.

49. Ibid., 4. Note also, The idea of nature screaming a song of human misery also has a certain nature exemplar, as explained in a book almost certainly familiar to Munch and that was well known to Strindberg, who writes the following (Strindberg; quoted in Carlson 1983: 10):

… that the death's head moth is called *Haïe* in French because of the sound it makes. What sound: "Ai": the universal human cry of pain; the scream that which the tree sloth laments the drudgery of existence; the expression of loss uttered by Apollo at the death of his friend Hyacinthus, and imprinted on the flower bearing his name.

50. K. Nahum, "'In Wild Embrace:' Attachment and Loss in Edvard Munch." In *Edvard Munch: Psyche, Symbol and Expression,* edited by J. Howe (Chicago: University of Chicago Press, 2001), 41.

51. R. Rosenbaum, "Edvard Munch: Some Changing Contexts." In *Edvard Munch: Symbol and Images,* edited by A. Eggum, R. Heller, T. Nergaard, R. Stang, et al. (Washington, DC: National Gallery of Art, 1978), 2.

52. O. Benesch, op. cit., 15.

53. C. Cernuschi, "Sex and Psyche, Nature and Nurture, the Personal and the Political: Edvard Munch and German Expressionism." In *Edvard Munch: Psyche, Symbol and Expression,* edited by J. Howe (Chicago: University of Chicago Press, 2001), 116.

54. R. Heller (1972), op. cit., 76.

55. Ibid., 78.

56. F. Zeri, op. cit., 8.

57. O. Benesch, op. cit., 15.

58. A. Young, *The Harmony of Illusions: Inventing Post-Traumatic Stress Disorder* (Princeton: Princeton University Press, 1997).

59. Ibid.

60. T. Knapp and M. Schumacher, op. cit.

61. F. Zeri, op. cit., 8.

62. O. Benesch, op. cit., 15.

63. E. Prelinger, "When the Halted Traveler Hears the Scream of Nature: Preliminary Thoughts on the Transformation of Some Romantic Themes." In *Shop talk: Studies in Honor of Seymour Slive.* (Cambridge: Harvard University Art Museums, 1995), 98.

64. A. Eggum et al., *Munch at the Munch Museum* (Oslo: Scala Books, 1998), 34.

65. G.A. Clum et al, "Validity and Reliability of the Panic Attack Symptoms and Cognition Quesitonnaire." *Journal of Psychopathology and Behavioral Assessment* 12 (1990).

66. R. Heller (1976), op. cit., 80.

67. See Hinton, 2001a, b, and c.

68. R. Hinoki, "Considerations on the Postural Reflex and Body Equilibrium—With Reference to Professor Fukada's Ideas on Equilibrium Function." In *Vestibular and Neural Front: Proceedings of the 12th International Symposium on Posture and Gait.* Edited by K. Taguchi, M. Igarashi, and S. Mori (Tokyo: Elsevier, 1994).

TILL M. MEYN

Panic in Modern Music

. . . terror of death cannot so much affright as the sound of trumpet, drum, fife, and suchlike music animates.

— Robert Burton, *Anatomy of Melancholy,* 1621

When I hear music, I fear no danger. I am invulnerable. I see no foe.

— Henry David Thoreau, *Journal,* 1857

O F ALL THE ARTS, music has the greatest power to incite panic or to soothe fear. A Stephen King novel may cause your heart to skip a beat as you read in the comfort of your favorite nook by the fire (safe from any *real* killer cars or bloody prom queens). *The Scream,* Edvard Munch's famous painting (p. vi) depicting a ghostly figure grasping his head in terror beneath blood-red clouds, might run chills down your spine as you tune in to your audio guide, strolling from temperature-controlled room to room at the National Gallery. Yet it is with the aid of music that the Saracens struck cold fear in the hearts of the Crusaders in the twelfth century;[1] with amplified loudspeakers that U.S. forces waged psychological warfare in the Gulf War of the 1990s; through familiar song that mothers are able to calm their children and lull them to sleep. The arts of painting, sculpture, dance, architecture, film, and literature can all inspire a wide range of feeling, including panic, but music has a special key to the realm of emotion, whether it be in a royal brass fanfare or a mother's song.

This chapter first explores music that exhibits panic, with a focus on three twentieth-century compositions: Arnold Schoenberg's opera *Erwartung; Renard: a Burlesque in Song and Dance* by Igor Stravinsky; and Sergei Prokofiev's musical tale *Peter and the Wolf.* To conclude is a brief discussion of music's power to soothe panic and a recommended list of selected modern music to that aim.

The word *panic* is defined by Webster as "intense, contagious fear affecting a body of people," or "intense, irrational fear felt by an individual."[2] The etymology of the word has musical roots: the Greek god Pan, with the torso of a man and the legs of a goat, was a player of pipes, and was said to incite panic in mortals. Whether the word describes mass upheaval and unrest or extreme fear in one person alone, its accepted meaning is essentially the same. When looking for works expressing panic in music, I sought pieces that exhibited extreme tension; for panic, as intense fear, is caused and complicated by the pull of emotional powers against each other. One of the driving forces behind nearly all styles and genres of music is the play between tension and release (or purposeful lack of release) from that tension, but it is important to note that panic in music is heightened tension of a very specific kind. Some of the other causes of extreme tension in a musical context are love/hate, joy/sadness, anger, war, dementia, and numerous other emotions and events that create strong pulls, often in different directions. Panic, however, tears at the very fabric of sanity, making rational decisions difficult; the fight-or-flight instinct brought on by panic wells up and consumes nearly all other emotional thought. Panic is a very specific heightened state of fear, not merely the anxiety in running a car out of gas or the thought of losing a job, but the fear of a threat against one's very existence, of losing life itself.

Before exploring panic in a musical setting, one must first determine how music conveys specific emotions, how an audience can be aware of the emotional message the music is designed to communicate. This can be a huge undertaking, and in fact many scholars through the ages have catalogued and written about the effects in music. More recently (1956) Leonard B. Meyer, a noted music scholar, wrote the groundbreaking *Emotion and Meaning in Music*, a work that has been a catalyst for many more opinions and ideas about interpreting emotions in music. However, his book and subsequent writings on the subject by authors both supporting and refuting his theories are concerned mostly with the expression of emotions in music without text. Such music carries emotion in its rhythms, harmonies, structure, instrumentation, dynamics, and melodies, but cannot easily communicate specific emotions to a general audience without well-defined support from sung or spoken words or a thorough, step-by-step narrative. The only way to know for certain what emotion the composer intended to convey at different points in a piece is to know what program is behind the music. In opera, song, choral, or other music with sung text the message to be represented by the music is generally clear. In theater or film, the music intensifies the emotions portrayed by the actors or written in the script, and so in these media it is usually also clear to understand the emotional ideas in the music. Even in music without text but with a program, such as a tone poem or programmatic symphony, the music and the story behind it can be compared and the sentiments explored. Occasionally, a composition without any program may exhibit musical themes that represent obvious references to situations or emotional states, such as the musical imitation of a siren, a scream, or another noise that could trigger specific emotional responses in the listener.

How does music express the tension and stress of panic, the push and pull of such intense emotion? By analyzing various facets of the musical content of selected works, at points where the intent of the composer is clearly the expression of panic, one can form a vocabulary of compositional traits that identifies panic in music. In the study of panic in music one could choose to take into account a comprehensive view of compositions for various instruments and ensembles, from opera, choral, and other texted music to purely instrumental pieces. Yet I have chosen to hone in on the very specific study of panic in these selected twentieth-century compositions for two main reasons. First, music with text, such as the works I discuss here, provides not only the program, the story behind the music, but also the narrative or dialogue at any given time in the work, therefore allowing a pinpointed approach to dissecting music that clearly reflects panic. Second, the struggles and conflicts of the twentieth century still resonate in our modern society, and the music of that period, fraught with a high level of tension, lends itself well to the examination of panic in a musical context.

The era preceding and surrounding the First World War, from the turn of the century through the late 1920s, was a time of apprehension and change in the world of art. In the visual and musical arts, a movement was formed that manifested the fear and uncertainty of the times, as well as a long-awaited break with tradition: expressionism. On the forefront of visual art, painters such as Nolde, Kandinsky, and Klee created works of dark subtlety and dreamlike abstraction, while in music, Schoenberg, Berg, and Webern composed pieces devoid of traditional tonality and teeming with tension, reflecting the direction of social and artistic thought in Europe. The piece that is widely considered to have been the prime inspiration for these expressionist composers is the opera *Salome* by Richard Strauss. Completed and premiered in 1905, the opera *Salome* is a musical representation of the biblical king Herod Antipas's lust for his wife's daughter; the story had been written by Oscar Wilde in French just over a decade earlier, then edited and translated into German, and set to music by Strauss. The musical language used by Strauss in *Salome* can be characterized as the use of extreme dissonance and rhythmic realism to evoke tension. Although panic is not a running theme in the work, other intense sinister emotions such as lust, horror, greed, and envy are displayed through dissonance in representation of those emotions that were a primary influence on the expressionist composers.

"bleed," 2001. **Anthony Lukens**

If Strauss's opera *Salome* was an inspiration to modern composers seeking a break with tradition, then Arnold Schoenberg's monodrama *Erwartung* of 1909 marked the demise of romanticism of the late nineteenth century.[3] Although *Erwartung* did not enjoy as celebrated a premiere as did *Salome*,[4] its innovative structure and musical language embodied the ideals of the emerging expressionist movement and it was quickly hailed as a work of genius. The close marriage of text and music in *Erwartung* link the two artforms in a powerful representation of panic, interwoven with and aided by the expressionistic subjects of night, insanity, and death. Schoenberg's librettist, Marie Pappenheim, wrote the text in a brisk three weeks, for Schoenberg then composed the half-hour opera in a mere seventeen days without much revision of the libretto. The feverish pace of writing could only have aided in the creation of a purposely disjunct and schizophrenic stage work that parallels the state of mind of the sole participant, the unnamed woman whose demented wanderings in the forest at night lead her to the lifeless body of her lover. Staged in four scenes, *Erwartung* (Expectation) leads the audience to understand that the subject is in search of her lover who she has not seen in three days, and through her disjointed cries of panic and fear as she searches for him, and her fitful sobbing over his body, we find that she may have been the murderer. Though her guilt is never confirmed, her anxious condition and hallucinations of death, as well as her anger at her lover's supposed infidelity, point to her culpability. Music historian Bryan Simms has this to say about the text of *Erwartung:*

> The Woman's fragmented outbursts, her disjointed eruptions of inner thoughts and emotions, the theme of violence as symptom of psychic and social disintegration, the nightmarish atmosphere, treatment of the main character as a symbolic type devoid of proper name, and a pervasive sense of impending doom all make the monodrama an important forerunner of German expressionist playwriting.[5]

Curiously, the libretto may have been inspired by true events that had unfolded in the personal life of the writer's relative, Bertha Pappenheim: she had become a case study for the neurologist Jean-Martin Charcot, whose clinical work on the subject of hysteria was followed up by none other than Sigmund Freud in his and Joseph Breuer's *Studien über Hysterie* (Studies on Hysteria) of 1895. In this work of Freud and Breuer, the analysis of hysteric patients, including that of Bertha Pappenheim, led to the discovery that cathartic therapy helped rehabilitate subjects who had experienced a traumatic event and were suffering symptoms such as severe speech impediments and even paralysis. The disjunct style of speech, amnesia, and hallucinations that the subject in *Erwartung* exhibits give validity to the idea that Marie Pappenheim likely used her relative's condition as a model for her character.[6]

The composer's musical interpretation of the libretto is less concerned with the events that unfold in the subject's journey through the forest in *Erwartung.* Rather, Schoenberg "repeatedly emphasized that the work was to be interpreted as a study of emotions in a heightened and momentary state of intensity."[7] Simms gives this description:

> ... the opera's music consists of a succession of disjunct and contrasting sections whose character mimics the rapidly changing emotional states of the Woman. A broad coherence is achieved primarily by the fluctuating expressive curve of her monologue, alternately fearful and reflective.[8]

A look at specific examples will help in understanding how Schoenberg musically expressed the subject's state of panic in his opera.

The musical language of the entire work can be characterized as an avoidance of tonality, a break with traditional tonal idioms that late romantic composers of the previous two decades had been building toward. Therefore, dissonant harmonies do not create the same tension in *Erwartung* as they would in tonal music. The monodrama is a journey through rapidly changing emotions, with fear as the primary mood expressed by the wandering woman. She expresses her fear of entering the dark forest toward the beginning of the first scene: "I am afraid . . . what heavy air presses out . . . Like a storm standing still. . . So horribly calm and empty . . . ."9 The woman sings these fragments in a speechlike manner, and as she expresses her fear, her voice becomes agitated and loud, and her words clipped. The tempo increases suddenly, and the instruments also play with more volume and intensity; the violins play a fast, short burst of notes, and the woodwinds trill, communicating the woman's trembling. The fear at this point in the drama is so sudden and intense that it is clearly an expression of panic, the text and the music heightening the mood. The panic is also tangible at points in the second scene. The woman, hallucinating, imagines someone touching her at measure 43, and her voice slides to a scream at its highest pitch yet, loudly, as the instruments utter fragmented bursts of harmony. Her panic builds moments later as she hears a rustling in the leaves above her, expressed by the fluttering of instruments rising in pitch and volume, and she again shrieks frantically. In the third scene, the woman titters fearfully at shadows portrayed by a quiet harp and clarinets at measure 91, but her greatest apprehension so far comes shortly thereafter: "But the shadow crawls! Yellow, wide eyes, popping out like stalks . . . How it stares . . . No animal, dear God, no animal . . . I am so afraid. . . ."10 The tempo again increases dramatically, as the pitch and volume crescendo, with all instruments playing at once. This also ends the third scene, as the instruments tremble and slowly come down to a whisper. The last scene, longer by far than the first three, represents the embodiment of her previously irrational fears, now made real. Her panic reaches its climax soon after the discovery of a body; she describes the features of the corpse's face (harkening back to Salome's grotesque admiration of the head of John the Baptist in Strauss's opera) and realizes that it is the face of her lover. With a terrifying and bone-chilling scream for help at measure 190, she and the orchestra reach the highest and loudest chord of the piece, held for a dramatic five seconds.

The musical interpretation of panic in *Erwartung* is not surprising. A scream is imitated by the instruments as deafening noise at a high pitch level, trembling is exemplified by trills and rapid fluctuations, and the increase of tempo and irregular rhythmic bursts reflect the pounding of a panicked heart and shattered nerves. Indeed, all of these characteristics can be found in many different styles, eras, and genres of music, but in *Erwartung* the sense of panic is so pervasive that it is not only the dominant emotion in the work, but it consumes the listener and creates a tense environment even for the audience. The avoidance of tonality and complete dissonance of harmony also affects an atmosphere where tension is always present; increased tempo, fluctuating tones and rhythms, and crescendo of pitch and volume, as well as the understood meaning of the sung text, all play on the emotions of the listener to cause a vicarious sense of panic.

In *Renard: a Burlesque in Song and Dance,* panic is sensed by the audience in a wholly different manner. Written by Igor Stravinsky in 1916 but not performed until 1922, *Renard* is a stylized, rather silly account of barnyard animals taken from a collection of folk tales by Afanasiev. As described by Robert Craft, biographer and friend to Stravinsky, "It is a 'burlesque in song and dance,' a morality play based on the medieval beast epic, in musical form a chamber cantata."[11] Stravinsky adapted the story for the stage, instructing that the four singers who give voice to the animal characters should stand with the orchestra while the action is mimed on stage. The men's voices represent the cock, the cat, the goat, and Renard the fox, and the music is tonally oriented and jolly. Panic in this play first comes about when the cock is coaxed down from his perch and attacked by the fox. The cock calls for his friends the cat and the goat to help him, as Renard begins plucking out his feathers. The cries of panic, repeated high notes represented by a tenor voice, are accentuated and the mood heightened by the chamber orchestra, playing loud, offbeat rhythmic chords between the voice at rehearsal 20. The cat and goat force the fox to release his prey and the three friends dance with joy at rehearsal 26. Yet the fox is successful in coaxing the cock from his perch once again and the victimized bird screams in terror to the same accompaniment as previously played. This time, however, the cock's friends do not come to the rescue until it is almost too late: the fox has dragged the unconscious bird to his lair. The tables are turned when the cat and goat beguile the fox out of his hole with a folk song and proceed to strangle him to death! The screams of all four singers at once, representing the panic-stricken Renard, accompanied by pointillistic, vehement chords from the instruments, give a simultaneous grotesque but comical cartoonlike depiction of panic. Once again the three friends exult in a joyful dance and the work is concluded with the same march ushering the actors off stage as had heralded them on.

The expression of panic in *Renard* is quite unlike that of *Erwartung.* The tonal language and farcical subject matter in the burlesque creates a listening environment where the audience is amused and entertained by the suffering of the cock and the fox, whereas in the monodrama the continuous dissonance and unsettling mental condition of the woman establish a dreamlike, fearful ambience that is not at all comic. There are similarities, however, in the musical techniques used to communicate the sense of panic expressed in both dramas.

Peter and the Wolf, by Sergei Prokofiev, offers yet another facet to the musical expression of panic. As in Stravinsky's *Renard,* the subjects are animals and the music is tonally oriented, but Prokofiev's piece is no morality play and the design of the story and characters brings across a wholly different message and listening environment. Anyone who is familiar with this famous narrated musical tale will probably admit that, although it was written for children, its appeal is universal. Composed in 1936 for chamber orchestra and narrator, *Peter and the Wolf* details the story of Peter, a boy living in Russia, and his bravery in capturing the dreaded gray wolf with the help of his friend the bird. The effectiveness of the work in communicating the story and emotions lies in its format: the narrator sets each scene with short commentary and deliv-

ers the dialogue of each character, between which a musical interpretation of the action is played by the orchestra. Each character is
depicted by his own instrument and musical theme, or leitmotiv
(a Wagnerian operatic technique), so that as the tale unfolds the
audience can follow the developing action and interaction of the
subjects.

There are three episodes of panic in *Peter and the Wolf*. The
first sign of disturbance is at rehearsal 13, as the little bird just
escapes the clutches of the wily cat; the strings play brisk rhythmic chords, like the pounding of a panicked heart and the bird's
theme in the flute becomes frantic. The bird escapes his fate, but
the duck jumps out of her pond at rehearsal 21 and is swallowed
whole by the wolf, who has just emerged from the forest. Panic

is clearly expressed here by the orchestra: the duck's theme, played by the oboe, rises ever higher and crescendos in terror while the other instruments play loud offbeat chords in imitation of the fast-approaching wolf nearing his prey. The offbeat rhythms "catch up" to the on-beat oboe melody, and at the point of ultimate panic upon her demise, the strings play tremulously in expression of the intense anxiety of the moment. The final depiction of panic occurs as the wolf is captured at rehearsal 34. Peter, who remains fearless throughout the story despite the worried warnings of his grandfather, asks his friend the bird to distract the wolf, who is circling the tree where Peter is perched. Peter then lowers a noose around the wolf's tail and pulls with all his might. As the panicked wolf struggles to pull free, his fear and anger intensify, expressed by the quickening tempo, clamoring woodwinds, frantic strings, military drum, and the blaring horns that represent his character. The exuberant Peter and his animal friends march the captive wolf to the zoo in a finale that incorporates all the themes and melodies of the work.

Each of the compositions discussed here has its own agenda: *Erwartung* pushes the bounds of tonality in a dreamlike representation of panic on many levels; *Renard* attempts to entertain through panic from the perspective of comedy; *Peter and the Wolf* tells an exciting children's tale where panic is ultimately resolved (even the duck can be heard quacking from the wolf's belly at the end). Yet all express panic in essentially the same musical terms, with ideas that are easily interpreted by the listener as intense. The extremes of volume, pitch, and tempo in the music reflect the same associations with panic in a non-musical context, where a scream, a pounding heart, and quick reflexes are some of the most common reactions to intense fear.

The experience of panic can cause extreme emotional distress, which quickly manifests in physical symptoms. It stands to reason that the way to alleviate panic is to quell the emotional turbulence and create stability. As we have seen, music can depict panic by intensifying elements such as tempo, volume, pitch, texture, and harmony. Logically, the easing of those tensions in the music will help pacify emotional distress felt by the listener. Therefore, if someone is experiencing true panic, not simply a vicarious thrill of fear through musical entertainment, then quiet, slow, harmonious music with little tension should also help to calm those fears. Following is a short, selective list of modern music that can calm panic through its meditative and peaceful melodies, harmonies, and moods. The power of music over the emotions has touched so many over thousands of years; from the chanting prayers of Gregorian monks to the solidarity in a national anthem, music is a language that speaks to everyone who is able to listen.

MODERN MUSIC TO CALM PANIC

Samuel Barber	*Adagio for Strings*
Claude Debussy	*Sirènes* from *Nocturnes*
Gabriel Fauré	*Cantique de Jean Racine*
Morten Lauridsen	*Se per havervi, oimé* from *Madrigali*
Gustav Mahler	*Adagietto* from *Symphony no.5*
Frank Martin	*Mass*
Jules Massenet	*Meditation* from *Thaïs*
Arvo Pärt	*Magnificat*
Sergei Rachmaninoff	*Vespers*
Maurice Ravel	*Adagio assai* from *Piano Concerto in G Major*
Erik Satie	*Gymnopédies*
Igor Stravinsky	*Andante: 'Sento dire no'ncè pace'* from *Pulcinella*
Ralph Vaughan Williams	*Movement II: Lento* from *A London Symphony*

ENDNOTES

1. The Saracens played shawms, shrill oboe-like instruments, which they blew by the hundreds as they approached their opponents in battle.

2. Bernard S. Cayne, *Webster's Dictionary of the English Language* (New York: Lexicon Publications, Inc., 1988), 725.

3. The author owes most of the ideas written here concerning *Erwartung* to the scholarship of Bryan R. Simms.

4. Strauss's opera was highly anticipated, but premiered amid controversy; the explicit sexual content led some major venues to delay their running.

5. Bryan R. Simms, *The Atonal Music of Arnold Schoenberg: 1908–1923* (New York: Oxford University Press, 2000), 92.

6. Ibid., 92–93.

7. Ibid., 94; Simms attributes this interpretation to Egon Wellesz's "Arnold Schönbergs Bühnenwerke" of 1920.

8. Ibid., 95–96.

9. Arnold Schoenberg, *Erwartung: A Monodrama in One Act* (Vienna: Universal Edition A. G., 1923), mm. 11–14 (all translations by Till M. Meyn).

10. Ibid., mm. 105–12.

11. Robert Craft, "Music and Words." In *Stravinsky in the Theatre*, edited by Minna Lederman (New York: Da Capo Press, 1975), 88.

Going Back for the Little Ones: Understanding Panic in Sexuality

S ELAH MARTHA has been the Director of Women's Programs at Body Electric School in Oakland, California, since 1996. Body Electric is a body-based process for core transformation of sexuality and sexual self-esteem. Selah likes to call it "sex re-education for grown-ups." The school draws on ancient principles and techniques to create a new context for eroticism. Brooke Warner, co-editor of this book, contacted Selah to share her experiences with Body Electric and lend her insight into the subject of panic in relation to sexuality, particularly in the context of working with people who want to learn a new language for sexual expression. Read more about Body Electric on their website, *www.bodyelectric.com*. In the meantime, join Selah and Brooke in the exploration and understanding of how panic plays gets played out in the sexual experience.

* * *

Brooke: Is the therapy you do considered "sex therapy?"

Selah: I have a private practice where I work with individuals and couples. I think of it not just as sex therapy, even though people come to me with sexual issues. I think of it on the whole as explorations of embodiment. In other words, what are the forces which cause us to constrict our bodies and not be fully present and fully alive. That's a huge subject, and a lot of it relates to sexuality because that's so core in the body.

Brooke: I'd like you to comment about how sexuality issues fall into panic and panic reactions in the sense that people can have very constrictive feelings around the actual physical experiencing of it.

Selah: It's a classic illustration of what I talk about. It's called constellations of muscle tension that we have learned over time for a variety of reasons. In their extreme expression, those constellations will result in real rigid contractions of which panic would be one. Panic's kind of neat in a way because it's not dissociation. With dissociation you don't even know you're doing it. You've gone to a place of tension where you aren't feeling anything; or you've gone into another realm that's not entirely new to the body out of necessity. But panic is a feeling. There's a lot going on in there.

Brooke: Though in extreme cases people often say they are so tight they can't breath or move—but you think it's more experiential?

Selah: Well you can't get away from it. It's a funny thing. It's a prison that you know you're stuck in. If you then go into dissociation, then you're in dissociation. On a body level, when you're feeling panic, you're still feeling—so you're actually connected to your body. I think that a lot of dissociation is actually because people don't want to feel panic because it is so frightening and because it connects to the fear of death, and they have no repertoire, no embodiment repertoire for experiencing that much fear and just staying with it.

Brooke: Statiscally women suffer from panic three times more than men. I wonder if this is something you can attest to in your practice?

Selah: I think there's a lot more permission culturally for women to feel fear or fear-related sensations. There's very little permission for men to actually feel it. They're taught to take action when those signals come in. They're taught to do things when there's a fear-generated situation. Women's training is not so much that. They have more of a moment that's both a permission and a problem at times. Men are trained in terms of the sensation to bring to action so that they're trained to skip the step of feeling it and go into action. So they're wiring is different.

Brooke: What are the types of backgrounds people come from that would lead to feelings of fear and panic around sex? Do you think socio-religious conditioning in our society is at the core of these panic reactions?

Selah: I would have to say so. My own sense, and my own personal experience in my body, is that the early training, not necessarily specific to sexuality, but the early training about our bodies—typically the lower parts of our bodies—our butts, our genitals—is that it's not okay; it's not a safe place to be and the muscles intuitively respond to those messages, even if they're not traumatic. If there's a bunch of people holding their breath, squeezing their butts, not feeling particularly innocent or shame-free about their genitals (and the fact that they're sexual beings), the whole lower half of the body just intuitively closes up and that's not even the trauma—a lot of people have real trauma, in which case the body slams shut. That's what I mean by life body. We're built to survive. We're built to go for as much life source as is available and if that means constricting a certain part of the body so that the rest of the being can go on more fully, then we'll do it.

I think even people in this culture have messages coming in all the time that we should cover up and hold it in and not express too much and certainly not express too much interest in erotic contact. Children are very individual. They're very sensuous. They're very curious. They touch their bodies. They want to know about their bodies. They feel, they want to check it out, and there's a natural curiosity about their genitals. And very early, even in the

"Young woman frightened by a thunderstorm which breaks a tree next to her," 1798. **Jean-Baptiste Stouf.**

nicest ways, we're told to tone it down, hold that in, watch where you do that. Even at that level the muscles start to hold on tighter. If you take those messages and tighten the lower half of the body, the very root of our energy and our creativity, and you start right out tightening that, and then you add in whatever shame-based trauma occurred, there's going to be a lot of tension. Then we see a bunch of images about how we're supposed to feel free and healthy and alive—we're supposed to feel easy and knowledgeable about sexuality with no inititiation, no information—no real information—given about the complexity and detail of it, and what might be fun and what might not be fun, and no permission for experimentation. And then we're told, *Go forward and have a happy sex life.* It's impossible, really difficult, because people don't know what the options are and their bodies are already really afraid. You put that kind of pressure on someone and at a certain point, and when the pressure gets too great, that's when panic results— cause there's nowhere to go. The body is doing everything you've asked it to do. You ask it to shut down, shut down, shut down, and then you ask it to enjoy something that is this powerful force— erotic energy, the most powerful energy source on earth, and the mixed messages are overwhelming.

Brooke: When you see panic-related issues emerging, is the source most often a specific trauma? Is it something that you would say is common in sexual experiences?

Selah: I work with pretty normally functioning people in the world in general who want more from their sex life and know that there's a whole other world that the culture has not offered them.

I would say that I see it, but not on the level of disorder very often. People are managing very well, because they're feeling their fear rather than going into panic seizures. But fear is a huge issue.

Brooke: One of the things that this book emphasizes is different levels of panic and variations of panic in our human experience. We have a list of symptoms that signify the onset of panic disorder and panic attacks, which is the most extreme panic sensation. But at the base of it all is intense fear, really.

Selah: That comes up a lot in sexuality. Panic and fear manifests as the ability to feel sensation. People know they would like to feel sensation either specifically in their genitals or in the act of sex, and they're not feeling sensation. And it's puzzling and confusing and discouraging, and it's rooted in fear. I work with people to bring awareness to those areas of numbness and sometimes, if they let themselves move, what's actually there is panic. That's what it is. The word panic is related some way etymologically to the god Pan. It's a little bit like the Chinese character of crisis and change being the same—about the energy really being away from stasis. It's a broad description about energy in flux, energy that has lost stasis, that is moving fast in a chaotic form. Again, as a culture we have no room for that, which is why we label a lot of this as disorder, when actually it's not. It's people trying to release energy and move in a transformative state, which we do not recognize. We're afraid of it, so we try to make it stop, or we make ourselves stop, which makes it worse. I have had clients who have severe fears for good reason. When they have been able to be in it, to panic, to scream, to run around, to kick in absolute and total chaos, it's a huge relief. The main relief is not necessarily that all the fears are gone, because that's not true. But they don't think they're crazy. They begin to trust their bodies again—*Oh, this is really real. I didn't make this up. I'm not crazy. There's a reason I feel like this. And the only thing crazy is that I didn't get to express how bad it was.* So there's a shift where the person realizes that it wasn't their neurosis. It was a fear that they needed to remove.

Brooke: So that's something that you might encourage? Can you say, go for it, let it go?

Selah: With panic disorder, it's a little different. If someone actually has panic, you need to work with that. There are situations where it wouldn't actually help to have them tap into a fear. In most people, the body will actually let go of chronic conditions, of muscle tension and pain. Women might be more susceptible because women are more trained to be more constantly accessible on what I call the relationship channel. So women tend to be feeling not just their own feelings, but the feelings of those around them. They're trained to be aware, very intuitive. Most women can walk into a room and they've kind of got the room. That's a fine intuitive

One need not be a Chamber—to be Haunted—
One need not be a House—
The Brain has Corridors—surpassing
Material Place—

Far safer, of a Midnight Meeting
External Ghost
Than its interior confronting—
That Cooler Host.

Far safer, through an Abbey gallop.
The Stone's chase—
Than unarmed, one's own self encounter—
In a lonesome Place—

Ourself behind ourself, concealed—
Should startle most—
Assassin hid in our Apartment
Be Horror's least.

The Body—borrows a Revolver—
He bolts the Door—
O'er looking a superior spectre—
Or more—

      —Emily Dickinson

skill and we need to use it more. On the other hand, women tend to channel and be more susceptible to the collective emotion than we can necessarily handle.

Brooke: The notion of panic with the god Pan brings up feelings of excitement as well as terror. Have you seen people with this kind of mixed notion of panic, who are enticed by sexuality and express it through acting out in dangerous or fear-based ways?

Selah: I need to make a distinction between exciting and actually threatening situations. In the latter case the appropriate body response is fear and panic and "get me the hell out of here." I think that can be a little confusing, especially if it's viewed as fear associated with arousal. Some people feel that they need the fear of threatening situations in order to get arousal going. At the same time, because they're so threatened internally, they're not getting full sensation. That's a whole category in itself of the association of fear with sexual arousal. I don't think it's healthy. It's different than excitement when you know you're safe and maybe needing a challenge, or meeting a forceful energy—that can be very exciting.

Originally, biologically, some women were actually selecting mates. They were controlling stuff like that, and there was actually danger involved, and even death. I think we have some of that in our cell memory. I spent many years separating out my fear from my sexual arousal, because for me fear was a shut-down. It meant that I couldn't actually let the juices in my body go, and I couldn't actually feel anything. Once I got that sorted out by discharging a lot of the residual fear that was in my body then I could move into a place which I would just call sensation; where there's some high-impact sensation of some forceful energy that can be very exciting when you're in the center of your body. If you're not in the center of your body than it's just the rehearsal of something old, or it's just really cruddy. But if you're in your body and your making choices every moment, then the challenge and the excitement can cause panic. If you're going beyond the known for you, going beyond what you know as reality, then there's always a little panic there. So that would be true sexually as well. When you go to the next level of excitement, to the next level of risk, the next scenario that you've never known before, there would be a little level of "oh my God, what am I doing"—holding your breath, squeezing your muscles, having second thoughts—I mean, this is all going on in flashes—before you decide for whatever reason that this is okay, I'm going to go forward. And that's what we were talking about as real panic as associated with the god Pan—that's the real enchantment of "come a little further into the mystery." But there has to be some sense of safety, either by really being in your own body or with some sort of agreement with whoever it is that you're playing with so that you both know what the rules are.

Brooke: Do you think that people who have more severe panic reactions are not "in their own bodies?"

Selah: Feeling yourself, feeling your circulation, feeling your organs, every minute, really being alive in every cell—that is often wildly frightening, as well as it is comfortable. The perception is that the comfortable part is the good part that we're supposed to be achieving and the uncomfortable part is something bad and we're making a mistake. I totally disagree with that notion. That's a value judgment we've created, but life itself is a full spectrum of those feelings. It goes from off-the-charts uncomfortable to the point of death to off-the-charts comfortable with bliss and ecstasy and happiness and joy. The interesting thing is to live all of that, but we've been trained in our bodies not to do that. We've been trained to walk the middle ground. And that's a real loss. As far as my own panic, I would say that the dialogue is: "Uh oh, I am about to have sensations which are going to overwhelm me and I'm going to feel out of control." Then I can't breathe as well, my muscles start contracting, my thoughts go crazy—literally bouncing around like pingpong balls. But the flip side of that is: "I must handle this. I must handle this." That's what we say to each other, "Get a grip."

So you're actually in a battle with yourself. If I were to just let myself go and just freak out, it would probably take me five minutes and I would be done. But we're not allowed to do that.

Brooke: Is that something that you allow in your practice or workshops?

Selah: Occasionally that happens in workshops, but we don't necessarily encourage that. We encourage to let happen whatever happens in a person's body. So people will go through panic and our instruction will be to support, and that they have control over their minds and over their breath. Or they can just go ahead and scream and thrash around a little. Usually within minutes the body will stabilize. The body really knows what it's doing. Children do this all the time. And the more we try to control this the more we let the charge build. The obsession with control in our culture automatically teaches the muscles of the body to hold. The repertoire of what one can do and say when that much charge is leaving the body is very narrow.

Brooke: What are your recommendations for that type of observation?

Selah: In the people I've worked with, panic has root in past experience, because the muscles at some point in time were taught to shut down, and the breath was taught to shallow itself. Animals in dangerous situations don't shit. The body functions just close down. People who've been holding back but want to express at that level often will be able to take the load off and they'll see that the muscles relax. The memory will open up and it will happen during the discharge of the body. The holding is usually linked to the past in some way, and my recommendation would be to try to access those memories. Nobody wants to go back. I call it "going back for the little ones." It's an easier, more compassionate way to think about it. It's the little person in you that got frozen in time cause it was just too scary. Just go back in and get 'em. Put your arms around them and bring them back. But that's a therapeutic process. In terms of daily life, the main thing is breath. Can you remember in a moment of panic that you're in charge of your breath? If nothing else? You can slow your breathing down and take deeper breaths so that you're inviting yourself back into your body to a level your capable of maintaining.

Brooke: Going back to the therapeutic process, is it often rooted in abuse, or is it much more simple than that? What most commonly makes people so tense and scared?

Selah: Personally and professionally I would say that it's usually linked to a time when an adult was coming at you with a lot of rage. Sexual abuse isn't even about sex. It's usually about adult rage being taken out on a child. A little soft child body has to handle this rage and confusion that's zooming out of an adult body. The same thing will happen at the core. The child will tense its core muscles. Sexual abuse is even more invasive and more penetrative because it literally penetrates your body, even though it's still out of control rage coming from a more powerful person to a child. When this happens the child feels overpowered and is afraid it's going to die. Of course, what the body does is lock up at the core to get through that particular challenge. And it's smart. The body is really really smart in terms of survival.

Brooke: So that can be something small, like being yelled at for masturbating?

Selah: Oh yeah. Any kind of startle response or sense that something is wrong. It could be linked to toilet training. If you have children, you have more of a chance to notice this, but if you take time to look at how soft children's bodies are—there's no tension there. There's no armor. They can't get out of the way. Even if there's a sudden irritation right when they were trying to use the body and do what you wanted them to, that can get set in at the muscular level. Sexual abuse is completely terrifying and overwhelming. It's the same set of core muscles. We record those events in our muscles. People are often afraid to go into their bodies and say, "Okay, what do you want to tell me? There's something we need to clean up in here." They're afraid they're going to find some really horrific abuse, and for some people that's true. But for a lot of people it's not the picture we have of really bad abuse. It could just be a really bad moment, when you were really vulnerable and someone was just being mean, but nevertheless it shocked your system. It's still horrific, because a child isn't differentiating; they're not labeling it abuse. They're just having an experience that they're fighting and there's a shock and they're being overpowered, but it all gets recorded in the muscles. So I think the degree of panic is relative.

There's what the muscles do when they're shocked, and then there's what the muscles do when they're repeatedly shocked and have to deal with it over time when there's no let up. The child, if you let them, will immediately clear it. They'll cry and cry and cry until they're done crying, or they'll scream or have a tantrum. But if that same child is repeatedly shocked in that way and has to hold it every time, then you start getting real chronic muscle holding patterns.

Brooke: And you think there are trigger mechanisms?

Selah: Yeah, I do. There will be things that will remind you of the constellation of things that were going on at that time.

Brooke: What's the process you go through? What's the next course of action you take with your clients in therapy?

Selah: Well, there's a couple ways you could go. First I recognize that the healer is in the person, so I don't make the decisions. When we reach those juncture points the person really has to decide which way they want to go with it, and I'll go there. It could be as simple as the physical release of a forbidden expression. That could be rage. That could be pounding the heck out of something and I have pillows and mattresses for that. It could be a tantrum where you pound your legs and arms. This is similar to bioenergetics. What I find, and this is related to what we recognize as sexual, is that we have orgasms of rage, of sorrow, of ecstasy, of fear. At the bottom of all of these expressions, if you let them happen, is this c-shaped contraction, right below the navel, where all of it distills into this aahhhhhh—tension-point release. The body takes care of it if you let the body do what it needs to do. It will always result in this final orgasm of whatever it's feeling, and you can't tell your body to do that. You have to make space for that and let your body do it in its own way. It's the core musculature. It's the root. Right down into the pelvic muscles and the sphincters and the anus and the genitals and the way the muscles radiate out from there and the way they interact.

Brooke: I noticed on the website for Body Electric that there was a workshop that focused on intent fire and the inability to surrender, the fear of being overpowered, and so forth. It seems like panic would come out during those workshops—surrender in particular being so related to the ways in which people react sexually.

Selah: On the simplest level I'm going to go back to this idea of repertoire. If we go back to our simplest knowledge of what's okay and what's not, what's important is what you've learned during those experiences and what you have not learned. So if you've had a very difficult time physically in your life, if you've been under stress and constant tension, then that's what you've learned to respond to. But what you have not learned feels safe because it's just missing information. What does it feel like to surrender to a loved one's touch? If you don't have that in your repertoire and you go into a relationship, then there is no repertoire with surrender, just bad feelings. There's dual paths. There's the clearing part, where you go after what's residual in your body and you clear it out by expressing it. Simultaneously, there's the retraining part, where you begin to build a repertoire of pleasure and surrender, but in really tiny ways. Do it by holding hands with a friend for two minutes. Your body will actually take in that information, and just like a computer begin to build up data that was not there before. You have to fill in the missing data. For that you have to use your adult brain and think about what gives you pleasure and develop the habit and the tolerance of pleasure. Often people who have suffered a lot of abuse have also developed a huge tolerance for fear and pain, or they wouldn't be alive. They don't have much tolerance for pleasure—and what are those submissions? And how do you manage those when they're arising in your body? How do you receive?

Brooke: There are different ways we categorize panic reactions. They can come about as a result of social phobia or appear concurrently with agoraphobia. There's a tendency toward fear and withdrawal in a person who suffers from panic. Does that have to do with not having prior experience with what it would mean to have a healthy reaction?

Selah: Yeah, so there's nowhere to go. People don't want to go into panic, but there's no other wiring established, no alternative response.

Brooke: Does the resistance to the onset of a panic or fear reaction cause an awareness that in turn makes a person more likely to fall into the reaction, or is awareness the first step that results in the reaction?

Selah: Well, I think resistance is different than awareness. Awareness is a positive step. You've got to know what's going on. Once you do recognize what's going on, your body will automatically start to change. Resistance is part of the cycle. We all have resistance a million times a day. I like to think of them as little resisters in the electrical circuitry that flow the charge down so that the wires don't fry. So when you experience that resistance as an emotional, physical being, it's the energy intensifying before it can flow freely again. Resistance is very interesting. Usually it contains a lot of old fears—again, lack of repertoire. When I worked in the movement community, called the Institute for Transformational Movement, we used to say that resistance is nothing more than movement waiting to come forth. So just to release the value judgment around resistance is important. For myself, I cannot use the idea that if we're afraid of something we draw it to us and create it. It seems so unkind to me.

Brooke: So you don't think it's true. Or it just feels blaming?

Selah: It feels like an idea, like a judgment, a construct, and it's not useful to me because you experience what you experience. And if you then think you're wrong for experiencing it, that will definitely not help you untangle the knot. I think anything that tells people that they're wrong is for what they're experiencing is a big waste of time.

Brooke: What do you think of the notion of labeling all of this? Do you think that that's detrimental, the whole idea of the disorder construct we have. There's this whole book of disorders. It seems pretty easy to look at the majority of them and say to yourself, "Oh, I experience that sometimes."

Selah: It depends on the person. If you've been laboring under the misconception that something you've been struggling with is something you should be able to handle by yourself and control, then I think it's really helpful to have a diagnosis, cause then there's the comfort of—*Oh, I'm joining a community of people. It's a problem, we're all doing the best we can to solve it, and all we can do is share information and see how it goes.* There's a softening in knowing that that's there. I think there's a continuum, and we label people and we're saying we can't handle their range of expressions and that's abnormal and that needs to be medicated, or institutionalized. I think there are times, however, that recognizing that you're struggle isn't personal helps.

Brooke: What's being unfolded in these chapters is that there's different panic reactions. On the one hand, there's that surge of having almost been in an accident—a panic explosion—and then there's the built-in, repetitive threat—recurring panic attacks—that people suffer with their entire lives. You can run the gamut of what it means to have a panic reaction, which is maybe why this is such a universal topic.

Selah: That's a good distinction. When you in an accident, and there's that shock and an adrenaline surge, all the biochemistry that gathers forces to get you through it—to me, that's fear. That's a normal fear reaction. If you then get out of the car and start running around screaming unintelligibly for a long period of time, and if you don't then come down from that, then you're caught in a loop and your body isn't finishing its expression and there's an incapacity to return to the present moment.

Brooke: Would you call that the inability to create closure, or to finish the cycle? Do you think there should be a full circle, a full-swing pattern, to have a surge and then to come down, in order to complete the cycle and prevent from getting stuck?

Selah: You might have an ongoing problem and there might be many cycles. So, maybe part of the repertoire that's missing is the completion of the cycle.

Brooke: Sexually that seems like it could come into play. Every time you engage in trying to have a sexual experience with your partner, that could be little mini-cycles, if that were our analogy.

Selah: From my personal experience, coming from a background with incest, that analogy really works. The difference now—after many years of work, after having processed it and forgiven everyone involved, and I still have to forgive myself, that's the one I forget most of all—is that when the negative reactive feelings would come up before, I would get stuck in the fear and could not proceed with the present-time encounter. And every once in a while it still comes up for me. But the difference is that now I stop and I say, "I'm in it," and my partner says, "let's breathe." I talk about it, I get comfort, and then I return to the present moment and my present-time reality, which is actually that I like to have sex. Sometimes my reality says, "let's not do that" and I may change my mind, whereas in the past I couldn't get to that closure.

* * *

Brooke: Selah and I ended with the conclusion that there are many provocations and triggers for panic reactions in relation to sexuality. The concept of completing a panic reaction—allowing ourselves to experience the surge and do what we need to do (thrash around, freeze up, freak out, run to the bathroom)—is important. This is in line with Peter Levine's Somatic Experiencing (see Panic, Biology, and Reason: Giving the Body Its Due, pp. 27–48). Feeling stuck and incomplete doesn't allow for the process and we stay in the panic moment, stuck in fear.

Another important message is that panic doesn't necessarily come out of abuse. It can come from experiencing a negative reaction in a vulnerable moment. It can come from witnessing a verbal or physical assault that resonates in the core muscles of the body to be triggered later in life. My experience has been that people who have come to terms with their panic don't feel the stigma that can be associated with suffering from a psychological disorder, but they are the lucky ones. Selah's wisdom of experience includes helping us recognize that letting go of blame is one of the essential stepping stones toward understanding panic, be it our own or others'.

INSIGHT

T R E A T M E N T

Drug Specific Treatment for Panic Disorder Diagnosis

TRICYCLIC ANTIDEPRESSANTS (TCAs):

The mechanism of action for Tricyclic Antidepressants is not well-established, but thought to be related to the action on the transmitter-uptake mechanism of monoaminergic neurons. Panic disorder patients are extremely sensitive to the early stimulating effects of TCAs, including anxiety, agitiation, and insomnia during initial treatment. Most TCAs are administered orally and are non habit-forming.

Side Effects: Thae adverse side effects limit the desirability of TCAs for treatment of panic disorder. Effects include tremors, dizziness, nervousness, sexual dysfunction, fatigue, cognitive impairment, weight gain, gastrointestinal problems, and low blood pressure. Caution should be exercised by those who suffer from cardiovascular disease, as TCAs can induce arrhythmia.

Drugs: **Clomipramine (Anafranil)**
Strongly serotonergic, this is labeled as an antiobsessional drug. Not many studies have been done to prove the efficacy of the drug over time, partly because of adverse side effects in panic patients, resulting in dropouts from studies.

Doxepin (Adapin, Sinequan)
Used to treat panic and anxiety. Administered orally and should be taken with food. Can be habit-forming. Caution should be used by those with liver and kidney disease.

Imipramine (Tofranil, Janimine)
The mainstay medication for the treatment of panic disorder. In the early 60s studies showed its efficacy in anti-panic treatment. Extensive studies confirmed its ability to block panic attacks and reduce the effects of panic disorder over time. Shown to reduce anxiety and agoraphobia.

BENZODIAZEPINES

Until recently, Benzodiazepines had been the standard treatment for most anxiety disorders. They function by reinforcing a chemical in the brain that inhibits nerve-cell excitability. SSRIs are preferred over Benzodiazepines because patients experience more side effects with Benzodiazepines and they are habit-forming, while SSRIs are not. Benzodiazepines are prescribed when there is a severe illness that necessitates rapid response to panic and for patients who are either unresponsive to or experience severe side effects from antidepressants. Certain drugs are also effective in treating Generalized Anxiety Disorder or lesser anxiety.* Benzodiazepines are a rapid and effective treatment for people so disabled by panic that they are unable to go about their daily routine. Patients with panic disorder usually require higher doses of benzodiazepines than other anxious patients.

Side Effects: Major concern with Benzodiazepines is physiological depenence. Adverse effects include daytime drowsiness, hung-over feeling, respiratory problems may be exacerbated, can stimulate overeating and weight gain. Dangerous when combined with alcohol and may be associated with birth defects and should not be used when pregnant.

Drugs: **Alprazolam (Xanax)**
For management of panic disorder with or without agoraphobia and short-term symptomatic relief of symptoms of excessive anxiety. Also effective in the treatment of phobic avoidance and lessening overall symptoms of panic. Originally thought to be non-addictive, but later discovered that withdrawal reactions can be quite forceful. Still thought to be safer than Valium.

Lorazepam (Ativan)
Shown to be equivalent to Xanax for anti-panic efficacy. The short-term relief of manifestations of excessive anxiety in patients with anxiety neurosis. Mild in comparison to Valium because its effects are shorter lived. Because it's absorbed in the stomach, it works more works more effectively on an empty stomach.

Clonazepam (Klonopin)
This is a high-potency drug whose studies have shown effectiveness in the reduction of the symptomolgy of panic disorder. The benefit of Klonopin is that it remains in the system longer than its counterparts, requiring less frequent dosing.

Diazepam (Valium)
Central nervous system depressant effective in the treatment of panic attacks. It remains in the system for a relatively long time in comparison to other drugs. Overprescribed in the 60s and later considered to be unsafe because of patient addiction.

Selective Serotonin Reuptake Inhibitors (SSRIs)

These are the treatment of choice for many sufferers of panic disorder because they cause fewer side effects. The introduction of these drugs into clinical practice marked a turning point in the treatment of panic disorder. Claims decreased adverse effects and increased safety, as well as safety in overdose. There are many similarities among the SSRIs, butsome of the differences are pinpointed in this overview. As a class, these drugs are not addictive

Side Effects: nausea, agitation, dizziness, exhaustion, depression, irritability, blurred vision, headaches, nervousness, dry mouth, and sexual dysfunction, including loss of libido (low sex drive) and ejaculatory problems. In general, SSRIs are reported to have fewer side effects than TCAs.

Drugs: **Fluoxetine (Prozac)**

First SSRI shown to have anti-panic effects. Studies have shown improvements significant reductions in panic symptoms. It blocks the reuptake of seratonin into the nervous system cells. Prozac has the potential of prolonging the effects of other medications in the body and caution should be used when mixing medications.

Sertraline (Zoloft)

Approved by the FDA for treatment of depression. Appears more effective for obsessive-compulsive disorder than panic disorder, but has less side effects than other drugs in this category. Recent studies have shown significant results in decreasing the frequency of panic attacks.

Paroxetine (Paxil and Paxil CR)

For treatment of panic disorder and obsessive-compulsive disorder. This drug inhibits serotonin and seemingly has few side effects than tricyclic antidepressants. Stuidies have shown Paxil's effect on acute symptoms, as well as overall reduction of panic symptomology, with few side effects.

Citalopram (Celexa)

Relatively new drug, introduced in the US in 1998 for treatment of depression, but used effectively in Europe for over a decade. It has been shown to be effective in treating panic disorder, and patients generally report feeling better anywhere from 1-4 weeks from initiating treatment. Celexa is not addictive, but its long-term effects have not been sufficiently studied.

Fluvoxamine (Luvox)

Used for the treatment of panic disorder and generalized anxiety disorder, but most successful with obsessive-compulsive disorder. Its efficacy in long-term trials has not been well evaluated because it was only released in 1995.

*See FDA approved indications from SSRIs on p. 288.

MONOAMINE OXIDASE INHIBITORS (MAOIS):

Because of potentially dangerous interactions with other drugs and some foods, MAOIs should be reserved as a treatment alternative when symptoms have failed to respond to other common antidepressants. SSRIs are among the contraindicated drugs. Although as effective as other pharmacological treatments, MAOIs pose a problem because of the negative, toxic effects they induce in combination with certain foods: Do NOT eat food or drink beverages with tyramine while taking MAOI's. Among the foods that should be avoided are: lox, pickled herring, snails, liver, dry sausage, fava beans, raisins, figs, avocados, soy sauce, cheese (cottage and cream cheese ok), sour cream, yogurt, alcohol, caffeine, yeasts, pickles, sauerkraut.

Side Effects: weight gain, drowsiness, dizziness, sexual dysfunction, insomnia, lightheadedness, sleep disturbances, hypotension and hypertension brought on by eating certain foods. Concurrent use with SSRIs must be avoided as severe serotonergic syndrome may be precipitated.

Drugs: **Phenelzine (Nardil)**
Used in the treatment of depressed patients who are considered "atypical" or "neurotic." Anxiety, depression, phobias, and hypochondria is often found in these patients and Nardil is prescribed for those who have not had success with other drugs.

Selegiline (Eldepryl)
Originally used to treat depression, this drug is considered the safest of the older MAOIs and has fewer side effects, not causing sexual dysfunction, anxiety, or insomnia.

ANTIEPILEPTIC MEDICATIONS:

Antiepileptic drugs have been adopted more recently in the treatment of panic disorder because of their effectiveness in the treatment of anxiety and depresssion. None has received an FDA indication for use in panic disorder, though trials are being run. See Atul Pande's chapter for Neurontin use in panic disorder.

Side Effects: memory lapses, gastrointestinal irritation, mood swings, dizziness, ataxia, fatigue, nausea, poor muscle control, and somnolence.

Drugs: **Gabapentin (Neurontin)**
Preliminary reports show that this drug, used to treat seizures, is useful in the treatment of patients with severe panic disorder. More studies need to be done in order to confirm these drugs are indeed effective for panic.

Clonazapam (Klonopin)
Anticonvulsive benzodiazepine that has been used to treat panic. This drug has been reported to be more effective than many SSRIs in relieving symptoms. Withdrawal symtoms can be very severe.

note: Warnings against smoking, consumption of alcohol, and use during pregnancy should be heeded in all cases.

*Benzodiazepines used in the treatment include Diazepam (Valium), Lorazepam (Ativan), Halazepam (Paxipam), and Chlordiazepoxide (Librium).

Drug Specific Treatment for Panic Disorder Diagnosis *(continued)*

THE VALUE AND LIMITATIONS OF FDA APPROVED INDICATIONS

It is common and often necessary to select strategies for care that combine the effects of several agents for treatment resistant patients. Moreover, such strategies often employ novel uses of drugs for an indication beyond those that are "labeled" safe and effective by the Food and Drug Administration. Decisions to seek labeled approval for use of a drug more often reflect an economic calculus by a drug's patent holder rather than emerging medical practice or scientifically based reasons. Because of this, the Federal Food, Drug and Cosmetics Act does not limit the manner in which a physician may use an approved drug. "Once a product has been approved for marketing, a physician may choose to prescribe it for uses or in treatment regimens for individual patients that are not included in approved labeling." (Physicians Desk Reference)

The SSRIs have the following approved indications for usage by the FDA

Fluoxetine (Prozac) — Free market without patent protection
> Depression
> Obsessive-Compulsive Disorder
> Bulimia Nervosa

Sertraline (Zoloft)
> Depression
> Obsessive-Compulsive Disorder
> Panic Disorder
> Posttraumatic Stress Disorder

Paroxetine (Paxil and Paxil CR)
> Depression
> Obsessive-Compulsive Disorder
> Panic Disorder
> Social Anxiety Disorder (Social Phobia)

Citalopram (Celexa)
> Depression

Fluvoxamine (Luvox)
> Obsessive-Compulsive Disorder

ATUL C. PANDE

Conventional Drug Treatment of Panic Disorder

S INCE THE TERM *panic disorder* was introduced into psychiatric terminology two decades ago, treatment for this condition has continued to evolve in multiple directions. Because the impairment in panic disorder consists of more than panic attacks alone, comprehensive treatment involves more than just the suppression or prevention of the attacks themselves. Typical treatment programs for panic disorder can include the use of medications, psychological ("talking") therapy, and behavioral therapy. The use of medications to treat panic disorder is important not only to control the symptoms but also to improve functional outcome. Increasingly, the medical community has begun to realize that the key goal of treatment should be symptom elimination rather than just reduction. In the case of panic disorder, reducing the rate of panic attacks is clearly beneficial but is unlikely to take away the constant fear of having more attacks or eliminate the tendency by many panic sufferers to avoid certain situations.

Medication Treatment

A panic attack is a form of very intense anxiety that typically occurs in short bursts of a few minutes to an hour or so. In theory, almost any medication that has anxiety-reducing effects can be useful in curbing panic attacks. Even alcohol, which in small doses reduces anxiety, can suppress panic, although this is hardly an advisable treatment approach. Many sufferers of panic attacks discover alco-

Table 1: Examples of Medications Used to Treat Panic Disorder

Drug Class	Examples
Tricyclic Antidepressants	Imipramine (Tofranil)
Serotonin Reuptake Inhibitors	Sertraline (Zoloft), paroxetine (Paxil)
Benzodiazepines	Alprazolam (Xanax), clonazepam (Klonopin)

hol as a readily self-administered treatment but then become prisoners to alcohol abuse and dependence.

There are currently several classes of medications in use for the treatment of panic disorder (Table 1; SEE PP. 284–287 for more examples). The first medication to be extensively studied, and approved by health authorities in many countries, as a treatment for panic disorder was alprazolam (originally marketed by the Upjohn Company as Xanax). Xanax was shown in several scientific studies to eliminate or reduce panic attacks and to suppress the fearfulness or avoidance of certain places or situations that is commonly a part of panic disorder. Being part of the class of medications known as benzodiazepines, Xanax has some potential problems. While it can be very helpful for the majority of people who receive it in an appropriate manner, some people may become dependent on the drug or be inclined to take increasing doses beyond what is prescribed for them. This effect of the benzodiazepines in some people has led to unnecessary fear and concern even about the legitimate medical use of these drugs. With appropriate caution, however, the vast majority of panic disorder sufferers can take Xanax and derive benefit without fearing the treatment itself.

Due to some of the concerns about benzadiazepines and their potential for misuse, the interest of doctors and patients has expanded to other classes of medications that work by altering a brain chemical called serotonin. These medications, selective serotonin reuptake inhibitors (SSRIs), of which fluoxetine (Prozac) was the first to hit the market, have been extensively studied over the past decade. Although SSRIs were originally approved as treatments for depression, subsequent studies have shown several of them to be effective in treating panic disorder. In the United States, the Food and Drug Administration has so far approved Sertraline (Zoloft) and Paroxetine (Paxil) among the SSRIs specifically for the treatment of panic disorder.

Studies have shown that SSRIs reduce or eliminate panic attacks, reduce fearfulness and worrying in between attacks, and thereby provide substantial relief to sufferers. Among the major differences between SSRIs and benzadiazepines is the time it takes to derive substantial benefit. Not many studies have directly compared these two classes of drugs, but the experience of clinicians and patients suggests that relief of symptoms begins within a few days with benzadiazepines, but may take two or more weeks with the SSRIs. On the plus side, SSRIs are not known to have the same risk of dependence and misuse as benzadiazepines do. A comparison of the features of these two classes of medication is shown in Table 2.

Given that many patients with panic disorder often also develop depressive symptoms either intermittently or chronically, the use of SSRIs has the dual benefit of relieving symptoms of panic and depression. Many experts believe that benzodiazepines are most suitable for patients who have minimal depression accompanying their panic disorder. Skillful clinicians often combine benzodiazepines with SSRIs to achieve optimal therapeutic benefit. This can be a useful treatment approach so long as the combined burden of side effects does not become unmanageable.

Table 2: Features of Medications Used to Treat Panic Disorder

Serotonin Reuptake Inhibitors

Positives:	Relief of panic and anxiety
	No noticeable sedation
Negatives:	Slower onset of anti-anxiety effects

Benzodiazepines

Positives:	Rapid relief of anxiety and panic symptoms
Negatives:	Drowsiness
	Dizziness
	Reduced attention and memory
	Psychological and physical dependence

Now mainly of historical interest, a class of medications known as the monoamine oxidase inhibitors (MAOIs) were often used in the treatment of panic disorder. Drugs included in this class, such as phenelzine (Nardil) and tranylcypromine (Parnate), are still marketed but infrequently used. Although data from studies and clinical experience clearly indicate these drugs to be effective in relieving panic and anxiety symptoms, there are several limitations associated with their use. Because of the way these drugs work, there is a likelihood of adverse interactions with some other drugs or foods. This requires constant vigilance on the patient's part to avoid those drugs and foods while taking the MAOI drugs. With the introduction of the serotonin medications, use of the MAOIs has gradually lessened to where they are predominantly being used for those situations where other treatments have failed.

Experimental Medications

Although the majority of patients with panic disorder who require medication treatment can be successfully treated with either benzadiazepines or SSRIs, some people either fail to get any meaningful relief, get only partial relief, or are unable to tolerate the side effects of the medications. Therefore, research is being carried out to develop new treatments for panic disorder.

Other than the benzadiazepines and SSRI classes of medications, there is some indication that medications which were originally used to treat seizure disorder may have some use in improving panic disorder. Reports in the scientific literature have suggested that sodium valproate (Depakote) may treat some patients with panic disorder. Similarly, a preliminary report on gabapentin (Neurontin) indicated that patients with a more severe type of panic disorder may benefit from this medication. Depakote and Neurontin have been approved for the treatment of seizure disorder and only limited evidence for their effect in panic disorder is available at present. Until further studies have been carried out, no definitive recommendation can be made about how, if at all, Depakote or Neurontin may be used in treating panic disorder. Such studies are required to confirm that these drugs are indeed effective for treating panic, and to establish what is the most effective and safe dosing regimen for this condition.

Some research is also going on to test the usefulness of drugs for panic disorder that work similarly to benzodiazepines but attempt to reduce some of their undesirable effects. These drugs selectively activate the neurotransmitter GABA and are aimed at reducing anxiety symptoms without evoking unwanted effects like drowsiness, memory lapses, and so on.

Long-Term Treatment

Panic disorder is a chronic, recurring disorder. Although some people may have limited bouts of panic and recover for an indefinite length of time, many will have periods of symptoms interspersed with intervals of partial or full recovery.

Several studies have followed patients with panic disorder for a number of years following initial treatment. Since many of the patients in these studies either discontinued treatment or had periods of being on and off treatment, a singular conclusion about long-term outcome is hard to make. Nevertheless, it is clear that a significant majority of patients continue to have symptoms even after as long as four years. The greater the level of functional impairment and phobic avoidance at the start of the follow-up the lower were the remission rates during follow-up. Unfortunately, little data exist on the best treatment approaches to minimize disability associated with panic disorder. In at least one study, cognitive behavioral therapy was helpful in reducing the relapse rates upon discontinuation of treatment. Thus, a combination of drug and cognitive therapy may provide synergistic benefits that are sustainable over time.

A few studies have tested whether the beneficial effects of drug treatment are sustained beyond the short-term. In a study of Paxil, patients with panic disorder who responded to three months of maintenance treatment were assigned to either continue paroxetine or switch to placebo for another three months. At the end of the study, 5 percent of Paxil-treated patients and 30 percent of placebo-treated patients had relapsed. Another study compared Paxil, clomipramine (Anafranil), and placebo treatment for nine months. It was found that patients continued to improve over the entire duration of treatment. These kinds of studies suggest that continuation of drug treatment beyond the initial few weeks is beneficial and patients may continue to improve over prolonged periods.

Although prolonged drug therapy is often beneficial, little data are available to support a clear recommendation on the optimal length of treatment. Some experts believe that prolonged treatment may be appropriate for most patients with panic disorder but is particularly essential when there are high levels of persisting symptoms, previous relapses have led to serious impairment, or multiple external stressors are present. Unfortunately, clinicians are often reluctant to consider long-term therapy even when clear signals indicate a need. Some of this reluctance may be based upon lack of understanding of the long-term course of panic disorder, lack of knowledge about the benefits of prolonged treatment, or the fear of "dependence." Clearly, more education is needed to encourage clinicians and patients to undertake prolonged treatment under the appropriate circumstances.

When and How to Stop Medication

After the symptoms of panic disorder have been adequately controlled, patients often find it difficult to stick with medication treatment. Certainly, after prolonged periods of treatment, it is important for patients and their doctors to evaluate whether discontinuation of treatment may be warranted. The persistence of intolerable side effects or a loss of therapeutic effect may necessitate stopping treatment in some cases.

In most situations, the decision to stop medication depends upon achieving a prolonged period of sustained remission during which time patients have acquired behavioral techniques aimed at anxiety management. If this occurs in the context of a stable life situation with few anticipated major life stressors, then discontinuation of medication may be considered.

Discontinuing medication treatment must invariably be carried out very gradually. This is essential in order to avoid the untoward effects of medication withdrawal. Even more importantly, gradual tapering off of medication allows for an opportunity to rapidly reinstitute treatment should symptoms of panic disorder reemerge. At least one study has shown that rapid reinstitution of treatment in early relapsers helped to avert full symptomatic manifestations of panic disorder. This approach may be particularly valuable where the disability associated with full relapse would have major consequences for the individual's work or family life.

Alternative "Medications"

A variety of natural and herbal remedies have been suggested for the treatment of anxiety and depression. None is specifically proposed for panic disorder.

Although remedies such as kava-kava are believed by many to have calming and anti-anxiety properties, the evidence in support of such claims is weak. Personal testimonials are often used to advance these remedies as legitimate treatments. Until these remedies are subjected to formal study in the same manner as medications described above, it is not possible to prove or disprove their utility in treating panic disorder.

HELEN RESNECK-SANNES

There Really Is Something to Be Afraid of: Body-Oriented Psychotherapy for the Treatment of Panic Disorder

Reality is the leading cause of stress for those in touch with it.

> —Jane Wagner, *The Search for Signs of Intelligent Life in the Universe*

TONY SOPRANO, the mob boss from the popular HBO series, *The Sopranos,* suffers from panic attacks. He becomes attached to a family of ducks who have settled in his swimming pool; when they leave, he faints. He is unaware of the triggers to these spells of anxiety and fear that have surfaced into his consciousness for the first time. Before the attacks he felt in charge; he was "the boss," king of the mob. Now he feels fragile and concerned enough to risk exposing his criminal secrets to a therapist if it will alleviate his distress. He enters psychoanalysis. His suffering becomes so severe that he even agrees to take the Prozac his psychiatrist pre-scribes. The incidence of people in our culture suffering from panic attacks is so common that television, the pervasive media of our time, portrays its debilitating effects in such an unlikely candidate as the boss of the mob. The purpose of this chapter is to present a treatment for this widespread disorder. The interventions I discuss use techniques from Bioenergetics, a somatically based analytic psychotherapy developed by Alexander Lowen, as well as some of the principles for the treatment of trauma developed by Peter A. Levine (see Chapter 3, page 27). These treatments encourage the client to pay attention to signals and impulses emanating from his or her body and to use these to understand intrapsychic and emotional concerns. In this context, the alarming physiological symptoms of panic attacks are viewed as the body's physical response to danger. A treatment approach is presented which encourages the sufferer to trust and attend to the messages from his body. Rather than trying to deny fear, the physiological arousal is viewed as an attempt to deal with a threat either in one's physical or intrapsychic world.

The symptoms of panic will be described, followed by case studies of how they affect the lives of five different people. The first person, though fictional, is Tony Soprano. Next, I present three case studies from my practice. Each of these cases demonstrate different aspects of the complex nature of this syndrome and the necessity for different treatment interventions. Identifying information of the clients is disguised to protect their identities. Lastly, I present myself. Although I did not experience a classic panic attack, I had been in a state of high arousal and fear. The help I received from a friend illustrates how supporting the body's impulses can help transform our physiological responses.

Tony Soprano's symptoms of panic are classic—heart palpitations, dizziness, and even fainting. Initially, he denies that there is anything in his life causing him anxiety. However, as the television series progresses, and the encounters with his psychiatrist unfold, he learns that his mother may have set him up to be "hit" and that his best friend is betraying his secrets to the FBI. Living this kind of life would make anyone anxious. The problem for Tony is that he is in denial about these real threats in his life. He protests to his therapist that mothers love their children, that it's unnatural for a mother to want to have her son killed. As for his best friend, Pussy, Tony suspects that he is talking to the Feds, but it is almost too unbearable to admit. Instead of facing the awful truth of these betrayals and the danger he faces, he suffers panic attacks—until one episode in which an actual attempt is made on his life. He is able to escape the bullet and for the first time in many months his depression lifts—he is no longer anxious. How can this be?

Tony now has a real threat to attach to his symptoms. His fight-or-flight responses are useful for keeping him away from danger. He no longer has to deny the messages that his body is telling him; he can identify an external threat. Later in the series his symptoms return, as he is still reacting physically to the fact his mother wanted to have him killed. Tony represents how cognitive denial does not prevent these intense bodily reactions which have been hard-wired into our biology to protect us from harm.

Panic is the body's physiological response to danger. When threatened, the body goes into the state of arousal, or sympathetic dominance. Heart rate increases and blood rushes to the extremities to prepare us to run or fight.

A panic attack causes the fastest and most complex reaction known within the human body. It immediately alters the functioning of the eyes, several major glands, the brain, heart, lungs, stomach, intestines, pancreas, kidneys and bladder, and the major muscle groups. Within the cardiovascular system the heart increases its rates of contraction, and the pressure it exerts as blood is pumped into the arteries. The vessels that channel blood into the vital organs and skeletal muscles expand, increasing their blood flow, while the blood vessels in the arms, legs, and other less vital parts of the body begin to constrict, reducing blood flow in those areas.[1]

When an animal senses threat, the primitive, reptilian brain constructed for survival takes over. Early persons living in Equatorial Africa didn't have the luxury of time to evaluate whether the movement in the brushes was a lion about to pounce or grass waving in the breeze. Survival demanded their bodies respond as if danger was present, to prepare for fight or flight. Modern peoples' physiological responses to threat shifts into the same highly charged energized state.

When the fight-or-flight responses are successful and a person is able to escape harm or kill her attacker, the body returns to homeostasis. The energy is discharged while actively and effectively defending against threat and the nervous system moves back toward a normal level of functioning. When an actual attempt was made on Tony's life and he successfully dodged the bullet, he was able to locate the source of the danger and defend himself. His defensive fight-or-flight response worked. His physiological responses were no longer perceived as alien entities attacking him. His body was on his side and his responses led to his survival.

One of the contributing factors to feeling overwhelmed during a panic attack is the inability to identify the precipitating event. The body is in a high state of activation ready for fight or flight, but the danger is not identifiable. The person can't find the stimulus to which his or her body is reacting and the symptoms (the state of arousal) become frightening—a source of anxiety in and of themselves. The body's arousal state seems out of proportion to the reality of the situation. If the situation is psychologically threatening, there may be strong intrapsychic forces preventing the person from seeking the escape or support which is needed. Because Tony Soprano could not face the fact that his mother wanted him killed, his flight-or-fight responses were thwarted—unable to be expressed.

His psychoanalyst (wisely) did not try to talk him out of his fear nor try to override his somatic reactions. Attempts to induce relaxation can further augment the thwarting by communicating to the person that the bodily reactions are the problem. Here Levine illustrates what can happen when a client who becomes aroused is encouraged to relax:

> Relaxation was not the answer. In our first session as I naively, and with the best of intentions, attempted to help her relax, she went into a full-blown anxiety attack. She appeared paralyzed, unable to breathe. Her heart was pounding wildly, and seemed to almost stop.[2]

I next present several cases showing how panic attacks can be successfully managed without trying to override the body's signals of danger. Let us examine the case of Bill. He was an assistant professor at the university and entered therapy with the complaint of panic attacks that were so severe they interfered with his work. He was experiencing overwhelming feelings of fear, accompanied by rapid heartbeat, shortness of breath, sweating, shaking, and fear of dying. These symptoms primarily occurred when he was on work-related trips with an influential member of his department. Further questioning revealed that his boss was placing Bill in life-threatening situations and then denying his concern. For instance, one time they were in a small boat during a storm. His boss refused to provide a short-wave radio. Another time they climbed an exposed rock without a rope and went scuba diving without partners. The message was: "Deny your fear and do not ask for support." Bill's head was telling him he was safe, but his body was sending him signals to the contrary.

With Bill I applied two interventions which I commonly use in the treatment of panic attacks. The first intervention is a technique common in the practice of Bioenergetic analysis. The therapist assists the client in identifying the bodily symptoms of panic and invites the person to investigate why they are appearing and what they might be communicating. For some reason the body is responding to danger. The threatening stimulus may not be known in the present, but there is usually a good reason for the body's behavior, and it needs to be heeded.

Once Bill agreed that his symptoms might be useful, that his body was telling him that he was in danger, I asked him if he was willing to experiment with coming in and out of the physiological state of panic in the office with my assistance. By learning to identify the physical state of arousal and how to change it, he felt less out of control, and thus less threatened by his panic states. This intervention was initiated when he was feeling safe and calm.

"If an agoraphobic patient who has been accompanied into the street is left alone there, he will produce an anxiety attack. Or if an obsessional neurotic is prevented from washing his hands after having touched something, he will become prey to almost unbearable anxiety. It is plain, then, that the purpose and the result of the imposed condition of being accompanied in the street and the obsessional act of washing the hands were to obviate the outbreaks of anxiety of this kind. In this sense every inhibition which the ego imposes on itself can be called a symptom."

—Sigmund Freud, *Inhibitions, Symptoms and Anxiety*

I next introduced a classic Bioenergetic grounding exercise. While sitting in a chair, I instructed him to place both feet on the floor, hip-width apart. I told him to place his left hand on his belly and his right hand on his heart and to notice his breath. Belly breathing is grounded, centered breathing. During panic attacks, people tend to primarily breathe into their chest, do not fully exhale, breathing again into a chest already inflated with air. There is no room for another breath and they start to feel like they can't breathe, becoming frightened, and trying to breathe in even harder.

I instructed him to concentrate on fully completing an exhale and as he released his breath, to gently push into the floor with his

T R E A T M E N T

feet. I told him to allow his eyes to be opened or closed but to not try to focus on anything in the room. I asked him to keep his mouth open—hang-dogged and slack-jawed. I demonstrated "the look" I intended, as people often feel foolish with their jaws hanging open.

Finally, and most importantly, I encouraged him to allow his belly move with his breath, expanding with the inhale and relaxing with the exhale. At first Bill, as do many people, had difficulty with this, so with his permission I placed my hand over his left hand, which was resting on his belly, and gently pushed down on the exhale and released my pressure during the inhale. Once he was able to master this breathing, I returned to my chair and encouraged him to take a few more breaths, concentrating on the exhale. People tend to tighten their stomachs during panic attacks as they try to breathe into the chest without fully exhaling.

Next I asked him if he was willing to try to consciously organize his body into the configuration he assumed during a panic attack, and then consciously reorganize it from that arrangement. At first he was hesitant, so I reassured him that he would not have a full-blown attack. I wanted him to be aware so that he could have some voluntary control over his body the next time he found himself having an attack.

I told him the story of two children at nursery school. A loud train goes by and the little girl shakes her hands and says, "I'm afraid." The little boy next to her says, "Suck in your belly button and you won't be afraid." I tell him that when we're afraid we tend to act like that little boy and suck in our belly buttons. This limits the amount of air we can have in our belly. I told him to tighten his belly and pull up his legs to experience the subtle tightening of the gluteus muscles. I instructed him to breathe into his chest and without fully exhaling to breathe in again and again. He began to gasp for air, his shoulders pulling up toward his ears and his eyes becoming wide with fright.

I told him to fully exhale while gently pushing into the floor with his feet. His shoulders dropped and his facial features softened in relief. He practiced this exercise several times in my office until he felt comfortable with the different states and could move in and out of them with ease.

Bill had one more panic attack before we terminated therapy. He had been raised in a family that refused to talk about their feelings. Bill was called home without warning and only told that his mother needed to see him. Once home, his sister told him that their mother had had open heart surgery the night before but was now feeling fine. She hadn't told him earlier because she hadn't wanted to worry him.

He entered his mother's hospital room and found her under an oxygen tent, unable to recognize him. He was afraid that she had suffered a stroke and was permanently brain damaged or was dying. He ran into the hall gasping for breath. He remembered the exercises we had rehearsed and was able to control his breathing and seek help. A nurse reassured him that by the next day she would likely be removed from the oxygen tent and be more cognizant (able to recognize him and converse).

Bill's family used denial as a defense mechanism to handle life's stresses and anxieties—the same mechanism his boss used to deny his fear. This was not a coping strategy that was useful for Bill, as his body knew when a situation was dangerous. Denial left him without resources for coping with his experience. Instead of allowing the feelings of panic to be the final definition of his experience, he sought help, talked to the nurse, received the necessary information, and was able to calm himself. He terminated therapy after sixteen sessions and has reported no new panic attacks.

The next client, who I will call Jim, was referred by my dentist. During one of those lovely times when everything was stuffed in my mouth, my dentist asked me my thoughts regarding panic attacks and panic disorder. He pulled the instruments out of my mouth long enough for me to explain to him my thinking about it as a blocked fight-or-flight response that left the body in a heightened state of arousal. He said that his friend Jim had begun experiencing severe panic attacks since the death of his wife and his treatment by a therapist had left him feeling worse. He wondered if I could help him; I replied that I would like to try. A week later Jim called for an appointment.

Jim's presentation differed from Tony and Bill in that no events in his current life appeared to be life-threatening. His case demonstrates how intrapsychic forces, primarily guilt and denial, can be precipitators for the constellation of panic disorder. He described seeing his previous therapist for two years, once a week, using a combination of cognitive therapy and relaxation. He had also tried the usual pharmaceutical treatment for anxiety, depression, and panic. He disliked the side effects and actually felt worse on the medication. In general, he said that he felt more anxious after this first therapy and was dubious that any treatment could help him.

Jim was experiencing severe grief after his wife's death. He had tried to date, but other women only reminded him of his wife and his loss. He felt guilty, as he had had a series of affairs during their relationship. She had suffered from a chronic illness which rendered her helpless and dependent on him. On the one hand, he liked this helplessness, as she needed him and wouldn't leave; on the other hand, he hated being trapped. Ultimately she did leave him when she died, but he still seemed trapped out of loyalty to her and the life they had planned together.

His panic attacks were severe, rendering him helpless—at times he actually became dizzy and fainted. The attacks occurred most often at work and sometimes at the grocery store. In both situations he had the sense of people approaching him and not being able to escape. He obsessed about selling his house, thinking that if he sold it he could leave his job and retire to a less expensive place to live. Other times he became fixated on buying a car, would spend all of his free time researching and finding the car, then shortly after buying it he would become disappointed and sell it.

During the first session I focused on his guilt. I told him about the book, *Necessary Losses*, by Judith Viorst. She reports that most happily married couples at some point in their relationship wish for their spouse to die. If the partner suffered an accidental death then there would be no responsibility or guilt and the person could be free. Jim was quite relieved to know about this statistic and after the first session he stopped taking his Xanax, saying that the medication made him "feel weird."

After our second session he brought me a picture of himself with his recently purchased red Camaro convertible. I admired it and asked him questions about how he felt about it. Buying a car represented being a single man. He actually referred to the convertible as a "chick magnet." But within three weeks he was already displeased with the idea of a convertible and began focusing on selling it and buying another car—a different Camaro, which he has continued to own and enjoy. Before his wife's death, he had been torn between buying a car that he liked and one that would satisfy his wife's needs. The second car represented his willingness to move forward and make a decision for himself. It was not a car to appease his wife or to attract to women, but a car that he enjoyed driving and owning. He has told me repeatedly that I don't understand that this is a big change for him. Since his wife's death he had bought and sold seven cars and had never felt calm about his purchases. Being able to buy a car he wasn't tired of within a few weeks meant that Jim had come to terms with being a single unattached man. He is no longer guilty about making a purchase on his own and can choose a car that fits his needs.

Jim was too frightened to attempt entering and leaving the panic state in my office. He suffered from attention deficit disorder and had difficulty staying with his bodily sensations. He needed constant support and reassurance from me regarding his decisions about changing jobs and moving. I reflected that selling his house without a plan of where to move scared him, as it would many people. We reviewed his financial situation and discovered that it was possible for him to keep his house and work half-time. Sitting behind the desk and having people approach him contributed to his feelings of being trapped and panicked. Once he was able to complete "the flight response" (getting out from behind the desk) and find a job working "in the field," his panic attacks dissipated. He no longer felt the need to sell his house and leave town. After ten sessions he reported that he was not experiencing panic attacks and was generally feeling less anxious.

We began to explore his current relationships with women. Shortly thereafter he learned that because he had switched jobs he had lost his insurance benefits—influencing his decision to terminate therapy. Although Jim no longer suffers from panic disorder, he has many issues that need to be addressed in psychotherapy. He was the child of an alcoholic mother. His father was rarely at home and many times he returned from school to find his mother passed out drunk on the couch. He suffers from

"Weeping woman, study for *Guernica*," c. 1937. **Pablo Picasso**

obsessive-compulsive disorder and is still drawn to women who are dependent and needing care with the unconscious hope that they won't leave him. As he is not currently experiencing panic attacks and has lost his benefits, he has terminated therapy and it is clear that he isn't motivated to explore other issues.

The next client differs from the other three in that nothing existed in her current situation to explain her symptoms of panic. Debbie was a twenty-four-year-old woman with a history of depression. She was in her third trimester of pregnancy and experiencing symptoms of depression, anxiety, and panic. She had episodes of dizziness and difficulty breathing, sometimes waking up from sleep gasping for breath. She reported that these panic attacks had flared three times before, always during December. They lasted about three months and then subsided. She was aware that her mother was depressed during her infancy and thought there might be a connection. She had a good relationship with her current therapist, who she was seeing weekly in psychotherapy that was initiated three years ago. Although Debbie felt that she had gained much from the treatment, she was still suffering from panic attacks. One of her friends, a colleague of mine, knew about my work with posttraumatic stress disorder and suggested that my treatment approach might be helpful to her.

Two days before our first appointment her husband brought her to the local mental health unit for medication to alleviate her symptoms. Because of her state of emotion and the recent news coverage on post-partum depression following the Andrea Yates case, in addition to the risk of maternal homicide and suicide, the staff at the mental health unit wanted to hospitalize her against her will. She was locked in a room while the staff went to find the psychiatrist. Fortunately, her husband talked the psychiatrist into releasing her into his custody and they left the hospital against medical advice. She received a prescription for Paxil and Imipramine, which was what she went to the hospital for in the first place.

I encouraged her to tune into her body and follow its processes. She sat rigidly in the chair saying that she felt her arms were held at her side and she couldn't move them. She complained that her spine felt like it was outside of her body, raw and exposed. This was accompanied by a stabbing pain in her back and she reported difficulty finding her breath. Her mother was able to validate that when she was four months old, during the winter months, she had been sick with scarlet fever. At first her mother said that she had taken Debbie to the hospital with a dangerously high fever. The next week her mother went back on that story and said that Debbie had been treated at home.

Debbie felt that her mother minimized her experiences as a child and was encouraging her to "put on a happy face" and deny her current distress. Debbie and I hypothesized that for the last three years she had been reliving some infantile trauma that occurred during the winter, perhaps her experience of suffering from the fever. She seemed to be experiencing an anniversary reaction to an infantile trauma, encoded in her body but not available to narrative memory.

Recent findings from observing caretaker/infant pairs have confirmed what body therapists have known for a long time—that early attachment experiences are encoded in the right brain where they remain unsymbolized and available through communication with the body. Allan Schore has summarized this work, focusing on the right brain to right brain communication that occurs between the infant and her caretaker. These empirical findings indicate that memories during these preverbal years are stored in the nonverbal right brain. They are remembered in terms of body states, without a story. Out of a desire to understand and apply coherency to these feelings the person may later construct a narrative for these feelings.[3]

As Debbie sat in the chair and followed her sensory processes, she seemed to be reliving an experience that occurred during her infancy. She felt as if her arms were tied to her sides and that she was being held down. As she stayed with her physical sensations she began to experience waves of anger and then rage. With physical support and encouragement she was able to throw off the bonds that held her trapped. On her third session, at my invitation, she stood up and began pounding a large pillow in my office with a tennis racquet I keep there to give clients the opportunity to release emotion. The purpose of hitting was not to rid herself of her angry feelings. Rather, I was encouraging her to express the fight responses that had been thwarted when she was tied down. These responses had probably been blocked during her life and hitting the tennis racquet encouraged her to feel the power of her aggression in a safe, contained environment.

The fourth session she talked about fears of being trapped at the hospital during labor. The previous session she had activated her fight responses. Now her body was feeling the desire to for flight or escape. I reminded her that during her visit to the psychiatric hospital she had been locked into a room, unable to escape.

Her husband had intervened, enabling her to leave; perhaps she could trust him to protect her during her labor. After a visit to the birth center we concocted a plan in which it would be okay for her to walk around during labor and even look out of window if she chose. Her husband was supportive and reassured her that he would be her advocate and enforce her requirement that she not be held down, that she be allowed to move as needed during the birthing process. By the fifth session she had lowered the dosage of her Paxil from 30 milligrams to 20 milligrams and had stopped taking the Imipramine. She returned for two more sessions and visited once after the baby was born. She was not taking medication and appeared to be a tired but happy mother. She returned for one more session almost a year later wanting to work on setting boundaries with a friend. She reports no anxiety, depression, or panic attacks.

The last person I will discuss is myself. Although what I experienced was not truly a panic attack, I was certainly frightened. The resolution of my fear demonstrates the principles of identifying the stressors and supporting the fight-or-flight responses. I also bring myself into this chapter because of an experience I had four years ago when writing an article for a journal and describing a treatment with a client. I gave her a copy of the article in which I described our work and was surprised that she was offended by my writing. She felt that I was distant and took the role of an observer in my writing, while during the therapeutic process I was much more present. Specifically, she didn't like being the object of treatment and needed to feel my vulnerability in the process. During the experience I am about to describe, I felt extremely vulnerable.

Early one morning about four years ago I was consulting with a colleague over the phone about a client of his. This person was someone whom I held in high esteem and cared about. His client was a member of a Bioenergetic training group; while working with her, I observed that she was disassociated much of the time. During the group, I intervened, using the techniques I had been

Internal Exile
Rachel Loden

What you will not grieve
is forced on you
in the mirror,
drags like an oar
in black water.

The scented boat
drifts empty
through the stars
Why must you lie down
where there are no flowers?

What you will not live
eats through the closet
like a moth,
is fattened
on a meal of dust.

You have gone
to that distant city
as some enter a shrine,
not to worship
but to be forgotten.

* * *

taught by Levine for dealing with trauma. I carefully modulated her arousal state, preventing her from becoming overwhelmed and disassociated. Afterwards she asked if I would be willing to see her for some individual work.

My colleague's response to me and my observations about his client were cold and hateful. Some of the feeling of coldness was augmented by his use of the speaker phone causing his voice to sound like Darth Vader, but I did not miss the chilling annihilation toward me. After I hung up I began to tremble and felt my heart pounding in my chest. My fear and my body's response to it was so intense that I didn't think I could manage my feelings on my own. I called up a friend, Raven Lang, who immediately came to my house carrying a Samurai sword and suggested that I hold it. She pointed out the dried blood on it, indicating that it was actually used to kill someone. The edge of its blade was sharp enough to graze my skin and the point honed enough to run someone through.

I stood up, holding the sword in front of me, and assumed the classic Bioenergetic grounded stance. My feet were hip-width apart, knees slightly bent, and weight evenly balanced between my left and right feet. I lifted the sword above my head and slowly bent my legs, breathing in and exhaling as I straightened them. Holding that sword I felt the power of my rage and aggression soar from my arms and become one with the silver blade. I then sat on the floor holding it in front of me while Raven told me stories of its power. My fear was replaced by the pleasure of the strength in my arms and the enjoyment of my own feelings of aggression. Instead of trying to contain my aggressive impulses to fight to preserve my self-esteem, which I perceived as being threatened, Raven encouraged me to acknowledge and take ownership of these impulses by giving me the Samurai sword. She suggested that I keep the sword as long as I needed it. During the week that I kept it I held the sword in front of me several times. I felt the muscles of my upper back soften and I could feel the power and strength of my arms.

Panic attacks are the body's response to danger, a response that doesn't allow the person suffering to identify the precipitating cause or causes. The threat may result from psychological mechanisms, such as guilt and object loss, or actual perils in the external world. Regardless of the trigger, the person is unable to identify the risk. Sometimes intrapsychic forces such as denial, guilt, and repression prevent the sufferer from being aware of the particular stress or stressors that are causing the reaction. Other times infantile traumas are stored in the body and may later be represented as panic states without the person's cognitive awareness of the threat to his or her safety.

When treating panic attacks, physiological arousal is viewed as an attempt to deal with a threat, either in the physical or intrapsychic world, of the sufferer. The fight-or-flight responses are supported, enabling the person to complete their defensive pattern and return to homeostasis. People suffering from panic are also encouraged to identify their responses to fear by making themselves aware of the holding patterns in their bodies. By being aware of those patterns and learning to change them, any of us who experience panic responses can begin to develop control over our own physiology of the panic reaction.

ENDNOTES

1. Reid Wilson, *Taking Control of Panic Attacks* (New York: Harper Perrenial, 1996).

2. Peter A. Levine, *Walking the Tiger: Healing Trauma* (Berkeley: North Atlantic Books, 1997), 29.

3. Helen Resneck-Sannes, "A Feeling in Search of Memory." *Women and Therapy* 16, no. 4. (1995).

Ron Robbins

Body Approaches to the Treatment of Panic

Sometimes things that seem easy turn out hard.
Other times, the hard seems easy.

JEANNIE DID NOT KNOW what to make of the sudden end of her panic attacks. They had come often. They were horrible events with body uproar and wild fantasies of dying—racing heart, trembling, choking feelings. When her panic attacks occurred at work she would flee to an empty room and call in a colleague. She would cling desperately to her, both emotionally and psychologically, until the feelings subsided. When at home, Jeannie would disappear to a place in the house where she could shield her family from what was happening to her until she felt better. Hiding the shame she felt about her uncontrolled behavior was all she could do to get back to her routine.

Jeannie had known, and learned to anticipate, these attacks for over seven years. She estimated their occurrence at three times a week, although at times they were less frequent. They ripped apart her sense of who she was. They were a vivid tear in her personal being. Though it is estimated that panic attacks strike as many as 10–15 percent of us in our lifetimes, most of us get by without having them develop into an ongoing frequent pattern.[1] If the panic attacks take over, however, as in Jeannie's case, the chances of them ending without treatment is unlikely. Untreated, there is little reason to expect panic attacks to simply go away.

It was only by giving great support that Jeannie's colleague was able to move her enough beyond her anxiety and convince her to participate in a one-session intervention that offered the possi-

Panic Attack
Amber Taylor

Panic Attack
tight chest
can't breathe
but why?
I feel like …
I don't know—
panicked?
stressed?
worried?
    forgotten?
alone?
I don't know,
and it worries me …
I'm always sick,
always hurt,
always rushing—
STOP!
stop with these feelings
self-pity?
stop with these pressures
stop …

    with everything

      *   *   *

bility of relief. The one session was part of a research program named The Rhythmic Integration Project on Panic. The project was formally studying and systematizing a method that had already shown a capacity to rapidly reduce, and typically eliminate, panic attacks.

Jeannie arrived at the session in obvious distress. Within ninety minutes, her panic attacks were gone. It all seemed too easy. What did it mean? Suddenly years of suffering and inner elaboration of the panic experience stopped. For Jeannie it was quite a before-after experience: "Who is it that is me?" she questioned.

Three months after the intervention, during a follow-up contact, Jeannie expressed her ongoing amazement about what had happened, but she was still grappling with the magnitude of the change and how to make sense of it. Her voice lowered as she spoke about the experience, "No one would believe it. I can't tell anyone. It seems so crazy—or like some kind of miracle."

Jeannie was not the only one to experience what seemed to be a personal miracle. When events occur in unexplainable ways and have profoundly desirable effects, they are apt to be called miraculous. But what Jeannie and other treated panic sufferers couldn't explain is explainable. In fact, it is an outgrowth of a carefully conceived and measured process with a clear rationale. The intervention that proved so helpful is a systematic integration of Bioenergetics and other body-oriented psychotherapies.[2]

The balance of this chapter will present clinical and research background material about panic attacks, as well as the rationale and study results of a process undertaken by The Rhythmic Integration Project on Panic to rapidly reduce the frequency of panic attack occurrence.

Background

It seems every level of analysis has been undertaken in our attempt to understand panic—except the obvious. There has been examination of chemical imbalances, measurements taken of oxygen levels,[3] hypothesizing of gene markers, and speculation about neurological and brain processes.[4] Even cholesterol levels[5] have been considered. Therapists have stressed the importance of patients' inner lives and childhood experiences.[6] In behavioral treatment, personal imagery has been stimulated, sensations noted, and emotions aroused to the point of flooding. Family dynamics have been probed, and cognitive thoughts and logical patterns have been closely examined and changed.

Observable body movements have been largely overlooked. It is a new variation on the story of the Blind Men and the Elephant. The blind men at least tried to perceive directly what was before them. They touched and felt the physical—the leg, the ear, etc. One touched the tail and thought the animal was rope-like. Another contacted the side and likened it to a wall. Only able to know a piece of what was before them, they couldn't comprehend a whole view.

In studying panic attacks, modern science does less than the blind men. It forsakes simple direct observation in favor of high-tech instrumentation and systematic inner probing through questions and verbal report. Sophisticated and well-researched techniques have replaced the natural human perceptive ability to open the eyes and observe. Though researchers rarely look to find and follow clues from the observable body, individuals who suffer from panic attacks are likely to know their body cues, having carefully observed their own bodies in panic reactions.

Panic sufferers don't have the perspective of seeing from the outside. They focus on the physical from the vantage point of within, often exaggerating their thoughts and emotions. "Research has shown that individuals with panic disorder are preoccupied with certain bodily sensations, such as heart palpitations, dizziness, or a sense of unreality. In particular, they attribute more threatening meanings to bodily sensations than do persons with other anxiety disorders."[7,8]

People with panic attacks also differ from those who suffer from other kinds of anxiety disorders in the amount of attention they give to their own physical sensations. They attend "vigilantly." They are trying to see something, but are seemingly unable to get it. This might suggest that research efforts directed toward helping sufferers might approach understanding and treatment by taking a look, from an outside view, at observable physical behavior. This, however, has not been a focus of research in the field.

The neglect of the directly observable is curious in light of how panic attacks have been defined for clinical purposes in the DSM-IV (p. v).[9] Of the thirteen listed panic disorder symptoms, ten involve clear physical sensations. These physical sensations, vividly sensed by the sufferer, may or may not be accompanied by cognitive experiences. Thoughts of losing control, going crazy, or dying are common occurrences for people suffering from panic attacks.

Though there are some exceptions, the research literature that focuses on the psychological treatment of panic attacks is heavily weighted by approaches concerned with changing irrational cognitions associated with the attacks. The importance of this emphasis grows out of society's emphasis on the significance of our thoughts and René Descartes's universally known philosophy, "I think, therefore I am." A strong cognitive and cognitive-behavioral establishment in academia also furthers it. Solid and extensive work on panic treatment has developed in these quarters. A number of studies have shown that panic attacks can be successfully treated in fairly reasonable time periods.

In these studies,[10] summarized by A. Arntz and colleagues, between 75–90 percent of panic-ridden subjects become panic-free after following a course of cognitive therapy designed to address their symptoms. The treatment times of the studies varied between eight to twelve sessions, sometimes involving homework that called on subjects to do personal work between sessions. These results were significantly better than those obtained by subjects who were put on a waiting list for future treatment, or for placebo treatments such as progressive relaxation or supportive help.

The Rhythmic Integration Project on Panic demonstrates the possibility that treatment can be effective in even less time, often in just one session. Its effectiveness originates from the original idea of intervening at a point in the panic process before panic-arousing thoughts creep in precognitively.

Support for the fact that panic attacks are initially precognitive comes from several sources. Historical meanings, diagnostic descriptions, research findings, and theoretical writings support the idea that the mind's thoughts do not play the primary role in the arousal of panic attacks. This is a concept that often seems counterintuitive to sufferers, as their thoughts, anticipation, and attempts to avoid are usually a major part of their experience.

A review of the history of the word panic identifies its early usage in English or French as having occurred in the sixteenth and seventeenth centuries: "the so-called 'panique terrors' or 'terreur panique:' Sudden Foolish Frights, without any certeine cause ... (England, 1603)." The

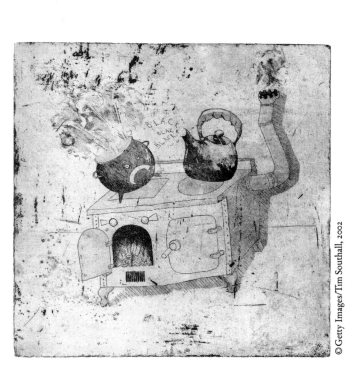

review concludes, "Many of the original meanings of the word "panic" seem relevant to the phenomenon — its sudden and groundless appearance, 'out of the clear blue sky.'"[11] In order to be diagnosed as clinically suffering from panic it's required that the individual have at least one panic attack that is unexpected[12]—or unanticipated. H. Waring, who collected data from panic sufferers as part of general medical practice reported that, "Nearly all patients stated that their first attack caught them unawares (97 percent)."[13] These observations strongly suggest that thoughts, cognitions, are not the catalyst to panic attacks. Something else comes first.

D. Klein, a major researcher and theoretician in the field, also presents a strong case for the source of panic attacks being a noncognitive event.[14] He argues that the anxiety that occurs during a panic attack significantly differs from that which occurs just prior to the attack. Klein based his argument on data that showed that two classes of psychiatric drugs, trycyclics and benzodiazipines, produced different results in relation to panic and anxiety. Trycyclics reduced panic attacks, but they did not affect anticipatory anxiety. Benzodiazipines reversed the situation; they reduced the anticipatory anxiety, but not the attacks. It appeared to Klein that there were two kinds of anxieties.

Klein's thinking is further elaborated in relation to the attacks themselves: "It is only after a series of such extremely unpleasant experiences that the person develops a 'secondary anticipatory anxiety' between panic attacks, often referred to as 'free floating anxiety.' Klein went on to hypothesize that panic attacks, and anticipatory anxiety, were basically different psycho-biologically. He believed that anticipatory anxiety, with its stimulation of worry and catastrophic thoughts had "followed, not preceded, panic attack."[15]

A further case can be made for arguing that fearful anticipation, and the arousal of worry and distressed thinking, may be the result rather than the cause of panic attacks. In the vast majority of instances, expectations that an attack will occur are not followed by the symptoms.[16]

Additionally, sufferers often have no explanation for what caused their first attack,[17] and between 20–40 percent of those suffering panic attacks, who have been seen in general medical rather than psychiatric settings do not have fearful cognitions associated with them.[18]

The Role of the Directly Observable

In relation to panic attacks, directly observable body signs have not often been a central scientific concern, nor have they played a large role in developing treatment methods. There are, however, several notable exceptions: Applied Relaxation, Breathing Retraining, and Eye Movement Desensitization and Reprocessing (EMDR). Each of these treatment methods grew out of scientific work. None of these methods emerged directly from the extensive clinical psychotherapeutic work done in the context of Body Psychotherapy. Here the body is carefully observed in individual sessions, typically in private treatment over an extended period of time. What is seen is worked with to gain understanding of the person and their functioning and in finding ways to change. Often the aims are spoken of in general terms: increased well-being, self-awareness and control, more feeling, and a fuller understanding of one's personal history.

The clinical field of body psychotherapy lacks the rigor of the scientific approach. It does not typically focus on removing specific and scientifically measurable symptoms, but it allows for a greater freedom range in looking at an individual and in dealing with what the client presents. It has a large and extended field of direct client experience on which to draw on for understandings.[19]

Interestingly, the three scientifically related methods that will be discussed as having a relationship to observable behaviors deal with variables that have been important in the approaches of body therapy. Where relevant, touchpoints drawn from the body therapy school of Bioenergetics[20] will be mentioned.

In Applied Relaxation,[21,22] people are taught to quickly progress to a state of relaxation and then instructed how to use the relaxation to cope, counteract, and eventually eliminate anxiety reactions. This method has been taught over a twelve-week period and studied in relationship to its effect on the frequency of panic attacks. The study utilized homework between sessions. Individuals were asked to relax fifteen to twenty times a day while doing natural activities such as talking on the phone, looking at their watch, and responding to prearranged cues.

As the facility to move quickly to relaxation developed, participants began to apply it during panic-provoking moments. At the end of treatment, 65 percent of the participants were panic-free. At a follow-up session one year later, 82 percent were panic-free.[23] They were encouraged to continue practicing relaxation on a regular basis.

A second form of directly observable bodily behavior studied in relation to panic attacks is disturbed breathing patterns. This is often an important part of body-oriented psychotherapy. Bioenergetic therapists, for example, are specifically trained to develop sensitivity to shifts in breathing patterns (i.e., when abdominal breathing is replaced by chest breathing). Disturbances such as shallow or held breathing or erratic rhythms are seen as indicators of therapeutic intervention. Practitioners use their observations to deepen breathing and to raise the individual's level of excitement in order to bring unconscious memories into awareness where they can be explored. Deep breathing is also used to vivify and strengthen emotional experience.

The method of Breathing Retraining, as described by R. Ley,[24] was designed from a source other than the field of Body Psychotherapy. Therapists and doctors took note of shifts in breathing patterns that occurred specifically during panic attacks. They observed that the symptoms of panic resemble those of hyperventilation.

Ley forwards a method of breathing retraining for panic sufferers. It involves sensitizing clients to their breathing difficulties by teaching respiratory mechanics and the physical and psychological effects of hyperventilating. Clients are also taught to control the panic effects of hyperventilation by slowing their rate of respiration, breathing through their nose, and using their diaphragm rather than their chest.[25]

Ley argued that hyperventilation was the central cause of panic attacks. Research and review, however, has not supported this. In studies where people with panic disorder voluntarily hyperventilated, panic attacks were not reported, although the symptoms were felt to be similar.[26]

There is a stronger argument against the idea that hyperventilation is the key cause of panic attacks. Many sufferers do not hyperventilate during panic attacks. Since hyperventilation can be part of a panic attack, but does not have to be, it can't be the central factor in the existence of an attack. Disturbed breathing patterns are still an important factor, however.

L. Papp and J. Gorman[27] suggest that Breathing Retraining can serve as a viable treatment for those panickers who do hyperventilate. Results from recent studies also indicate benefits for those who do not hyperventilate; perhaps this is a result of correcting other breathing distortions.[28] L. Lum[29] specifically makes the point that chest breathing may be a mechanism which heightens the possibility that a panic attack will occur, while not leading to hyperventilation.

The real crux for Breathing Retraining as a method lies in the question of whether or not it reduces panic attacks. Ley's results[30] show subjects dropped on average from 1.89 to 1.43 panic attacks per day following eight sessions of Breathing Retraining. This is statistically significant and demonstrates that the method can play a role in reducing panic attacks. However, the reduction found is relatively small, and the technique might not have been powerful in actual terms for any particular individual. Two of the sixteen subjects actually experienced an increase in panic attacks.

The technique of Eye Movement Desensitization and Retraining (EMDR)[31] has been applied to and researched for a variety of anxiety disturbances, including panic attacks.

This third observable body process that has resulted in the development of a treatment method focuses on the eyes. Bioenergetic practitioners observe and work with the eyes and their surrounding musculature. The eyes are noted for signs of aliveness, emotional expression, and character attitudes. In a poetic metaphor, they are seen as "the windows of the soul."

EMDR developed from a personal discovery by its originator, F. Shapiro. While remembering some her own traumatic memories, she noted that as her eyes spontaneously shifted from side to side. She experienced a decrease in the emotional charge that she was feeling. She developed a treatment method that was initially based on the observation that these kinds of eye movements could lessen the experience of painful emotional memories.

Shapiro first applied her method to people who suffered from traumatic stress disorders. As they recalled troublesome memories, they were instructed to follow her finger as it moved from side to side. They were then asked to report their thoughts, sensations, and emotions. The process was repeated until clients reported that their level of discomfort had dropped significantly. Next, clients were instructed to form a positive thought about themselves or their trauma and work with it until there were signs that the thought was accepted.[32]

Shapiro's first study reported dramatic results.[33] It reported improvements from single sessions in clients who suffered from posttraumatic stress disturbance to the point of no longer suffering from the disorder. Shapiro's work came under strong scientific criticism for a variety of reasons and from a number of sources (see end notes 31–34). It has been argued that she was the sole practitioner in her study. It has been pointed out that the one-session results have not been replicable by other practitioners, while other methods have been more effective. It has been stated that the extensive claims of success in treating a variety of anxiety problems by EMDR practitioners are said to lack sufficient scientific support. Most importantly, studies have shown that factors other than the eye movements could have been responsible for the changes reported. In fact, Shapiro eventually abandoned eye movements as the necessary variable in her method. She began using other techniques, such as alternately tapping the sides of the body or using audio tones while arousing memories of the trauma. Though Shapiro's original eye movement intervention continues as a technique, its centrality has given way to a more general technique of bilateral stimulation that involves alternately stimulating both sides of the body.

Shapiro's method is now characterized as "an integrated form of therapy incorporating aspects of many traditional psychological orientations."[34] These include using imagery, behavioral desensitization, cognitive restructuring, rating inner experiences, and keeping a journal. EMDR treatment is now spread out over a three-session application (or more) rather than the one-session approach originally thought sufficient. For people with multiple traumas, it is suggested that several months of sessions may be necessary.[35]

The posttraumatic stress disorder application of EMDR has been applied in the treatment of panic disorder. Here it can be measured against a clear criterion, the reduction or cessation of panic attacks. Research evaluation has measured the efficacy of the technique—whether attacks are reduced, if eye movements are important, and how it fares in comparison to other methods that involve desensitization and cognitive therapy.

Research by U. Feske and his colleagues[36] found that six sessions of EMDR significantly helped people reduce panic attacks. Subjects went from an average of 3.6 attacks to .96 attacks in a two-week period. Feske's extended results led to the question of whether eye movements mattered or not. After three months it was found that there was no difference in the results of the EMDR group whose eye movements followed the therapist's moving finger as they recalled traumatic memories and a second group who provided an eye experience that was not believed to have an effect:

EMDR without eye movements. Here subjects were aided to hold their eyes steady by focusing on a therapist's stationary finger while recalling and reporting the traumatic memories.

In fact, both these groups did significantly better than an untreated control group. Feske suggests that EMDR's eye technique was not critical because the stationary eyes yielded the same result as laterally moving eyes. The possibility is forwarded that a different factor, the repetition of traumatic memories that was common to both groups, may have been the crucial factor causing the results. The argument suggested is that the memories aroused associated feelings. By repeating them a number of times the subject gradually lost sensitivity to them, until they no longer aroused traumatic feelings. Desensitization, not eye movement, was the critical factor.

This explanation may not suffice for body therapists. They might argue that both rapid and fixated eye movements would lead to observable changes in the body's natural dynamics. They are both, so to speak, body techniques. Both introduce a means of physical control while memories are recited. Both fall under the general goal of helping people gain self-control. The experimental control of the client's eyes as they recalled memories may well have been the important factor in producing the result. Control rather than desensitization may be what's relevant for change. With greater self-control the traumatic memories no longer result in highly intense and disturbing emotional recall.

The Rhythmic Integration Project on Panic emerges from a clinical viewpoint that looks directly at the movement and structure of the physical body. It grew from a background that emphasized the importance of body experience in the therapeutic process.

Rhythmic Integration intervention consists of two major components. It works to find what it calls "The Body Starter," and to make the client aware of it. Then the client is guided through a series of steps designed to change their physical expression so that panic attacks don't occur.

Rhythmic Integration looks for the spontaneous body movements that provide the physical beginning of a panic attack. The word "Starter" is carefully chosen. Often the literature uses the word "trigger" in relationship to a panic attack. Trigger provides the metaphor of a gun—pull the trigger, the bullet is fired. The response is instantaneous. For panic attacks, a trigger has been thought to be an encounter with a location, an event, a thought, or a physical sensation. Once the moment is triggered, it is suggested, the panic explodes. But in reality, often the so-called triggering response occurs, and no panic attack follows: "I was sure I'd have a panic attack but nothing happened." Starter evokes a different metaphor—the starter of a car. A starter gets the engine to turn over; but it will take engaging the gears and pumping the gas for the car to really get going.

In panic attacks, the Starter readies the organism for panic, but it is not enough to get it going. It is the first observable physical event in a process that may lead to an attack. If the person is aware of their Body Starter, the physical aspect of the panic process can be shut down before it gets moving. Even better, if the Starter doesn't occur, if there is no first physical event, there is no chance for a panic attack—without a start a process can't occur.

Telling an individual that panic attacks often begin with a Body Starter is typically met with disbelief. People with panic attacks are quite aware of the role of their thoughts in the process. Many have developed cognitive strategies, "self-talk," to try to anticipate, modify, or control their symptoms. Some blame outside situations for their plight. They come up with avoidance possibilities to stay away from scenes similar to those where attacks have previously occurred. In the individual's mind, these strategies are creative coping mechanisms devised to meet the challenge of panic attacks. People are often invested and proud of their solutions, even though they are usually not effective in preventing attacks.

Our clinical experience has shown that the disruptive movement pattern, the Body Starter associated with the beginning of the panic attack, is outside the person's immediate awareness until it is clearly and repeatedly pointed out to them as it occurs. The statement that a physical movement starts panic seems to put the body in charge. Thought and consciousness are secondary. This very idea is typically an affront to the person's meaning system.

It's often first met with defense—"I don't believe it," or "Doesn't everyone do that?"

In about half the cases, after the person perceives and accepts their Body Starter, there is a spontaneous report that someone in their family, or a friend, has previously noted the movement and commented on it (i.e., "My husband teases me about that," or "I remember my mom asking me why I move like that?").

A Body Starter that some people use appears to be the same one that Shapiro personally discovered—spontaneous eye movement. Shapiro had tried to stimulate a response in her clients by having their eyes follow her finger as it moved from side to side. This is an imprecise method. It does not guarantee a spontaneous movement as Shapiro experienced it.

There is a somewhat similar technique described in the literature of body psychotherapy[37] that has the client's eyes tracking a moving penlight as it moves in varied directions. The aim is to break through chronic muscle holding. After a while, the greater part of a session, the eyes may lose track and spontaneously go from side to side of their own accord. Often at this moment a powerful emotional catharsis accompanied by significant memories occurs. Therapists experienced with this eye-tracking method know from experience that the spontaneous movement and its aftermath may not occur. Spontaneity is a key aspect of the Body Starter. In the Rhythmic Integration Project there is no attempt to experimentally induce it. Rather the facilitator watches for the natural occurrence of the movement as the client speaks about their panic. As it occurs in the flow of conversation, and it inevitably does, it is brought to the client's attention before identifying it as the Starter.

In the intervention session, once the Body Starter has been identified, a process of change needs to be undertaken in order to make a difference. Rhythmic Integration (RI)[38] follows a model based on the early physical and psychological developments humans undergo. As our bodies mature, new psychological potentials become available and new experiences occur. RI describes seven stages that make up the Cycle of Change,[39] as well as the body dynamics and psychological outgrowths of each. The stages are named for their respective psychological process: Dreaming, Creating, Communicating, Inspiring, Analyzing, Solidifying, and Achieving.

Treating Panic

Working to help a person change their use of the Body Starter involves moving through the Cycle of Change and dealing with any stopping points that might occur. The session calls for considerable skill on the part of the practitioner. Body movements must be registered and evaluated. Each stage of the change process must be negotiated. The aim is to have the intervention completed within ninety minutes. Difficulty arises from any of a variety of resistances that may emerge to deflect or stop progress. These must be perceived by the therapist and efficiently worked with until the entire process is completed.

To concretize this, consider the following example: Early in the session the therapist requests memories of panic episodes. Help is provided to enable the client to activate a Dreaming quality that underlies this type of memory recall with heightened physical and emotional responsiveness. Already at this beginning point, resistance can arise which can stop and/or end the course of change if not successfully brought to the surface and addressed.

CASE STUDY

Mary was excited to be in the study. She had experienced several panic attacks a week for the past seven years. Yet near the beginning of the session she stated that she couldn't evoke memories of any of the attacks. As having a memory was crucial to the Dream Phase of the process, little could be done.

Instead of remembering, Mary kept talking about how she felt during her attacks—trembling, rapid heart, desperate fears of losing control, etc. She was very dramatic in her presentations. Specifics of an incident, however, were lacking. Attempts to awaken them proved unsuccessful for over half the session.

Finally, she spontaneously revealed, "The truth is, I don't want to remember specifics." She had vowed to herself beforehand that she would prevent an attack in the session at any cost. Her strategy was to not remember—not to allow scenes of the past to emerge. Without the scenes, she reasoned, she would not have the sensations and emotions that accompanied them. She could be secure that nothing uncontrollable would happen.

Her strategy went a step further. She focused her eyes on a spot on the wall in front of her as she talked. She knew from the past that this kind of focus prevented anything from starting. In fact, her plan supported the thinking of the research. Her focus allowed her to control her movements, preventing her Starter from occurring. In her everyday life she couldn't always focus and control her thoughts, prevent her Starter. In everyday life she was often caught unawares, unable to control her Starter, and experienced panic attacks.

Once she had revealed the reasons for not remembering, the resistance to the process could be addressed. Mary was reassured that the method did not involve having a panic attack in the session. She was able to give up her defense and remember an event that led to the discovery of her Body Starter and set her on the way to pursue the course of change. Mary was able to let down her guard and proceed. Her panic attacks stopped occurring and she has remained panic-free.

Let's continue to examine the course of change beyond the stage of Dreaming, to give an overview of the change process. Each of the stages of the Cycle of Change is capitalized to highlight it. During the Dreaming phase, the Body Starter becomes outwardly observable (the eyes, for example, moving from side to side). As the therapist directs attention to the Starter, the situation changes for the client. They move beyond memories and begin to tell their story while working toward awareness of their Body Starter.

This is a naturally awkward time. The client is doing two things at once: recalling their attacks and noticing their movements. They are split between two tasks, two pieces, and are noticeably in a state of physical tension because of the disjunction. It's a bit like the challenge of the childhood game of tapping your head while rubbing your stomach. The tension that arises serves as an impetus for a Creative moment to bring back a sense of unity. Different approaches are tried. To get there requires allowing both fragments to exist until something new occurs, something bigger takes over, and the separate pieces blend into one harmonious and new response.

As the session proceeds, the client and therapist, through joint observation and back and forth Communicating, make the experience of identifying the Starter easily observable for them both. Eventually the Starter, previously unconscious, becomes an integrated part of the client's conscious experience. The therapist and client then work through the dynamics of Inspiration, exploring the hopes and despairs that accompany the panic attack experiences.

The next stage involves the client Analyzing their situation closely in order to become aware of the link between different parts of their specific memories and the occurrence of the Body Starter. During high-charged moments of their story they will take notice of the Starter.

The individual will be asked to recall several panic situations and work with them until they can tell their story without it being accompanied by the movement of the Body Starter. When this has been Solidified, the change aspect of the session concludes by working physically to Achieve a way for their body to have a fluid way of expression without arousing the physical dysfunctions that mark the Body Starter.

Rhythmic Integration Project Results

The complete cessation of panic attacks, which occurred within a week for four of our five subjects, was profound for them. It was experienced as a stunning change. Panic attacks are extremely powerful experiences. To limit them, sufferers quickly develop an elaborate inner dialogue to understand and develop strategies. The experience of ending panic attacks after only a 90-minute session is hard to believe.

Figure 1 shows the dramatic reduction in attacks for all participants, though not all of them experienced immediate ongoing cessation. Those patients who did not report complete cessation were all panic-free for the month prior to the one-year follow-up.

It is interesting to consider what happened to those who did not cease their panic attacks immediately. In the routine one-week

Panic Frequency Before and After Intervention

Subject	Month Prior	Week After	Month After	2 Months After	3 Months After	Year After
Client A	2	0	0	0	0	0
Client B	18	0	0	0	0	0
Client C	5	3	2*	0	0	0
Client D	3	0	4*	0	0	0
Client E	20	0	0	1	7*	0
Total Attacks	48	3	6	1	9	0

* Explanations of disparities are outlined in the following paragraphs:

follow-up call by a staff member of the project, Client C reported having had three panic attacks in the first week after the session. Review of a videotape of the intervention revealed a second Starter, a choking response, that hadn't been identified in the session. The study was designed to provide participants additional support if there were signs of difficulty. For Client C, two more panic attacks occurred in the several days leading up to the therapist's phone call, at which point the problem was addressed. Drawing on what occurred during the interventions, the interaction took only five minutes. In subsequent follow-up calls over the following year Client C reported no further attacks.

Client D experienced a burst of attacks the week before she was to undergo major surgery. This was to be the last of a series of surgeries that she had undergone as a result of an injury. She attributed the injury to the beginning of her panic attacks. She reported that in her stress she had completely forgotten to make use of her Starter. After her operation, she was given a one-hour session to reinforce her learning. A year later she reported no attacks.

The experience with Client E was particularly instructive. It demonstrated the psychological complexities that can come into play around treatment. A middle age man, Client E had suffered with a history of frequent panic attacks since early adolescence. Initially, after participating in the project, he dropped to no panic attacks. However, the very day he was contacted for his two-month follow-up he had an unexpected attack while exercising— "It came out of nowhere." Though early results had brought a two-month period of dramatic and unexpected change for him, he became convinced the method didn't work. He was angry and ready to give up on it. There were seven more attacks over the next days before the outbursts subsided, and his rate again dropped to zero.

Client E's experience makes evident that the method does not necessarily prevent the Starter from occurring. Nor is it certain that when it does occur that it will not escalate into an attack. It is possible, however, and seemed to ring true for all the participants, that over time awareness of the Starter fades into the background; the body learns how to take care of itself without conscious effort.

This study, as are many studies that begin to research a new method, was small and simply designed. There were five subjects, one therapist (the author), and a critical variable measured over time—the number of panic attacks reported. Still, the dramatic nature of the change after the intervention, in people with long histories of frequent panic attacks, is sufficient to show that the intervention was significant by research standards.[40]

Meanings

This is the first research study of this method. The results are strong enough to conclude that the one-session Rhythmic Integration intervention made a significant difference in the occurrence of panic attacks. The findings are further supported by similar results in experiences that took place in teaching, and clinical applications that were done before or outside the design of this study.

Certain generalities are important to note: The size of the sample was small; panic attacks are often associated with other emotional difficulties (i.e., depression, night terrors, agoraphobia, specific and social phobias, etc.); knowledge of how broadly, and under what conditions the results will be upheld, will also necessitate further study.

Another reason for caution about the method's applicability is fundamental. It arises from the fact that one therapist saw all subjects. Should the results be attributed to the method, or the therapist? A second study, currently in process, addresses this question under supervision of another therapist. The one-month follow-up results, collected at the time of this writing, again show a high level of success: eight subjects went from having a combined total of 146 attacks (mean=16, median=20, mode=20) to a combined total of six attacks. Five subjects became panic-free. The three others saw reductions in the number of attacks by 82 percent, 90 percent, and 95 percent respectively. The results at the time of this writing offer strong evidence of the effectiveness of the method. Follow-ups will continue. Also, a manual and training module are being developed which will lay the ground for further research and clinical application.[41]

The method suggests that the role of the body and its observable movements are highly significant in affecting the occurrence of panic attacks. Can this thinking be applied to other anxiety categories with similar results? The field of Bioenergetics and body-oriented psychotherapies has found that along with psychological improvement comes more fluidity of motion in the body. In considering the mind-body connection the reverse is also seen as true—a more natural flow pattern results in improved psychological functioning. The method used here demonstrates that changes toward natural movement patterns can be made in a systematic and rapid way.

Finally, there is the disbelief factor. Even experiencing the cessation of panic attacks after having them for years is not enough to negate the disbelief in those who have undergone the change. It takes time for the mind to accept the fact that the body's movements are a stimulus for attacks, that the mind may have a less critical role than previously thought. If the results prove to be widely applicable and frequently reported, the view that body movements play a key role in initiating panic attacks can become part of a consensus of understanding—believed as part of commonplace knowledge.

With a different belief system permeating society, panic attacks can move out of the murky arena of emotional disease to be understood more simply as a reaction started by a physically disruptive body movement. The mystique, and the shame that accompanies this malady, would be over. Like a golfer who works to eliminate a hitch in his swing, the sufferer of panic attacks might simply train themselves to break the troublesome link between disruptive movement and charged emotions. Their bodies then would flow more smoothly and avoid setting the physical conditions that can start a process headed toward inner uproar and the life-limiting experiences that accompany panic reactions.

ENDNOTES:

1. J. Gorman, *Understanding Panic Disorder Finding Hope, Gaining Control*, pamphlet from Freedom From Fear, Stanton Island, NY (a Pfizer, Inc. publication, 2000).

2. Body Psychotherapy is a general term that encompasses a number of therapeutic schools. Most owe their origin to the seminal psycho-analytic work of Wilhelm Reich and share many commonalities. The author's own training is in Bioenergetic Analysis and examples from this method are used in the balance of this paper. The reader interested in learning about the range of schools is referred to *www.usabp.com*.

3. L. Papp and J. Gorman, "Respiratory Neurobiology of Panic." In *Panic Disorder: Clinical, Biological, and Treatment Aspects,* edited by G. Asnis and Herman Meier van Praag (New York: John Wiley & Sons, 1995), 255–75.

4. S. Windmann, "Panic Disorder from a Monistic Perspective: Integrating Neurobiological and Psychological Approaches," *Journal of Anxiety Disorders* 12, no. 5 (1998): 485–507.

5. T. Shioiri, K. Fujii, T. Someya, and S. Takahashi, "Serum Cholesterol Levels and Panic Symptoms in Patients with Panic Disorder: A Preliminary Study," *Journal of Affective Disorders* 58, no. 2 (2000): 167–70.

6. S. Bouchard, M. Pelletier, J. Gautheir, G. Côté, and B. Laberge B., "The Assessment of Panic Using Self-Report: A Comprehensive Survey of Validated instruments," *Journal of Anxiety Disorders* 11, no. 1 (1997): 89–111.

7. A. Hoffart, S. Friis, and E. Martinsen, "Assessment of Fear Among Agoraphobic Patients: The Agoraphobic Cognitions Scale," *Journal of Psychopathology & Behavioral Assessment* 14, no. 2 (1992): 175–87.

8. N. Khawaja, P. Oei, and L. Evans, "Comparison Between the Panic Disorder with Agoraphobia Patients and Normal Controls on the Basis of Cognitions Affect and Physiology," *Behavioural & Cognitive Psychotherapy* 21, no. 3 (1993): 199–217.

9. American Psychiatric Association: *Diagnostic and Statistical Manual of Mental Disorders, Fourth Edition.* Washington, DC, American Psychiatric Association, 1994.

10. A. Arntz, and M. van Den Hout, "Psychological Treatments of Panic Disorder without Agoraphobia: Cognitive Therapy versus Applied Relaxation," *Behaviour Research & Therapy* 34, no. 2 (1996): 113–21.

11. R. Baker, *Panic Disorder Theory and Therapy* (London: Wiley Press, 1989).

12. American Psychiatric Association: op. cit., 1994.

13. H. Waring, "The Nature of Panic Attack Symptoms." In R. Baker. op. cit., 1989.

14. R. Baker, op. cit., 1989.

15. Ibid., 5.

16. J. Kenardy and C. Taylor, "Expected Versus Unexpected Panic Attacks: A Naturalistic Prospective Study," *Journal of Anxiety Disorders* 13, no. 4 (1999): 435–45.

17. W. Jacobs and L. Nadel, "The First Panic Attack A Neurobiological Theory," *Canadian Journal of Experimental Psychology* 53, no. 1 (1999): 92–107.

18. M. Kushner and B. Beitman, "Panic Attacks Without Fear: An Overview," *Behaviour Research & Therapy* 28, no. 6 (1990): 469–79.

19. http://www.eabp.org/scientific_answers.htm#Anchor
http://www.eabp.org/correction.htm

20. Author Ron Robbins is a trainer in the method of Bioenergetics. For further description of it see Alexander Lowen, *The Language of the Body* (New York: Collier Press, 1958).

21. L. Öst, "Applied Relaxation: Description of a Coping Technique and Review of Controlled Studies," in *Behaviour Research & Therapy* 25, no. 5 (1987): 397–409.

22. L. Öst and B. Westling, "Applied Relaxation versus Cognitive Behavior Therapy in the Treatment of Panic Disorder," *Behaviour Research & Therapy* 33, no. 2 (1995): 145–58.

23. Ibid.

24. Ronald Ley, "The Efficacy of Breathing Retraining and the Centrality of Hyperventilation in Panic Disorder: A Reinterpretation of Experimental Findings," *Behaviour Research & Therapy* 29, no. 3 (1991): 301–04.

25. Ronald Ley, "Agoraphobia, the Panic Attack and the Hyperventilation Syndrome," *Behaviour, Research & Therapy* 23, no. 1 (1985): 29–81.

26. R. Rapee, "Differential Response to Hyperventilation in Panic Disorder and Generalized Anxiety Disorder," *Journal of Abnormal Psychology* 95 (1986): 24–28.

TREATMENT

27. L. Papp and J. Gorman, "Respiratory Neurobiology of Panic, Respiratory Neurobiology of Panic." In *Panic Disorder: Clinical, Biological, and Treatment Aspects*, edited by G. Asnis and H.M. van Praag (New York: John Wiley & Sons, 1995) 255–75.

28. G. Hibbert and M. Chan, "Respiratory Control: Its Contribution to the Treatment of Panic Attacks," *British Journal of Psychiatry* 154 (1989): 232–36.

29. L. Lum, "Hyperventilation and Anxiety State," *Journal of the Royal Society of Medicine* 74 (1988): 1–4.

30. R. Ley, "The Efficacy of Breathing Retraining and the Centrality of Hyperventilation in Panic Disorder: A Reinterpretation of Experimental Findings," *Behaviour Research & Therapy* 29, no. 3 (1991) 301–04.

31. Francine Shapiro, *Eye Movement Desensitization and Reprocessing: Basic Principles, Protocols, and Procedures* (New York: Guilford Press, 1995), xviii, 398.

32. S. Cahill, M. Carrigan, and C. Frueh, "Does EMDR Work? And If So Why? A Critical Review of Controlled Outcome and Dismantling Research," *Journal of Anxiety Disorders* 13, nos. 1-2 (1999): 5–33.

33. Francine Shapiro, "Efficacy of the Eye Movement Desensitization Procedure in the Treatment of Traumatic Memories," *Journal of Traumatic Stress* 2, no. 2 (1989): 199–223.

34. Francine Shapiro, op. cit., 1995.

35. F. Shapiro, "Eye Movement Desensitization and Reprocessing (EMDR) and the Anxiety Disorders: Clinical and Research Applications of an Integrated Psychotherapy Treatment," *Journal of Anxiety Disorders* 13, nos. 1-2 (1999) 35–67.

36. Ulrike Feske and Alan J. Goldstein, "Eye Movement Desensitization and Reprocessing Treatment for Panic Disorder: A Controlled Outcome and Partial Dismantling Study," *Journal of Consulting & Clinical Psychology* 65, no. 6 (1997): 1026–35.

37. E. Baker, *Man in the Trap* (New York: Collier Press, 1980).

38. R. Robbins, *Rhythmic Integration: Finding Wholeness in the Cycle of Change* (New York: Station Hill Press, 1990).

39. Ibid.

40. Murray Sidman, *Tactics of Scientific Research* (New York: Basic Books, 1960).

41. Contact *panic-ri@bigfoot.com* for information.

MICHAEL MUFSON WITH SANA JOHNSON-QUIJADA

Panic and Anxiety in Relation to Sleep

Overview

IF YOU FEEL that you are having difficulty falling asleep or staying asleep, if you suspect that anxiety may be ruining your rest, or if you think that regular sleep hygiene techniques have been ineffective, this chapter can be your guide to better sleep. In fact, most anxiety-related sleep problems can be successfully recognized so that you can seek appropriate treatment.

The most extreme form of anxiety is panic. People who experience panic describe it as a combination of frightening sensations that may include chest pain, ringing in the ears, numbness in the arms and hands, feelings of impending doom, etc. ... and it comes on suddenly! Out of the blue! In fact it comes on so unexpectedly and out of control that it often wakes people up from sleep. Panic can feel like a heart attack and many people go to the emergency room repeatedly seeking medical explanations for their symptoms. These individuals can be convinced that there is something "medically wrong" with them.

This chapter will focus on *sleep-panic*, a panic attack that abruptly awakens the individual to complete alertness and is usually unassociated with dreams. This is in contrast to most other sleep forms of anxiety which disturb sleep and are commonly associated with dream activity.

It is important to know that anxiety can also be caused by a variety of medical problems, which will in turn disrupt sleep. Examples include seizures, sleeping medications, stimulating medications, reflux esophagitis, and alcohol or drug addiction. This chapter

TREATMENT

will help you understand your anxiety better, especially as it relates to your sleep.

Introduction

Sleep begins in utero for humans. Sleep is a physiologic state, necessary for both physical and emotional well-being. We all know what it feels like if we don't get enough sleep. Sleep has been extensively studied and its architecture is well described.

Sleep Stages

Sleep architecture is a biological phenomenon, unique to each of us. Sleep architecture refers to the phases of normal sleep that are revealed during polysomnographic testing. During sleep there are two states, non-REM sleep and REM sleep (see Table 1). Non-REM sleep has four stages and alternates with REM sleep cyclically through the night in periods of approximately ninety minutes. Sleep disorders as well as age and medications can disrupt normal sleep architecture and impair sleep efficiency. Scientists have been able to study sleep through the use of a technique called *polysomnography*, which uses scalp electrodes to measure electrical brain activity. In this way, sleep stages have been identified to help understand normal and abnormal sleep. Even though we have "standardized" sleep stages, it doesn't mean that we all sleep the same. This is important, for example, when you observe that one person may function optimally with only four hours of sleep while another can barely get by without nine hours each night.

In general, normal sleep has two major parts: REM (Rapid Eye Movement) sleep and NREM (nonREM) sleep. NREM sleep is divided further into sleep stages 1 through 4.

As adults, we spend at least half of our total sleep time in stage 2 sleep, a fifth in REM sleep, and the rest in the other stages of sleep. Infants, however, spend about half their sleep time in REM sleep, and the elderly sleep mostly in the lighter stages. This is helpful with our understanding of sleep-anxiety disorders, which can

Table 1:

Sleep Stages	Polygraph Recordings of Brain Activity	Clinical Features and Abnormalities
Awake	Alpha waves	*Awake, alert, calm, and with eyes closed.*
Stage 1	Theta waves	*Drifting in and out of sleep. Hypnic myoclonia—a sudden jerk that feels like a startle response.*
Stage 2	Sleep spindles	*Eye movements stop.* **Sleep-panic attacks.**
Stage 3	20% Delta waves	*Brain activity slows down.*
Stage 4	>50% Delta waves	*Deep sleep. Difficult to awaken from. Some children bed-wet (enuresis), have night terrors, or sleep walk (somnambulism).*
REM (Rapid Eye Movement)	Saw-tooth waves	*Dreams occur. Muscles become paralyzed. Increased heart rate and blood pressure. Penile erections. Nightmares. REM-panic may occur.*

occur differently depending on age and genetic makeup.

We've all heard of *circadian rhythms*. This term refers to our internal sleep-wake clock. The neurobiologic apparatus of it includes the different parts of our central nervous system, pictured on page 338.

The core of our circadian system is the *retinohypothalamic-pineal axis*. Light acting on the *retina* is the most important regulator of the circadian system. Light sends a message through the optic nerve to the brain's circadian pacemaker, the suprachiasmatic nucleus of the *hypothalamus*. The hypothalamus, in turn, communicates with the *pineal gland* to turn off the production of the hormone melatonin. Melatonin, which is produced in the pineal gland, normally increases when it gets dark, making people feel sleepy, and then decreases when there is light.

The hypothalamus also works with the *hypothalamic-pituitary adrenal axis*, in the *endocrine system* along side the *autonomic nervous system* to further synchronize other functions associated with our sleep-wake clock, including body temperature, hormone secretion, urine production, and changes in blood pressure. We think of these functions less often when we think of our circadian rhythm, but they can be very important to a good night's rest, and plays a role in sleep-panic as well. Some people with sleep-panic wake up with a feeling of urinary urgency, which may be related to a dysregulation of their sleep-wake clock.

This is why sleep doctors recommend sleep hygiene (i.e., regular sleep schedule, no caffeine, no nicotine) as an essential element of maintaining proper sleep. Sleep hygiene can be the simplest route to better sleep and works with natural circadian rhythms.

Insomnia (difficulty falling asleep, multiple awakenings) is very common. About 30 percent of the population suffers from insomnia, and sleep-panic can be one of the causes. Sleep hygiene, while helping to resolve insomnia, may not be the only treatment necessary for a problem as intense as sleep-panic.

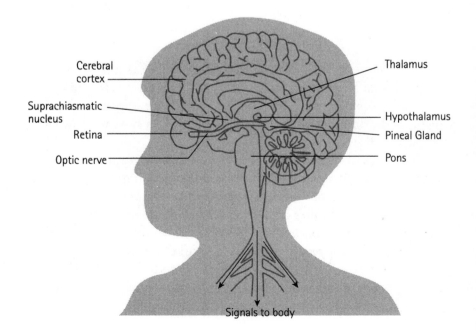

Anxiety Disorders and Sleep

SLEEP-PANIC ATTACKS

A sleep-panic attack is a panic attack that occurs during sleep. It awakens the individual from sleep to full alertness, often causing awakening after having suffered at least through the beginnings of a panic attack. The person experiencing a sleep-panic attack has a very difficult time getting back to sleep and can remember the panic episode vividly the next day. The attack is dream-free because it occurs in stages 2 or 3 of sleep for the majority of sufferers. (Compare to REM-panic below.)

SLEEP-PANIC AS A SYNDROME

Researchers suspect there is a sleep-panic syndrome, which represents a variant of panic disorder. They have found that this population suffers recurrent sleep-panic attacks, even predominantly over daytime panic attacks. These sleep-panic attacks, which awaken people to full alertness from sleep, are associated with people who have less efficient sleep, who overreact to small sleep disruptions, and who have insomnia.

In this variant of panic disorder, patients report sleep-panic brought on by relaxation and sleep deprivation. It can be a vicious cycle of losing sleep from sleep-panic attacks to sleeplessness inducing more sleep-panic attacks.

Also, studies suggest that sleep deprivation may trigger people with panic disorder to have sleep-panic attacks. There is a behavioral pattern that connects sleep-panic attacks, insomnia, sleep deprivation, and daytime panic attacks.

People with sleep-panic syndrome often have more associated depressive disorders and primary insomnia than do people with only panic disorder. In fact, sleep-panic syndrome is similar to anxious major depressive disorder in that both have decreased total REM and decreased delta sleep (see Table 1). This possibly suggests there is a common etiology between these disorders related to deregulation of the autonomic nervous system responses.

Interestingly, individuals with sleep-panic have less social or occupational disability, and less phobic limitations, like agoraphobia.

Table 2:

Anxiety Disorder	Clinical Features	Sleep Features
Sleep-Panic Syndrome	Recurrent sleep-panic attacks, which awaken the person suddenly to full alertness with a feeling of intense fear, and other symptoms of a panic attack.	Sleep-panic attacks are the predominant symptom; usually awaken from stages 2 or 3 of sleep. There is sleep-panic attack recall. There is no dream recall.
Panic Disorder	Recurrent unpredictable panic attacks which generally last less than ten minutes. Often have fear about having another attack. Some people change their behavior related to the attacks even though their behavior didn't "cause" the attack.	Generally have few sleep-panic attacks. When sleep-panic attacks are present, they are as described above. About 10 percent of people with panic disorder have sleep-panic syndrome.
Generalized Anxiety Disorder	Ongoing inner tension, worry. Feeling keyed up. Irritable, tense, difficulty with concentration. May be associated with psychophysiological insomnia.	Difficulty falling asleep or staying asleep, or don't feel rested in the morning after sleep. Decreased amount of delta and REM sleep stages.
Stress Response Disorders (Includes posttraumatic stress disorder, adjustment disorder, and grief)	Reoccurring frightening thoughts and memories of a threatening stressor. Avoidance behavior, numbing, and hyperarousal symptoms. Requires an external event.	Repetitive stereotyped anxiety dreams that usually resemble exact memories of the trauma. Awaken out of REM sleep stage.
Obsessive-Compulsive Disorder	Intrusive, distressing thoughts, which cause anxiety. People may perform rituals to relieve the anxiety. These rituals are called compulsions.	Acting out the rituals and the associated sleep anxiety often keeps the person from sleeping.

Panic Disorder

One panic attack does not mean that you have panic disorder. In fact, about one-third of people who have or have had panic attacks do not develop this disorder. Panic disorder emerges when panic attacks become recurrent and at least one of three things happen: a) *anticipatory anxiety,* in which a person starts worrying constantly about having another panic attack, b) the individual worries about the consequences of the anxiety attack (i.e., having a heart attack, going crazy), c) *phobic avoidance*, in which a person starts changing their behaviors related to the panic attacks (i.e., changing their profession, not going to specific places where they've experienced the panic attacks).

Because panic attacks can be incredibly frightening, people who suffer them often develop agoraphobia, a fear and avoidance of places or situations from which the person cannot escape (i.e., being outside the house alone, in a crowd, on a bridge). Interestingly, although the sleep-panic attacks are just as terrible to experience as the daytime panic attacks, sleep panickers don't have the same degree of agoraphobia as daytime panickers.

Also, before panic disorder can be diagnosed, it should be determined by a physician that the anxiety symptoms are not secondary to drug use, a medical condition, or another psychiatric disorder.

Studies suggest that the majority of people with panic disorder do experience sleep-panic attacks, although less frequently than daytime panic attacks. About 10 percent of people with panic disorder may have the variant called sleep-panic syndrome as described above, in which sleep-panic attacks are more common than daytime panic attacks.

People with panic disorder have more insomnia than the general population, but even more specifically, more middle-of-the-night and early morning awakenings. These awakenings are not necessarily related to sleep-panic attacks.

GENERALIZED ANXIETY DISORDER

Generalized anxiety disorder is characterized by excessive anxiety lasting at least six months, combined with three of six additional symptoms (restlessness or feeling keyed up or on edge, being easily fatigued, difficulty concentrating or mind going blank, irritability, muscle tension, and sleep disturbance). These people are often called "worry warts."

People with generalized anxiety disorder often have difficulty falling asleep because their muscles are tense and their mind won't relax. Also, like sleep-panic, their quality of sleep suffers with decreased amount of REM sleep (see Table 2), but they don't have

"Untitled," 1999. **Steve Markwell**

sleep-panic attacks. It isn't unusual, however, for people with generalized anxiety disorder to develop a comorbid anxiety illness such as panic disorder.

Related to generalized anxiety disorder is *hyperarousal insomnia*, a type of insomnia connected to personality traits. The person is "on edge" frequently and worrying constantly about multiple details of their lives which keep them from sinking into a good sleep. The treatment for hyperarousal insomnia includes things like regular exercise, progressive relaxation exercises, or a hot bath before bed. Traits of hyperarousal insomnia are also shared with other types of anxiety-induced sleep problems, such as those found in stress response syndrome and obsessive-compulsive disorder.

Also related to generalized anxiety disorder is *psychophysiologic insomnia*, an anxiety disorder that develops from behavioral conditioning. These people become conditioned so that everything about sleep eventually becomes a trigger to their anxiety about falling asleep or staying asleep. If and when they do fall asleep they are too anxious to fall into a deep sleep and thus are easily awakened. When they do awake, they feel a lot of anxiety again about getting back to sleep, causing a vicious circle of anxiety and insomnia.

Stress Response Syndrome

Stress response syndrome includes such problems as posttraumatic stress disorder and adjustment disorder.

Stress response syndrome is related to REM sleep, which is the sleep stage when we experience dreams. The person often will wake up in a sweat, vividly remembering a horrible dream related to their initial traumatic experience. This is different, as you will recognize, from sleep panickers, who will wake up without dream recollection. Also, people with stress response syndrome have hyperarousal, making it difficult to fall asleep in the first place, leading to initial insomnia.

Obsessive-Compulsive Disorder

Obsessive-compulsive disorder is a chronic disorder that results in individuals having disabling obsessions and/or compulsions.

Obsessions are uncontrollable spontaneous intrusive thoughts. Compulsions are repetitive ritualistic behaviors (i.e., checking, handwashing) or mental acts (i.e., counting, repeating words) that the person is driven to do in response to the obsession, to avoid something terrible they believe will happen if they don't perform the ritual.

Obsessive-compulsives view their symptoms as "ego-dystonic" —against their nature, and they are able to recognize their fears as unrealistic. They don't want to do the compulsions over and over again, but by force of the obsession they cannot help it.

These obsessive thoughts are often terrifying and keep people from sleeping. Even once they fall asleep, their sleep quality can be poor because their anxiety doesn't necessarily fall asleep when their bodies do. This has similarities to hyperarousal insomnia.

Compulsions can also interfere with sleep by their task-driven command over time. The arduous rituals make it difficult to initiate sleep because people with obsessive-compulsive disorder are always too busy!

Parasomnias

Parasomnias are sleep disorders that occur during specific stages of sleep or during the transition from wakefulness to sleep.

People may have more than one parasomnia, which may be stress-related or due to irregular sleep schedules. Although there are several different parasomnias, we will focus on those related to sleep-panic. Most of them occur in children, who often outgrow them. However, some do not and parasomnias can continue into adulthood.

NIGHTMARE DISORDER

Formerly called dream anxiety disorder, nightmare disorder is similar to sleep-panic in that the person awakes from sleep fully alert and oriented. However, there are differences between nightmares and sleep-panic. It is a dream, a nightmare, that wakes the person up in nightmare disorder. This is because it involves a different stage of sleep—REM versus Stages 2 and 3. Also, it usually occurs during the last half of sleep and with a less intense degree of fright upon awakening from sleep than is experienced in sleep-panic.

SLEEP TERROR DISORDER

In contrast to nightmare disorder, sleep terror disorder awakens the person during the first third of the night in Stage 4, which is deep sleep (slow brain waves) and difficult to awaken from (see Table 1). Those who hear the scream of a person experiencing a sleep terror are generally alarmed and try to arouse the person, finding them unresponsive to arousing efforts. They will awaken confused and disoriented. Similar to sleep-panic, the person expe-

Table 3:

	Dreams	Nightmares	Sleep Terror	Sleepwalking	Sleep-Panic
Sleep Stage	Light non-REM and REM sleep	REM sleep	Stages 3-4	Stages 3-4	Stages 2-3
Responses to Stimulus	Easily awakened and reoriented	Easily awakened and reoriented	Very little	Very little	Easily awakened and reoriented
Motor Movement	Little or none	Little or none	Purposeless	Purposeful	Purposeless
Memory of the Event	Yes	Yes	No	No	Yes

riences intense fear, sweating, fast heart rate, and fast breathing. They cannot remember their dreams. Unlike sleep-panic, they fall asleep quite easily soon after awakening and won't remember having the episode the next day.

SLEEPWALKING

The sleepwalker gets out of bed while sleeping and walks around (somnambulism). Like sleep terror disorder, the person is unaware and unresponsive to attempts at communication. It is very difficult to awaken the sleepwalker and the event usually occurs during the first third of the night, during Stage 4. The person will not remember sleepwalking.

In comparing the similarities and differences between sleep-panic and parasomnias, as well as the similarities and differences between sleep-panic and anxiety disorders, researchers try to figure out which class of disorders sleep-panic belongs to. The question remains: Is sleep-panic a syndrome variant of panic disorder? Is it a symptom of panic disorder? Or is it a new parasomnia?

Sleep, Anxiety, and Drug Disorders

People suffering from anxiety disorders have statistically higher comorbid rates of alcohol problems. Many people who use alcohol like to rationalize that they use it to treat their anxiety symptoms. Hippocrates once said, "Wine drunk with equal quantity of water puts away anxiety and terror." Well, that's not necessarily true. Studies have shown that alcohol use for social phobia often follows the onset of the anxiety symptoms, not the other way around. This leans toward the panic and anxiety disorders stemming from alcohol usage.

The effects of alcohol on sleep are dramatic. Not only does it disrupt sleep architecture and decrease REM sleep, it also can create a psychological dependence. Alcohol is effective as a sedative, but as tolerance develops the dose must be increased to get the same effect. When the sleep architecture becomes more and more impaired causing fragmented dreams and sleep, the alcohol user subsequently experiences more daytime sleepiness and fatigue.

Alcohol is not the only common offender. Nicotine, drugs (i.e., cocaine, amphetamines), caffeine, over-the-counter diet aids and decongestants, and stimulants in the form of prescription medicines can all induce anxiety symptoms.

Prescription medication that commonly cause anxiety include stimulants such as Ritalin, cardiovascular medications, corticosteroids, and anticonvulsants. Even anti-anxiety medications like benzodiazepines can cause anxiety, especially when used incorrectly. Anxiety symptoms can result from taking medications, and also from withdrawals once a person stops taking the medications. The way medicine affects our bodies is complicated and needs close monitoring by a physician and compliance with treatment protocol.

Anxiety and Medical Illness

If you think you suffer from sleep anxiety, see your doctor for a complete medical exam to rule out physical disorders with symptoms similar to anxiety. This will include ruling out any substances that may trigger anxiety symptoms.

To help diagnose your anxiety, your doctor will begin by asking you to describe your anxiety symptoms and your sleep. You will need to identify any stressors in your life, your personal and family medical history, and then start the physical exam that will look for medical illnesses whose symptoms mimic anxiety disorders.

You may benefit from screening tests, which will require a

blood sample and perhaps a sleep study (polysomnogram). If there is indeed an underlying medical disease, its treatment will relieve the panic-anxiety symptoms.

If a medical cause is then ruled out, your primary care provider may often be the one who will refer you to a psychiatrist to help with diagnosis and medication management. A psychiatric evaluation is important to rule out anxiety disorders or comorbid psychiatric illnesses. Your anxiety disorder may not get better until the comorbid psychiatric illness is also treated. After that you may consider behavioral or psychotherapy therapy.

Treatment

Getting patients into treatment for panic-anxiety can be as easy as giving a cat a bath. This is because of both the nature of the illness, which leaves the individual avoidant of others, and because of the social stigma. Most people feel a certain amount of shame about confusing feelings of anxiety, such as uncontrollable fear or thinking they're going crazy. Family and friends can play a crucial role in providing a supportive environment for the individual to seek professional help. Without medication, these chronic debilitating disorders can progress and lead to such unnecessary tragedies as isolation, divorce, and even suicide.

To treat sleep-panic, treat the underlying problem, which is what is causing the panic-anxiety. Problems in this context, such as poor sleep, are the symptoms of the disorder, not the focus of the treatment. This includes avoiding alcohol or other drugs to relieve your anxiety symptoms, giving you what may initially feel like better sleep but ultimately worsening your anxiety symptoms.

If you have sleep-panic secondary to alcohol or drug use, or from another medical cause, targeting the cause will most effectively treat the symptoms.

Differential Diagnosis

- Medications
- Epilepsy (person awakes from sleep with confusion and disorientation—postictal), especially complex partial seizures
- Vestibular dysfunction (illness of the inner ear system)
- Cardiovascular; Arrhythmia (irregular heartbeat or rapid heart-beat), Angina Pectoris (chest pain)
- Pulmonary—Asthma
- Sleep apnea—panic attacks relieved with CPAP
- Hyperventilation Syndrome
- Pain Syndromes
- Ulcer Disease
- Endocrine Disorders Hyperthyroidism (overactive thyroid), Hyperparathyroidism, Pheochromocytoma (catacholamine secretion)
- Primary Anxiety Disorders
- Drug or Alcohol Disorders

For sleep-panic, there are three primary modes of treatment: medication, behavioral therapy (cognitive-behavioral therapy), and psychotherapy.

Medications are the first line of treatment to block sleep-panic attacks, and although they are helpful tools which can block the panic-anxiety completely, they are not cures. Panic-anxiety is a chronic disorder that can be managed well with appropriate treatment and even go into remission, but will not necessarily disappear forever, especially if treatment is stopped. Psychiatrists now recommend "maintenance therapy," meaning staying on medication even after you are symptom-free. Treatment will also reduce the chance of a person developing a second anxiety disorder.

If one medication doesn't work, be patient and try others. There are many good medications for anxiety and each person responds uniquely. Also, more medications are being developed all the time and we are fortunate to be have many options.

Antidepressants work most effectively for treating sleep-panic. In fact, these medications can also function as anxiolytics. It is important to recognize that medication may initially worsen anxiety symptoms before helping them to go away. Anxiety symptoms often get worse for about a week before they get better. Antidepressants include seratonin reuptake inhibitors such as Fluoxetine, Sertraline, and Citaopram, as well as tricyclics such as Disipramine and Amitriptline, and MAO inhibitors such as Parnate and Nardil.

Benzodiazepines are often used in concert with antidepressants for the first four to six weeks until the antidepressants begin to take full effect. They should then be tapered down and discontinued because they cause rebound insomnia and anxiety, and in some people create dependence and even abuse. They impair memory and concentration. They can also exacerbate sleep apnea and other breathing disorders during sleep, which may preclude their use. Only in atypical cases will physicians elect to maintain someone long-term on benzodiazepines.

Benzodiazepines must be used under clear medical supervision. Because they make people with panic-anxiety feel incredibly good so quickly, and yet because of the negative side effects already described, benzodiazepines are a double-edged sword. Discontinuing benzodiazepines once they are started can be a real challenge. They can provide real relief, though, particularly when used appropriately, getting off them after four to six weeks.

Never stop taking medication without consulting with your doctor. Because of the effects these medications have on mood and the way they affect anxiety centers in the brain, stopping them can leave you in an acute state of severe anxiety—and it won't feel good. If you are having side effects, talk it over with your doctor to make adjustments in a way that is less traumatic for you.

Melatonin can be taken in pill form to help advance the onset of sleep, and is especially good for sleeping problems, like those that result from jetlag. It can be useful for people who have trouble getting to sleep, like people who have hyperarousal insomnia. Its role in sleep-panic, however, is yet to be determined. Cognitive behavioral therapy can enhance treatment with medication. It is useful in diminishing anxiety and teaching strategies.

Psychotherapy is also an important treatment option for panic-anxiety, especially in combination with medication. There are many different therapy techniques that are helpful. Examples are relaxation therapy, cognitive-behavioral therapy (used to treat the anticipatory anxiety of avoidance), and psychotherapy focused on the psychosocial causes of anxiety.

Conclusion

Sleep is a complex state affected by many factors. If it is disturbed, it has a profound effect on an individual's life. Sleep-panic has a physiological effect on sleep that can be diagnosed and treated, effectively restoring your sleep. Untreated, sleep-panic leads to impaired cognition, depressed mood, and decreased energy. Treatment for sleep-panic and other anxiety disorders is available, and the vast majority of individuals can significantly improve their sleep.

If you think anxiety may be impairing your sleep, discuss it with your doctor. You deserve good sleep. Give yourself the chance to achieve consistent, sound sleep.

MARTA HELLIESEN

Sexual Manifestations of Panic and Its Treatment

Introduction

PANIC IS ONE OF THE MOST commonly diagnosed anxiety disorders. It is a psychological and physiological experience that, when triggered by certain stimuli, emerges as a function of an interactive brain/body physiology. The experience of a panic attack involves strong emotional arousal and a series of somatic (bodily) events. It can be triggered by external stimuli like places, people, and things, but it is usually related to internal stimuli, such as memories or visceral signals (heart rate, blood pressure, etc.). Panic is an expression of fear, which is—evolutionarily speaking—one of our primary mechanisms of survival. Once we navigate danger we can then turn our attention to other deeper needs such as reproduction, sleep, and nourishment—and, if possible, experience some pleasure, which tends to prolong our survival.

During sexual arousal a number of neurological, endocrine, musculoskeletal, and emotional events take place. As with panic, sexual arousal is a function of an interactive physiology between brain and body. This chapter discusses the interconnected qualities of sexual arousal and the panic response from a neurophysiological point of view.

I propose treatment modalities for sexual manifestations of panic and discuss how breathing patterns, hands-on work, and a trusting therapist/client relationship can affect the brain and thus behavior. The use of neuroscientific methods is essential for the healing of deep trauma and the transformation of destructive sexual behavior into healthy patterns. Yet this neuroscientific approach does not eschew the mystery at the heart of sexuality, or the workings of the brain.

I stress the importance of working with the whole person, emphasizing the integration of the erotic body with the mind, using both the clarity of science and the heart-based qualities of therapy. This is critical to understand, since a division in the holistic human organism can result in a vicious circle of anxiety, panic, sexual dissatisfaction, and sexual dysfunction.

Understanding the Autonomic Nervous System (ANS)

Most of the physical symptoms (heart palpitations, sweating or chills, shortness of breath, dizziness, nausea, chest pain, etc.) of panic are mediated by the ANS, which plays a significant role in the sexual arousal response. The ANS is a subdivision of our nervous system (brain, spinal cord, and nerves), and its primary role is to maintain internal homeostasis (i.e., heart rate, blood pressure, temperature regulation, digestive processes, etc.).

The regulation of the ANS is unconscious, but can be influenced by conscious mental functions. The ANS is divided into two subdivisions, the Parasympathetic Nervous System (PNS, rest and digestive processes) and the Sympathetic Nervous System (SNS, fight-or-flight response). These two parts operate together like the yin and yang, creating optimal balance in a relaxed, awake body.

The PNS and SNS secrete different neurotransmitters, but in this context I will refer only to norepinephrine, which is released from the sympathetic nerve endings, referred to as adrenergic. The inner section of the adrenal glands (adrenal medulla) is a part of the SNS. It releases adrenaline and norepinephrine (catecholamines) into the blood stream and contributes to the overall effect of sympathetic nerve activation.

During sexual activity both the PNS and SNS are activated. The ratio of PNS/SNS activation is a function of the particular needs of the different parts of the body at any given point in time. During panic, the SNS is put into overdrive—a response that is often times incompatible with sexual arousal.

Anatomy and Physiology of Panic

As human beings we all have experienced some degree of fear or panic in our lives. Many people experience frequent panic attacks, living in fear of repeating another attack. This can have a severe impact on the quality of life for the person suffering, as well as family and friends. By explaining the brain as a malleable structure, and giving an outline of the physiology of fear and of sexual arousal, I hope to convey a tangible cure for panic and sexually associated issues.

Fear and anxiety are closely related and are both normal responses to danger. Anxiety is usually thought of as coming from within us (i.e., a reaction to a memory or anticipation of something unpleasant), while fear is triggered from an external stimulus (i.e., snakes, dark alleys, terrorists). Panic is described as intense anxiety and discomfort. Based on previous experience, the initial registration of visceral stimuli, like increased blood pressure or heart rate, can be interpreted by the brain as the onset of a panic attack. This will trigger the unconscious fear response as well as the learned fear associated with the panic attack itself, and thus results in a full-fledged panic attack.[1]

Panic disorder, agoraphobia, posttraumatic stress disorder, obsessive-compulsive disorder, and generalized anxiety disorder are all anxiety disorders categorized in DSM-IV, based on different clinical symptoms. From a neuroscientific point of view, I concur with LeDoux, who claims that the underlying mechanisms in all these disorders are very similar. "Anxiety disorders reflect the operation of the fear system of the brain."

Fear and panic responses are not located in one particular site in the brain. Rather these responses seem to be mediated by a "fear network" that produces defensive behavior necessary to survive. Given that this ability to react is a function of evolution, it is hardy, quick to learn, and doesn't easily forget. Among the structures involved in the fear response, the amygdala is considered to be central (a small almond-shaped region in the forebrain). Other important structures are the thalamus (the main relay center for sensory input), the hippocampus (temporal lobe cortical structure, famous for its role in learning and memory), the medial prefrontal cortex (best known for its role in planning and inhibition of inappropriate responses), and the cerebral cortex (cognitive processes).

Nerve fibers from the amygdala, activated in response to a fear stimulus, are responsible for coordinating autonomic and behavioral responses. Some of these alert the hypothalamus (major control center for endocrine functions, mood, sexual pleasure, rage, etc.), which activates the SNS and increases the release of steroid stress hormones from the adrenal glands. Other fibers go to the brainstem nuclei and cause an increase in respiratory rate, increased blood pressure, and heart rate, as well as behavioral fear response, defensive behaviors, and postural freezing.[2,3]

The fine-tuned operation of this nerve network produces a general anxiety or panic response that includes rapid heartbeat, sweaty hands, dry mouth, tight stomach, etc. Variations in our responses are due to learned stimuli that initiate these responses. Depending on where we live and our past experiences with danger and fear we will each have a particular list of triggers that will degenerate the cells in the hippocampus, the prime structure for formation of memory. These changes are reversible if the stress subsides. However, exposure to anxiety over long periods causes irreversible degeneration of hippocampal cells.

The practical implications of this can be temporary impairment of memory formation to permanent memory loss. In human trauma survivors, researchers have often found a shrunken hippocampus and impaired memory,[4] indicating that stressful life events can have a permanent, debilitating effect on the hippocampus and its functions. This damage seems to be caused by the adrenal steroid hormone cortisol, which travels through the blood to the brain where it binds to cells in the hippocampus. Initially this binding helps regulate the release of steroid (stress) hormones, but as the stress persists, the hippocampus falters in its regulatory role and damaging effects take place.[5]

It is established that amygdala functions are enhanced when hippocampus function is impaired during stress. In other words, a retrievable memory of a traumatic event might not be formed because of a temporary halt in the hippocampal memory formation, yet the amygdala-mediated fear response (bodily, emotional) created by the same trauma is amplified and stored. If the trauma happens very early in life, the hippocampus may not have been developed enough to have formed a conscious memory, while amygdala—which develops earlier—is active in mediating the fear response.[6] This is especially relevant to sexual trauma at an early age.

Another factor affecting memory formation is dissociation, the focusing attention on a non-traumatic aspect of the environment or on imagination, during a traumatic event. This divided attention can impair the formation of a memory in the hippocampus, while the memory formation involving the amygdala stays intact.[7]

Fear responses established during traumas like incest, rape, or similar incidents can manifest during sexual encounters later in life where the person might go from arousal and excitement to a state of panic within moments. The physical changes involved can range from relaxed to tight muscles throughout the body, from slow and deep breathing to shallow and fast, from an open and well-lubricated vagina to tight and dry, or from a firm, erect phallus to flaccid and unaroused. Mentally there could be a sense of extreme anxiety and suffocation. Individuals who experience this suffer greatly as they are often unable (due to the above-mentioned mechanisms) to access a conscious memory of any event associated with their reaction, but the fear response is very real to them. They often withdraw from sexual contact due to fear and judgment from sexual partners. This becomes a vicious circle in which just the thought of sex might lead to a panic attack.

These response patterns are not permanent and can be transformed. If the suffering person is willing to commit to a process involving specifically designed body and breath work, parallel to a psychodynamic process to enhance cognitive awareness, behavioral changes and integration of trauma (even if not recalled) will take place.

©Getty Images/Tim Southall, 2002

TREATMENT

Using Tools: Breathing and the Brain

Breath, the intake of oxygen and the exhalation of carbon dioxide, is the essence of our life. We are born with a natural rhythmic breath—in infants, breath can be observed moving through the body from mouth to anus. Early on we start to develop our list of potential dangers or discomforts and as part of a survival response we start holding our breath to be quiet, invisible, and to feel less. Holding the breath affects the tightly measured balance between oxygen and carbon dioxide, which determines the pH levels in the blood. An increase in the level of carbon dioxide in blood leads to several unpleasant somatic sensations (dizziness, racing heart, feeling of suffocation) and is interpreted in the brain as danger, often resulting in a panic attack, thus creating a conditioned stimuli for future panic attacks.[8]

In my work with panic-related sexual issues, I emphasize the breath as a main tool in reconditioning the client's fear network. By using touch to guide the client to a state of deep relaxed breathing there is an increase in oxygen uptake, balancing the oxygen/carbon dioxide levels and signaling to the brain to release the stress response. A change from chest to abdominal breathing changes the muscular contraction patterns throughout the body, resulting in different proprioceptive information from the muscles to the motor control centers in the brain, causing the release of muscular tension. The key to this process is for the client to remain aware and in contact with the therapist while the breathing patterns are changed. Eventually a parallel unconscious and conscious counteracting of conditioned response patterns associated with anxiety and intimacy is achieved.

This process is likely to involve modulation of cortical and sub-cortical projections involving the amygdala, hypothalamus, hippocampus, prefrontal cortex, brainstem nuclei, and other areas of the brain. More research is needed to map the neurophysiological mechanisms involved in this modulation. Meanwhile, magnetic resonance studies of the brain during meditation have shown activation of neuronal structures involved in attention and control of the ANS.[9] Studies of yoga and meditation have shown a reduced stress response through modulation of the sympathetic response and by lowering stress hormones levels,[10] as well as affecting the level of adrenaline and norepinephrine.[11]

During sex, yoga, and meditation the goal is to stay fully focused on the experience of breath and body sensation and stay present to the unknown. The moment we activate our cognition we interrupt the organic flow of the bodily processes, which during sex can mean loss of erection, premature ejaculation, vaginal dryness, or interruption of a building orgasm.

Sexual Arousal in the Male

The physiology of sexual arousal (erection) in men involves the regulation of blood flow to and from the penis, and is dependent on nerve impulse regulation from both the central and peripheral nervous system. In the brain, there is an integration of visual, olfactory, tactile, and imaginative stimuli that modulate the spinal cord regulation of erections. The result of this process decides whether there will be an erect or flaccid penis. For many men over fifty, the physiological aging process affects the erectile ability in such a way that visual or imaginative stimulation does not necessarily manifest in the penis. Direct stimulation of the sensory nerve endings in the penis is needed to activate the nerves responsible for an erection that will match the desire or lust a man is feeling in his head.

During an erection there is an inflow of blood into the central artery and the erectile tissue in the penis. Parasympathetic nerve endings, together with the vascular endothelium, release nitric oxide and possibly other vasodilating peptides into the corpus cavernosum of the penis. The nitric oxide activates a cascade of events that produces the second messenger, cyclic Guanosin Monophosphate, which mediates smooth muscle relaxation of the penile arteries and the erectile tissue, causing increased blood flow into the penis. (Viagra works by enhancing the nitric oxide mediated mechanisms.)

As the erectile tissue gets filled with blood it compresses the veins and blood is trapped in the penis. When the male reaches a peak in sexual pleasure (orgasm and ejaculation) there is a release of norepinephrine and adrenaline from the SNS. This causes contraction of the smooth muscles in the ductus deferens (which carries sperm cells from the testes to the prostate gland), and the urethra (which carries semen from the prostate gland out of the penis). This, together with contraction of the skeletal muscles in the floor of the pelvis and the muscles at the base of the penis, forces semen out of the penis during ejaculation.

The catecholamines released during orgasm also cause the arteries in the erectile tissue to contract; blood drains from the penis and subsiding erection results, aided by adrenergic mechanisms to a nonerect state. A penis in a flaccid state inhabits a tonic contraction of the arterial smooth muscles, causing higher arterial resistance and reduced blood flow into the penis.[12,13]

Sexual Arousal in the Female

Sexual arousal in women, as in men, is a function of vasocongestion in the genital area. There is an increase in blood flow to the clitoris, vagina, vulva, uterus, and possibly urethra. The clitoris has similar erectile tissue to that of the penis. During sexual arousal there is an increase in clitoral erectile tissue artery inflow, which leads to tumescence and the extrusion of the clitoris. Vasodilation and vasocongestion of the vaginal capillary network leads to increased intra-arterial pressure, which contributes to lubrication of the vaginal wall.[14]

During arousal there is a lengthening of the anterior vaginal wall and the uterus rises, but does not increase in volume as previously thought.[15] It is possible that nitric oxide, vasoactive intestinal polypeptide, and prostaglandin E play a role in the smooth muscle relaxation in the clitoral erectile tissue,[16,17,18] but the neurotransmitters involved remain undetermined.

Through stimulation of the clitoris, vaginal wall, or G-spot, the muscular body tension and the pelvic engorgement builds to a climax and an orgasm is reached. This pleasure can involve few to many rhythmic contractions of the uterus, vagina, and pelvic floor muscles, including the anal sphincter, which helps pump blood in the pelvic area back into main circulation. In men, adrenergic systems are responsible for ejaculation and flaccidity, while in women, adrenergic mechanisms are active during and following sexual activity.[19,20] It has been shown that following intense exercise (which heightens SNS activity) there is an increase in vaginal pulse amplitude response to erotic stimulation. It is suggested that there might be an optimal level of SNS activation for facilitation of female sexual arousal.[21]

Case Study I:

My first case study is my client Sara. She had worked with me for two years and was working intensely to resolve her trauma around paternal incest by an alcoholic father and an emotionally absent mother. Sara was highly functional and a strong, independent thirty-two-year-old woman who had lived a productive and successful life. She had been sexually active with men and women since the age of sixteen, but was aware that during most of her sex life she had been in a dissociated state.

Over the last year she had experienced a number of flashbacks and nightmares from her childhood trauma. The theme of her dreams was that she was falling into a dark abyss or walking down a dark narrowing tunnel. Through weekly meetings with me Sara slowly gained the emotional strength to embody this darkness as opposed to alienating it. Despite the struggle this involved, she became very curious about what the darkness was about. She started to search for manifestations of it in the outside world. She read Marquis de Sade as well as the *Story of O* and was surprised to discover how these books stirred her emotions and turned her on. We spent many sessions processing the feelings (fear, desire, disgust, anger) that emerged during her reading. It was with my support that she eventually found her way to a dominant man who took her on as a mentee.

> "I found that outbreaks of anxiety and a general state of preparedness for anxiety were produced by certain sexual practices such as *coitus interruptus,* undischarged sexual excitation or enforced abstinence—that is, whenever sexual excitation was inhibited, arrested or deflected in its progress towards satisfaction. Since sexual excitation was an expression of libidinal instinctual impulses it did not seem too rash to assume that the libido was turned into anxiety through the agency of these disturbances."
>
> —Sigmund Freud, *Inhibitions, Symptoms and Anxiety*

TREATMENT

In the first session with her mentor, Sara fainted. She came to, found her mentor caring and supportive, and they continued the session. Sara saw her dominant weekly for about a year. In her own words she describes the following process. "By going into the darkness that submission represented to me, I could experience that dark part of myself fully. I discovered that by breathing deeply and reminding myself about the truth and safety of the present moment, I was able to transform my conditioned fear response—which included fainting—into both pleasure and excitement. It enabled me to fully trust another intimate human being for the first time since I can remember. It also helped me integrate the incest as part of who I am. I wish it didn't happen, but I have been able to accept it and work with it. I stopped seeing my dominant as my needs changed. Now I am able to get turned on and have an orgasm from regular sex, and when I occasionally play it's in a different version, no more pain." This is not to suggest that everybody with sexual trauma should engage in Domination/Submisson, but is presented as an example of an experiential approach to growth and healing.

Psychology and Physiology: Exploring the Process

From a scientific point of view, Sara's case can be explained partially in terms of conditioned fear response, which is a variation of the classical conditioning model first discovered by Ivan Pavlov around the turn of the century. Fear conditioning turns meaningless stimuli into warning signs—cues that signal a potentially dangerous situation based on similar past experiences.[22] Sara's process involved a change of the conditioned fear response that was probably established very early in her life. Being forced into sexual encounters at a young age there were most likely several conditioned stimuli involved in Sara's fainting. For example, being commanded and immobilized by a male, not knowing what the next move would be, and not being able to fight back or scream (at this point by consensual submission). To faint (which Sara started doing early on in life when exposed to danger) can be compared to the innate response in animals to freeze or play dead when they sense danger.

This action is mediated by subcortical (unconscious) mechanisms including the amygdala and brainstem nuclei. As these conditioned stimuli were repeated many times (but without the sexual assault) the fear reactions (fainting, sweating, nausea) diminished and extinction took place. The process of extinction prevents expression of the fear response but does not erase it altogether. The original fear response can be reinstated by reexposure to an assault or similar stressful events associated with the conditioned stimuli.[23]

Parallel to the work with her dominant, Sara worked intensely with me to process, in an interactive dynamic way, what she was going through. My intention was to support and teach her to stay present in her body and to her contact with me, and to recognize and transform the dissociative response pattern. This meant that in her relationship with me she had to tolerate intimate, nonsexual contact, which was another breach of her old behavioral patterns. Sara's nightmares might reflect her brain's attempt to consolidate memory configurations that, due to dissociation and lack of verbal processing of the trauma at the time, were blocked from being consolidated in her cerebral cortex (which is necessary for permanent storage). Dream stages of sleep are thought to be important for reorganizing memory and for connecting memory and emotion.[24]

I believe that heightened awareness of the body and cognitive recognition of present circumstances coupled with repeated exposure to conditioned stimuli modifies the subcortical and cortical projections (including the medial prefrontal cortex which is implicated in the extinction process) to the amygdala. This "reworking" of the brain's configuration inhibits the automated fear response, allowing alternate processing of sexual nerve impulses (involving brainstem nuclei, hypothalamus, amygdala, hippocampus, and other forebrain structures) so the sensations can be experienced as sexual and pleasant. Sara's subsiding desire for pain over time is a multi-layered phenomenon which is beyond the scope of this chapter to discuss. However, I will suggest as one possible explanation a sensitization of her sensory nerve pathways (enhancing sensations) due to less stress and fear, which reduced stress release of opiates and in turn lowered stress-induced analgesia.

Sexual Arousal versus Panic

Intense and/or chronic anxiety, as well as sexual arousal, stimulates cardiovascular responses—increasing the heart rate and blood pressure.[25,26] In both males and females, there is a significant increase of norepinephrine during sexual arousal as well as during a fear response.[27,28,29] It's also been found that there is a positive correlation between blood level of norepinephrine, sexual arousal, and orgasm.[30] An increase in norepinephrine signals that the SNS is activated. While it's known that the SNS is active during sexual arousal in women, and that it's involved in ejaculation and maintenance of a nonerect state in men, the exact role of norepinephrine in sexual arousal remains unknown. However, for both genders the above reports indicate a strong activation of the adrenergic system in both sexual arousal and anxiety, suggesting that similar mechanisms are active in both. The key is to find the right balance on the arousal/anxiety curve.

The question is how do we sustain the proper balance? Our high-stress, anxiety-provoking society (further heightened in fast-paced cities) can cause a tonic activation of the stress response. This involves increased activity of the brainstem nucleus, Locus Coeruleus, which sends norepinephrine-containing nerve projections to a number of brain sites, some of which are implicated in the fear response. Directly and indirectly the activation of the brainstem nucleus leads to an increase in heart rate, blood pressure, and activation of the SNS. Exposure to stressful situations is also associated with an increased release of the stress hormone cortisol from the adrenal glands. Sustained over time, high levels of cortisol can affect sexual function and compromise the immune system, as well as the growth and reproductive systems, and can cause brain damage. Activation of stress systems like these will cause many people to live on the anxious side of the curve, causing anxiety and sexual dysfunction.

Sexual Dysfunction

Very often sexual dysfunction is rooted in a person's heightened state of anxiety. Suffering from sexual dysfunction can lead to depression, which often times amplifies sexual problems by inducing lack of desire and lust and creating more anxiety; the circle goes round and round.[31,32] Finding which symptom came first—anxiety, dysfunction, or depression—can be difficult. Many people run from gynecologist to urologist to psychologist to psychiatrist without getting any answers.

I believe sexual dysfunction is a manifestation of imbalance. Often these symptoms are ignored or forgotten prior to the body's last scream for help. My approach is to bring the person to a baseline and from there to investigate the sequence of events leading to the symptoms, eventually finding the obstacle causing the imbalance. Some of the manifestations of sexual dysfunction in men are premature or rapid ejaculation and erectile dysfunction in women include vaginal dryness and pain. Both genders share the problems of delayed orgasm or an-orgasm, tight anal canals, hemorrhoids, lack of desire, and numbness.

Sexual panic in men can often revolve around the penis and its features—how big is it, how hard it gets, how long the erection lasts, how deep it thrusts, how well it make their partner come. The porn industry, locker room philosophy, and multiple other aspects of our culture emphasize and reward size versus quality. When size does not measure up to the current norm, humiliation, shame, and panic can follow. Many men on the small side have gone through tremendous trauma because of it, and have subsequently found their own unique creative adjustments that have enabled them to survive. The idea of being seen in the bedroom with a small soft penis has led many men to train themselves to be hard the moment the pants come off. However, the fact that they are already fantasizing about sex with their partner (or somebody else) in order to become erect usually results in an orgasm either before or immediately after penetration. Not only are they struggling with the "shame" of a small penis, they now have a problem with premature ejaculation.

Working Together: Case Study II

My client Steve was one of these men. He called me but could only tell me that he had a "problem"—fear of being heard prevented him from talking about details on his cell phone. The man who arrived for his appointment was a typical successful-looking New Yorker. He carried himself in a confident way, wore a tailor-made suit, and was perfectly groomed. He told me about his problem with premature ejaculation and how it recently had gotten very bad. He really needed to impress his new lover, but as soon as he was inside he would come and she was getting pissed off.

At this point he was so nervous about her reaction that he even had problems getting hard. He needed a quick fix. I was observing him as he was talking to me. His upper body was puffed up, he was holding his stomach in to look younger and slimmer then his forty-seven years; his breathing was shallow. His lifestyle included a pack of cigarettes a day, a few cocktails and a bottle of wine with dinner every night, followed by "wild" sex. His pain was palpable and I was thinking to myself, I have to make him breathe, his problem will not be solved through talking.

I asked Steve to lie down on his back on the massage table. I told him to close his eyes, do as little as possible, and relax. I gently put my hand on his belly and encouraged him to try to breathe into my hand with no further agenda. The quietness of the room, the soft table underneath his worn body, and my warm hand on his tight stomach slowly started to melt away the layers of protection. I could feel his breath deepening and could see his face starting to relax. I moved to the end of the table and cupped his head between my hands in a firm but gentle grip. I let my breath be audible next to his ear to encourage him to deepen his breath.

As the breath started to enter his body, he could no longer maintain his conditioned tight posture, and his body started to get looser and softer. I asked Steve to tell me what he was aware of in his body. He told me how tired he felt, and how good it felt to be touched without having to do anything. He could not remember the last time he had felt this relaxed. I noticed that he looked very sad. He was soon sobbing, telling a story that moved from locker room harassment to his current failing business and the pressure of maintaining his high lifestyle and image. In other words, Steve was living a lifestyle that kept his body in a tonic state of fear. He had conditioned himself to fantasize to create a premature erection, which caused a premature ejaculation and an unsatisfactory sex life for both himself and his partner. He had compensated with a very assertive, confident demeanor and by frequenting places that he could no longer afford. Essentially he was terrified of being exposed. Obviously Steve was a complex client with deep-rooted wounds that would take time to heal. We worked with reconditioning so he could feel the sensation of touch without thinking about it. He began to relax with me.

We also worked on the sexual needs and desires of women. He came to understand that it takes more than a large penis to please a woman—as long as you have hands, tongue, and sensitivity you can make any woman happy. If she is a real "size queen" you can always strap on a big dildo for the occasion. He came to accept (not necessarily like) that his penis was on the small side and his premature ejaculation ended. He was devoted to doing his home-work, which included breathing exercises and different masturbation rituals without fantasies. We worked together for four months, and although Steve is still working to complete his healing process, he has accomplished much.

The essence of the work I did with Steve was to help him become aware of some of the physical and mental defense mechanisms that he was using, and transform these into mechanisms that were more constructive. Although we did talk during our sessions, the main work was for Steve to develop trust and be able to relax with me. We worked to change his breathing pattern from tight and shallow to deep and relaxed. By experiencing the effect of the breathing while he was with me, he was able to start applying it elsewhere both in his private and professional life. He discovered how it helped him stay more grounded when he was with women, and to appreciate sober sex.

Erectile Dysfunction

Erectile dysfunction, defined as the inability to obtain and maintain an erection sufficient for satisfactory intercourse or other sexual expression, affects over 50 percent of men between the ages of forty and seventy.[33] Erectile dysfunction means: 1) blood is not entering the penis adequately, 2) blood is retracting from the penis too fast, 3) the erectile tissue in the penis is unable to expand and fill with blood. There can be many causes underlying these conditions (i.e., vascular disease, heart disease, neurological dysfunction, diabetes, side effects of HIV medication and other medications, or psychogenic factors). I mostly encounter the latter in my work, which is treatable without pharmacology.

Based on my own practice, 99 percent of the cases with erectile dysfunction are caused by psychological reasons, with anxiety being the number one cause. Men tend to forget that the penis is not an isolated entity that should be able to perform anytime anywhere. The simple fact that the penis is connected to a body and mind and is affected by everything that goes on is easily forgotten. Most of the men who come to me are not aware that they are anxious. All they know is that "things are not functioning as they used to." Some of the issues that surface are fear of not being a good enough lover, of not lasting long enough, or of not being big enough.

Many men feel constantly stressed and exhausted; many feel disconnected from their wives. Some men have gained weight and are self-conscious about their bodies, and others are struggling with after-effects of previous trauma, which interferes with sexual function.34 The common factor for these various causes is that it involves too much thinking and activation of the fear system, which interferes with the blood flow into the penis. As I described in both case studies, I work with my clients to help them stay present in their bodies and to their contact with me. I help them understand that we have limited capacity as human beings and can focus fully on only one thing at a time.

Our habit of doing at least three things simultaneously to raise our efficiency does not apply to sex—you have to be there with all your faculties. Men with psychological-based erectile dysfunction can always get an erection if they are able to relax and feel the erotic stimulation of their skin and genitals. The challenge is to stay focused on the breath and the sensory experience. In cases where fantasies interfere with erection, the work is to trust that the body will respond to touch and practice masturbation and erotic contact without fantasies. Relying on fantasies to get an erection can easily result in premature ejaculation, as well as interfere with intimacy.

Many men lose their erection the moment they penetrate a bodily orifice, as they get too excited or too worried about not lasting long enough. By staying where they are, breathing and concentrating on the feeling versus the thought, they discover that they can get erect again. If the men I work with have a partner I always encourage them to work together in the process, as it takes two to tango, and the man's erectile dysfunction can be a function of what is going on in the relationship. It can deepen the intimacy if the partner participates in the homework. Single men rely more on the relationship with me during the process, and do the homework by engaging in various self-pleasuring rituals. As soon as my clients discover that they get erect when they relax, they start to trust their bodies and the process of healing accelerates.

Sexual Dysfunction in Women

Sexual dysfunction in women can, as for men, be caused by physical factors like vasculogenic, neurogenic, or endocrine problems, post-surgery trauma, or side effects of medications.[35] Again, I will address the psychogenic causes. The problems I encounter most frequently are lack of orgasm or pain during intercourse. One aspect of the latter is referred to as vaginismus, which is an involuntary contraction of the outer third of the vagina in response to attempted penetration. This is a muscular fear response controlled by the brain, established as a protective measure following one or many painful, perhaps non-lubricated, penetrations, early or later in life. A non-medical healing process for this is done through creating a safe environment, free of performance pressure or other threats and by supporting the woman in staying aware and relaxed through touch and breath. Through exposure to a very slow, gentle, and lubricated penetration and by gradually increasing the size of the object (fingers, dildo, penis), women can relax their pelvic floor, open up, and be free of their vaginismus. Depending on the individual, this process can take from a day or two to many months.

For a woman who describes herself as an-orgasmic, the first step is to help her define her unique experience of an orgasm. Many women define orgasm according to the Hollywood version where a hard pumping man sends the moaning woman through the ceiling within two minutes. Wrong. There are as many orgasms as there are women, they come in all sizes, sounds, and rhythms, and they are different from day to day and week to week. The key is that we don't know what our orgasm is going to look or feel like when we start an erotic event. The challenge is to engage fully in the erotic process while not worrying about the duration or the "result." Women often feel the buildup to an orgasm, and can be very close, but are unable to let go of the last bit of control. Instead, they feel the energy implode in their bodies. This can be rooted in emotional as well as physical trauma early or later in life. The fear conditioning system in the brain has established a muscular holding pattern that protects against the vulnerability that comes with letting go at the time of orgasm. Again, the breath is the main tool. When reaching the point where fear of "losing control" threatens an orgasm, a woman can, with support, choose to breathe into that experience, focus on her body, and trust that she will not be hurt—and before she knows it she's riding the waves of an orgasm. By repeating this over and over in similar and different versions, the fear conditioning will be extinct and new orgasmic response patterns will develop in the brain.

Women frequently struggle with self-consciousness about their bodies, as few women fit the twiggy version that's promoted by the media and fashion industry. The essential part of my work with women is to gently support their acceptance of their own bodies. Women have a tendency—when they don't accept their bodies—to hold their breath in order to look thinner. The result can be an activation of the stress response, which can lead to panic attack and numbness throughout the body. None of this goes well with sex. The key is to accept and celebrate the body as is, let the curves of the belly, breasts, and hips be manifestations of eroticism and not of imperfection.

It is hard for women to take the time at home to be with themselves and to indulge in self-exploration and self-stimulation. However, it is essential to be familiar with your body to get beyond the mystery and taboos associated with the vagina. By getting to know the uniqueness of your erotic body, the more and less sensitive spots, and what kind of stimulation can bring you to orgasm, you can smoothly guide your partner to do the right things, avoiding hurt and frustration. Like men, many women experience performance angst, activating the fear network and interrupting pleasure. It often takes women longer than men to resolve their sexual issues. This is due in part to earlier and deeper sexual wounds. Women have also had to fight against the many societal and religious voices that have tried to suppress their sexual selves. Believing these voices is the cause of much sexual guilt and shame. However, due to the amazing plasticity of the brain, we can change and commit to the healing process. Integration will take place and women can come to live fully in their sexual bodies.

Concluding Remarks

Based on the neurophysiology underlying fear conditioning, I've proposed treatment forms to change conditioned fear responses related to sex. In my practice, I utilize a combination of touch, breath, and relaxation techniques, coupled with bodily and cognitive awareness while empathizing the connection between the client and myself. The parallel conscious and unconscious processing of conditioned stimulus under safe circumstances can slowly modulate the conditioned fear response to the point of extinction. I suggest that over time and through repetition, bodily and cognitive stimuli associated with sexuality and intimacy can be integrated into a new neurological configuration. This can mediate healing of sexual wounds as well as transform anxiety-related sexual dysfunction.

Endnotes:

1. J.E. LeDoux, *The Emotional Brain: The Mysterious Underpinnings of Emotional Life* (New York: Simon & Schuster, 1996), 258–61.

2. Ibid., 138–78.

3. J.M. Gorman et al., "Neuroanatomical Hypothesis of Panic Disorder, Revised," *American Journal of Psychiatry* 157 (2000): 493–505.

4. J.D. Bremner et al., "MRI-based Measurements of Hippocampal Volume in Patients with Combat-Related PTSD," *American Journal of Psychiatry* 31, no. 2 (1992): 973–81.

5. B.S. McEwen and R. Sapolsky, "Stress and Cognitive Functioning," *Current Opinion in Neurobiology* 5, no. 2 (1995): 205–16.

6. J.E. LeDoux, op. cit., 200–09

7. D.J. Siegel, *The Developing Mind: Toward A Neurobiology of Interpersonal Experience* (New York: Guildford Press, 1999), 50–55.

8. J.E. LeDoux, op. cit., 258–61.

9. S.W. Lazar et al., "Functional Brain Mapping of the Relaxation Response and Meditation," *Neuroreport* 11, no. 7 (2000): 1581–85.

10. N. Yardi, "Yoga for Control of Epilepsy," *Seizure* 10, no. 1 (2000): 7–12.

11. J.R. Infante et al., "Catecholamine Levels in Practitioners of the Transcendental Meditation Technique," *Physiology & Behavior* 72, nos. 1–2 (2001): 141–46.

12. C.M. Meston et al., "The Neurobiology of Sexual Function," in *Archives of General Psychiatry* 57 (2000): 1012–30.

13. K.E. Andersson, "Pharmacology of Penile Erection," *Pharmacological Reviews* 53 (2001): 417–50.

14. C.M. Meston and P.F. Frohlich, op. cit.

15. W.W. Schultz et al., "Magnetic Resonance Imaging of Male and Female Genitals during Coitus and Female Sexual Arousal," *British Medical Journal* 319 (1999): 1596–1600.

16. R.J. Levin, "VIP, Vagina, Clitoral and Periurethral Glans—An Update on Human Female Genital Arousal," *Experimental and Clinical Endocrinology* 98, no. 2 (1991): 61–69.

17. K. Min et al., "Sildenafil Augments Pelvic-Mediated Genital Sexual Arousal in the Anesthetized Rabbit," *International Journal of Impotence Research* 12, no. 3 (2000): S32–39.

18. K. Min et al., "Experimental Models for the Investigation of Female Sexual Function and Dysfunction," *International Journal of Impotence Research* 13, no. 3 (2001): 151–56.

19. M.S. Exton et al., "Cardiovascular and Endocrine Alternations After Masturbation-Induced Orgasm in Women," *Psychosomatic Medicine* 61 (1999): 280–89.

20. C.M. Meston and P.F. Frohlich, op. cit.

21. Ibid.

22. J.E. LeDoux, op. cit., 141.

23. Ibid., 145.

24. D.J. Siegel, op. cit., 50–55.

25. M.S. Exton et al., op. cit., 280–89.

26. T.C. Buckley and D.G. Kaloupek, "A Meta-Analytic Examination of Basal Cardiovascular Activity in Posttraumatic Stress Disorder," *Psychosomatic Medicine* 63 (2001): 585–94.

27. T. Kruger et al., "Neuroendocrine and Cardiovascular Response to Sexual Arousal and Orgasm in Men," *Pschoendocrinology* 4 (1998): 401–11.

28. M.S. Exton et al., op. cit.

29. J.D. Bremner, "The Neurobiology of Posttraumatic Stress Disorder: An Integration of Animal and Human Research." In *Posttraumatic Stress Disorder: A Comprehensive Text,* edited by P.A. Saigh and J.D. Bremner (Boston: Allyn & Bacon, 1999), 103–43.

30. C.M. Meston and P.F. Frohlich, op. cit.

31. S.N. Seidman and S. Roose, "The Relationship between Depression and Erectile Dysfunction," *Current Psychiatry Reports* 2 (2000): 201–05.

32. S.N. Seidman and S.P. Roose, "Sexual Dysfunction and Depression," *Current Psychiatry Reports* 3 (2001): 202–08.

33. H.A. Feldman et al., "Impotence and Its Medical and Psychosocial Correlates: Results of the Massachusetts Male Aging Study," *Journal of Urology* 151 (1994): 54–61.

34. M. Kotler et. al., "Sexual Dysfunction in Male Posttraumatic Stress Disorder Patients," *Psychotherapy and Psychosomatics* 69, no. 6 (2000): 309–15.

35. J. Berman and L. Berman, *For Women Only: A Revolutionary Guide to Overcoming Sexual Dysfunction and Reclaiming Your Sex Life* (New York: Henry Holt and Company, LLC., 2001).

ANDREW GAEDDERT

Herbal Treatment for Panic Disorder and other Anxiety-Related Disorders

EVERYONE EXPERIENCES FEAR AND ANXIETY. Fear is a response to an external threat, whereas anxiety can erupt from external events and a person's own thoughts. Anxiety is a stress response that can arise suddenly as in panic, or can occur gradually.

According to the *American Heritage Dictionary*, anxiety is a state of apprehension, uncertainty, and fear resulting from the anticipation of a realistic or fantasized threatening event or situation, often impairing physical and psychological functioning. Panic is a sudden overpowering terror.

Generalized anxiety disorder pertains to persistent daily anxiety or worry that interferes with one's life. In addition, there may be three or more of the following symptoms: restlessness, fatigue, concentration problems, irritability, muscle tension, and insomnia. Three to five percent of adults have generalized anxiety disorder during a given year. Women are twice as likely as men to suffer from this disorder. It has not been proven that repressed conflicts or chemical imbalances cause anxiety although these are popular theories among mental health professionals.

Panic attacks are acute and extreme anxiety in response to a specific situation. Common symptoms include the sudden appearance of shortness of breath, feelings of being smothered or "closed in," heart palpitations, shaking, fear of going crazy or losing control, feeling detached from the environment, dizziness, sweating, and chest pain. All of these symptoms lead people to worry that they have a dangerous medical problem. Although panic attacks themselves are not dangerous, it is a good idea to seek a physician to rule out other disorders.

Posttraumatic stress disorder is an anxiety disorder caused by exposure to an overwhelming traumatic event. This is often seen in combat veterans and victims of violent acts, where the person repeatedly reexperiences the event that is the origin of their stress. Sometimes a person's symptoms don't begin until months or years after the traumatic event took place. Symptoms include intense fear, hopelessness, and horror. The person may reexperience the trauma in nightmares or flashbacks. The person may have difficulty sleeping or be easily startled. Oftentimes posttraumatic stress disorder becomes less severe over time.

Conventional Treatments

Conventional therapies include behavior modification, where the sufferer is exposed to the situation that causes the fear, panic, and worry in an attempt to counter their fears. Cognitive behavioral therapy emphasizes self-help assignments and examines one's thoughts, and can be very effective for anxiety, panic, and posttraumatic stress disorder.[1] Psychiatrists typically recommend drugs such as SSRIs, MAO inhibitors, or trycyclic antidepressants alone or in addition to counseling or behavioral therapy. Typical side effects of medications include anxiety, fatigue, gastrointestinal symptoms, insomnia, headaches or migraines, and sexual dysfunction.

Herbal Approaches

There are several reasons why clients may want to explore herbal approaches. Some individuals are afraid of being on antidepressants and other medications for long periods of time. Other people have not had satisfactory results with typical conventional medications or treatment. Finally, some men and women try conventional drugs, but find their side effects intolerable.

The best way to begin herbal therapy is to have herbs administered by a trained herbalist. You may obtain the name of an herbalist from a friend or loved one or see resource list. For example, herbalists trained in Traditional Chinese Medicine (TCM), in addition taking account of symptoms of anxiety and panic, may be especially interested in other symptoms such as nightmares, sweating during the day and at night, mood swings, digestive symptoms, muscle aches, joint pain, and sensations of hot and cold. Women may be asked about their period, as well as hormonal changes. A TCM practitioner may examine the patient's face and determine if the client seems especially fearful, timid, or angry. Qualities of the pulse and the tongue are measured. Clinicians may also pay attention to the individual's body type and speed of movement.

"Untitled," 1999. **Katie Meier**

According to TCM, certain lifestyle habits and constitutional factors would predispose one to suffer from panic disorder more than another. For example, without adequate sleep and mind rest such as T'ai Chi or meditation, one would be more likely to suffer from panic attacks. A poor diet may lead to symptoms such as hot sensations and confusion. Although herbal antidepressants or sedatives can be administered, well-trained herbalists keep in mind constitutional factors when they select herbs. The following examples demonstrate how different patients with panic disorder and posttraumatic stress disorder are treated differently by Chinese medicine.

CASE ONE

Bob has a hot energetic pattern. He suffers from posttraumatic stress disorder. He feels explosive rage at times (this by itself creates heat). Heat symptoms include his face becoming red, migraines, and headache. Furthermore Bob is always thirsty, which he alleviates by drinking sodas to quench his thirst. Sodas, however, contain sugar which is warming, and caffeine which removes water and is cooling; thus, over time he is getting dehydrated. In addi-

Panic's Quick Mock Death
Douglass Blazer

Just as I start to strip talk's
hagiography to revelation's bare
shine, envisioning the epiphany
of irony's masked tease,
my mind vastly walks out.

A rising elevator stalls about to touch
the furthest floor. A moon rocket
suspends its thrust a mile into takeoff.
Sperm, an inch from paradise, stops.

The alphabet turns narcoleptic.
Colossal words breach like calcium whales
to mineral-sleep a closed beach.
My brain-sponge is squeezed by brute machines
to an empty wafer of sandy paper.

Listeners wait with ears in their eyes.
Ultra-sonic insects nest in my head.
A carcass of ketchup slaps my face.
The puzzled look of a shell-shocked soldier
pocks my complexion red.

Such loss is cryogenics. I cast heat
sidetrackedly as hooks without bait.
Water in a stream warbles a decomposed
foot deftly running rock-to-rock
like disordered vowels on a crucial test.

I tug the foot. Yank it. Pull
from the deep of my back. Defeatedly
I admit what I was saying is lost.
Moments later, fat with apologies,
the corpse is saturating my lap.

*   *   *

tion, Bob drinks alcohol at night to help him relax and go to sleep. Alcohol is both warming and a diuretic. Alcohol is known to interfere with sleep, so Bob's rest is less than satisfactory. No wonder he wakes up irritable and groggy in need of his morning coffee (which is heating) to get going—and the whole cycle starts all over again. During the day, Bob eats fast food, fried foods, an excessive amounts of meat, and sweets. These are all heating, making Bob's body crave something cooling. In addition to "chilling out" and relaxing, he also needs more rest. For Bob, Chinese herbal formulas that have cooling properties, as well as moisture rich herbs called yin tonics, are recommended.

CASE TWO

Eleanor suffers from nervous exhaustion. She is largely housebound because she is fearful. When she goes outside, she is reminded of the time she was mugged. Eleanor is said to have a cold constitution. She was sickly as a child with bedwetting, asthma, eczema, and frequent bronchial infections. Her body type is thin; she is underweight. Eleanor does not work or do volunteer work.

She has only recently been able to go out of the house twice a week to see a counselor. Previously, all trips out of the house resulted in panic attacks. Her pulse is slow and weak, her tongue is pale; she has sallow complexion. For Eleanor, kidney and lung herbs are recommended. The herbs are traditionally used to warm the body and boost energy levels. It is thought that as the body is warmer and energetic, functions are restored and the individual is able to act with more courage.

Case Three

Jeannette was involved in serious auto accident, which necessitated many surgeries and the almost constant use of pain-killers such as Vicodin and Ibuphron. She is also taking the antidepressant Trazadone. She has panic attacks whenever she has to drive on the freeway. Jeannette uses food to comfort herself; she is fifty pounds overweight. She wakes up tired after ten hours of sleep. In fact, bed is one of the few places she feels safe. However, once the day gets going she does begin to pick up energy. She is a teacher who enjoys her work, though she has difficulty saying "no," and sometimes feels on the verge of having panic attacks when she thinks of all the things she has to do. Physical symptoms include frequent diarrhea, indigestion, and bronchial and urinary tract infections. Her tongue is pale with a red tip and a heavy white coating. Her pulse has a slippery quality. Jeannette is said to have a damp condition. Herbs are used to warm her up and remove extra water and phlegm, along with an exercise program and dietary counseling. Jeanette will feel stronger in facing the world, able to say "no" to excess foods, as well as excessive work and extracurricular commitments.

Herbs work best when combined with a general health program, which include a good diet, adequate rest, stress reduction, and daily exercise to one's constitution. For example, seniors or persons incapacitated by anxiety and other disorders may need gentle exercise such as walking, gardening, swimming, or water aerobics. More robust individuals may find more vigorous activity more effective. Allowing adequate time to eat and saying a prayer or giving thanks before eating can help promote the calm lacking in so many people's lives.

Can Herbs Be Combined with Drugs?

At The Get Well Foundation, our clinic in Oakland, California, clients frequently combine herbs and drugs. For example, clients may take sleep medication at night but use herbs during the day for other discomforts due to anxiety, panic, or other symptoms. Some of our clients with anxiety disorders are on various prescribed medicines for hypertension, anti-anxiety drugs, pain medication, etc. However, they often have side effects from the medication, which we help them reduce. If clients and their mental health professionals agree, we incorporate an herbal program to assist the client in reducing their medications. Herbalists should be comfortable treating patients on medication. If your practitioner is reluctant, it's best to seek a referral and find someone who is experienced in this area. To avoid herbal/drug interactions, it is important to take herbs and drugs two hours apart.

It is important to find an herbalist who can recommend or prescribe herbs in a form you prefer, be it tea, alcohol extracts, or pills. It is not uncommon to start out with teas or alcohol extracts and switch to pills, as they are easier to take long-term. As herbs are not drugs, it is common to drink several cups a day of infusion, eight to sixteen ounces of brewed decoction, or nine or more pills per day. Some herbalist may even recommend herbal baths or bathing with aromatherapy, which can have immediate benefits.

What if you cannot find an herbalist to work with? Although there are many over-the-counter herbs sold for anxiety, these should be used cautiously with medications. Perhaps the safest are lavender essential oil, which can be applied topically to the inner wrists or added to a bath, and Rescue Remedy, a gentle herbal medicine which can be added to water and sipped on throughout the day.

In our experience, the following popular herbs work best for treatment of anxiety and panic when combined with professionally prescribed constitutional tonic herbs. Like foods, herbs work best when used in combination. The well-known herbal antidepressant, St. John's Wort, has been found to interact negatively with a variety of pharmaceutical drugs, so it is best used by clients who are not taking medications. In a few cases, it has also caused a photosensitive skin reaction. Gingko leaf can be used to promote blood flow. It has also been used to help alleviate the side effects of sexual dysfunction caused by antidepressants. Clients need to take gingko for at least six weeks to observe clinical benefits. It has been reported to interact with blood thinning medications, including aspirin and coumadin. Kava Kava has natural sedative and muscle relaxant properties. Clinical studies have demonstrated it to be safe and effective. It should only be used under professional supervision if clients are taking sedating drugs. It should not be used before driving or operating heavy machinery as a general precaution.

Herbal therapy, when used appropriately, can offer many benefits to people suffering from anxiety and panic disorder. Botanicals are often more suitable than drugs for highly sensitive patients and individuals who have previous herb experience. They should be combined with other treatments, such as cognitive behavioral therapy. Herbal therapy is an attractive alternative for many people who suffer from anxiety and panic disorder. Our advice may lead you to discover a more natural alleviation from your symptoms. If you're just getting started, please, whenever possible, use herbs under the direction of a professional herbalist.

ENDNOTES

1. Judith Beck, *Cognitive Therapy: Basics and Beyond* (New York: Guilford Press, 1995).

ANDREW LANGE

Homeopathic Treatment of Panic Disorder and Anxiety-Related Disorders

Just remember that sickness is the means by which an organism frees itself of foreign matter, so that one must just help it to be sick, to have its whole sickness and break out with it, for that is progress.

—Rainier Maria Rilke, *Letters to a Young Poet*

I N ORDER TO ADDRESS ANXIETY we must find where the individual separates the experience of life from its unacceptable disappointments. The resolution of anxiety comes when we can integrate both the conscious and the murky, forgotten fears that we have chosen to suppress over years of defending our lives. Carl Jung based his process of psychological individuation on the alchemical process, which begins with the negredo, the darkness. He described the fundamental beginning process as the integration of the shadow, that we must first address the unacceptable aspects of our personalities before we can move forward.

The medicine in homeopathic work is the shadow. Like Silver, which is used in the making of mirrors, homeopathy finds medicines that reflect our state. The remedy is a meeting with the image of the fear we have been running from. It is our opportunity to turn around and face the fear that is chasing us, thus dissolving its power.

There is a trance induction that begins, "Imagine you are on an island, someplace you feel safe. It could be a place in your memory or in your imagination. You must see the colors, smell the smells, and feel the sensations of being there." The importance of this induction is not that such a place exists physically; rather it is that the power of our imagination itself is healing. It begins with our ability to expand our awareness into a larger frame of reference. There is great value in the invocation of sensation-based processing, because sensation is the language of the autonomic nervous system. The imagination has the capacity to create sensory experience, but imagining a visual image would have less trauma-resolution value than imagining the touch of warm sand or smell of fresh air. This is the power of imagination. Our physical body hardly exists beyond our skin, yet our minds are certain of the reality that we have built in defining the world around us. All of us have our own unique world in which we live with certainty and determination. As Proverbs states, "Every man in his own mind thinks he's right, but God looks to the heart."

The island of our imagination is unlimited. The isolated island of our "real world" has more restricted definitions. The egoistic island we live on is dominated by an identification with our personalities. We have developed this island over our whole lives. Like any republic we have defined its borders and secured its defense. Yet any island is surrounded by vast seas and is connected ultimately with the ocean floor and therefore the whole earth.

There is a dream. In the dream we are being chased and can't get away. We try to find some alley or stairwell to escape, but we are helplessly pursued. It is the same in our lives. We may be pursued by expectations or an individual. In terms of finding resolution, it doesn't matter. But when we finally turn around and face our fear it no longer carries the same threat.

In primitive cultures the name of a person or thing carried its potency, its magic, its power. When we define our fear, or turn around and demand, "What is your name, what do you want?" suddenly its potency is dissolved. By naming the bully, the robber, or the oppressor, we then have power over their hidden insecurity of being identified.

We can become too identified with our problems. In one sense naming the problem can bring hidden knowledge to consciousness. This is the positive aspect of diagnosis. By naming a disease or a dysfunction we can then approach it. We need a language to bring to consciousness our experiences, feelings, and fears. On the other hand, excessive identification and attachment to the pathology can maintain its dominance over our lives. When the children of alcoholics are identified with the title of "Adult Child of an Alcoholic," (or the acronym ACOA) it may help them to understand their history. Their difficulties in achieving a successful adulthood may have its source in unsuccessful parent models. Yet at any age we find those who still blame their parents. An adult is someone who takes responsibility for life; it is no longer projecting upon the mother, the father, the world, or the stars. It is no longer the government, our teachers, or our spouses who cause our pain and dysfunction. If the explanation for our unhappiness is that the world outside ourselves is to blame, then we have forgotten how to direct our lives. Identification with the name of a diagnosis can make us codependent with our healthcare providers and create another layer of protection where we become enabled and dependent on the role of the victim.

A profound fear is generated when we find our identities threatened, our failures exposed, our naked wisp of being hanging from a thread like a seed cast upon the wind.

We restrict our lives, limiting the possible opportunities and responses. We're so sure of our duties and responsibilities, our need to be right, we forget that we have cornered ourselves. Anxiety comes from not being able to accept who we are and how we are responsible for our lives.

Our response to fear creates even more fear. We have increased the metabolism and reactivity of our lives. Anxiety is the natural product of a life lived in the future rather than the present, the realm of possibilities rather than the task at hand. Our reactivity is stimulated by the sounds and rhythms of modern life that impinge on our senses. The daily input of images and information has grown exponentially as part of our modern world, including images that are not only disturbing, but also conflicting.

When we watch action films, our moods are regulated by the music as well as the images. Formulas are applied to media that are known to pull the strings of our emotions. The pace of the film is outside of any real time frame. Relationships are rapidly formed and sex is performed intertwined with acts of violence. These are not the relationships that we experience in our lives.

If most of the relationships we see or fantasize about are based on such superficial contact, we are in deep trouble. If these images were only entertainment, there would probably not be so much damage, but they form deep impressions on our psyches and culture. In fact, our cultural experiences are becoming more limited due to the pervasive influence of corporate mass media as smaller, independent voices become conglomerated.

If through media we are exposed as a voyeuristic act to sexuality in the context of violence and aggression, intimacy in our lives can become associated with violence and aggression. We think we can separate them, yet in our bodies these responses can become confused.

Sexual arousal and capacity for intimacy are expressed in social contexts. Sex hormones by themselves do not evoke behavior, rather they make it more likely that behavior will occur when the appropriate stimuli are present. Sexual arousal is associated with activity of both the parasympathetic and sympathetic nervous system.

The parasympathetic system governs relaxation and surrender. It allows the erotic responses of arousal. It is the sympathetic system that is responsible for ejaculation and the orgasmic response in men and women. Knowing that fear and anger can effect sexual feelings, we can try to recognize when emotions unrelated to our capacity for love are influencing our behavior. Often sex is used as a release for underlying unresolved emotions that have accumulated throughout the day. This runs the risk of using what is an act of intimacy for the resolution of anger and anxiety. While it is a pleasure, it does not deal with our emotions directly any more than violence would effectively resolve anger. Our emotions are not fooled by temporary diversions. They need to be engaged rather than dismissed.

Change comes from becoming more engaged in life. So when we feel angry at the end of the day it is better to resolve these feelings independent of our intimate relationships. The resolution of anger is best enacted either through communication or physical exertion. Anxiety and depression can inhibit sexual function and desire, triggering a vicious circle of failure to perform and feelings of inadequacy. Because anxiety, anger, fear, or other defense reactions can activate the sympathetic nervous system, and because

this can lead to an inhibition of the parasympathetic nervous system, these emotional states can cause a block or cessation of sexual feelings.

In hypnosis, there is a technique of anchoring experiences and their memories through touch. When positive inductions are stated the body is touched in a pre-established spot in order to engage these memories in future sessions. In therapy, touch becomes a positive mode in which resolution or positive experiences are set in our bodies.

A negative experience or conflicting messages can be anchored in our bodies as well. Violations of our physical boundaries remain latent in our memories of physical and emotional traumas. Acts of aggression that are confused with intimacy set unconscious defenses. Touch can become a trigger for old memories and silent rejection.

Double Bind Theory, developed by Paul Watzliwick and Gregory Bateson in the 1950s, is one of the leading theories of schizophrenia and its causes. Watzliwick and Bateson found that mixed messages that mask the true emotional content of communication had the potential of driving someone to schizophrenia. We are all a little crazy when we are not being real, when we don't say what we really feel, when we hide behind our fears. Imagine a mother who in a sweet voice tells her child, "Johnny, we don't do that do we?" Imagine the frustration instilled in a child who receives the conflicting message of ridicule and disgrace behind his mother's smiling face. This contradictory communication is a recipe for confusion and fear.

Like the theme in the novel *Catch 22*, by Joseph Heller, the Double Bind Theory shows how conflicting double messages result in irresolvable conflict. Another common example of this conflict is the rigidity of bureaucrats. Even when they agree that your situation is unique, they still cannot go outside the rules: "If we did it for you, we'd have to do it for everyone." This is a conflict between truth, at the level of justice, and societal restrictions.

In *The Politics of Experience*, R.D. Laing proposed that insanity is a normal response to an insane society. How else could we organize such disinformation? The rate of psychological adaptation required in modern life has exposed us to a constant reinvention of expectations.

The Storm of Cultural Transitions

The greatest historical parallel to today's rapid cultural change is the transformation that transpired from the Dark Ages to the Renaissance. During the Dark Ages, the Arabic world had maintained an open society toward ideas and learning, while European society remained closed for centuries. Diet alone showed the fundamental change in the minds of the society. Since it was difficult to find uncontaminated water, the people of the Dark Ages depended on drinking alcoholic beverages and living in a state of intoxication. They hadn't yet figured out the value of boiling water to kill bacteria. The old monasteries were known for their ale as much as their knowledge. The crusades brought the growth of trade and the introduction of caffeinated teas and coffees, which in turn led to the Enlightenment. Suddenly stimulants were the primary drink rather than depressants. This was a major shift in consciousness, one which supported Renaissance thinking. This was an internal change, embedded in the diet, yet it had an impact that surpassed many external changes of the era.

Stimulants are still the primarily accepted form of drug use in Western society, since they engender productivity and suppress emotions. It is exactly the acceptance of suppressed emotion that generates the simmering of the volcanic fire that produces fear and anxiety. Caffeine can have longer lasting effects on our biorhythms, sleep cycles, and sugar metabolism than we might think. Caffeine has been shown to disrupt our ability to go into an alpha state, the brain activity measured as a wave frequency associated with meditation and relaxation, for eight or more hours. Caffeine acts as a heart stimulant, increasing arterial pressure and often producing palpitations. The buzz and agitation are the sought and valued outcome. The effect of this agitation and its ability to mask forgotten stimuli creates anxieties that pervade our modern lives.

Fear and Trembling

Finding our place in society can become a difficult task when we feel like invading hordes could destroy our lives at any time. Throughout history, and still in much of the underdeveloped world today, these threats are a daily reality. War, famine, and disease are still a personal experience for many populations. Wars are being fought for economic development. By the seventeenth century, weapons evolved from the personal grit of hand-to-hand combat to the use of explosives and guns. This increased primary distance of personal contact, reduced the sense of responsibility for acts of violence, and perpetuated fear. In modern times, the distance has become even greater. We bomb from the sky and watch mass destruction repeatedly shown on television. We know what "collateral damage" and "acceptable losses" mean even if we do not see the actual events.

In primitive societies, the threat of attack was more immediately physical or projected upon the universe through myth. Abstract fears were caused by gods and goddesses, sacred animals, and totems. Other fears were direct threats and were engaged instinctually as survival mechanisms. When a jaguar darted from the bushes, the hunter would draw his spear, thrust it into the jaguar's heart, and vanquish his opponent. In the today's world, a modern Jaguar car may approach us with the same degree of threat, yet our response would be limited to honking our horn or swearing at our opponent. We understand why the modern Jaguar poses less of a threat. After all, we are okay, whatever that means to us. Yet our modern internal response is the same as primitive defenses. We carry the effects of this in our body as tension. Lactic acid, adrenaline, and testosterone surge through our systems. Voluntary muscles shorten to strike back and our sympathetic nervous systems prepare for fight or flight.

With little outlet for our tension, we proceed to work. The threat of a car pulling out in front of us is over and perhaps we have even "gotten over it." Then our supervisor comes up to us complaining, "Blah, blah, blah, by two o'clock!" In a primitive society, we would have gotten out our spear, thrust it through the supervisor's chest, and been promoted. But in today's society we remain passive, afraid of losing a job, and without any true security. By the time we come home, our nervous systems are on fear mode.

The nervous system is divided into two components. One is the voluntary nervous system. It is expressed through our muscles that voluntarily control movement. The second and more pervasive aspect of the nervous system is involuntary. The involuntary, or autonomic, nervous system regulates respiration, heart rhythm, control of bladder and bowels, and adaptive responses.

If by the end of the end of the workday we have not responded adequately to our stresses, the chemicals of fear in our body accumulate in response to subtle and overt threats throughout the day. Without an adequate physical release they remain unresolved, building a state of tension in the body. Then we go home and try to relax. We might have a drink or a smoke. Maybe we have even begun practicing meditation. And while this may resolve our minds, it does not directly impact the capacity of our bodies to discharge this tension. This particular aspect of our embodied fear must be resolved through action. That means we must find some sort of exercise to release our physical tension at the end of the day. Meditation has many extraordinary benefits that have physical results and can help us to become more balanced in our emotional responses, but it does not replace movement.

There are two major experiences of anxiety—personal and collective. Collective anxiety arises from our identification with society and its events. Global reporting of instant news, with its emphasis on fear and negativity, creates cultural beliefs based on limited or misinformed perspectives. This is not quite a recommendation for throwing out the television; it's more to raise the point that the mute button may be the greatest invention since the wheel. This collective fear is no different than primitive myth, as it is based on cultural abstractions from our personal experience.

Our own limited perspectives enhance the personal roots of anxiety, which derive from our inability to expand our identities beyond the need to defend and protect ourselves. There are appropriate fears that exist to instinctually protect us, but the overwhelming defenses that we have maintained are mostly antiquated and unnecessary. These anxieties become our pervasive response to threats that no longer exist, but like a car with a stuck accelerator propel us helplessly forward. To address these anxieties requires that we shift the set point, the overactive thermostat that we have set too high, before we suffocate from our own combustion.

Homeopathic Approaches to Anxiety and Panic

The homeopathic approach to anxiety considers that the regulation of the response is unconscious, even if we know its cause. The solution is not to just eliminate or suppress the signal. Instead we want to trigger the body to reduce or regulate its amperage. Homeopathy as a therapeutic method does not address anxiety at a cognitive level. The explanation from personal history itself does not resolve the inner conflict. We only provide a corresponding reflection of the inner state through medicine that mimics it and allows the psyche to self-correct.

The following are a few important examples of how to treat anxiety from the *Homeopathic Materia Medica.* By understanding the clinical pictures of the medicines we begin to develop a deeper comprehension of the unique situations from which anxiety arises. Our collective experience of healing helps us understand how the world of nature reflects our state of mind, helping us to discover and reveal appropriate medicines.

ACONITE

Aconite is a beautiful and poisonous plant. The flowers are shaped like a monk's hood. Its symmetrical form is suggestive of higher forms of life in the animal kingdom. The higher invertebrates, as well as all vertebrates, possess bilateral symmetry as their fundamental morphological developmental pattern.

Aconite is often mentioned in mythological history. It was supposed to be the principal ingredient in the deadly draught given to the old men of Ceos when they had become too old to be serviceable to their country. Medea was said to have used it in concocting the poisonous drink she intended for Theseus. It is told that Hecate caused Aconite to spring from the mouth of Cerberus. Theophrastus relates that there was a method of preparing the Aconite so that its action would be delayed, killing its intended victim at the end of one or two years.

The huntsmen of the Alps are said to have dipped their arrows into the juice of this plant when hunting wolves; hence the common name Wolfsbane. In later times, it was employed in attempts to destroy whole armies; the Indian poison Bikh or Bisch, with which natives poisoned tanks in the Burmese war, is supposed to have been a prepared from one of its species, *Aconitum ferox.*

As a medicine, the ancients used it chiefly to relieve pain. Diogenes Laertius states that the philosopher Aristotle killed himself with a draught of Aconite. The great historian Pliny says it proves fatal when applied to the genital organs of women.

Paradoxically, in Poland, Russia, and Lapland, Aconite was considered harmless, and was used to fatten geese and quails, while some other varieties are said to be eaten as a salad in Sweden.

The classical clinical picture of someone who requires Aconite is extreme restlessness and fear. These people feel they will die from their condition and are so certain of the proximity of their death that they can even predict its imminent approach.

They experience attacks of panic and terror, unreasonable and unaccountable fear, and palpitations. The pathology of someone who requires Aconite can be elicited from a sudden shock or frightening incident, an earthquake, a car accident, or being stuck in an elevator. It can develop into a chronic state of fear. War veterans and police can require Aconite as a result of posttraumatic stress disorder. It is indicated in fears following natural disasters, such as earthquakes, fires, and floods. It was the single most important medicine required for survivors in the aftermath of the attack on the World Trade Center in New York City.

The patient requiring Aconite may have fear in crowds or claustrophobia. They will insist on sitting on an aisle seat in a theatre or near an exit. It is useful for women who have the fear of death during pregnancy, especially during labor. The indication for Aconite is recognized by its urgency and immediacy. When it is used in a childhood fever that has come on suddenly, it may also be indicated for the child's caregivers who are fearful and agitated.

SILVER

Mythologically, Silver has been associated with the feminine principle and lunacy. The argentums are characterized by phobias and impulsive responses to things, being useful in bringing an uncontrolled imagination into order. Silver, like *Gelsemium sempervirens*, is useful for anxiety before examinations. The main theme is anticipation. Reflecting its capacity to conduct electricity, Silver is a medicine for the overactive impulses of the nervous system. Like the Silver in photographic film and papers, it helps retain memories, strengthening the coherent organization of the mind.

As the moon relates to water and to the tides, so Silver relates to emotional fluxes and periodic cycles. Silver has a significant relation to the female organs, the menstrual cycle, and the ovaries and testes. Reflecting the etymological associations of lunacy and the moon, the womb was associated with causing hysteria. Thus hysterectomy, the removal of the uterus, was a radical yet all too common procedure until recently. There is still a preoccupation in our modern culture with premenstrual syndromes and hormonal fluctuations as an explanation for feminine behavior, rather than an imbalance that may need to be addressed. Silver is one remedy that can bring balance to menstrual cycles.

Silver has an important role to play in the processes of reproduction and gestation. It is used in swelling of the testes and swelling of the urethra in men. In women it is indicated in excessive uterine bleeding, ovarian swelling and pain, especially in young widows or women who have not borne children

The water organs, the kidney and bladder, are also prominently affected in the pathology of Silver. There may be profuse urination, symptoms suggestive of diabetes or pre-diabetic states, and chronic inflammation of the urethra. Silver Nitrate (*Argentum nitricum*) was traditionally used for the treatment of gonorrhea. It has been used as a disinfectant in the eyes of newborns.

Silver in colloidal preparations, suspended particles in minute concentrations, has remarkable antibiotic properties.

Silver is a primary remedy in the treatment of common neurotic states. The patient requiring Silver is usually warm-blooded. They are constantly in a hurry, accomplishing little or nothing. They worry about being late when there is plenty of time. They may have suicidal thoughts or irrational impulses that appear suddenly. There can be mental exhaustion from worry, with nervous excitement and trembling. They may pace back and forth or take long walks to discharge their anxieties.

The use of Silver preparations helps to reestablish a rhythmic order between the internal cycles and the surrounding environment. It reduces the state of reactivity that perpetuates senses of anticipation and fear.

CANNABIS

This remedy is prepared from Indian hemp, *Cannabis sativa* or *Cannabis indica*, a hallucinogenic plant that is widely distributed throughout the world, both by natural dispersion of their seeds and commerce. Today marijuana is one of the most widespread social drugs.

Cannabis is found throughout history. The Ismaili sect contacted by the Crusaders in the eleventh and twelfth centuries were a society known as the Hashishin, Hashish eaters, or the Assassins. The drug was employed to drive cult members to undertake political assassinations, carried out with fanatical ruthlessness and a reckless disregard of death. In modern use, the patient requiring Cannabis as a remedy may present in several ways. The themes found in the effects of Cannabis are fantasy, theorizing, and amnesia. There is inappropriate laughter and paranoia.

The spacey types of people who might be prescribed Cannabis have a tenuous connection to their bodies and a tendency to feel they are out of their bodies. They may have used a lot of marijuana or other psychedelic drugs in the past.

Cannabis patients can present tremendous belief systems that are not supported by any action in their lives. Like marijuana users, they may associate their experience with spiritual exploration and awareness; however, it is almost a polarity to true spiritual exercise. Cannabis use promotes the dispersal of awareness. This drawing out of the ego that one experiences may in fact seem like a revelation or release of anxiety, but the Cannabis effect is also the enhancer of paranoia and delusional perceptions.

True spiritual experience is based on the focusing of awareness rather than its dispersion. Cannabis and hallucinogens can produce self-aggrandizing ideations, projecting the experience of enhanced sensory experiences into cosmological fantasies. While the loss of inhibition experienced under hallucinogens may release suppressed emotions or experiences, it is not the replacement for a sustained integration of a transcendent experience. The litmus test for the division between psychosis and mystical experience is our ability to act on it in our daily lives.

This is the central pathology of Cannabis; it creates a state in which fantasies can become the guiding experience of life. As the Cannabis patient's imagined worldview expands, their ability to ground their emotions and thoughts and function consistently in the world around them is subverted. This separation from society may serve as a verification of the uniqueness of their perceptions. This can be a form of imagination, which gives them a feeling of spiritual inflation.

The reality of spiritual experience can be detected by its ability for the individual to function more creatively and effectively in life. It's grounded in the ability to find happiness in life rather than in escapist theories.

There is another presentation of the Cannabis type. It is the other polarity of the attempted dissolution of the ego. In fact, Cannabis patients can have very defined ego boundaries. There is a great fear in losing control. The controlled person who requires Cannabis as a medicine appears very similar to the clinical picture requiring *Arsenicum album*.

Arsenicum is one of the main homeopathic medicines used in anxiety states. Arsenicum patients want order in their world to compensate for their fears that something will go wrong. They can be very fastidious and compulsive. They are uptight worriers whose fears and anxieties drive everyone around them crazy. Like Woody Allen, they can be extreme hypochondriacs. They won't go into bathrooms at restaurants because they are worried about contamination and filth. They may have extreme diets or theories about what may cause cancer.

In the controlled type of Cannabis patient we frequently see great anxiety about health and fear of death. These people tend to have avoided marijuana for fear of losing control, or they may have had paranoid and fearful experiences smoking it. Some may feel that they have never been well since a period of marijuana use.

Another hallucinogen used in homeopathic practice is *Agaricus muscarius*, or Amanita, a mushroom that was used by Siberian shamans to induce ecstatic states. The clinical picture of Amanita is similar, with extreme anxiety states and fear of disease, especially cancer.

It is as if the loss of inhibition brings us closer to deathlike experiences and the fear of our loss of identity. On the other hand, we may experience a sense of freedom from dissociating from our ego personalities. It is this polarity that is enhanced by the use of Cannabis and other hallucinogenic plants. The deep association between the pathological effects of hallucinogenic drugs and their ability to produce both deep anxieties and psychotic experiences leads us to their indications in clinical practice.

This is a clinical picture of patients who require Cannabis as a medicine. It is not meant to judge an individual's use of marijuana or serve as a justification for the incarceration of marijuana users any more than a clinical description of Tobaccum would be. There is no medical justification for such biases or controls. The pathological effects of marijuana elicit the pervasive mental state in which we are trying to escape, to create an idealistic life, rather than engage in the culture at large.

These represent a few of the central themes in the psychological profiles used in the homeopathic treatment of anxiety and panic. By understanding the roots of anxiety and its pathogenesis in the individual we can elicit fundamental changes in behavior and experience.

TREATMENT

ORIGINS

Historical Instances of Panic / DANIEL USSISHKIN

Berrios, German E., and Christopher Link. "Anxiety Disorders: Clinical Section." In *A History of Clinical Psychiatry*. Edited by German E. Berrios and Roy Porter. New York: New York University Press, 1995. pp. 545–62.

Boulenger, Jean-Phillipe, and Thomas W. Uhde. "Crises Aigües D'angoisse Et Phobies: Aspects Historiques Et Manifestations Cliniques Du Syndrome D'agoraphobie." *Annals Médico-Psychologiques* 145, no. 2 (1987): 113–31

Clark, Michael J. "Anxiety Disorders: Social Section." *A History of Clinical Psychiatry*. Edited by German E. Berrios and Roy Porter. New York: New York University, 1995. pp. 545-62.

Friedrich, Carl, and Otto Westphal. *Westphal's "Die Agoraphobie" with Commentary: The Beginnings of Agoraphobia*. Commentary by Terry J. Knapp and translated by Michael T. Schumacher. New York and London: University Press of America, 1988.

Gay, Peter. "On the Bourgeoisie: A Psychological Interpretation." In *Consciousness and Class Experience in Nineteenth-Century Europe*. Edited by John M. Merriman. New York: Holms and Meier Publishers, 1979. pp. 187-203.

Goldstein, Jan E. *Console and Classify: The French Psychiatric Profession in the Nineteenth Century*, 2nd ed. Chicago: University of Chicago Press, 2001.

Leed, Eric. *No Man's Land: Combat and Identity in World War I*. Cambridge: Cambridge University Press, 1979.

Lewis, Aubrey. "Problems Presented by the Ambiguous Word 'Anxiety' as Used in Psychopathology." *Israel Annals of Psychiatry and Related Disciplines* 5, no. 2 (1967): 105-21.

Pichot, P. "Panique: Attaque et trouble historique du mot et des concepts." *L'Encéphale* 22, no. 5 (1996): 3-8.

Porter, Roy. "The Body and the Mind, the Doctor and the Patient." In *Hysteria Beyond Freud*. Edited by Sander Gilman et al. Berkeley and Los Angeles: University of California Press, 1993. pp. 225–85.

Sedgwick, Eve Kosofsky. *Epistemology of the Closet*. Berkeley and Los Angeles: University of California Press, 1990.

Showalter, Elaine. *The Female Malady: Woman, Madness, and English Culture, 1830-1980*. New York: Pantheon Books, 1987.

Stone, Martin. "Shellshock and the Psychologists." In *The Anatomy of Madness: Essays in the History of Psychiatry*. Edited by W. F. Bynum et al. London: Routledge Kegan & Paul, 1985. pp. 242–71.

Stonebridge, Lyndsey. "Anxiety at a Time of Crisis." *History Workshop Journal* 45 (1998): 172–82.

Vidler, Anthony. "Agoraphobia: Spatial Estrangement in the Work of Georg Simmel and Siegfried Kracauer." *New German Critique* 54 (1991): 31–45

Zal, Michael H. "From Anxiety to Panic Disorder: A Historical Perspective." *Psychiatric Annals* 18, no. 6 (1988): 367–71.

Tracing the Roots of Panic to Prenatal Trauma / FRANZ RENGGLI

Castellino, Ray. *Resolving Prenatal and Birth Trauma*, training manuscript. Santa Barbara: 1995-98.

Ibid. *The Polarity Therapy Paradigm, Regarding Preconception, Prenatal and Birth Imprinting*. Santa Barbara: BEBA, 1996.

Ibid. *The Caregivers' Role in Birth and Newborn Self-Attachment Needs*. Santa Barbara: BEBA, 1997.

Chamberlain, David. *The Mind of Your Newborn Baby*. Berkeley: North Atlantic Books, 1998.

Emerson, William. *Collected Works I: The Treatment of Birth Trauma in Infants and Children*. Petaluma, CA: Emerson Training Seminars, 1996.

Ibid. *Birth Trauma: The Psychological Effects of Obstetrical Interventions*. Petaluma, CA: Emerson Training Seminars, 1997.

Ibid. "The Vulnerable Prenate." *International Journal of Prenatal and Perinatal Psychology and Medicine* 10 (1998): 5–18.

Ibid. *Shock: A Universal Malady*. Petaluma, CA: Emerson Training Seminars, 1999.

Ibid. *Collected Works II: Pre- and Perinatal Regression Therapy*. Petaluma, CA: Emerson Training Seminars, 2000.

Ibid. *Shock and Spirituality, How our Earliest Wounds Affect the Capacity for Universe*. Mawah, NJ: Paulist Press, 2002.

Fodor, Nandor. *The Search for the Beloved. A Clinical Investigation of the Trauma of Birth and Prenatal Conditioning*. New York: University Books, 1949.

Grof, Stanislav. *Beyond the Brain*. Albany, NY: New York State University, 1985.

Janus, Ludwig. *The Enduring Effects of Prenatal Experience, Echoes from the Womb*. Heidelberg, Germany: Mattes Press, 2001.

Levine, Peter. *Waking the Tiger: Healing Trauma*. Berkeley: North Atlantic Books, 1997.

Linn, Sheila Fabricate. *Remembering our Home, Healing Hurts, and Receiving Gifts from Conception to Birth*. Mawah, NJ: Paulist Press, 1999.

Maret, Stephen M. *The Prenatal Person, Frank Lake's Maternal-Fetal Distress Syndrome*. New York: University Press of America, 1997.

Mott, Francis John. *The Nature of the Self*. London: Allen Wingate, 1959.

Ibid. *Mythology of the Prenatal Life*. London: The Integration Publishing Company, 1960.

Ibid. *The Universal Design of Creation*. Edenbridge: Mark Beech, 1964.

Nathanielsz, Peter. *Life in the Womb, The Origin of Health and Disease*. Ithaca, NY: Promethean Press, 1999.

Ibid. *The Prenatal Prescription, The Ground Breaking Program to Safeguard Your Child's Future Health*. London: Vermilion, 2001.

Piontelli, Alessandra. *From Fetus to Child: An Observational and Psychoanalytic Study*. London: Routledge, 1992.

Renggli, Franz. *Angst und Geborgenheit, soziokulturelle Folgen der Mutter-Kind-Beziehung im ersten Lebensjahr, Ergebnisse aus Verhaltensforschung, Psychoanalyse und Ethnologie*. Hamburg: Rowohlt Press, 1974.

Ibid. *Selbstzerstörung aus Verlassenheit, die Pest als Ausbruch einer Massenpsychose im Mittelalter, zur Geschichte der frühen Mutter-Kind-Beziehung*. Hamburg: Rasch und Röhring, 1992.

Ibid. *Der Ursprung der Angst, Antike Mythen und das Trauma der Geburt*. Düsseldorf: Walter Press, 2001.

Taylor, Steven. *Understanding and Treating Panic Disorder, Cognitive-Behavioral Approaches*. Chichester and New York: John Wiley & Sons, 2001.

Van der Kolk, Bessel A., Alexander C. McFarlane, and Lars Weisaeth, eds. *Traumatic Stress*. New York: Guilford Press, 1996.

Other Resources:

Renggli, Franz, "The Sunrise as the Birth of a Baby: The Prenatal Key to Egyptian Mythology, in Deference to the Dutch Historian of Religion, Bruno Hugo Stricker." *Journal of Prenatal and Perinatal Psychology and Health*, 16, no. 3: 2002.

Other Journals:

Journal of Prenatal and Perinatal Psychology and Health

The Official Journal of the Association for Pre- and Perinatal Psychology and Health (APPPAH) USA

The International Journal for Prenatal and Perinatal Psychology and Medicine, Heidelberg, Germany

The Official Journal of the International Society of Prenatal and Perinatal Psychology and Medicine (ISPPPM)

A Personal Account of Thyroid Disease with Panic Disorder /

LESLIE BERGER BLUMENBERG

Arem, Ridha. *The Thyroid Solution: A Mind-Body Program for Beating Depression and Regaining Your Emotional and Physical Health.* New York: Ballantine Books, 2000.

Balch, James F., and Phyllis A. Balch. *Prescription for Nutritional Healing.* New York: Avery Penguin Putnam, 2000.

Barnes, Broda. *Hypothyroidism: The Unsuspected Illness.* New York: Ty Crowell Co., 1976.

Ford, Gillian. *Listening to Your Hormones.* Roseville, CA: Prima Publishing, 1997.

Langer, Stephen, and James Scheer. *Solved: The Riddle of Illness, 3rd ed.* Columbus, OH: McGraw Hill, 2000.

Rosenthal, M. Sara. *The Thyroid Sourcebook: 3rd ed.* Columbus, OH: McGraw Hill, 1999.

Shomon, Mary J. *Living Well with Hypothyroidism: What Your Doctor Doesn't Tell You ... That You Need to Know.* New York: Harper Resource, 2000.

Vliet, Elizabeth. *Screaming to Be Heard: Hormonal Connections Women Suspect ... and Doctors Still Ignore.* New York: M. Evans & Co. Inc., 2001.

Thyroid Disease and Panic Disorder Resources on the Internet

http://thyroid.about.com/mbody.htm
Thyroid Disease Website

http://thyroid.about.com/blchklst.htm—hypo symptoms checklist
hypothyroid check list

http://www.thyroidmanager.org
Thyroid Manager, written for doctors and patients, continuously updated

http://panicdisorder.about.com/mbody.htm
Panic/Anxiety Disorders Website

http://bearpaw8.tripod.com/pd.html
Panic Disorders: A Comprehensive Overview

http://www.nimh.nih.gov/anxiety/upd.cfm
National Institute of Mental Health on Panic Disorder

http://www.drrind.com/adrenal.asp
Adrenal Insufficiency and Thyroid Disease

Other information of interest:
http://www.soyonlineservice.co.nz/
Excellent Overview on the Dangers of Soy

http://www.krispin.com/magnes.html
A Comprehensive Overview on Magnesium Deficiency

http://www.mercola.com/article/hypothyroid/diagnosis.htm
How To Know If Your Thyroid Is Working Properly With Blood Tests
(FT3 & FT4)

INSIGHT

A Lacanian Perspective on Panic and Fragmentation /

MARSHALL ALCORN

American Psychiatric Association: *Diagnostic and Statistical Manual of Mental Disorders, Fourth Edition.* Washington, DC, American Psychiatric Association, 1994.

Chapman, A.H. *Harry Stack Sullivant's Concepts of Personality Development and Psychiatric Illness.* New York: Brunner/Mazel Publishers, Inc., 1980.

Elenberger, Henri. *The Discovery of the Unconscious.* New York: Basic Books, 1970.

Evans, Dylan. *Dictionary of Lacanian Psychoanalysis.* London: Routeledge, 1996.

Fine, Reuben. *A History of Psychoanalysis.* New York: Columbia University Press, 1979.

Freud, Sigmund. *Inhibitions, Symptoms, and Anxiety.* New York: W.W. Norton & Company, 1932.

Harari, Roberto. *Lacan's Seminar On Anxiety.* New York: Other Press, 2001.

Hecker, Jeffrey E., and Geoggrey Thorpe. *Agoraphobia and Panic: A Guide to Psychological Treatment.* Boston: Allyn and Bacon, 1992.

Klein, Melanie. *Envy and Gratitude.* New York: Basic Books, 1957.

Zizek, Slavoj. *Looking Awry: An Introduction to Jacques Lacan Through Culture.* Cambridge: M.I.T. Press, 1992.

The Short Story in the Age of Anxiety / Robert Combs

Auden, W.H. "Notes on Music and Opera." In *On Music*. Edited by Dan Halpern and Jeane Wilmot Carter. Hopewell, NJ: The Ecco Press, 1994. pp. 25–33.

Charters, Ann. *The Story and Its Writer: An Introduction to Short Fiction, 4th ed.* Boston: St. Martin's Press, 1995.

Charters, Ann. *The Story and Its Writer: An Introduction to Short Fiction, 5th ed.* Boston: St. Martin's Press, 1999.

O'Connor, Flannery. *Short Story Theories*. Athens, OH: Ohio University Press, 1976.

O'Connor, Flannery. "A Good Man Is Hard to Find." In *The Short Story and Its Writer, An Introduction to Short Fiction, 5th ed.* Boston: St. Martin's Press, 1999.

O'Connor, Flannery. "Writing Short Stories." In *Charters, 5th ed.* pp. 1616–20.

Wilkie, Brian, and James Hurt. *Literature of the Western World, Vol. II Neoclassicism Through the Modern Period, 5th ed.* Upper Saddle River, NJ: Prentice Hall Press, 2001.

Wolff, Tobias. *Matters of Life and Death: New American Stories*. Green Harbor, MA: Wampeter Press, 1983.

Wolman, Benjamin B., and George Stricker, eds. *Anxiety and Related Disorders: A Handbook*. New York: John Wiley & Sons, 1994.

Munch, Agoraphobia, and the Terrors of the Modernizing Urban Landscape / Devon Hinton

American Psychiatric Association: *Diagnostic and Statistical Manual of Mental Disorders, Fourth Edition*. Washington, DC, American Psychiatric Association, 1994.

Aretaeus. *The Extant Works of Arataeus, the Cappdocian*. Edited and translated by F. Adams. London: Sydenham Society, 1856.

Balaban, C., and R. Jacob, "Background and History of the Interface Between Anxiety and Vertigo." *Journal of Anxiety Disorders* 15 (2001): 27-51.

Barlow, D. *Anxiety and Its Disorders*. London: Guilford Press, 1988.

Benesch, O. *Edvard Munch*. New York: Phaidon, 1960.

Berenson, B. "The Florentine Painters of the Renaissance." In *Michelangelo: The Sistine Chapel Ceiling*. Edited by C. Seymour. New York: Norton, 1972. pp. 166–70.

Berman, P., and J. Van Nimmen. *Munch and Women: Image and Myth*. Alexandria, VA: Art Services International, 1997.

Berrios, G. "Anxiety Disorders: A Conceptual History." *Journal of Affective Disorders* 56 (1999): 83-94.

Bischoff, U. *Edvard Munch 1863-1944.* New York: Barnes & Noble, 2001.

Bjerke, O.S. *Edvard Munch, Harald Sohlberg: Landscapes of the Mind.* New York: National Academy of Design, 1995.

Bjornstad, K. *The Story of Edvard Munch.* London: Arcadia, 2001.

Bouillon, J.P. "Arabesques." In *Lost Paradise, Symbolist Europe.* Edited by Pierre Theberge. Montreal: Montreal Museum of Art, 1995. pp. 376–84.

Bowen, A.M. "Munch and Agoraphobia: His Art and His Illness. RACAR: Revue d'Art Canadienne 15, no. 1 (1988): 23–50.

Brettell, R. *Impressionism, Painting Quickly in France 1860-1890.* New Haven and London: Yale University Press, 2001.

Brown, G., and T. Harris. "Aetiology of Anxiety and Depressive Disorders in an Inner-City Population." *Early Adversity. Psychological Medicine* 23 (1993): 143–54.

Callen, A. *The Art of Impressionism: Painting Techniques and the Making of Modernity.* New Haven: Yale University Press, 2000.

Carlson, H. "Introduction to August Stringberg." In *Strindberg: Five Plays*, translated by H. Carlson. Berkeley: University of California, 1983.

Cernuschi, C. "Sex and Psyche, Nature and Nurture, the Personal and the Political: Edvard Munch and German Expressionism." In *Edvard Munch: Psyche, Symbol and Expression.* Edited by J. Howe. Chicago: University of Chicago Press, 2001. pp. 134–67.

Clum, G.A., S. Broyles, J. Borden, and P. Watkins. "Validity and Reliability of the Panic Attack Symptoms and Cognition Quesitonnaire." *Journal of Psychopathology and Behavioral Assessment* 12 (1990): 233–45.

Craske, M. "Phobic Fear and Panic Attacks: The Same Emotional States Triggered by Different Cues?" *Clinical Psychology Review* 11 (1991): 599-620.

Craske, M. *Anxiety Disorders: Psychological Approaches to Theory and Treatment.* Boulder: Westview Press, 1999.

Deknatel, F. *Edvard Munch.* Boston: Institute of Contemporary Art, 1950.

Eggum, A., and R. M. Rapett. *Munch et la France.* Paris: Spadem, 1991.

Eggum, A., G. Woll, and M. Lande. *Munch at the Munch Museum.* Oslo: Scala books, 1998.

Haugen, E. *Norweigian-English Dictionary.* Madison: University of Wisconson, 1974.

Heller, R. *Edvard Munch: The Scream.* New York: Viking Press, 1972.

Heller, R. *Munch: His life and Work.* London: Murray, 1984.

Herbert, R. *Monet on the Normandy Coast. Tourism and Painting, 1876–1886.* New Haven: Yale University Press,1994.

Hinoki, R. "Considerations on the Postural Reflex and Body

Equilibrium—With Reference to Prof. Fukada's Ideas on Equilibrium Function." In *Vestibular and Neural Front: Proceedings of the 12th International Symposium on Posture and Gait*. Edited by K. Taguchi, M. Igarashi, and S. Mori. Tokyo: Elsevier, 1994.

Hinton, D., and S. Hinton. "Panic Disorder, Somatization, and the 'New Cross-Cultural Psychiatry:' Reflections on Panic Disorder Among Southeast Asian Refugees." *Culture, Medicine, and Psychiatry,* special issue. (forthcoming).

Hinton, D., K. Um, and P. Ba. "A Unique Panic-Disorder Presentation Among Khmer Refugees: The Sore-Neck Syndrome." *Culture, Medicine, and Psychiatry* 25, no. 3 (2001a): 297–316.

Hinton, D., K. Um, and P. Ba. "*Kyol Goeu* ("Wind Overload") Part I: A Cultural Syndrome of Orthostatic Panic Among Khmer Refugees." *Transcultural Psychiatry* 38, no. 4 (2001b): 403–32.

Hinton, D., K. Um, and P. Ba. "*Kyol Goeu* ("Wind Overload") Part II: Prevalence, Characteristics, and Mechanisms of *Kyol Goeu* and Near-*Kyol Goeu* Episodes of Khmer Patients Attending a Pyschiatric Clinic." *Transcultural Psychiatry* 38, no. 4 (2001c): 433–60.

Hinton, D., S. Hinton, K. Um, and A. Chea. "The Khmer 'Weak Heart' Syndrome: Fear of Death From Palpitations. *Transcultural Psychiatry* (forthcoming).

Hodin, J. *Edvard Munch*. London: Thames and Hudson Ltd., 1972.

Howe, J. "Nocturnes: The Music of Melanchology, and the Mysteries of Love and Death." In *Edvard Munch: Psyche, Symbol and Expression*. Edited by J. Howe. Chicago: University of Chicago Press, 2002. 48–74.

Kerman, J. *Listen*. Berkeley: Worth Publishers,1972.

Kern, S. *The Culture of Time and Space: 1880-1918*. Cambridge: Harvard University Press, 1983.

King, D. *The Age of Technology*. Cambridge: Discovery Enterpises, 1997.

Knapp, T., and M. Schumacher. *Westphal's "Die Agoraphobie" with Commentary*. London: University Press of America, 1988.

Larson, B. *Microbes and Maladies: Bacteriology and Health at the Fin de Siècle*. Montreal: Montreal Museum of Fine Arts, 1985.

Nahum, K. "'In Wild Embrace:' Attachment and Loss in Edvard Munch." In *Edvard Munch: Psyche, Symbol and Expression*. Edited by J. Howe. Chicago: University of Chicago Press, 2001. pp. 31–47.

Nergaard, T. "Despair." In *Edvard Munch: Symbol and Images*. Edited by A. Eggum, R. Heller, T. Nergaard, R. Stang, et al. Washington, DC: National Gallery of Art, 1978.

Nochlin, L. *The Body in Pieces: The Fragment as a Metaphor of Modernity*. New York: Thames and Hudson, 1994.

Pepall, R., ed. *Lost Paradise: Symbolist Europe*. Montreal: Montreal Museum of Fine Arts, 1995.

Perron, J. *Between Fear and Sex: The Odyssey of Edvard Munch.* Copenhagen: Galeri Faurschou, 2000.

Porter, R. "The Rage of Party: A Glorious Revolution in Psychiatry." *Medical History* 27 (1983): 35-50.

Prelinger, E. "When the Halted Traveler Hears the Scream of Nature: Preliminary Thoughts on the Transformation of Some Romantic Themes." In *Shop talk: Studies in Honor of Seymour Slive.* Cambridge: Harvard University Art Museums, 1995.

Prelinger, E., and M. Parke-Taylor. "The Symbolist Prints of Edvard Munch." In *The Symbolist Prints of Edvard Munch.* Edited by E. Prelinger and M. Parke-Taylor. London and New Haven: Yale University Press,1996.

Rabinbach, A. "Neurasthenia and Modernity." In *Incorporations.* Edited by J. Crary and S. Kwinter. Cambridge: The MIT Press, 1992. pp. 178-89.

Rachman, S. *Anxiety.* London: Psychology Press, 1998.

Rapee, R., M. Craske, and D. Barlow. "Assessment Instrument for Panic Disorder that Include Fear of Sensation-Producing Activities: The Albany Panic and Phobia Questionnaire." *Anxiety* 1 (1995):114-44.

Rosenbaum, R. "Edvard Munch: Some Changing Contexts." In *Edvard Munch: Symbol and Images.* Edited by A. Eggum, R. Heller, T. Nergaard, R. Stang, et al. Washington, DC: National Gallery of Art, 1978.

Saslow, J. *The Poetry of Michelangelo.* New Haven: Yale University, 1991.

Schapiro, M. *Impressionism, Reflections and Perceptions.* New York: Braziller, 1997.

Scott, J. *Seeing Like a State.* New Haven: Yale University Press, 1998.

Seidman, S. *Romantic Longings:1830–1980.* New York and London: Routledge, 1990.

Smith, J.B. *Munch.* London: Phaidon Press, 1992.

Stand, R. *Edvard Munch.* New York: Abbeville Press, 1997.

Stringberg, A. *Strindberg: Five Plays.* Translated by H. Carlson. Berkeley: University of California Press,1983.

Street, L., C. Michelle, and D. Barlow. "Sensations, Cognitions, and the Perception of Cues Associated with Expected and Unexpected Attacks." *Behav. Res. Ther.* 27 (1989): 189-98.

Tojner, P.E. *Munch, Edvard: In His Own Words.* Munich: Prestel, 2001.

Torjusen, B. Words and Images of Edvard Munch. White River Junction, VT: Chelsea Green Publishing Company, 1986.

Tucker, P. *Impressionists at Argenteuil.* New Haven, CT: Yale University Press, 2000.

Tweed, J., V. Shoenbach, L. George, and D. Blazer. "The Effects of Childhood Parental Death and Divorce on the Six-Month History of Anxiety Disorders." *British Journal of Psychiatry* 154 (1989): 823-28.

Varnedoe, K. *Gustave Caillebotte*. New Haven: Yale University Press, 2000.

Woll, G. *Edward Munch: The Complete Graphic Work*. Oslo: Gerd Woll Abrams, 2001.

Wood, M.H., ed. *The Frieze of Life*. New York: National Gallery Publications, 1992.

Young, A. *The Harmony of Illusions: Inventing Post-Traumatic Stress Disorder*. Princeton: Princeton University Press, 1997.

Zeri, F. *Munch: The Scream*. Ontario: NDE Publishing, 2000.

Panic in Modern Music / TILL M. MEYN

Cayne, Bernard S. et al., eds. *Webster's Dictionary of the English Language*. New York: Lexicon Publications, Inc., 1988.

Craft, Robert. "Music and Words." In *Stravinsky in the Theatre*. Edited by Minna Lederman. New York: Da Capo Press, 1975. pp. 88–89.

Davies, Stephen. *Musical Meaning and Expression*. Ithaca: Cornell University Press, 1994.

Kennedy, Michael. *Richard Strauss: Man, Musician, Enigma*. Cambridge: Cambridge University Press, 1999.

Meyer, Leonard B. *Emotion and Meaning in Music*. Chicago: University of Chicago Press, 1956.

Prokofiev, Sergei. *Peter and the Wolf: A Musical Tale for Children*. London: Boosey & Hawkes, 1942.

Schoenberg, Arnold. *Erwartung: A Monodrama in One Act*. Vienna: Universal Edition A. G., 1923.

Simms, Bryan R. *The Atonal Music of Arnold Schoenberg: 1908-1923*. New York: Oxford University Press, 2000.

Simms, Bryan R. "Whose Idea was *Erwartung*?" In *Constructive Dissonance: Arnold Schoenberg and the Transformations of Twentieth-Century Culture*. Edited by Juliane Brand and Christopher Hailey. Berkeley: University of California Press, 1997.

Stravinsky, Igor. *Renard: A Burlesque in Song and Dance*. London: J & W Chester, Ltd., 1917.

White, Eric Walter. *Stravinsky: The Composer and His Works*. Los Angeles: University of California Press, 1966.

TREATMENT

There Really Is Something to Be Afraid of: A Body-Oriented Psychotherapy for the Treatment of Panic Disorder / HELEN RESNECK-SANNES

American Psychiatric Association: *Diagnostic and Statistical Manual of Mental Disorders, Fourth Edition*. Washington, DC, American Psychiatric Association, 1994.

Levine, Peter A. *Waking the Tiger: Healing Trauma*. Berkeley: North Atlantic Books, 1997.

Lowen, Alexander. *Bioenergetics*. New York: Penguin Books, 1975.

Resneck-Sannes, Helen. "A Feeling in Search of a Memory." *Women and Therapy*, 16, no. 4 (1995): 97-105.

Schore, A.N. *Early Trauma and the Development of the Right Brain*. Unpublished keynote address, Royal Australian and New Zealand College of Psychiatrists, Faculty of Child and Adolescent Psychiatry, 11th Annual Conference. Sydney, Australia, October, 1998.

Toronto, E. "The human touch: An Exploration of the Role and Meaning of Physical Touch in Psychoanalysis." *Psychoanalytic Psychology* 8, no. 1 (2001).

Viorst, Judith. *Necessary Losses*. New York: Simon and Schuster,1997.

Wagner, Jane. *The Search for Signs of Intelligent Life in the Universe*. New York: Harper & Row, 1985.

Wilson, Reid. *Taking Control of Panic Attacks*. New York: Harper Perennial, 1996.

Panic and Anxiety in Relation to Sleep / MICHAEL MUFSON WITH SANA JOHNSON-QUIJADA

Abramson, L., M.S. Keshavan, and N. Sitaram. "Elevated Sleep and Waking Heart Rates in Anxious Depressions." *Biology Psychiatry* 26 (1989): 496–99.

Aldrich, M. *Sleep Medicine*. New York: Oxford University Press, 1999.

American Psychiatric Association: *Diagnostic and Statistical Manual of Mental Disorders, Fourth Edition*. Washington, DC, American Psychiatric Association, 1994.

Branch, W.T. *Office Practice of Medicine*. Philadelphia: W.B. Saunders Co., 1994.

Canetti, A., J. Ramon de la Fuente, R. Salin-Pascual, and R. Gutierrez. "Caracteristicas del Sueno en Pacientes con Crisis de Angustia." *Acia Psiquiatrica Amer. Latina* 33 (1987): 21–26.

Christie, K.A., J.D. Burke, D.A. Regier, D.S. Rae, J.H. Boyd, and B.Z. Locke. "Epidemiologic Evidence for Early Onset of Mental Disorders and Higher Risk of Drug Abuse in Young Adults." *American J. Psychiatry* 145 (1988): 971–75.

Fisher, C., E. Kaha, A. Edwards, D.M. Davis, and J. Fine. "A Pschophysiological Study of Nightmares and Night Terrors." *The Journal of Nervous and Mental Disease* 158, no. 3 (1974): 174–88.

Freedman, R.R., P. Janni, E. Enedgui, R. Pohl, and J.M. Rainy. "Psychophysiological Factors in Panic Disorder." *Psychopathology* 17, no. 1 (1984): 66–73.

Hauri, P.J., M. Friedman, and C.L. Ravaris. "Sleep in Patients with Spontaneous Panic Attacks." *Sleep* 12, no. 4 (1989): 323–37.

Horne, J. *Why We Sleep*. New York, Oxford, Tokyo: Oxford University Press, 1988.

Insel, T.R., J.C. Gillin, A. Moore, W.B. Medelson, R.J. Loewenstein, and D.L. Murphy. "The Sleep of Patients with Obsessive-Compulsive Disorder." *Arch Gen Psychiatry* 39 (1982): 1372–77.

Kales, J.D., A. Kales, C.R. Soldatos, A.B. Caldwell, D.S. Charney, and E.D. Martin. "Night Terrors." *Arch Gen Psychiatry* 37 (1980): 1413–17.

Koenigsberg, H.W., C.P. Pollak, and D. Ferro. "Can Panic Be Induced in Deep Sleep? Examining the Necessity of Cognitive Processing for Panic." *Depression and Anxiety* 8 (1998): 126–30.

Kushner, M.G., K.J. Sher, and B.D. Beitman. "The Relation Between Alcohol Problems and the Anxiety Disorders." *American J. Psychiatry* 147 (1990): 685–95.

Lancel, M. "Role of GABAa Receptors in the Regulation of Sleep: Initial Sleep Responses to Peripherally Administered Modulators and Agonists." *Sleep* 22: (1999) 33–42.

Lesser, I.M., R.E. Poland, C. Holcomb, and D.E. Rose. "Electroencephalographic Study of Nighttime Panic Attacks." *The Journal of Nerves and Mental Disease* 173, no. 12 (1985): 744–46.

Ley, R. "Panic Attacks During Sleep: A Hyperventilation-Probability Model." *J. Behavioral Therapy & Exp Psychiat* 19, no. 3 (1988): 181–92.

Mellman, T.A., and T.W. Uhde. "Electroencephalographic Sleep in Panic Disorder." *Arch Gen Psychiatry* 46 (1989): 178–84.

Mellman, T.A., and T.W. Uhde. "Patients with Frequent Sleep Panic: Clinical Findings and Response to Medications Treatment." *J. Clinical Psychiatry* 51 (1990): 513–16.

Mellman, T.A., and T.W. Uhde. "Sleep Panic Attacks: New Clinical Findings and Theoretical Implications." *American J. Psychiatry* 146 (1989): 1204–07.

Pollack, M.H., and M.W. Otto. *The Psychiatric Clinics of North America: Anxiety Disorders: Longitudinal Course and Treatment*, Vol. 18, no. 4. Philadelphia: Harcourt, Brace & Company, 1995.

Regestien, Q., and D. Ritchie. *Sleep Problems and Solutions*. Edited by Consumer Reports. New York: Consumer Union, 1990.

Roehrs T,. and T. Roth. "Sleep-Wake State and Memory Function." *Sleep* 23, no. s3 (2000): 64-68.

Ross, H.E., F.B. Glaser, and T. Germanson. "The Prevalence of Psychiatric Disorders in Patients with Alcohol and Other Drug Problems." *Arch Gen Psychiatry* 45 (1998) 1023–31.

Ross, R.J., W.A. Ball, K.A. Sullivan, and S.N. Caroff. "Sleep Disturbance as the Hallmark of Posttraumatic Stress Disorder." *American J. Psychiatry* 146 (1989): 697–707.

Sadock, B.J., and V.A. Sadock, eds. *Comprehensive Textbook of Psychiatry, 7th ed.* Philadelphia: Lippincott, Williams & Wilkins, 2000.

Stockwel, T., R. Hodgson, and H. Rankin. "Tension Reduction and the Effects of Prolonged Alcohol Consumption." *British Journal of Addiction* 77 (1982): 65–73.

Uhde, T.W., P. Roy-Byrne, J.C. Gillin, W.B. Mendelson, J.P. Boulenger, B.J. Vittone, and R.M. Post. "The Sleep of Patients with Panic Disorder: A Preliminary Report." *Psychiatry Research* 12 (1984): 251–59.

Woodward, S.H., M.J. Friedman, D.S. Charney, and A.Y. Deutch, eds. *Neurobiological and Clinical Consequences of Stress: From Normal Adaptation to PTSD.* Philadelphia: Lippincott-Raven Publishers, 1995.

Sexual Manifestations of Panic and Its Treatment / Marta Helliesen

Andersson, K.E. "Pharmacology of Penile Erection." *Pharmacology Review* 53 (2001): 417–50.

Berman, J., and L. Berman. *For Women Only: A Revolutionary Guide to Overcoming Sexual Dysfunction and Reclaiming Your Sex Life.* New York: Henry Holt and Company, LLC., 2001.

Bremner, J.D. "The Neurobiology of Posttraumatic Stress Disorder: An Integration of Animal and Human Research." *Posttraumatic Stress Disorder: A Comprehensive Text.* Edited by P.A. Saigh and J.D. Bremner. Boston: Allyn & Bacon, 1999, 103-43.

Bremner, J.D., et al. "MRI-based Measurements of Hippocampal Volume in Patients with Combat-Related PTSD." *American Journal of Psychiatry* 31, no. 2 (1992): 973–81.

Buckley, T.C., and D.G. Kaloupek. "A Meta-Analytic Examination of Basal Cardiovascular Activity in Posttraumatic Stress Disorder." *Psychosomatic Medicine* 63 (2001): 585–94.

Exton, M.S, A. Bindert, T. Kruger, F. Scheller, U. Hartman, and M. Schedlowski. "Cardiovascular and Endocrine Alterations after Masturbation-induced Orgasm in Women." *Psychosomatic Medicine* 61 (1999): 280–89.

Feldman, H.A., I. Goldstein, D.G. Hatzichristou, R.J. Krane, and J.B. McKinlay. "Impotence and Its Medical and Psychosocial Correlates: Results of the Massachusetts Male Aging Study." *Journal of Urology* 151 (1994): 54–61.

Gorman, J.M., J.M Kent, G.M. Sullivan, and J.D. Copland. "Neuroanatomical Hypothesis of Panic Disorder, revised." *American Journal of Psychiatry* 157 (2000): 493–505.

Heim, C., and C.B. Nemeroff. "The Role of Childhood Trauma in the Neurobiology of Mood and Anxiety Disorders: Preclinical and Clinical Studies." *Biological Psychiatry* 49, no. 12 (2001): 1023–39.

Infante, J.R., M. Torres-Avisbal, P. Pinel, J.A. Vallejo, F. Peran, F. Gonzalez, P. Contreras, C. Pacheco, A. Roldan, and J.M. Latre, "Catecholamine Levels in Practitioners of the Transcendental Meditation Technique." *Physiology & Behavior* 72, no. 1-2 (2001): 141-46.

Kotler, M., H. Cohen, D. Aizenberg, M. Matar, U. Loewenthal, Z. Kaplan, H. Miodownik, and Z. Zemishlany. "Sexual Dysfunction in Male Posttraumatic Stress Disorder Patients." *Psychotherapy and Psychosomatics* 69, no. 6 (2000): 309–15.

Kruger, T., M.S. Exton, C. Pawlak, A. von zur Muhlen, U. Hartman, and M. Schedlowski. "Neuroendocrine and Cardiovascular Response to Sexual Arousal and Orgasm in Men." *Psychoendocrinology* 4 (1998): 401–11.

Lazar, S.W., G. Bush, R.L. Gollub, G.L. Fricchione, G. Khalsa, and H. Benson. "Functional Brain Mapping of the Relaxation Response and Meditation." *Neuroreport* 11, no. 7 (2000): 1581–85.

LeDoux, J.E. *The Emotional Brain: The Mysterious Underpinnings of Emotional Life.* New York: Simon & Schuster, 1996.

Levin, R.J. "VIP, Vagina, Clitoral and Periurethral Glans—An Update on Human Female Genital Arousal." *Experimental and Clinical Endocrinology* 98, no. 2 (1991): 61–69.

McEwen, B.S., J. Angulo, H. Cameron, H.M. Chao, D. Daniels, M.N. Gannon, E. Gould, S. Mendelson, R. Sakai, R. Spencer, et al. "Paradoxical Effects of Adrenal Steroids on the Brain: Protection Versus Degeneration." *Biological Psychiatry* 31, no. 2 (1992): 177–99.

McEwen, B.S., and R. Sapolsky. "Stress and Cognitive Functioning." *Current Opinion in Neurobiology* 5, no. 2 (1995): 205–16.

Meston, C.M., and P.F. Frohlich. "The Neurobiology of Sexual Function." *Archives of General Psychiatry* 57 (2000): 1012–30.

Min, K., N.N. Kim, I. McAuley, M. Stankowicz, I. Goldstein, and A.M. Traish. "Sildenafil Augments Pelvic-Mediated Female Genital Sexual Arousal in the Anesthetized Rabbit." *International Journal of Impotence Research* 12, Supplement 3 (2000): S32–39.

Min, K., L. O'Connell, R. Munarriz, Y.H. Huang, S. Choi, N. Kim, I. Goldstein, and A. Traish. "Experimental Models for the Investigation of Female Sexual Function and Dysfunction." *International Journal of Impotence Research* 13, no. 3 (2001):151–56.

Schultz, W.W., P. Van Andel, I. Sabelis, and E. Mooyaart. "Magnetic Resonance Imaging of Male and Female Genitals During Coitus and Female Sexual Arousal." *British Medical Journal* 319 (1999): 1596–1600.

Seidman, S.N., and S. Roose. "The Relationship Between Depression and Erectile Dysfunction." *Current Psychiatry Reports* 2 (2000): 201–05.

Seidman, S.N., and S.P. Roose. "Sexual Dysfunction and Depression."
Current Psychiatry Reports 3 (2001): 202–08.

Siegel, D.J. *The Developing Mind: Toward A Neurobiology of
Interpersonal Experience.* New York: Guildford Press, 1999.

Yardi, N. "Yoga for Control of Epilepsy." *Seizure* 10, no. 1 (2000): 7–12.

Herbal Treatment for Panic Disorder and other Anxiety-Related Disorders /
ANDREW GAEDDERT

Gaeddert, Andrew. *Chinese Herbs in the Western Clinic.* Berkeley: North
Atlantic Books, 1994.

Kaptchuk,Ted. *The Web That Has No Weaver.* Chicago: Contemporary
Books, 2000.

Mills, Simon, and Kerry Bone. *Principles and Practic of Phytotherapy.*
London: Churchill Livingstone, 2000.

Homeopathic Treatment of Panic Disorder and Anxiety-Related Disorders /
ANDREW LANGE.

Erickson, Milton H. *The Collected Papers of Milton H. Erickson on
Hypnosis.* New York: Irvington Publishers, 1980.

Feher, Michael. *Fragments for a History of the Human Body.* New York:
Zone Books, 1989.

Hauschka, Rudolf. *The Nature of Substance.* London: Vincent Stuart Limited, 1966.

Kelso, J.A. Scott. *Dynamic Patterns: The Self-organization of Brain and
Behavior.* Cambridge and London: Massachusetts Institute of Technology,
1995.

Krishnamurti, Jiddu. *The Awakening of Intelligence.* New York: Harper &
Row, 1973.

Pearce, Joseph Chilton. *Evolution's End.* San Francisco: HarperCollins,
1992.

Pelikan, Wilhelm. *The Secrets of Metals.* Spring Valley, NY: Anthro-
posophic Press, 1973.

Taussig, Michael. *The Nervous System.* New York: Routledge, 1992.

Uyldert, Mellie. *Metal Magic.* Wellingborough: Turnstone Press Limited,
1980.

Winfree, Arthur T. *When Time Breaks Down: The Three-Dimensional
Dynamics of Electrochemical Waves and Cardiac Arythmias.* Princeton:
Princeton University Press, 1987.

Zaren, Ananda. *Core Elements of the Materia Medica of the Mind, Volume
I.* Germany: Ulrich Burgdorf Homoeopathic Publishing House, 1994.

About the Contributors

Authors

MARSHALL ALCORN, PH.D.

Marshall W. Alcorn, Jr. is Associate Professor of English, Humanities, and the Program in the Human Sciences at The George Washington University. He is Executive Director of the Association for the Psychoanalysis of Culture and Society and Secretary for the Forum on Psychiatry and the Humanities. He has published two books: *Narcissism and the Literary Libido* (New York University Press, 1994) and *Changing the Subject in English Class* (Southern Illinois University Press, 2000).

LESLIE BERGER BLUMENBERG

Leslie Berger Blumenberg has spent years researching thyroid disease and panic disorder. At an internet forum for thyroid disease patients, Leslie readily provides medical and anecdotal information describing the nature of thyroid disease and its treatment. As a thyroid patient advocate, she is hoping that patient awareness will force the medical community to rule out thyroid disease before dismissing symptomatic patients.

Blumenberg resides in coastal Maine with her husband Bennett, with their daughters Vanessa and Rachael living close by. She graduated from Lesley College, in Cambridge, and worked as a teacher of young children with special needs. Blumenberg enjoys freelance writing, creating original digital artwork, painting, gardening, and walking. She credits her good health today to her family's continuous love, support, and understanding.

Colin Clarke, Ph.D.

Colin A. Clarke is Assistant Professor of English in the field of Post-World War II American Literature at Louisiana Tech University. He has published critical work on James Fenimore Cooper, has an essay on Robert Lowell forthcoming, and is a published poet. He is currently at work on a book-length project dealing with issues of confinement in mid-twentieth-century American poetry. He received his doctorate from The George Washington University.

Robert Combs, Ph.D.

Robert Combs is Associate Professor of English at The George Washington University, in Washington, DC, where he teaches courses in American drama and short fiction. He is the author of *Vision of the Voyage: Hart Crane and the Psychology of Romanticism*, as well as articles on Eugene O'Neill, Harold Pinter, David Mamet, and others. He lives in Baltimore.

Andrew Gaeddert, A.H.G.

Andrew Gaeddert is the author of *Chinese Herbs in the Western Clinic* and *Healing Digestive Disorders* (North Atlantic Books). He has been on the protocol team for several scientific studies on herbal medicine sponsored by the NIH Office of Alternative Medicine and the University of California. He sees clients at the Get Well Clinic in Oakland, California. He can be reached at 510-635-9778, or *gwfclinic@aol.com*.

Richard Grossinger, Ph.D.

A native of New York City, Richard Grossinger attended Amherst College and the University of Michigan, from which he received a B.A. in English and a Ph.D. in Anthropology, respectively. In the late 1960s and early 1970s he did ethnographic fieldwork among Hopis and Euro-Americans in Arizona and fisherman in downeast Maine. He taught college in Maine and Vermont until 1977, when he and his family moved to the San Francisco Bay Area of California, where he founded North Atlantic Books.

Grossinger is the author of many titles, including a trilogy that includes *Planet Medicine, The Night Sky,* and *Embryogenesis.* His two nonfiction novels are *New Moon* and *Out of Babylon*. He has edited and co-edited several anthologies, including *The Alchemical Tradition in the Late Twentieth Century*, *Baseball I Gave You All the Best Years of My Life*, and *Ecology and Consciousness*.

Marta Helliesen, M.S.

Marta Helliesen is a practicing New York City psychotherapist specializing in sexuality. Born in Norway and trained as a neuro-scientist at the University of Bergen, she was a fellow for the Norwegian Research Council at the University of Washington in Seattle. She completed her psychotherapy training at the Gestalt Center for Psychotherapy and Training. A licensed massage therapist trained in a variety of modalities, Helliesen was a faculty member at the Swedish Institute of Massage as well as a founder of the women's chapter of the Body Electric School in New York City. She is a sex educator and currently a core community member at the Institute for Authentic Process Healing, where she contributes frequently to their website. Helliesen has developed unique treatment modalities based on neuroscientific principles, hands-on techniques, breath work, and Gestalt-oriented psychotherapy.

Devon Hinton, M.D., Ph.D.

Devon Hinton is a psychiatrist who received his doctorate in Anthropology at Harvard University. He is currently the Medical Director of two Southeast Asian Clinics and an Instructor of Psychiatry at Harvard Medical School. He has published extensively on the topic of culture and panic disorder, especially among Cambodian refugees.

Hinton received his psychiatric training and Anthropology doctorate at Harvard University. For his fieldwork, he spent three years in Thailand working in a Laotian-speaking part of the country. Hinton has edited a special journal issue on cross-cultural aspects of panic disorder (to appear in the journal "Culture, Medicine, and Psychiatry"), and in collaboration with Dr. Byron Good is just completing an edited book on this same topic. He presently acts as the medical director of two Southeast Asian clinics in the Boston area and is on the faculty at the Massachusetts General Hospital.

Ilona Jerabek, Ph.D.

Ilona Jerabek is the president and CEO of Plumeus Inc., a hi-tech company specialized in psychological test development and related products and services. Plumeus runs several large high-traffic websites, the most renown being Queendom.com, PsychTests.com, and QuizCards.com with combined traffic reaching 1.5 million unique visits a month. Queendom earned the position of the most visited website in the world in the Mental Health and Psychology categories and is one of the Top 10 sites for women and among the Top 50 health sites.

Jerabek has a doctoral degree in clinical sciences with a specialization in psychiatry. Throughout her graduate studies, she conducted multidisciplinary studies on anxiety disorder and worked on psychological genotyping of types of alcoholism during her postdoctoral fellowship in psychiatric genetics. She has numerous publications in the field of psychology, psychiatry, and neuroscience, and has earned several awards and distinction scholarships.

Sana Johnson-Quijada, M.D.

Sana Johnson-Quijada received a B.S. in biology from La Sierra University in 1994, and went on to Loma Linda University School of Medicine, where she graduated in 1998. She is currently a chief resident on the medical psychiatry service at the West Roxbury Veterans Administration Hospital, completing her residency at the Harvard South Shore Training Program. Her interests include women's mental health, the interplay between psychiatry and spirituality, anxiety disorders, and forensic psychiatry.

Andrew Lange, N.D.

Andrew Lange served as Chair of the Department of Homeopathic Medicine and Supervising Clinical Physician at Bastyr University in Seattle. He has taught internationally, serving on the faculty of the College of Homeopathy in London and lecturing at numerous conferences. Lange is currently the Director of the Homeopathic Research Institute and practices in Boulder, Colorado.

Peter A. Levine, Ph.D.

Peter A. Levine is co-founder of the Foundation for Human Enrichment and Director of the Foundation for Human Enrichment. Levine is the author of *Waking the Tiger: Healing Trauma* (North Atlantic Books, 1997). He received his Ph.D. in Medical and Biological Physics from the University of California, Berkeley. During his thirty years study of stress and trauma, he has contributed to a variety of scientific and medical publications. More information about Levine and his work can be found at www.traumahealing.com.

Selah Martha

Selah Martha's work has been dedicated to sexual healing through tantric yoga, Reichian Transformational Movement, and gestalt therapies since 1980. A Yale graduate and eco-feminist, she is the director of women's programs at Body Electric School and the mother of three daughters. She has been Director of Women's Programs at Body Electric School since 1996.

Martha's background is in feminist and movement therapy. She trained at the Institute for Transformational Movement in Seattle and started a private practice in 1992 at the Center for Movement Arts and Therapy in Seattle. She has recently moved her practice to Port Townsend, Washington, assisting people in a variety of somatic therapies to regain their wholeness sexually. She will continue to direct Body Electric's programming from Washington and teach events nationally.

Till M. Meyn, D.M.A.

Till Meyn was born in Cologne, Germany, and studied music from an early age. He earned his Doctarate of Musical Arts in Composition at the University of Southern Califonia's Thornton School of Music, his Master of Music in Composition at Indiana University, and his B.A. in Music at the University of California, San Diego. Meyn studied composition with Roger Reynolds, Rand Steiger, Frank Ticheli, Frederick Fox, and Don Freund among others.

Meyn has taught at the University of Southern California, Pepperdine University, Saddleback College, and Irvine Valley College.

He is currently Assistant Professor of music composition and theory at Youngstown State University's Dana School of Music in Ohio. He has received several commissions for new music and has earned the Sadye J. Moss Endowed Music Composition Prize, the Alchin Scholarship, and has composed for the Ernest Bloch Festival. Meyn is a baritone singer and has performed with numerous choral ensembles, notably the Los Angeles Master Chorale and the Indiana University Pro Arte Early Music Ensemble.

MICHAEL MUFSON, M.D.

Micheal Mufson is Assistant Professor of Psychiatry at Harvard Medical School. He completed his residency in psychiatry at the Yale University School of Medicine. He trained in medical psychiatry at the Brigham and Women's Hospital and joined the staff in 1983. Since that time he has been a consultant to the Sleep Clinic at the Brigham and Women's Hospital. He is Director of Psychiatry at the West Roxbury, Veterans Administration Hospital where he is a consultant to the Sleep Clinic.

Mufson is active in the education of Harvard medical students and is a co-director of an integrated neuropsychiatry course for medical students. He is also active in the teaching of psychiatric residents with a special expertise in the diagnosis of problems at the neurology-medicine-psychiatry interface and psychopathologic diagnosis. He has received teaching awards in both medical school education and psychiatric residency education. His clinical expertise includes complex medical psychiatric problems, chronic pain disorders, sleep disorders, and forensic psychiatry.

KIM NEWMAN

Newman is a freelance film writer, critic, and radio broadcaster. He has written TV scripts, radio scripts, short stories, and novels. Newman attended the University of Sussex, where he studied English. He moved to London by 1989 and joined the Sheep Worrying Theatre Group at the Arts Centre, Bridgwater. They produced many plays, musicals and assorted projects, and Kim even moonlighted as a kazoo-player in a cabaret band, Club Whoopee.

Newman became successful as a film reviewer and critic, and soon his short stories were being picked up by magazines like Interzone. In 1985 his first published work, *Ghastly Beyond Belief: The Science Fiction and Fantasy Book of Quotations*, co-authored with Neil Gaiman, was published. Shortly thereafter, Newman published *Nightmare Movies: A Critical History of the Horror Film since 1968*. During this period, Newman amassed impressive credentials as a reviewer and fiction writer, having written for almost every publication possible in the UK, and many more overseas. For more information, see Dr. Shade's Laboratory at: http://indigo.ie/~imago/newman.html.

ATUL C. PANDE, M.D.

Atul Pande joined Parke-Davis Pharmaceutical Research Division of Warner-Lambert Company in 1994 as Director of Psychopharmacology Research in 1994. He was promoted to Senior Director of Psychiatric Research in 1996 and remained in that position until Warner-Lambert merged with Pfizer, Inc. in 2000. In September 2000, he joined the Global Project Management department of Pfizer Global R & D, assuming the position of Vice-President and Worldwide Portfolio Leader for CNS products.

Pande is trained as a psychiatrist and was on the faculty of the University of Michigan, Ann Arbor until 1992 when he joined Lilly Research Laboratories. He served as the global research physician supporting the post-marketing development of Prozac. His career in academic and industry research has been marked by numerous original peer-reviewed scientific publications and presentations at national and international scientific meetings. Pande is certified as a specialist in psychiatry by the Royal College of Physicians of Canada. He is a fellow of the Collegium Internationale Neuro-Psychopharmacologicum and the Canadian College of Neuropsychopharmacology.

FRANZ RENGGLI, PH.D.

Franz Renggli was born in Switzerland in 1942. Having studied for a Ph.D. in Zoology, he later turned to psychoanalysis in the early 1970s. He counsels couples, families, and practices body psychotherapy. He is specialized to resolve birth and pregnancy traumata in babies —together with their families—and in adult patients.

Renggli has published three books about the early mother-child-relationship: *Angst und Geborgenheit* (Anxiety and Security), *Selbstzerstörung aus Verlassenheit* (Self-destruction out of Loneliness), and *Ursprung der Angst, Antike Mythen und das Trauma der Geburt* (The Origin of Anxiety, Antic Myths and the Trauma of Birth). Renggli lives in Basel, Switzerland.

HELEN RESNECK-SANNES, PH.D.

Helen Resneck-Sannes is a psychologist who specializes in cognitive therapy treatment for patients with panic disorder. Resneck-Sannes is a licensed psychologist in private practice in Santa Cruz, California. She is a certified Bioenergetic Analyst, a trainer for the International Institute for Bioenergetic Analysis, and leads training groups in California, Canada, Germany, and New Zealand.

Resneck-Sannes is co-editor of the next issue of the journal for the Institute, covering research in Bioenergetic Analysis. Her publications in the field of psychology include: "Embarrassment and Its Relation to the Body Image and Self-concept of the College Freshman," "Shame, Sexuality, and Vulnerability," "A Feeling in Search of a Memory," "Sensory Dysfunction in Subtypes of Schizophrenia," and "Passive into Active." She has a chapter appearing in the book, *Love is Ageless: Stories about Alzheimer's Disease*, edited by Jessica Bryant.

RON ROBBINS, PH.D.

Ron Robbins is a clinical psychologist with over forty years' experience working with change and therapeutic processes. He has trained psychotherapists in many countries across the world. He is the author of numerous professional articles as well as the book, *Rhythmic Integration: Finding Wholeness in the Process of Change*. Alexander Lowen described this book as "one of the most original contributions to the theory of personality."

Robbins has worked to transfer insights about the process of change that have been gained through therapeutic practice to other settings where change and development are important (i.e., schools, businesses, and athletics). He currently serves as a trainer and trustee of the International Institute of Bioenergetic Analysis and has served on the Steering Committee of the United States Association of Body Psychotherapy during its period of early development. Robbins is a past president of the Hudson Valley Psychological Association. He has been a Visiting Lecture and Research Associate at Vassar College, and a Visiting Lecturer at the State University College of New York at New Paltz. He practices in Poughkeepsie, New York.

DANIEL USSISHKIN

Ussishkin received his B.A. from Tel Aviv University in 2000. He received his M.A. in History at the University of California, Berkeley, and is currently working toward a Ph.D. in the same department. He is specializing in French and British nineteenth- and twentieth-century social and cultural history. His main interests are conceptions of the self and history of the body and health and how this relates to notions of citizenship and the social body, as well as the experience of war. His work lies within the framework of comparative history.

Poets:

DOUGLASS BLAZER's latest book, *We Sleep as the Dream Weaves Outside Our Minds*, was published by Alantansi Press in 1994. His poems have appeared in *American Poetry Review, New Directions, TriQuarterly*, and *Poetry*.

JACK FORBES, Powhatan-Delaware, is the co-founder of Native American Studies at the University of California, Davis and of D-Q University. He is a poet, essayist, and historian who has been writing since the 1950s and has some many books to his credit, including a long poem entitled "WHAT IS SPACE?"

RACHEL LODEN's book *Hotel Imperium* won the Contemporary Poetry Series competition of the University of Georgia Press and was named one of the ten best poetry books of 2000 by the San Francisco Chronicle Book Review. Her poems have appeared in the Pushcart Prize series, *Best American Poetry, The Bedford Introduction to Literature,* and many other journals and anthologies.

AMBER TAYLOR is seventeen years old and has been writing since she was fourteen. This is Taylor's debut publication. She spends her spare time reading, writing, and playing soccer and basketball with her friends.

Artists:

ANTHONY LUKENS lives and works in San Diego, California. In addition to painting, he enjoys making music, skateboarding, and living with his two cats, Egon and Olive.

STEVE MARKWELL is a fine artist, musician, and writer, currently living in Fort Collins, Colorado. In addition to his work in the arts, he is very active in wildlife and animal rights issues, both on local and national levels.

KATIE MEIER is founder of the studio art program at Eastside College Preparatory, a school in California for economic and racial minority students grades six through twelve. Meier studied art as an undergraduate at the University of California, Berkeley while also completing a degree in religion. She is now a Graduate Scholar of Religion at Arizona State University and is pursuing Holy Orders with the liberal Sophia Divinity School.

TIM SOUTHALL is a London-based artist who uses print-making as a medium for creating visual puns, using humor, satire, language, and literature to portray familiar phrases in a more literal sense. A graduate of the Royal College of Art, Southall's etchings have been exhibited at numerous London galleries as well as in Scotland, France, Belgium, and the United States. He has taught widely at schools in the United Kingdom, including the University of Northumbria, John Moores Liverpool, Ravensbourne College of Art, and the University of Sunderland, where he is currently senior lecturer.

Credits